D0855892

Special Days

Special Days

RUTH W. GREGORY

The Citadel Press   Secaucus, N.J.

First paperbound printing, 1978
Copyright© 1975 by American Library Association
All rights reserved
Published by Citadel Press
A division of Lyle Stuart, Inc.
120 Enterprise Ave., Secaucus, N.J. 07094
In Canada: George J. McLeod Limited, Toronto

Originally published as *Anniversaries and Holidays*

Manufactured in the United States of America
ISBN 0-8065-0659-8

Dedicated to the memory of Mary Emogene Hazeltine
(May 5, 1868–June 16, 1949), director of the
Library School of the University of Wisconsin
from 1906 to 1938; author of the first two editions
of Anniversaries and Holidays.

Contents

Preface

ANNIVERSARIES AND HOLIDAYS is a book of days. Its purpose is to identify the significant days that are celebrated by the nations of the world or recognized in some way by people with common backgrounds or mutual interests.

It has been planned as an information tool for the use of public and school libraries, reference centers in library systems, writers in the communication fields, teachers and club chairmen planning programs or exhibits for notable days, and individuals curious about holidays as an aspect of the history of mankind.

This volume is a complete revision of the second edition of *Anniversaries and Holidays* by Mary E. Hazeltine, published by the American Library Association in 1944.

The scope of the third edition is international. Many new nations have been established and new holidays created since the publication of the second edition.

The extent to which the practice of observing holidays for national purposes and for the public benefit has increased in all parts of the world may be seen in a statistical comparison of the third edition with the second. The 1975 edition includes 1,690 full or partial holidays and special-events days. The 1944 edition included 377 holidays and special-observance days. The names of outstanding men and women associated with historic events and major contributions to society predominated in the second edition, with 1,387 entries for birth dates. Because of the heavy increase in holidays, the birth dates in the third edition have been limited to 1,046. The total number of entries in the third edition is 2,736, as compared with 1,764 in the second edition. These entries identify anniversaries and holidays in 152 countries.

The third edition follows the pattern of the second in including holy days and religious festivals, days which commemorate the lives of famous men and women, civic holidays, and special-events days. It does include holidays that last beyond a one-day period, as in the case of religious festivals. It does not include such week- or month-long observances as National Pay Your Bills Week or Bourbon Month. Sources for information on the scheduling of promotional or special-interest weeks and months are listed in the bibliography under the heading Almanacs and Dictionaries of Days.

Organization of the Third Edition

The text of the third edition is divided into three major sections, preceded by an introduction that reviews the relationship of calendars to holidays and the place of holidays in history.

Part 1 is a Calendar of Fixed Days, based on the Gregorian calendar. It includes four groups of days in the following order under the successive dates of each month:

Religious days—holy days or feast days
People days—commemorative days for notable men and women
Patriotic or civic holidays—great days in a nation's history
Special-events days—the unique occurrence days.

The entries under each group, where there are more than one, are alphabetical.

Feast Days and Religious Holidays

The feast days of saints, as illustrated by Saint Patrick's Day in Ireland, significant weekday Christian holy days such as Corpus Christi, and the Mondays following Easter, Whitsunday, and Christmas, are major holidays in Europe and Latin America. Feast days as holidays are innumerable. In Roman Catholic countries they are celebrated in every town that pays tribute to a patron saint. There are also ten festivals universally observed in the name of the Virgin Mary, and the many regional memorials and pilgrimages dedicated to the Virgin's honor throughout the world greatly increase the total of religious days that are partial or full holidays.

The preponderance of religious holidays necessitated a limitation in the listing to those that are the most popular or unusual. The names of all of the countries observing the selected feast days and holy days as holidays are not included because of their great numbers. Ascension Day, for example, is a holiday in at least forty-two nations; Good Friday is a holiday in sixty-four nations. Information on specific countries that observe holy days as holidays may be found in sources listed in the bibliography, such as title number 12, *Europa Year Book*.

Religious holidays may be either fixed or movable days. The key to their location in this volume is the index.

People Days

The commemorative days of notable men and women included in this revision are, of necessity, arbitrary selections based upon the contribution an individual has made to a nation, to a profession, or to the progress of mankind. The selection was limited to persons who died before November 1974. The descriptive entries for special events may include the name of a living man or woman, but the relationship of the event to observances was the factor that determined its inclusion. The entries are by birth or death date. The people include thirty-six presidents of the United States; the men and women elected to the Hall of Fame for Great Americans through 1970; the majority of the citizens chosen for representation in Statuary Hall in the Capitol of the United States; world statesmen and United Nations leaders; selected Nobel Prize winners and other name-award winners; contributors to world music, literature, architecture, and art; first presidents of well-known associations; notable religious leaders; explorers who have enlarged man's knowledge of the earth; outstanding pioneers; and heroes. Space alone limits the inclusion of illustrious men and women of all nations who are honored in their specialized fields or by their countrymen.

The awareness of the importance of commemorative days that pay tribute to men and women of the entire world is demonstrated by the 1958 action of the United Nations in authorizing UNESCO to arrange for the celebration of important anniversaries in the fields of education, science, and culture in order to focus attention on the work of outstanding individuals of all nations and "to assert that these works are the common patrimony of all humanity." Career information on the men and women listed in this volume is available in biographical reference books, biographies, and histories available in libraries and through library systems.

The dates for the large majority of notable men and women are set dates and are included in the Calendar of Fixed Days in Part 1. The exceptions are religious leaders associated with movable feasts and festivals in Part 2. All are to be located through the index.

Patriotic or Civic Holidays

The first evidence of a legal holiday in the sense of suspension of business is a record that the Emperor Constantine forbade the holding of courts, markets, and the customary activities of business on Good Friday.

Contemporary patriotic or civic holidays reflect the history of nations and point to the ideas, the heroes, or the events that are the subject of their admiration or homage. Every country has civic holidays that are free days for all citizens except those in the public-protection fields, such as members of the armed forces, policemen, firemen, and hospital attendants.

In many countries the civic or public holiday is called a national day since a proclamation from the central government applies to the entire country. The United States does not have national holidays in this sense. Federal holidays are legally applicable only to the District of Columbia and to the federal employees who work in federal offices in all of the fifty states. Each state in the United States has the right to establish the dates of its own holidays. The legal holidays established by Congress for its jurisdiction are: New Year's Day, Washington's Birthday, Memorial Day, Independence Day, Labor Day, Columbus Day, Veterans Day, Thanksgiving Day, and Christmas.

In 1968 the Congress of the United States passed a bill to be effective in 1971 changing the time of observance for four existing holidays under its jurisdiction from the original date to Mondays. These were Washington's Birthday, Memorial Day, Columbus Day, and Veterans Day. Each of the fifty states has the option to conform to the change or to keep the original date. Since some states have preferred the traditional dates, there are some holiday calendar differences in the United States affecting the so-called national holidays. This edition makes use of the federal dates for the nine legal public holidays as established by Congress. Variations by states for these dates are not entered separately by specific dates, with the exception of Memorial Day, which had traditional time variations before the 1968 Act of Congress.

A survey of the holidays of the states in the United States was made to try to determine those days which are holidays as a release from a work schedule and those which are called holidays but which are actually days of observance by schools, patriotic or historical societies, or other organizations. The result was not definitive, since in many states local option is granted to governmental units and to school districts for recognition of a holiday and even the day of its observance. Consequently, one community within a state may or may not observe a holiday that is celebrated in another part of the state.

Variations in the observance of special days also prevail in the United States. Arbor Day is observed in various months in different areas of the United States, depending upon the seasons. Regional history determines the observance of some famous birthdays. The South, for example, chooses to observe the birthday of Robert E. Lee, but the North observes the birthday of Abraham Lincoln.

Paralleling the legal holidays of the United States are comparable days in other nations using different terms. For example, legal holidays in Canada are called statutory days. There are nine that are generally observed in all of the Canadian provinces: New Year's Day, Good Friday, Easter Monday, Victoria Day, Dominion Day, Labour Day, Thanksgiving Day, Remembrance Day, and Christmas. Great Britain is well known for its holidays occurring on Monday: Easter Monday, Whitmonday, August Bank Holiday, and Boxing Day. Such holidays in the United Kingdom are known as bank holidays. Legal holidays in other parts of the world are designated as national or civic days.

Sunday in Christian countries is a day of worship, and ordinary governmental and business affairs are not conducted. In many nations Sunday is a legal holiday.

Special-Events Days

Special-events days are days of recognition. Most special-events days in the United States, for example, are occasions for special programs rather than holidays. These recognition days have developed in the history of nations for definite reasons. Some special-events days, Child Health Day as one illustration, were established to call attention to a movement of universal value. This type of special-events day, in a sense, is a public-information day. Still others commemorate the completion of a project that stimulated economic progress in a nation, such as Golden Spike Day. The birthday of a famous person may be a special-events day, as in the case of January 15, when students and groups honor Dr. Martin Luther King, Jr., with school programs or out-of-school observances. The 1944 edition of *Anniversaries and Holidays* pointed to Commencement day as an important special-events day.

The third edition does not claim to be exhaustive. The number of special-events days continues to grow as new nations become conscious of the making of history and older communities dig into their collective memories. Every region of all continents has observances that depict the history and the development of a country or an area. This edition includes some of the "firsts" among these days as representative of this type of historical pageantry, such as the first Pioneer Day celebration in the United States. The agricultural fairs that are annual events in all sections of the United States are limited to an entry on the first fair, since there are over 2,000 county, regional, and state fairs in the United States alone. The countless annual-events days all over the world that are dedicated to sports are represented only by the day of the revival of the Olympics, several historic racing days, and the first of the popular New Year's Day football games. This edition does not list all of the special days of each of the fifty states of the United States, the provinces of Canada, or the colonies and protectorates of the great nations. It includes those that are best known or are typical in public interest and observance.

Part 2 is made up of the calendars of movable days divided into five sections: the Christian church year; the Islamic year; the Jewish year; and, one section each on the movable festivals of the Eastern and Western worlds. Each of the sections is preceded by a brief commentary on the unique calendars that regulate the movable feasts.

The movable feasts in all but one section are organized by the months of the Gregorian calendar, which appear on the left-hand side of the page. The festivals within each month are arranged alphabetically by the name of the festival. The one section that is not organized by the Gregorian months is the Islamic calendar. The entries in that section are alphabetical without a translation into a Gregorian time equivalent. The nature of the Islamic lunar calendar does not lend itself to such translation. (See the Islamic Calendar, page 149.)

There are a few festival days which are movable feast days in the Far East but which have become fixed days in countries utilizing the Gregorian calendar. Although Buddha's birthday is celebrated in Hawaii on or near a fixed day, it is celebrated on movable days in Asia. Both may be located through the index.

Part 3 is an annotated bibliography of books related to anniversaries and holidays. The purpose of the section is to gather together materials useful in a study of holidays and observances; to indicate a variety of materials that may be of value in developing an individualized approach to the observance of a particular holiday; and to suggest resources from the general literature that are pertinent to the observance of days on which little is written.

The bibliographies include books for all age groups, with one exception. Holiday picture books written for very young readers are excluded, unless the text of a particular book goes beyond a few words and many pictures to contribute to an understanding of the origins and customs of a holiday. This scheme admittedly excludes some very attractive picture books useful in work with small children and a number of colorful volumes suitable for display. However, for the purpose of this edition, the bibliographies that have been included were selected because of the treatment of the text rather than the beauty of the illustrations. The titles included in the bibliographies are not graded, since a designation of a reading level often creates barriers to the examination and use of printed material.

The major criteria for the inclusion of a title were quality and usefulness. The bibliography does not constitute a selection of best books on any holiday subject, although a check with reviews indicated an affirmative approval for each title from one or more critics. To apply a "best books" criterion to books related to holidays is not feasible. There are more than five thousand books written about Abraham Lincoln, for example, and many would be valuable in preparing programs for Lincoln's Birthday. Every expert in Lincolniana could quarrel over an omission on a "best books" list. On the other hand, there are annual observances, such as Kosciuszko Day, for which publications are extremely limited and there is little choice. The suggestions of titles on individuals associated with holidays about whom much has been written cover various aspects of their lives simply as reminders of the diversity of approaches that are possible in planning holiday observances.

The copyright dates for books on anniversaries and holidays included in the bibliography range from an 1899 source book to works published in the fall of 1974. The recentness of a copyright date does not provide a clue to the value of a book on traditional observances. A late-nineteenth- or early-twentieth-century holiday historian may offer much more in-depth information on the origin and the customs of a particular holiday than a contemporary author. But a deterrent to the use of older histories, in some cases, is the overabundance of minutiae about holidays. Such books, however, are prime sources of detailed data on the origins and early customs of holiday observance.

Anthologies containing fondly remembered poems and stories about holidays are perennial favorites regardless of dates of publication. The bibliography does exclude early-twentieth-century anthologies in which the sentiment of less familiar material seems to be out of touch with the interests and responses of today's readers.

The bibliography is divided into six sections. The first begins with source books for the verification of dates in various fields and interpretations of the calendar and the measurement of time. The first section also includes readings on commemorative events and historic fetes for the history buff or the planner of unusual events.

The second section deals with background readings on religious years, beliefs, and customs of value in an era of ecumenicity and interfaith program activities.

The next two sections deal with holidays. The first group consists of books covering more than one holiday in their presentations. This is followed by suggestions of books to use for sixty-nine individual days, such as Veterans Day, or for combined observances for occasions such as sports anniversaries.

The fifth category includes books that offer ideas for planning the observance of holidays and special days. It is subdivided into holiday foods, costumes and crafts, and holiday poems, songs, and observance ideas.

The final section of the bibliography lists books about selected persons named in the calendars.

The bibliographies as a whole include many titles which are related to the themes of days of observance or to the people associated with them but which were written for purposes other than holiday observance use. As Miss Hazeltine wrote in the introduction to the second edition, "All forms of literature contribute to holiday observance."

Keys to the Use of the Third Edition

The Entries

Specific names of the holidays of the countries around the world are entered as they appear in English translation. For example, the holiday in Burundi called Assassination of the Hero of the Nation Day is used exactly as it is found in the source material without any tampering to Americanize or abbreviate it.

The general names for civic holidays are another matter. There is a growing tendency in some handbooks and lists to label all public holidays as national days. An attempt has been made in this edition to distinguish one particular national holiday from another. Consequently, a specific name, such as Afghanistan Independence Day, has been used as a means of identifying the origin of a holiday that is commonly designated on calendars and lists simply as a national day.

The spelling of the names of the Islamic and the Far Eastern holidays vary in encyclopedias, histories, and travel books. There are even varied opinions on preferred spellings. An arbitrary decision was made on the spelling of such holidays when at least two sources agreed. The decision on the spelling of Jewish holidays was made in consultation with a rabbinical scholar.

The trend toward moving fixed holidays to a weekend adds to the difficulty of assigning specific dates. In this edition a c (meaning "circa") before a date, such as Washington's actual birth date, indicates that the birthday is observed at a time near that date. Many days of observance have been shifted slightly from the date of establishment. This edition enters those days, such as Mother's Day or Boy Scout Day, under the founding date with a c to indicate that the observance is not fixed to the date of establishment but remains within the same time period.

This edition follows the 1944 edition in the use of the "New Style" calendar for dates that follow 1752, the year that the Gregorian calendar was adopted by England and her colonies. As Miss Hazeltine pointed out, "This may make some dates seem in error with dates appearing elsewhere, especially the Founding Fathers, who belong to this period. George Washington, by the old reckoning, was born February 11, 1732, but according to the New Style calendar, which was adopted in his lifetime, his birthday fell on February 22."

The Bibliographies

The books in the bibliographies have been given numbers. Where appropriate, these numbers have been correlated with the entries in Parts 1 and 2 to suggest readings related to the holiday, person, or event cited by the main entry.

The Index

The volume concludes with a general index, which is the most important key to the location of any entry in the text. Holidays are entered under their proper names unless the popular name is more quickly identifiable, as in the case of Bastille Day, which is used for the French Independence Day. Cross references are included to facilitate the use of ANNIVERSARIES AND HOLIDAYS. The index entries refer to dates for Part 1 and to pages for the introductory material, Part 2, and the bibliographies.

Sources

The sources used in research for this edition were varied. The first findings revealed many discrepancies in dates related to modern holidays in printed source material. Some are due to confusion over the international date line or to instant reporting of events occurring before or after midnight which affect the preciseness of an official date record. The dates used for holidays in this edition have been verified wherever possible by government records, United Nations publications, and direct inquiry of foreign embassies, agencies of state governments, and specialists in history and current events. Official records were supplemented by the news-media reports on changing international situations which create new holidays or indicate that a current civic day will soon be replaced by another. A prime source of information and advice was a series of consultations with priests, rabbis, and ministers on the selection of holy days, with American citizens who have lived abroad on the importance of international festivals and secular observances, and with librarians and program planners on the selection of titles for the bibliography.

Acknowledgments

Any compilation the size of ANNIVERSARIES AND HOLIDAYS involves the cooperation of many people. Appreciation is due the staff of the Waukegan Public Library for their help in research and in suggesting titles for the bibliographies. Acknowledgment must also be given to the North Suburban Library System reference center for verification of essential data, and to the librarians across the United States who responded to inquiries about holidays in their respective states.

A special word of thanks goes to Herbert Bloom, senior editor of the American Library Association Publishing Services, for his advice and counsel.

Introduction

Holidays and the Calendar

A calendar is a device for reckoning the beginning, length, and divisions of a year and for locating a holiday or any other particular day. It is one of the essential tools of daily life and one that is taken for granted. It seems simple. However, upon examination, a calendar is found to be an ingenious and complicated system of reckoning and recording time.

The major problem in determining the date of a holiday is that there are three basic kinds of calendars in use in the twentieth century: the solar, the lunar, and the lunisolar. In addition, there are local or regional variations of these calendars.

The solar calendar is based on the solar or seasonal year, the time taken by the earth to go once around the sun. It consists of 365.2425 days, divided into twelve months of unequal length. To compensate for the quarter-day differential between the ordinary and the astronomical years, it is necessary to introduce a year with 366 days every fourth year. The Gregorian calendar, utilized by the Western nations for public and private purposes and by world nations for civil or commercial purposes, is a solar calendar.

A lunar calendar represents a year composed of twelve months determined by complete cycles of phases of the moon. Each month totals approximately the time required for the moon to wax and wan from a new moon to a full moon and back again to a new moon. The Islamic calendar (see page 149) is a modern example of a lunar calendar.

The lunisolar calendar is well illustrated by the Jewish calendar, in which the months are reckoned by the moon and the years by the sun. A month is reckoned as the time from the period when the moon is directly between the sun and the earth to the next period when this phenomenon occurs. (See also the Jewish Calendar, page 150.)

The solar calendar allows for fixed days, which may be identified by a recurring date, year after year, within the same time frame. New Year's Day, for example, is always January 1 in the Gregorian calendar, although the day of the week upon which it falls may vary slightly from one year to another.

The lunar and lunisolar calendars consist of movable days and dates. A specific festival in a lunar calendar moves into all months within the established cycle of lunar years. This is called "wandering through the calendar." In a lunisolar calendar, the movement of a festival is confined within a season, since the lunar cycles are adjusted to the solar agricultural seasons.

The Sumerians of Babylonia have been credited with the creation of the first lunar calendar and the Egyptians with the first solar calendar. In 46 B.C., Julius Caesar established the calendar that has been known for centuries as the Julian calendar. That year, 46 B.C., has been described by some historians as "the year of great confusion." Nevertheless, the Julian calendar became the calendar of the early Western world and is still used by the Eastern Orthodox churches.

There were weaknesses in the Julian calendar. Consequently, in 1582, Pope Gregory XIII promulgated a calendar for the purpose of reconciling the civil and Church calendars. Pope Gregory decreed that the day following Thursday, October 4, 1582, was to be Friday, October 15, 1582, thus advancing all dates in the calendar by eleven days. The Gregorian calendar came to be known as the New Style calendar, and the Julian calendar as the Old Style calendar.

If it is true, as some historians say, that the Julian calendar created a year of confusion, then the Gregorian calendar bears responsibility for generations of confusion in the recording of births, deaths, and historic dates because of the advancing of all dates by eleven days back in the sixteenth century. The confusion would not have occurred had the Gregorian calendar been immediately acceptable in all of the Western world.

The Gregorian calendar was adopted by Roman Catholic countries in 1582. However, it was not adopted by England and the British Empire, including the American colonies, until 1752. Russia started with the Gregorian calendar in 1918, then experimented with a calendar of its own at the end of the Bolshevik Revolution, and did not return to the use of the Gregorian calendar until 1940. The Chinese had made use of the Gregorian calendar for governmental purposes as early as 1912 but did not enforce its use in public life until 1930. It was not until after the end of World War II that the Gregorian calendar took a dominant position among world calendars, and its widespread use has facilitated world trade and intergovernmental relations. However, it has not replaced the lunar and lunisolar calendars for domestic and religious date calculations on a worldwide basis. This means that many nations use both the Gregorian calendar and their own time-honored calendars, and holy days and holidays are tied to local or national time-measurement customs.

Ideas for calendar reform have been advanced in the twentieth century and are described in some of the books listed in the bibliography in the section Calendars and the Measurement of Time on page 164. Such reforms have been suggested to provide months and quarters of equal length and to create a permanent time frame in which the same date will fall on the same day in successive years. Up to the early 1970s, calendar reform proposals have been opposed on the basis of some legal complexities but primarily by religious bodies whose fixed Sabbaths and holy days are irreconcilable with the proposed changes.

The fact remains that a compilation of anniversaries and holidays finds its basic source verification for dates in the New and the Old Style solar calendars, in the many regional lunar and lunisolar calendars, in calendars of religious years, and in historic books of days.

Holidays in History

Centuries ago, the word *holiday* was written as *holy day*, signifying, and limited to, a religious commemoration. In the course of history, the meaning of holiday broadened to encompass civic and secular as well as religious observance. It even came to be used to designate a vacation period, days of individual freedom from routine obligations. In the strictest sense, holidays are those days set aside by nations, or groups within nations, for the purpose of religious, civil, or secular observances on a universal or optional free-day basis.

A compilation of holidays provides an insight into life situations that mankind has considered important enough to cherish with carefully preserved customs and continued recognition. Holidays evolved through the centuries as a human response to at least six distinct factors: the mysteries of nature; the inherent awareness of the existence of a supreme deity; respect for the dead; hero worship; the growth of a tribal or national spirit; and an unusual event.

Nature and the mystery of the changing seasons were responsible for the most ancient of celebrations, especially at the time of the equinoxes. The favorite period was the spring equinox, which brought into being the welcome-to-spring festivals that are observed even in a sophisticated twentieth century. Gratitude for a good growing season was, and still is, expressed with harvest festivals and thanksgiving days. The modern communication media engage in seasonal commentaries on the ancient weather-prediction days, such as Groundhog Day or Saint Swithin's Day, even though the prophecies associated with such days are predictably inaccurate.

Primitive man's veneration of nature merged with his worship of deities, at least in terms of the calendar. Many early religious festivals coincided with seasonal observances. However, religious holy days and festivals came to be a visible affirmation of the beliefs and traditions of all faiths. A large proportion of the holidays observed throughout the modern world are related to religious customs and practices. For example, Corpus Christi is a holiday in twenty-two nations, Good Friday is a holiday in sixty-four nations, and Ascension Day is a holiday in forty-two nations. Each community in the Roman Catholic countries of Europe and Latin America has its own special saint's day, which usually is a local holiday. A noteworthy example of the dominance of religion in holiday observances is to be seen in the Islamic nations, where relatively few civic days are observed and the most important holidays are those directed by the tenets of the Moslem faith.

Holiday festivals honoring the dead are an ancient and universal custom. Days of tribute to ancestors have carried over through generations into the festivals of the modern nations of the Far East. Every country in the contemporary world has some kind of a memorial day as a separate observance, combined with a religious festival, or centered around a day of commemoration for a single individual.

Commemorative days honoring rulers and national heroes go back to the cradle of civilization in Mesopotamia. Hero worship initiated and sustained many holidays, as in the case of Saint Olaf's Day in Norway. In the twentieth century, commemorative days tend to honor men and women who have made a contribution to society. Some anniversary days, such as Washington's Birthday in the United States, are celebrated by an entire nation. Other commemorative days, such as Stephen Foster Day, are observed by groups with common interests. More and more commemorative days are being established by professions and organizations to honor the innovators and pace-setters whose work merits lasting recognition.

Victory celebrations that are holidays are common to all nations. The ancient Greeks observed the anniversary of their victory at Marathon in 490 B.C. Many South American countries honor battles of the nineteenth century that were of importance in the establishment of their boundaries or their independence. All modern nations observe the end of World War II, either as a kind of armistice day or as a liberation day, celebrating the exodus of foreign troops from their countries.

Prominent among civic holidays on a worldwide scale are the independence days observed by 92 of the 135 countries who were members of the United Nations in the early 1970s. The noteworthy contribution of the twentieth century to the list of civic holidays is Labor Day, which spread all over the globe with the advance of technology and industry and the recognition of the rights of workers.

Important days have been added to the world calendar by the United Nations. These include World Literacy Day, World Health Day, and others that confirm the importance of the goals that all mankind hold in common. The United Nations days have become holidays in many new nations and are observed in other parts of the world as special-events days.

Special-events days ordinarily are not holidays in the usual sense. They are days of recognition or commemoration of events that have significance in the history of a nation, an organization, a profession, or a technological development. Some, such as Moon Day, occur only once in history as a first-time day. However, there are special-events days that have become holidays in some parts of the world. An example is Arbor Day, which has its counterpart in the tree planting days in various countries of Africa where reforestation is not only essential but also a matter of national pride.

Anniversaries and holidays have a history of varied life spans. Some, like Christmas, are a basic part of the fabric of life. Others, such as civic holidays, are vulnerable to changes in government and may be wiped off the calendar or completely altered in purpose in any one year. Still others diminish in public interest until some event or major anniversary recalls their significance. Although the fact remains that holidays are generally popular, a particular holiday will last only as long as people want it to last. This may be for a decade or it may be for hundreds and even thousands of years.

Calendar of Fixed Days

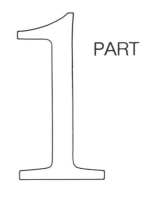

January

January, the first month in the Gregorian calendar, begins with the most popular single day of the entire year. At least 125 sovereign nations and their territories celebrate New Year's Day as a public holiday.

The name *January* was derived from the Latin *Januarius Mensus*, or the month of Janus. In the old Roman year, it was a festival month honoring Janus, the god of gates and doorways. Janus is depicted on coins and works of sculpture as a deity with two faces, one looking into the past, the other into the future. Janus is associated in mythology with new beginnings for all human enterprises. January, consequently, is one of the most appropriately named months of the year.

January has thirty-one days and two official flowers. The chief flower is the carnation and the snowdrop is the alternate. The January birthstone is the garnet.

The Fixed Days of January

1 The Circumcision of Our Lord Jesus Christ is the major feast observed by the Western church on January 1, a holy day of obligation celebrating Christ's submission to Jewish law. 73, 80.

1 Saint Basil's Day is celebrated in Greece along with New Year's Day. It honors the fourth-century bishop of Caesarea. The eating of Basil cakes is traditional.

1 Birthday of William Henry Harrison Beadle (January 1, 1838–November 13, 1915). American educator, superintendent of public schools in the Dakota territory. Represents South Dakota in a Statuary Hall sculpture done by H. Daniel Webster. 242.

1 Birthday of J(ohn) Edgar Hoover (January 1, 1895–May 2, 1972). American law-enforcement officer, author, and director of the Federal Bureau of Investigation, 1924–72.

1 Anniversary of the baptism of Bartolomé Esteban Murillo (January 1, 1618–April 3, 1682). Spanish painter, the first to become famous outside his own country. His great creations are the depiction of the Immaculate Conception and the portrayal of Christ and Saint John as children. 986.

1 Birthday of Paul Revere (January 1, 1735–May 10, 1818). American patriot and craftsman whose famous ride in the spring of 1775 placed him among the immortals in the American tradition. 648–50, 653, 739.

1 Birthday of Elizabeth (Betsy) Ross (January 1, 1752–January 30, 1836). American colonial woman who is reputed to have made the first American flag. On January 1, 1952, a three-cent postage stamp was issued by the United States government in commemoration of her two-hundredth birthday. 459, 739.

1 Birthday of Manuel Roxas y Acuña (January 1, 1892–April 15, 1948). Philippine statesman and first president of the Philippines, which came into being as an independent republic on July 4, 1946. 18, 521.

1 Birthday of Anthony Wayne (January 1, 1745–December 15, 1796). American Revolutionary War officer whose brilliant action in storming an almost impregnable fort at Stony Point, New York, lifted the hearts of his countrymen; known as "Mad Anthony." 739, 759.

1 Cameroon Independence Day, a national holiday bringing together the people of over one hundred tribes, including the Pygmies, to celebrate the beginning of the republic's independent status on January 1, 1960.

1 Haiti Independence Day, a public holiday honoring Jean Jacques Dessalines, the nation's founder, who proclaimed a state of independence on January 1, 1804, and restored the original Indian name *Haiti*, "land of mountains," to the country.

c1 Handsel Monday, Scotland's New Year's holiday observed on the first Monday in January. Old Year's Night and New Year's Day were once called "daft days" in Scotland. 164.

1 Independence Day for Western Samoa, consisting of the South Pacific islands of Savaii, Upolu, Manono, and Apolino; honors with Polynesian enthusiasm the declaration of independence from New Zealand, which occurred on January 1, 1962.

1 Sudan Independence Day, a nationwide celebration with major events held at Khartoum in honor of Sudan's sovereignty, established on January 1, 1956.

1 New Year's Day, a legal holiday in Canada, in the 50 states of the United States, and in 123 other nations of the world.

1 Anniversary of the Emancipation Proclamation freeing the slaves, issued by President Abraham Lincoln on January 1, 1863. 8.

1 Coon Carnival, a traditional holiday festival held on January 1 and 2, in Cape Town, Union of South Africa; famed for colorful dancing, music, and revelry; an attraction comparable in style to the Mardi Gras in the United States.

1 Mobile Carnival, in Mobile, Alabama, starts off the New Year with an elaborate fun-making celebration that has a history dating back to 1831. 8.

1 The Mummers Day parade held on January 1 in Philadelphia is an event dating back to 1876 and characterized by unusual costuming, string bands, clowns, and mummers. 8.

1 The Tournament of Roses, Pasadena, California, has been held annually since January 1, 1886, with flower-decorated floats forming processions that are hours—and miles—long. The climax of the day is the Rose Bowl football game held annually since January 1, 1902. The Rose Bowl preceded the other well-known annual American bowl games by three decades. 8.

2 Feast of Saint Macarius, patron saint of pastry cooks and confectioners, famous for sugarplums. 705.

2 Feast of the Martyrs for the Holy Scriptures, commemorating the slaughter of an English community that refused to surrender the New Testament to Diocletian's men.

2 Birthday of Count Folke Bernadotte (January 2, 1895–September 17, 1948). Swedish statesman, Red Cross official, United Nations mediator in Palestine, May 20 to September 17, 1948, when he was assassinated by terrorists. 784.

2 Birthday of Justin Winsor (January 2, 1831–October 22, 1897). American historian, an authority on the early history of North America, and librarian of the Boston Public Library and of Harvard University.

2 Birthday of James Wolfe (January 2, 1727–September 13, 1759). English general who died on the Plains of Abraham at the hour of victory against Montcalm, in a battle that assured the future of Canada as a member of the English family of nations. 18.

2 Georgia Ratification Day, commemorating Georgia's entry into the Union, January 2, 1788, as the fourth state among the original thirteen. 741.

2 Berchtold's Tag, observed in Switzerland with neighborhood parties in honor of the twelfth-century Duke Berchtold V, who founded the city of Berne with a promise to name it for the first animal killed in a hunt. Thus a bear provided not only the city's name but also its coat of arms.

2 Day of the Revolution, a holiday in Cuba celebrating the 1959 triumph of the Castro-led revolt that removed Fulgencio Batista as dictator. 18.

2 Granada Day in Spain, commemorates the recapture of the city from the Moors in 1492.

2 Hero's Day in Haiti, a public holiday paying tribute to the Haitians' ancestors.

2 Shigoto Hajime, or Beginning of Work Day, observed in Japan with belief in good omens for work begun on this day.

3 Feast day of Saint Geneviève, patron saint of Paris, and of secretaries, actors, lawyers, and the Woman's Army Corps. 5.

3 Birthday of Joseph Damien de Veuster (January 3, 1840–April 15, 1889). Belgian Roman Catholic missionary who, as Father Damien, brought hope to the leper colony on Molokai Island. 5.

3 Birthday of Larkin Goldsmith Mead (January 3, 1835–October 15, 1910). American sculptor who executed the Lincoln Monument in Springfield, Illinois, completed in 1883. 592.

3 Birthday of Lucretia Coffin Mott (January 3, 1793–November 11, 1880). American abolitionist and advocate of woman's rights who, with Elizabeth Cady Stanton, organized the convention at Seneca Falls in 1848, a major factor in the growth of the feminist movement in the United States. 825, 837, 990.

3 Birthday of J. R. R. Tolkien (January 3, 1892–September 2, 1973). Oxford professor, linguist, author of *The Hobbit* and *The Lord of the Rings*, honored by Tolkien societies and student groups.

3 Alaska Admission Day, statehood celebration held throughout Alaska to commemorate the admission of Alaska as the forty-ninth state on January 3, 1959. 741.

3 Anniversary of the Battle of Princeton, which forced Cornwallis to return to New York on January 3, 1777; commemorated at Princeton, New Jersey. 8.

3 Anniversary of the establishment on January 3, 1938, of the March of Dimes to raise funds for polio research.

4 Birthday of Louis Braille (January 4, 1809–January 6, 1852). French educator of the blind who originated the Braille system of printing and writing.

4 Birthday of Jacob Grimm (January 4, 1785–September 20, 1863). German philologist and writer who, with his brother William, published the famous *Grimm's Fairy Tales*. 986.

4 Birthday of Sir Isaac Newton (January 4, 1643–March 31, 1727). Physicist and mathematician; leader in the seventeenth-century scientific revolution; discoverer of the law of gravity. 977.

4 Burma Independence Day, a public holiday in Burma commemorating its establishment as a free nation on January 4, 1948.

3

4 Utah Admission Day. Utah entered the Union on January 4, 1896, as the forty-fifth state. 741.

5 Epiphany Eve, or Twelfth Night, has a history of centuries of merry-making. Shakespeare's play *Twelfth Night* was specifically written for this celebration, and some ceremonies, such as cutting the Baddeley, or Twelfth Night, cake at the Theatre Royal in London are still carried on. 8, 164.

5 Anniversary of the death of George Washington Carver on January 5, 1943. American chemist noted for his research in the industrial uses of vegetable crops; founder of the Carver Foundation for Research at Tuskegee. 1, 977, 984.

5 Birthday of Stephen Decatur (January 5, 1779–March 22, 1820). American naval officer who is remembered for his proclamation "My country—may she ever be right, but right or wrong, my country." 992.

5 Birthday of Rudolf Christoph Eucken (January 5, 1846–September 14, 1926). German philosopher of activism based on idealism and ethics; awarded the Nobel Prize in literature in 1908. 227.

5 Birthday of Cyrus Hamlin (January 5, 1811–August 8, 1900). American educator and missionary who helped establish and administer Robert College in Turkey.

5 Birthday of Zebulon Montgomery Pike (January 5, 1779–April 27, 1813). American general who commanded an early exploring expedition into the West. Pike's Peak, one of the highest summits in the Rockies, is named in his honor. 760.

5 The Glastonbury Thorn in England blooms on Old Christmas Eve, January 5, and is an occasion for pilgrims to go to Glastonbury, Somerset, to see the thorn and to visit the cradle of Christianity in England. 164.

5 Anniversary of the opening of the first American library school on January 5, 1887, at Columbia University.

5 Bird Day, anniversary of the incorporation of the National Association of Audubon Societies on January 5, 1905, with the purpose of protecting bird life. Bird Day is frequently observed with Arbor Day, which has varying dates of observance. 8, 257–65.

5 Nellie Taylor Ross became the first woman governor in the United States with her installation as governor of Wyoming, January 5, 1925. 22.

6 The Feast of the Epiphany, observed on January 6, the twelfth day after Christmas, is the oldest festival on the Church calendar, going back to the second century in Asia Minor and Egypt. Epiphany, meaning "manifestation," commemorates the star's leading of the Magi to the manger at Bethlehem. The day is also called the Feast of Kings, Twelfth Day, Twelfthtide, Three Kings' Day, Day of the Three Wise Men, or Old Christmas.

Three religious events are commemorated on January 6: the coming of the three wise men to Bethlehem; the miracle of the changing of the water into wine at the marriage feast; and the baptism of Christ in the Jordan by John the Baptist. 5, 67, 73, 80.

6 Greek Cross Day, observed particularly at Tarpon Springs, Florida, is one of the most beautiful events of the Epiphany season in the United States. It includes mass at the Greek Orthodox Church of Saint Nicholas, a solemn procession, and ceremonies on the banks of the bayou, from which symbolic doves are released and a gold cross is cast into the water to be recovered by divers.

6 Birthday of Joan of Arc, the Maid of Orleans (January 6, 1412–May 30, 1431). The national heroine of France whose life is commemorated on her birthday, or on May 30 when she was burned at the stake, or on May 16, 1920, when she was named a saint. 125, 705.

6 Birthday of Carl Sandburg (January 6, 1878–July 22, 1967). American poet, historian, folklorist, and biographer of Abraham Lincoln. 595, 986.

c6 "Birthday" of Sherlock Holmes, fictional detective in the works of Sir Arthur Conan Doyle. Celebrated on or near this date by the Baker Street Irregulars, a society of Holmes enthusiasts, and other aficionados.

6 Army Day, a holiday in Iraq.

6 New Mexico Admission Day. New Mexico entered the Union on January 6, 1912, as the forty-seventh state. 741.

6 Anniversary of the first around-the-world commercial flight, completed by Pan American Airways, January 6, 1942.

6 Four Freedoms Day, commemorating Franklin Roosevelt's message to Congress of January 6, 1941, which defined the national goals of the United States as "Four Freedoms: Freedom of Speech, Freedom of Worship, Freedom from Want, and Freedom from Fear." 8.

7 Ganna, Christmas Day in Ethiopia, with special celebrations for children at the royal palace in Addis Ababa.

7 Christmas, observed by the Russian Orthodox church on January 7 in accordance with the Julian calendar.

7 Birthday of Millard Fillmore (January 7, 1800–March 8, 1874). English ancestry; New York lawyer; thirteenth president of the United States, 1850–53. Episcopalian. Buried at Forest Lawn, Buffalo, New York. 667–72, 674–75, 678–79.

7 Anniversary of the opening on January 7, 1782, of the first commercial bank in the United States, the Bank of North America in Philadelphia.

7 Anniversary of the first election held under the United States Constitution, on January 7, 1789.

7 Liberian Pioneers' Day, a national holiday in Liberia honoring the nineteenth-century pioneers who came, mostly from the United States, to establish a black nation.

8 The Feast of Saint Gudula, patron saint of Brussels, celebrates with great solemnity the anniversary of the seventh-century saint who is always portrayed in the company of an angel who is lighting her lantern. 705.

8 Birthday of Jacob Collamer (January 8, 1791–November 9, 1865). United States senator from Vermont and postmaster general in 1849–50. Represents the state of Vermont in a Statuary Hall sculpture by Preston Powers. 242.

8 Birthday of William Wilkie Collins (January 8, 1824–September 23, 1889). English novelist remembered for *The Woman in White* and *The Moonstone.* 986.

8 Birthday of John Curtin (January 8, 1885–July 5, 1945). Australian editor, statesman, and prime minister. 18.

8 Birthday of Lowell Mason (January 8, 1792–August 11, 1872). American music educator and hymn writer who composed such familiar hymns as *Nearer, My God, to Thee* and *From Greenland's Icy Mountains.*

8 Battle of New Orleans Day, or Old Hickory's Day, or Jackson Day. A legal holiday in Louisiana commemorating the historic battle with the British won by Andrew Jackson, commander of United States forces, in 1815; as Jackson Day, January 8 is observed by the Democratic party in the United States with banquets and speeches. 244–48.

8 World Literacy Day, observed by a number of member countries of the United Nations to foster universal literacy. 845–49.

8 Anniversary of the first State of the Union message, delivered by President Washington on January 8, 1790.

9 Feast day of Saint Julian, patron saint of hospitality, pilgrims, hotelkeepers, and travelers.

9 Birthday of Carrie Lane Chapman Catt (January 9, 1859–March 9, 1947). American suffrage reformer, founder of the National League of Women Voters in 1919. She was a moving force behind the adoption of the nineteenth amendment to the United States Constitution. 827, 838.

9 Birthday of John Broadus Watson (January 9, 1878–September 25, 1958). American psychologist, founder of the behaviorist school of psychology in the United States. 977.

9 Connecticut Ratification Day. Connecticut entered the Union as the fifth state on January 9, 1788. 741.

9 Anniversary of the first successful balloon ascension in the United States, made on January 9, 1793, in Philadelphia, by a Frenchman, Francois Blanchard.

10 Anniversary of the establishment on January 10, 1429, of the Order of the Golden Fleece, celebrated order of knighthood in Austria-Hungary and Spain.

10 Anniversary of the founding of the League of Nations on January 10, 1920, in a worldwide movement toward peace and cooperation between nations. 789.

10 Anniversary of the first session of the General Assembly of the United Nations, held on January 10, 1946, in London. 784.

11 Birthday of Ezra Cornell (January 11, 1807–December 9, 1874). American capitalist and philanthropist who established and endowed Cornell University. His birthday is observed as Founder's Day at Cornell.

11 Birthday of Eugenio Maria De Hostos (January 11, 1839–August 11, 1903), Puerto Rican philosopher and patriot, commemorated in Puerto Rico.

11 Birthday of Philipp la Renotiere von Ferrary (January 11, 1848–May 20, 1917). International philatelist honored by societies of stamp collectors.

11 Birthday of Alexander Hamilton (January 11, 1755–July 12, 1804). First United States secretary of the treasury; birthday observed by the United States Department of the Treasury. He was elected to the Hall of Fame for Great Americans in 1915. 237, 479, 991.

11 Birthday of William James (January 11, 1842–August 26, 1910). American psychologist and philosopher. His most noted work is *Pragmatism*. 986.

11 Birthday of Sir John Macdonald (January 11, 1815–June 6, 1891). First prime minister of Canada. 995.

11 Albania Proclamation of the Republic Day, a holiday commemorating January 11, 1946, when Albania was established after years of resistance against foreign interests.

11 Chad Independence Day, the official day for the nationwide celebration of independence gained by Chad on August 11, 1960; scheduled for January 11 to avoid the torrential August rain season.

12 Birthday of John Hancock (January 12, 1737–October 8, 1793). American Revolutionary patriot, signer of the Declaration of Independence whose name has become synonymous with the word *signature* because of his distinctive handwriting on that document. 478, 479, 487, 489.

12 Birthday of Johann Heinrich Pestalozzi (January 12, 1746–February 17, 1827). Swiss educational reformer whose beliefs and system laid the foundations for elementary education. 15.

12 Birthday of John Singer Sargent (January 12, 1856–April 15, 1925). Distinguished American portraitist and muralist. A series of Sargent's decorative panels was executed for the Boston Public Library. 986.

12 Birthday of John Winthrop (January 12, 1588–March 26, 1649). American colonial leader; first governor of the Massachusetts Bay Colony. 760.

c12 Meitlisunntig, a Swiss festival held on the second Sunday of January in the Seetal district of Aargau, Switzerland, featuring a military procession of girls re-enacting the roles of women in the Vill-mergen War of 1712.

12 Anniversary of the election on Jan-uary 12, 1932, of Hattie Caraway of Arkansas as the first woman senator in the United States. 822.

12 Anniversary of the establishment on January 12, 1777, of the Mission Santa Clara De Asis in California, dedi-cated to work with the Indians.

12 Anniversary of the establishment of the first museum in the United States at Charleston, South Carolina, Jan-uary 12, 1773.

13 Saint Knute's Day, the twentieth day after Christmas, January 13, the occasion for the dismantling of Christmas trees in Sweden and for celebrating with dances.

13 Tyvendedagen, the twentieth day after Christmas, January 13, the official end of Yuletide in Norway, ob-served in some regions with the traditional "Christmas Race" on sleighs, which carries out the old folk saying that "Saint Knute drives Christmas away."

13 Birthday of Salmon Portland Chase (January 13, 1808–May 7, 1873). American lawyer and statesman, secretary of the treasury under Lincoln; sixth chief justice of the Supreme Court. 15.

13 Anniversary of the death of George Fox (July 1624–January 13, 1691). English founder of the Society of Friends; honored by all Quaker societies. 992.

13 Birthday of Charles Perrault (Jan-uary 13, 1628–May 16, 1703). French lawyer and author; famous for *Les Contes de Perrault*, through which he gave immortality to the folk tales *Cinderella, Sleeping Beauty, Little Red Riding Hood*, and others.

13 Anniversary of the death of Ed-mund Spenser, January 13, 1599. English poet best known for *The Faerie Queene*. 987.

13 Stephen Foster Memorial Day, com-memorating the anniversary of Fos-ter's death, January 13, 1864; permanently established as a memorial by presidential proclamation in 1952; observed by the Stephen Foster Memorial Association and musical organizations. 986, 1002.

14 Feast of Saint Sava, a children's festival in Serbia in honor of Saint Sava, a king's son, who built schools and monasteries all over Serbia and died on January 14, 1237. The day is observed in schools and by communities with feasting, music, and dancing. 705.

14 Birthday of Matthew Fontaine Maury (January 14, 1806–February 1, 1873). American hydrographer and naval officer. He was the first to give a complete description of the Gulf Stream and to chart specific routes for Atlantic crossings. He was elected to the Hall of Fame for Great Americans in 1930. 237, 977.

14 Birthday of Albert Schweitzer (Jan-uary 14, 1875–September 4, 1965). Author, organist, theologian, and medical missionary who established hospitals at Lambaréné, now in Gabon; recipient of the 1952 Nobel Peace Prize for his work for the brotherhood of nations. Among his writings are *The Quest for the Historical Jesus* and *Out of My Life and Thought*. 992.

14 Maryland Ratification Day, com-memorates the ratification by the Continental Congress of the Treaty of Paris officially ending the Revolutionary War and establishing the United States as a sovereign nation. The ratification took place at the Maryland State House, 1784.

15 Feast of Christ of Esquipulas, the Black Christ Festival, observed on January 15 at Esquipulas in Guatemala, named for the famous figure of Christ carved out of dark brown balsam.

15 Anniversary of the death of Mathew B. Brady on January 15, 1896. American photographer who made the first photographic war records on the battle-fields of the Civil War. 587.

c15 Martin Luther King, Jr., Day. Birthday of Martin Luther King, Jr. (January 15, 1929–April 4, 1968). Black champion of civil rights, minister, author, Nobel Peace Prize winner in 1964, proponent of nonviolence. His birth is commemorated as a holiday in Michigan on the second Sunday of January, and his birthday is a holiday in the Virgin Islands. It is a commemorative day in many states in the United States and is observed as Human Relations Day. 546–56.

15 Birthday of Sonya Kovalevski (January 15, 1850–February 10, 1891). Russian mathematician who pioneered in a field that was hostile to women; received the Prix Bordin of the Paris Academy for her achievements.

15 Anniversary of the baptism of Molière (Jean-Baptiste Poquelin) on January 15, 1622. French dramatist recognized as the greatest French writer of comedy. His finest comedy is considered to be *Le Misanthrope*. 986.

15 Birthday of Ella Flagg Young (January 15, 1845–October 26, 1918). American educator, superintendent of the Chicago school system, first woman president of the National Education Association.

15 Adults Day, or Seijin-No-Hi, observed in Japan as a special day in tribute to young men and women who have reached adulthood; observed by families and organizations.

15 Arbor Day, a holiday in Jordan.

c15 Church and Economic Life Day, observed for several days in mid-January by the National Council of Churches to study the problems of applying religious principles to modern business life.

15 Historic Fraunces Tavern Day, a tribute to the 1762 purchase by innkeeper Samuel Fraunces of the DeLancey mansion; twentieth-century Manhattan's oldest building.

15 Teachers' Day, Dia Del Maestro, observed annually in Venezuela on January 15; a national day of tribute to educators.

15 Anniversary of the opening of the British Museum on January 15, 1759, a gift to the nation through the will of Sir Hans Sloane.

15 Anniversary of the incorporation of the Ford Foundation on January 15, 1936, to administer funds for scientific, educational, and charitable purposes.

16 Birthday of Samuel McIntire (January 16, 1757–February 6, 1811). American architect and woodcarver known as "the architect of Salem" for his design and construction of the mansions of Salem shipping merchants.

17 Feast day of Saint Anthony the Abbot, patron saint of butchers, brush makers, and domestic animals; invoked against erysipelas, the disease called "burning fire"; patriarch of all monks. The feast of Saint Anthony is observed throughout the Christian world as the day of the Blessing of the Animals. In California, Switzerland, Mexico, Spain, and other countries, domestic animals are decorated with flowers and bells and are blessed at the church door in the name of Saint Anthony, patron of four-footed beasts. 5, 705.

17 Birthday of Benjamin Franklin (January 17, 1706–April 17, 1790). American printer, statesman, inventor, and diplomat who was America's first world citizen. It has been customary for schools in some areas to start Thrift Week on Franklin's birthday. He was elected to the Hall of Fame for Great Americans in 1900. His birthday is observed annually by the city of Philadelphia, the Franklin Society, and other organizations. 237, 739, 990, 991.

17 Birthday of David Lloyd George (January 17, 1863–March 26, 1945). British statesman, one of the great figures in twentieth-century British history. 15.

17 Birthday of Glenn Luther Martin (January 17, 1886–December 4, 1955). American pioneer aviator and airplane manufacturer who developed several of the most famous military planes; awarded the aeronautics industry's highest award, the Collier Trophy, in 1933, and the Guggenheim Medal of the Institute of Aeronautical Science in 1944.

17 Nautilus Day, anniversary of the launching of the United States submarine the *Nautilus*, the world's first atomic-powered vessel, on January 17, 1955.

18 Peter's Chair at Rome, the major feast of the Roman Catholic church on January 18, commemorates the time when Saint Peter ascended the throne as bishop of Rome and as the first Pope; the beginning of "the church unity octave."

18 Santa Prisca Day in Taxco, Mexico, a holiday honoring the village saint and climaxing one of the most colorful fiestas in Latin America; features the dance of the Moors and the dance of the shepherds in costumes of the Moors and Christians.

18 Birthday of Rubén Darío (January 18, 1867–February 6, 1916). Nicaraguan poet and short-story writer recognized as one of the outstanding poets of Latin America. 987.

18 Birthday of Alan Alexander Milne (January 18, 1882–January 31, 1956). English poet and playwright who is best known for his volumes of verses and prose for children, including *Winnie-the-Pooh*, which became available in 1961 in a Latin translation called *Winnie Ille Pu.*

18 Birthday of Peter Mark Roget (January 18, 1779–September 12, 1869). English physician, author of books on physiology, remembered for the famous *Thesaurus of English Words and Phrases.*

18 Birthday of Daniel Webster (January 18, 1782–October 24, 1852). American statesman, lawyer, and orator whose birthday is observed in Massachusetts. He was elected to the Hall of Fame for Great Americans in 1900. 237, 739.

18 Tunisia National Revolution Day, a holiday in Tunisia, the smallest country of North Africa, honoring the nationalist movements of the 1930s and 1940s that led to independence in 1956 and the abolishment of the monarchy in 1957.

c18 Arbor Day in Florida, observed on the third Friday in January. 163.

19 Feast day of Saint Henry of Uppsala, patron saint of Finland.

19 Birthday of David Starr Jordan (January 19, 1851–September 19, 1931). American educator and biologist; first president of Leland Stanford, Junior, University.

19 Birthday of William Williams Keen (January 19, 1837–June 7, 1932). American surgeon, pioneer in operations on the brain and nervous system.

c19 Robert E. Lee Day. Birthday of Robert Edward Lee (January 19, 1807–October 12, 1870). American soldier and educator; commander of the army of Northern Virginia; president of the college known today as Washington and Lee University. He was elected to the Hall of Fame for Great Americans in 1900. He represents the state of Virginia in Statuary Hall in a sculpture done by Edward Virginius Valentine. Lee's Birthday is observed as a holiday in Alabama, Arkansas, Florida, Georgia, Louisiana, Mississippi, North Carolina, and South Carolina on the day of his birthday or on the third Monday of January. A Robert E. Lee birthday celebration is held annually at Stratford Hall, Virginia, the ancestral home of the Lees, where school children hold special exercises. 580–84.

19 Birthday of Edgar Allan Poe (January 19, 1809–October 7, 1849). American poet, short-story writer, and critic whose influence upon poetry and fiction has been extensive. Elected to the Hall of Fame for Great Americans in 1910. Edgar Allan Poe awards are presented annually by the Mystery Writers Association for the best mystery novel written by an American author, for the best mystery novel published in America, and for radio, motion picture, and television writing in the field. 8, 234, 237, 986.

19 Birthday of James Watt (January 19, 1736–August 25, 1819). Scottish engineer and inventor who developed a separate condensing vessel for the steam engine. The watt and the kilowatt units of power are named in his honor. 15, 977.

19 Confederate Heroes Day, observed in Texas in memory of the Confederate forces of the American Civil War.

c19 Lee-Jackson Day, observed in Virginia on the third Monday of January; combines Lee's birthday of January 19 with Stonewall Jackson's, which falls on January 21.

20 Feast day of Saint Sebastian, patron saint of archers, soldiers, and athletes, a holiday celebrated in Rio de Janeiro with church services, colorful religious processions, and festivities. 705.

20 Birthday of André Marie Ampère (January 20, 1775–June 10, 1836). French physicist, mathematician, and discoverer of "Ampère's law." 977.

20 Birthday of Johannes Vilhelm Jensen (January 20, 1873–November 25, 1950). Danish novelist and lyric poet whose series of epic novels describing the northern peoples from the Ice Age to the fifteenth century brought him the Nobel Prize in literature in 1944. 227.

20 Mali Army Day, a national holiday in Mali, formerly the French Sudan.

20 Presidential Inauguration Day, observed in the capital of the United States every fourth year; a legal holiday in the District of Columbia. 8.

20 Babin Den, Grandmother's Day, observed in Bulgaria. Festivities include ducking of girls by boys in anticipation of good health.

20 Anniversary of the first basketball game, played in Springfield, Massachusetts, on January 20, 1892, under the supervision of Dr. James Naismith, the inventor of the game.

20 Anniversary of the announcement of the "Point Four" program in President Truman's January 20, 1949, inaugural address extending the benefits of American scientific advances to the underdeveloped areas of the world. 18.

21 Feast day of Saint Agnes, patron saint of Girl Scouts, patroness of chastity and young girls. It is the day the Pope blesses two lambs whose wool is used to make circular bands called pallia, which the Pope sends to his archbishops. 5, 125, 705.

21 Altagracia Day, a holiday celebrated in the Dominican Republic on January 21 with a pilgrimage to the Saint Altagracia shrine.

21 Feast day of Saint Meinrad, hermit martyr, celebrated at the Hermitage of Einsiedeln in Switzerland, attracting pilgrimages from all parts of Europe. 705.

c21 World Religion Day, sponsored by the National Spiritual Assembly of the Baha'is of the United States; observed around January 21 "to demonstrate the fundamental oneness of all revealed religion."

21 Birthday of Ethan Allen (January 21, 1738–February 12, 1789). American Revolutionary commander, organizer of the "Green Mountain Boys." Represents the state of Vermont in a Statuary Hall sculpture done by Larkin Goldsmith Mead. 242, 739.

21 Birthday of John Charles Frémont (January 21, 1813–July 13, 1890). American surveyor and army officer who made official expeditions into the American West; frequently called "the Pathfinder." 15, 992.

21 Birthday of Thomas Jonathan Jackson (January 21, 1824–May 10, 1863). American Confederate general known as Stonewall; famous for strategy and tactics in the Civil War. He was elected to the Hall of Fame for Great Americans in 1955. 237.

21 Anniversary of the death of Lenin on January 21, 1924, revolutionary leader of Russia; observed on January 21 in Moscow with processions before the Lenin mausoleum, military displays, and speeches.

21 Anniversary of the death of George Orwell on January 21, 1950. British author best known for *Animal Farm* and *Nineteen Eighty-Four.* 986.

21 Anniversary of the founding of Kiwanis International, a community-service organization for business and professional men, on January 21, 1915, at Detroit, Michigan.

22 Feast day of Saint Vincent of Saragossa, patron saint of winegrowers; celebrated in Europe with processions, prayers, and weather-omen ceremonials. 79.

22 Birthday of Francis Bacon (January 22, 1561–April 9, 1626). English essayist, philosopher, and jurist who developed the inductive method of inquiry. 986.

22 Birthday of George Gordon Byron (January 22, 1788–April 19, 1824). English poet famous for *Childe Harold*. 986, 992.

22 Birthday of August Strindberg (January 22, 1849–May 14, 1912). Swedish novelist and dramatist who influenced the development of expressionistic drama. 986.

22 Birthday of Beatrice Potter Webb (January 22, 1858–April 30, 1943). English economist who collaborated with her husband Sidney Webb on many works on economics.

22 Ukrainian Day, marks the January 1918 proclamation of the free Ukrainian Republic, now a part of the Union of Soviet Socialist Republics.

23 Feast day of Saint Ildephonsus, Doctor of the Church, Archbishop of Toledo, for whom the New Mexican pueblo of San Ildefonso is named and whose feast day is celebrated there with the buffalo dance and other ceremonial dances combining pagan rites and Christian ceremonies. 705.

23 Feast day of Saint Raymund of Penafort, patron saint of confessors and medical-record librarians. 5, 705.

23 The Grand Duchess' Birthday, a national holiday in Luxembourg, one of the smallest and oldest independent countries in Europe; observed with parades and fireworks.

23 Anniversary of the record ocean descent on January 23, 1960 of the United States Navy's bathysphere *Trieste* to the bottom of the Mariana Trench in the Pacific.

24 Feast day of Saint Timothy, patron saint of second- or third-generation clergy; patron saint of those who suffer from stomach trouble.

24 Birthday of Edith Newbold Wharton (January 24, 1862–August 11, 1937). American novelist whose *Ethan Frome* has become an American classic. Her *Age of Innocence* received the Pulitzer Prize in 1921, and *The Old Maid* the Pulitzer Prize in drama in 1935. Edith Wharton was the first woman to receive an honorary degree from Yale University. 229, 986.

24 Alacitis Fair, an annual celebration of the Aymara Indians of Bolivia. It has been held at La Paz for hundreds of years in honor of their god of prosperity, to whom miniature replicas are offered of all the goods the Aymaras would like to have.

24 Anniversary of the discovery of gold in California, January 24, 1848.

25 Feast of Saint Ananias of Damascus, who baptized Paul and brought him into the Church.

25 Feast of the Conversion of Saint Paul, celebrated in the Roman Catholic, Anglican, and Lutheran churches. 73.

25 Birthday of Robert Boyle (January 25, 1627–December 30, 1691). Irish physicist and chemist who set forth the famous Boyle's law. 977.

25 Burns Day, commemorates the birth on January 25, 1759, of Robert Burns, with celebrations in Scotland, England, and Newfoundland. The Scottish-Americans of Minneapolis, St. Paul, and other sections of the United States gather on this date to honor the national poet of Scotland. Burns Clubs around the world hold Burns Night celebrations toasting "The Immortal Memory" and concluding with the singing of Burns's famous *Auld Lange Syne*. 8, 986.

25 Birthday of James Marion Sims (January 25, 1813–November 13, 1883). American surgeon, pioneer in the treatment of women's diseases.

11

26 Feast day of Saint Polycarp, one of the Apostolic Fathers whose martyrdom created the tradition of observing saints' days. 125.

26 Birthday of Roy Chapman Andrews (January 26, 1884–March 11, 1960). American natural scientist, explorer, and author famous for his finding of dinosaur eggs, new geological formations, and the remains of the largest mammal known to have existed. 977, 992.

c26 Australia Day, or Foundation Day, a public holiday in commemoration of the landing on the Australian continent of Captain Arthur Phillip and his company of men and women on January 26, 1788; celebrated on the 26th or on the first Monday after the 26th.

26 Duarte Day, a holiday in the Dominican Republic honoring Juan Pablo Duarte, a founder of the republic and a leader in its fight for liberation from Haiti.

26 India's Republic Day, Basant Panchmi, celebrated in commemoration of the proclamation of the republic on January 26, 1950. It is observed at Delhi with several days of pageantry and military parades.

26 General Douglas MacArthur Day, observed in Arkansas as a memorial day and in tribute to the birthday of the renowned World War II general and Arkansas' most famous son. 998.

26 Michigan Day, commemorates Michigan's admission to the Union as the twenty-sixth state on January 26, 1837. 741.

27 Feast of Saint Devote, patron saint of Monte Carlo. 5, 705.

27 Feast day of Saint John Chrysostom, the "golden-tongued church father," patron saint of preachers of the Word of God. 705.

27 Birthday of Charles Lutwidge Dodgson (January 27, 1832–January 14, 1898). English mathematician and author who wrote under the pseudonym Lewis Carroll; the author of the classic *Alice's Adventures in Wonderland*. 986.

27 Birthday of Samuel Gompers (January 27, 1850–December 13, 1924). American labor leader, first president of the American Federation of Labor. 563, 570, 976.

27 Birthday of Jerome Kern (January 27, 1885–November 11, 1945). American composer who composed almost exclusively for the theater and whose most popular achievement was the score for the musical version of Edna Ferber's novel *Show Boat*. 1002.

27 Birthday of Wolfgang Amadeus Mozart (January 27, 1756–December 5, 1791). Austrian concert pianist and world-renowned composer. In appreciation of his work, Mozart's birthday is celebrated by musical societies in all nations. The annual Salzburg Festival, held in late July through August in Salzburg, honors Mozart. 986.

27 Vietnam Day, the anniversary of the official signing, on January 27, 1973, of the peace agreements to terminate the Vietnam War.

28 Saint Charlemagne's Day, an annual French college celebration, honoring the great emperor at a speechmaking, champagne-drinking breakfast.

28 Birthday of Charles George Gordon (January 28, 1833–January 26, 1885). British soldier and military hero known as Gordon Pasha, Gordon of Khartoum, or Chinese Gordon.

28 Anniversary of the death of John McCrae on January 28, 1918. Canadian physician and poet best remembered for the poem *In Flanders Fields*, frequently used in Veterans Day observances. 801, 992.

28 Birthday of José Marti (January 28, 1853–May 19, 1895). Cuban patriot and writer whose birthday is a national holiday in Cuba.

28 Birthday of Sir Henry Morton Stanley (January 28, 1841–May 10, 1904). Anglo-American explorer remembered for his fulfillment of the mission to find the explorer David Livingstone. 992.

28 Rwanda Democracy Day, a holiday in Rwanda, which is called the African Switzerland; a civic day concerned with equality for all peoples in the nation.

28 Anniversary of the establishment by Congress of the United States Coast Guard on January 28, 1915, combining the Life Saving Service and the Revenue Cutter Service.

29 Feast day of Saint Francis de Sales, patron saint of writers and journalists, and author of the classic *Introduction to the Devout Life*. During his lifetime, he was known as "the Gentle Christ of Geneva."

29 Birthday of Anton Pavlovich Chekhov (January 29, 1860–July 14, 1904). Russian dramatist and short-story writer. 986.

29 Birthday of William McKinley (January 29, 1843–September 14, 1901). Scotch-Irish ancestry; Ohio lawyer; Civil War officer; twenty-fifth president of the United States, 1897–1901. Methodist. Buried at Canton, Ohio. Carnation Day, January 29, was created in honor of President McKinley, and a William McKinley banquet is held annually at Canton, Ohio, on his birthday. 667–79.

29 Birthday of Thomas Paine (January 29, 1737–June 8, 1809). American Revolutionary propagandist and author of *Common Sense, The Rights of Man*, and *The Age of Reason*. Elected to the Hall of Fame for Great Americans in 1945. January 29 was named Common Sense Day in his honor to encourage the use of good sense in appreciating and protecting the rights of all people. 237, 986.

29 Birthday of Romain Rolland (January 29, 1866–December 30, 1944). French novelist, dramatist, and biographer, best known for his novels *Jean-Christophe* and *The Soul Enchanted*. He was awarded the Nobel Prize in literature in 1915. 227.

29 Kansas Day, a statewide holiday commemorating the admission of Kansas as the thirty-fourth state in the Union on January 29, 1861. The anniversary of statehood has been a special day of celebration by the Republicans of Kansas since 1892 and is a popular day for political meetings. 741.

29 Anniversary of the establishment of the American College in Rome on January 29, 1860, by Pope Pius IX.

29 Anniversary of the establishment of the Baseball Hall of Fame on January 29, 1936; the first five men included were Ty Cobb, Walter Johnson, Christy Mathewson, Honus Wagner, and Babe Ruth. 734.

29 Anniversary of the institution by Queen Victoria of the Victoria Cross, the most coveted of all British orders, on January 29, 1856, to reward individual acts of bravery. 228.

30 Saint Charles Day, observed by Anglican churches in commemoration of King Charles the martyr. The Society of Charles the Martyr holds an annual service on January 30 commemorating the execution of King Charles I on the scaffold site in the courtyard of the Royal United Services Museum; commemorative services are held at the church of Saint Martin-in-the-Fields and Trafalgar Square in London on or near February 2. 125, 164.

30 Holiday of the Three Hierarchs, an Eastern Orthodox holy day commemorating Saint Basil, Saint Gregory, and Saint John Chrysostomos.

30 Birthday of Franklin Delano Roosevelt (January 30, 1882–April 12, 1945). Dutch ancestry; lawyer; New York governor; statesman; assistant secretary of the navy under Wilson; thirty-second president of the United States, 1933–45. First president to be elected to a third term. Episcopalian. Buried at Hyde Park, New York, where his house and library are under the jurisdiction of the federal government. Franklin D. Roosevelt Day is a holiday in Kentucky and the Virgin Islands. 667–79.

13

30 Birthday of John Henry Towers (January 30, 1885–April 1, 1955). American naval officer and aviator who, in 1912, established a world's record for endurance in a seaplane; commander of the *Langley*, the first American aircraft carrier; the first naval aviator to reach the rank of admiral.

30 Woman Peerage Day, anniversary of the passage of a bill by the House of Lords on January 30, 1958, and by the House of Commons on February 13, 1958, establishing lifetime peerages for both men and women, thus admitting women into the House of Lords for the first time in its six-and-a-half-century history.

30 Anniversary of the purchase on January 30, 1815, of Thomas Jefferson's library for use by the Library of Congress.

31 Feast day of Saint John Bosco; founder of the Salesians; friend of boys; patron saint of editors. 705.

31 Birthday of Irving Langmuir (January 31, 1881–August 16, 1957). American chemist who is credited with the development of the basic scientific principle and discoveries that have been applied in the atomic age. He received the 1932 Nobel Prize in chemistry for his many contributions to science. 225.

31 Birthday of Alfonso Lopez (January 31, 1886–November 20, 1959). Colombian statesman; president of the United Nations Security Council in 1948.

31 Birthday of Robert Morris (January 31, 1734–May 7, 1806). American merchant, financier of the American Revolution, and signer of the Declaration of Independence. 478, 739.

31 Birthday of Theodore William Richards (January 31, 1868–April 2, 1928). American chemist who won the 1914 Nobel Prize in chemistry for his research in the determination of atomic weights. 225.

31 Birthday of Jackie Robinson (January 31, 1919–October 24, 1972). First black man to play in major-league baseball; recipient of the Spingarn Medal in 1956. Elected to the Baseball Hall of Fame in 1962. 1.

31 Birthday of Franz Peter Schubert (January 31, 1797–November 19, 1828). Austrian composer, famous for *The Unfinished Symphony* and for such songs as *Who Is Sylvia?* 986.

31 Nauru Independence Day, a holiday in Nauru, an island in the Pacific Ocean, commemorating the achievement of independence on January 31, 1968.

c31 Dicing for the Maid's Money Day, a ceremony held near the end of January in Guildford, Surrey, England, to fulfill the terms of a seventeenth-century will providing for the casting of lots by two maidservants for the interest from a trust. 164.

c31 Up-Helly-Aa, an old Norse fire festival, observed with all the old ceremonials at Lerwick in the Shetland Islands on the last Tuesday of January. 164.

February

February, the second month of the Gregorian calendar, gets its name from *Februarius* through the verb *februare*, meaning "to purify." It is the shortest month, with twenty-eight days, except in Leap Year when it has twenty-nine. In ancient Rome it was the month of purification, with special ceremonies of repentance held at the festival of Februa on February 15. In the twentieth century, it is a period for many Christians of preparation for Easter. It is frequently, but depending upon the date of Easter, the month of Mardi Gras and other pre-Lenten carnivals. It is also the month of great sports events. In the United States, February is sometimes called Presidents' Month because of the observance of the birthdays of two great American presidents, Washington and Lincoln.

The flowers for February are the violet and the primrose. The birthstone is the amethyst.

The Fixed Days of February

1 Feast day of Saint Brigid, or Bride, patroness of Irish nuns, dairy workers, and of Ireland, Wales, Australia, and New Zealand. 5, 705.

1 Birthday of Thomas Campbell (February 1, 1763–January 4, 1854). Irish religious leader who founded, with his son, the Church of the Disciples of Christ in America.

1 Birthday of Sir Edward Coke (February 1, 1552–September 3, 1634). English jurist, an eminent legal specialist on the supremacy of the common law. 18.

1 Birthday of Granville Stanley Hall (February 1, 1844–April 24, 1924). American psychologist, an authority on child and educational psychology; first president of the American Psychological Association.

1 Birthday of Victor Herbert (February 1, 1859–May 26, 1924). American composer and conductor whose operettas *Babes in Toyland, Naughty Marietta*, and others are a part of the musical heritage of the United States. 1002.

1 Birthday of Langston Hughes (February 1, 1902–May 22, 1967). Black American poet; innovator in the interpretation of the black experience in the United States. Known also for his anthologies *The Poetry of the Negro* and *The Book of Negro Folklore*, compiled with Arna Bontemps. 860, 1000.

1 Air Force Day, a holiday in Nicaragua honoring the achievements of the nation's airmen.

1 National Freedom Day, commemorates the signing by President Lincoln on February 1, 1865, of the thirteenth amendment to the Constitution, which abolished slavery. A presidential proclamation of 1949 established the perpetuity of this observance.

1 People's Day, stresses the importance of the individual and underscores the precedence of people over property.

1 Anniversary of the first meeting of the Supreme Court of the United States on February 1, 1790, with Chief Justice John Jay presiding.

2 Candlemas Day, or Feast of the Purification of the Blessed Virgin Mary, observed in Roman Catholic and Anglican churches. The blessing of candles is one of the great traditions of this day. The Dia de la Candelaria is a particularly popular festival in Mexico and other Latin American countries. 80, 125.

2 Birthday of Christian Gauss (February 2, 1878–November 1, 1951). American educator and writer in whose name Phi Beta Kappa presents an annual award for an outstanding book published in the United States on literary scholarship or criticism. 234.

2 Birthday of Solomon R. Guggenheim (February 2, 1861–November 3, 1949). American capitalist and philanthropist; founder in 1937 of the Guggenheim Foundation, which maintains the Solomon R. Guggenheim Museum in New York.

2 Birthday of James Joyce (February 2, 1882–January 13, 1941). Irish poet and novelist, author of *Ulysses*, considered to be a masterpiece in world literature. 986.

2 Birthday of Gabriel Naudé (February 2, 1600–July 30, 1653). French librarian, administrator of the Mazarin Library.

2 Anniversary of the death of Giovanni Palestrina on February 2, 1594. Italian composer celebrated for his masses and other sacred music. 986.

2 Groundhog Day, a traditional day of observance. According to folklore, if the groundhog, or woodchuck, comes out of his burrow on this day and sees his shadow, he will go back for another six weeks. In Canada, the bear is sometimes substituted for the groundhog.

2 Anniversary of the signing of the Treaty of Guadalupe Hidalgo, ceding Texas, New Mexico, Arizona, and California to the United States; signed by Mexico and the United States, February 2, 1848.

3 Feast day of Saint Anskar, or Ansgar, missionary to Denmark, Sweden, Norway, and Northern Germany; patron saint of Denmark. 5, 705.

3 Feast day of Saint Blaise, patron saint of people who suffer from sore throats, of wool combers, and of waxchandlers; throats are blessed on this day; a public holiday in Paraguay. 5, 705.

3 The Fiesta of San Blas, protector of the harvests, celebrated in Puerto Rico in the sugar-harvest towns, with outstanding religious observances at Coamo, whose patron saint is San Blas.

3 Birthday of Elizabeth Blackwell (February 3, 1821–May 31, 1910). First woman doctor in the United States, founder of the New York Infirmary for Women and Children, and lecturer on hygiene and preventive medicine. An American Women's Medical Association Award for distinguished service has been named in her honor. 843, 990.

3 Anniversary of the death of Johann Gensfleisch Gutenberg on February 3, 1468. German inventor of movable type; publisher of the Gutenberg Bible, "the finest example of printer's art ever known." 977.

3 Birthday of Elisha Kent Kane (February 3, 1820–February 16, 1857). American physician and Arctic explorer for whom the Kane Basin is named.

3 Birthday of Sidney Lanier (February 3, 1842–September 7, 1881). American poet, musician, and critic. Elected to the Hall of Fame for Great Americans in 1945. 237.

3 Birthday of Felix Mendelssohn-Bartholdy (February 3, 1809–November 4, 1847). German romantic composer famous for piano and violin concertos, oratorios, and chamber music. 986.

3 Birthday of Gertrude Stein (February 3, 1874–July 27, 1946). American author whose *Making of Americans* led to a heated literary controversy over style and meaning. *The Autobiography of Alice B. Toklas* was actually Gertrude Stein's autobiography. 837.

c3 The Bean-throwing Festival, or Setsubun, observed in Japan on or near February 3 with good fortune bean-throwing ceremonies that have come down from ancient times to the present. Setsubun marks the last day of winter in the lunar calendar.

3 Four Chaplains Memorial Day, honoring Alexander Goode, Jewish chaplain; Father John P. Washington, Roman Catholic chaplain; and George L. Fox and Clark V. Poling, Protestant chaplains, who gave up their life jackets to others and went down with the *Dorchester* on February 3, 1943.

c3 Homstrom, a Swiss festival celebrating the end of winter with the burning of straw men as a symbol of the departing Old Man Winter; observed on the first Sunday in February.

3 Anniversary of the issuance on February 3, 1690, of the first paper money in America; issued by the American colonists to pay soldiers fighting in the war with Quebec.

4 Feast day of Saint Andrew Corsini, bishop of Fiesoli, mediator between quarrelsome Italian states; a saint invoked to compose quarrels and discords. 705.

4 Anniversary of the death of Miguel Covarrubias on February 4, 1957. Mexican painter and illustrator of such books as *The Eagle, The Jaguar,* and *The Serpent.*

4 Birthday of Mark Hopkins (February 4, 1802–June 17, 1887). American educator and moral philosopher who served as president of Williams College. He was elected to the Hall of Fame for Great Americans in 1915. 237.

4 Birthday of Charles Augustus Lindbergh (February 4, 1902–August 26, 1974). American aviator known as "the Lone Eagle" for his pioneering solo flight across the Atlantic on May 20–21, 1927; the first American private citizen to become a public hero. 219, 200.

4 Sri Lanka Independence Day, a national holiday commemorating the granting of independence on February 4, 1948, to the former British colony which changed its name in 1972 from Ceylon to Sri Lanka.

4 Kosciuszko Day, observed by Polish-American communities in the United States to honor the February 4, 1746, birth of Tadeusz Kosciuszko, who fought with the colonists in the American Revolutionary War. 557–59.

4 Anniversary of the incorporation of the National Institute of Arts and Letters on February 4, 1913, with the objective of furthering literature and the fine arts in the United States.

4 Anniversary of the founding of the United Service Organizations (USO) on February 4, 1941, to serve the social, educational, religious, and welfare needs of the United States armed forces. The February 4 anniversary is observed annually at service centers.

4 Anniversary of the organization of the first Winter Olympic games on February 4, 1932.

5 Feast day of Saint Agatha, patron saint of Malta; patroness of nurses, bell founders, jewelers, and fire fighters; invoked for protection against fire in homes. 5, 705.

5 Japanese Martyr Day, memorializing Saint Peter Baptist and his companions, who were killed by the Emperor Tagosama in 1597.

5 Birthday of Hiram Stevens Maxim (February 5, 1840–November 24, 1916). Anglo-American inventor whose most important invention was the automatic single-barrel rifle; honored by gun and rifle societies. 977.

5 Birthday of Dwight Lyman Moody (February 5, 1837–December 22, 1899). American evangelist who built the first YMCA building in America in Chicago, conducted revivals all over the world with Ira Sankey, organist, and founded the Chicago Bible Institute, now known as the Moody Bible Institute.

5 Birthday of Robert Peel (February 5, 1788–July 2, 1850). English prime minister, nineteenth-century orator, advocate of liberal reforms. The British police became known as "bobbies" as a result of his interest in public safety and criminal-investigation reforms. 15.

5 Birthday of Adlai Ewing Stevenson (February 5, 1900–July 14, 1965). Lawyer; governor of Illinois; United States representative to the United Nations. 15, 447.

5 Mexican Constitution Day, a legal holiday in Mexico honoring the anniversaries of the constitutions of 1857 and 1917.

5 Anniversary of the Liberation of the Republic, a public holiday in San Marino.

5 Roger Williams Day, observed by American Baptists to celebrate the arrival of Roger Williams, their American founder, on the North American continent on February 5, 1631. Roger Williams represents Rhode Island in a Statuary Hall sculpture done by Franklin Simmons. 8, 242.

5 Runeberg's Day, observed in Finland to honor Johan Ludvig Runeberg, Finland's leading poet, on the day of his birth, February 5, 1804.

6 Feast day of Saint Dorothea, patroness of gardeners and florists. 705.

6 Birthday of Sir Henry Irving (February 6, 1838–October 13, 1905). English actor-manager who made his reputation in the role of Hamlet. He was knighted in 1895, the first actor to receive this honor; buried in Westminster Abbey.

6 Birthday of Károly Kisfaludy (February 6, 1788–November 21, 1830). Hungarian romantic poet and dramatist who inspired his fellow Hungarians to voice their national cultural heritage.

6 Birthday of Milton Bennett Medary (February 6, 1874–August 7, 1929). American architect whose work is represented by the Washington Memorial Chapel at Valley Forge and the Edward A. Bok Carillon Tower at Mountain Lake, Florida.

6 Birthday of George Herman (Babe) Ruth (February 6, 1895–August 16, 1948). American baseball player whose home-run record was not exceeded until 1974 with the triumph of Henry Aaron, black player with the Atlanta Braves. 729, 731.

6 Massachusetts Ratification Day. Massachusetts entered the Union on February 6, 1788, as the sixth state of the original thirteen. 741.

6 New Zealand Day, or Waitangi, commemorates the signing of the 1840 Waitangi Treaty between the Maori and the Europeans; a national holiday in New Zealand.

6 Anniversary of the accession of Elizabeth II to the British throne on February 6, 1952, recognized annually by the royal salutes fired by the Queen's Troops of the Royal Horse Artillery.

7 Birthday of Alfred Adler (February 7, 1870–May 28, 1937). Austrian psychiatrist, author, and major proponent of the "inferiority complex" theory. 977.

7 Birthday of John Deere (February 7, 1804–May 17, 1886). American inventor and manufacturer of the steel plow.

7 Birthday of Charles Dickens (February 7, 1812–June 9, 1870). English novelist whose major works, which include *Oliver Twist, David Copperfield*, and *A Tale of Two Cities*, are still popular. Dickens is buried in Westminster Abbey. 986.

7 Birthday of Frederick Douglass (February 7, 1817–February 20, 1895). Leader in the abolition movement and first black citizen to hold high rank in the United States government as a consultant to President Lincoln and United States minister to Haiti. 1, 990, 993.

7 Birthday of Sinclair Lewis (February 7, 1885–January 10, 1951). American novelist and playwright. The first American to receive the Nobel Prize in literature; presented to him in 1930. 226, 227.

7   Birthday of Sir James Augustus Henry Murray (February 7, 1837–July 26, 1915). Scottish philologist and lexicographer whose lifework was the *New English Dictionary on Historical Principles*, now known as the *Oxford English Dictionary*.

7   Birthday of John Rylands (February 7, 1801–December 11, 1888). English merchant and philanthropist whose memorial is the treasure-rich John Rylands Library in Manchester, England.

7   Grenada Independence Day, a holiday in the Caribbean island of Grenada honoring the attainment of complete independence on February 7, 1974.

7   Anniversary of the authorization on February 7, 1936, of a flag for the office of the vice-president of the United States.

8   Birthday of William Tecumseh Sherman (February 8, 1820–February 14, 1891). American Union general remembered as the leader of the march through Georgia during the Civil War and famous for the phrase "War is hell." Elected to the Hall of Fame for Great Americans in 1905. 237.

8   Birthday of Jules Verne (February 8, 1828–March 24, 1905). French novelist famous for *Twenty Thousand Leagues under the Sea*, an author whose writings stimulated the development of science fiction. 986.

c8   Boy Scouts Day, commemorates the incorporation of the Boy Scouts of America on February 8, 1910. A Boy Scouts of America Sabbath is usually scheduled for a Sunday near this date. Boy Scouts Day is scheduled annually near the date of the organization's birthday and is followed by week- or month-long activities.

8   Narvik Sun Pageant Day, celebrates the return of the sun after its winter absence, observed on February 8 at Narvik, Norway.

9   Feast day of Saint Apollonia, patron saint of dentists; invoked against toothaches and all dental troubles. 705.

9   Birthday of George Ade (February 9, 1866–May 16, 1944). American playwright and humorist who was famous for his *Fables in Slang*.

9   Birthday of Mrs. Patrick Campbell (February 9, 1865–April 9, 1940). English actress and great friend of George Bernard Shaw, who wrote *Pygmalion* as a vehicle for her talents.

9   Birthday of William H. Harrison (February 9, 1773–April 4, 1841). English ancestry. Ohio lawyer and soldier; congressman; ninth president of the United States, 1841. Died in the White House after one month in office. Episcopalian. Buried at North Bend, Ohio. 667–72.

9   Birthday of Sir Leander Starr Jameson (February 9, 1853–November 16, 1917). South African statesman; prime minister of Cape Colony. 15.

9   Birthday of Amy Lowell (February 9, 1874–May 12, 1925). American poet, biographer, and critic, a leader among the imagist poets; author of a monumental life of Keats. 986.

9   Birthday of Samuel Jones Tilden (February 9, 1814–August 4, 1886). American politician and philanthropist whose will established the Tilden Foundation, one of the integral components of the New York Public Library. 573.

9   Anniversary of the proclamation of the Confederate States of America on February 9, 1861. Jefferson Davis became the provisional president on February 18, 1861.

9   Anniversary of the establishment of the United States National Weather Service as a unit of the United States Army on February 9, 1870.

10   Feast of Saint Paul's Shipwreck off the coast of Malta in A.D. 60, commemorated in Malta.

10   Feast day of Saint Scholastica, sister of Saint Benedict and special patroness of the Benedictine nuns; patron saint of children in convulsions. 5, 705.

10 Birthday of Charles Lamb (February 10, 1775–December 27, 1834). English essayist and critic whose works include a variety of material from *Tales from Shakespeare* to the miscellaneous *Last Essays of Elia*. 720, 986.

10 Birthday of Boris Leonidovich Pasternak (February 10, 1890–May 30, 1960). Russian poet, novelist and translator who was awarded the 1958 Nobel Prize in literature but was forced to refuse it because of political opposition; the author of *Doctor Zhivago*. 227, 986.

10 Birthday of William Allen White (February 10, 1868–January 29, 1944). American journalist and author, editor of the Emporia *Gazette*, who was known as "the Sage of Emporia." Among the editorials for which he was noted were "To an Anxious Friend," which won a Pulitzer Prize, and the one on his daughter Mary at the time of her accidental death. The William Allen White Children's Book Award is given annually for a children's book chosen by Kansas school children. 234.

c11 The Feast of Our Lady's Miraculous Apparitions to Saint Bernadette Soubirous at Lourdes, a major religious weeklong celebration at Lourdes. The Philippine Catholics observe the anniversary of the apparition with a spectacular fete including religious rites, long processions, and a fiesta. 125.

11 Birthday of Lydia Maria Child (February 11, 1802–October 20, 1880). American author and abolitionist; editor of *Juvenile Miscellany*, the first children's periodical of literary merit. 825.

11 Birthday of Thomas Alva Edison (February 11, 1847–October 18, 1931). American inventor who took out over a thousand patents. His best-known inventions are the phonograph and the incandescent lamp. He was elected to the Hall of Fame for Great Americans in 1960. The Thomas Alva Edison Foundation presents four awards annually in honor of Edison: for the best science book for children and youth and for books that contribute to character development and to an understanding of American history. 237, 977.

11 Birthday of Melville Weston Fuller (February 11, 1833–July 4, 1910). American lawyer; eighth chief justice of the United States.

11 Birthday of Josiah Willard Gibbs (February 11, 1839–April 28, 1903). American physicist and chemist. Elected to the Hall of Fame for Great Americans in 1950. 237.

11 Cameroon Youth Day, a public holiday in Cameroon, a republic on the west coast of Africa, dedicated to the children and young people of the nation.

11 Giorno della Conciliazione, Day of Conciliation, a holiday in Italy commemorating the treaty between the Holy See and Italy confirmed on February 11, 1929. The state of Vatican City, an independent sovereign country under papal temporal government, was accorded international status on this day.

11 Japanese National Foundation Day, a national holiday in Japan commemorating the founding of the nation of Japan in 660 B.C. by the first emperor.

11 Liberia Armed Forces Day, a public holiday honoring the professional army and navy and the militia of Liberia.

c11 The Gasparilla Carnival, recreating the days of the pirates, has been held in Tampa, Florida, since 1904. The carnival is held in mid-February and revives the nineteenth-century Gasparilla, the Spanish pirate, his buccaneers, and their three-masted sloop with welcoming ceremonies at the harbor, pirate parades, fireworks, and balls. 8.

11 National Inventors Day, honors the work of all inventors; observed by programs and exhibits of societies of inventors.

c11 Pageant of Light, held at Fort Myers, Florida, near the time of Edison's birthday on February 11; honors the great inventor who built a laboratory in Fort Myers in 1884.

11 White Shirt Day, a day of recognition marking the end of the 1937 sit-down strikes at the plants in Flint, Michigan; observed through the wearing of white shirts by "blue-collar" workers as a symbol of the dignity of work.

12 Birthday of Peter Cooper (February 12, 1791–April 4, 1883). American industrialist and civic leader whose name lives in the Cooper Union for the Advancement of Science and Art, which he founded and endowed. He was elected to the Hall of Fame for Great Americans in 1900. 237.

12 Birthday of Charles Robert Darwin (February 12, 1809–April 19, 1882). English biologist whose theory of evolution by natural selection came to be known as Darwinism. His most-noted work is *On the Origin of the Species by Means of Natural Selection, or the Preservation of Favored Races in the Struggle for Life.* 977, 986.

12 Birthday of Abraham Lincoln (February 12, 1809–April 15, 1865). English ancestry; Illinois lawyer and debater; sixteenth president of the United States, 1861–65. Assassinated in office. Called "the Great Emancipator." No formal religious affiliation. Buried in Oak Ridge Cemetery, Springfield, Illinois. Lincoln was elected to the Hall of Fame for Great Americans in 1900. Lincoln's Birthday is celebrated in thirty-one states of the Union on his birthday or on the first Monday of February. 585–97, 667–79.

12 Birthday of Cotton Mather (February 12, 1663–February 13, 1728). American colonial minister, man of letters, and author of the most important literary work produced in the colonies, the *Magnalia Christi Americana,* an "ecclesiastical history of New England." 986.

c12 Race Relations Sunday, observed on the Sunday nearest Lincoln's birthday, dedicated to understanding among all races.

12 Burma Union Day, a public holiday in Burma commemorating the 1947 conference of national and ethnic leaders which led to the formation of the Union of Burma.

12 Chile Independence Day, a day of tribute recognizing February 12, 1818, when Chile achieved complete independence from Spain after seven years of bitter warfare; the Independence Day celebrations are held on September 18, honoring the first declaration of independence issued on September 18, 1810.

12 Georgia Day, or Oglethorpe Day, a legal holiday in Georgia commemorating the landing of James Edward Oglethorpe and his colonists at Savannah on February 12, 1733.

12 Nancy Hanks Lincoln Memorial Day, observed at Booneville, Indiana, on February 12, and at Lincoln City, Indiana, on May 30.

12 Anniversary of the establishment of the National Association for the Advancement of Colored People (NAACP) on February 12, 1909.

13 Birthday of David Dudley Field (February 13, 1805–April 13, 1894). American jurist and pioneer codifier of laws.

13 Birthday of Robert Houghwout Jackson (February 13, 1892–October 9, 1954). American lawyer, associate justice of the United States Supreme Court, member of the War Crimes Commission, and chief United States prosecutor at the International Military Tribunal at Nuremberg. 573.

13 Anniversary of the initial issue of the first magazine published in the United States, *The American Magazine, or a monthly review of the political state of the British Colonies,* dated February 13, 1741.

13 Anniversary of the establishment of the American Society of Composers, Authors and Publishers (ASCAP) on February 13, 1914.

13 Anniversary of the establishment of the Boston Latin School, oldest public school in America with a continuous existence, which opened on February 13, 1635.

13 Anniversary of the opening of the first state university in the United States, the University of North Carolina, in 1795.

13 Fiesta de Menendez, observed in Saint Augustine, Florida, to honor the 1565 birthday of the city's founder.

14 Feast day of Saint Valentine, patron saint of lovers, invoked against epilepsy, plague, and fainting diseases; commemorated by the secular Valentine's Day.

14 Birthday of Richard Allen (February 14, 1760–March 26, 1831). American clergyman, founder and first bishop of the African Methodist church. The first black to be regularly ordained in the Methodist Episcopal church. 1.

14 Birthday of Nicolaus Copernicus (February 14, 1473–May 24, 1543). Polish doctor and scientist who is known as the "Founder of Modern Astronomy"; creator of the Copernican system. 977.

14 Birthday of George Jean Nathan (February 14, 1882–April 8, 1958). American editor, drama critic, cofounder of *The American Mercury*, prolific author, and mentor of such playwrights as Eugene O'Neill, Arthur Miller, and William Saroyan.

14 Birthday of Anna Howard Shaw (February 14, 1847–July 2, 1919). American suffrage leader, physician, and minister, the first woman ordained in the Methodist church.

14 Birthday of Joseph Thomson (February 14, 1858–August 2, 1895). Scottish geologist and naturalist who conducted explorations into Africa that yielded important data on the flora, fauna, and geology of the African continent. Thomson's gazelle, an East African species, was named for him.

14 Birthday of Israel Zangwill (February 14, 1864–August 1, 1926). English author whose best work deals with Jewish subjects, as in *Children of the Ghetto: A Study of a Peculiar People.*

14 Admission Day in Arizona, a legal holiday commemorating February 14, 1912, when President Taft signed the proclamation admitting Arizona as the forty-eighth state. It is celebrated by schools and patriotic groups. 741.

14 Day of national mourning in Mexico commemorating the death of Vincente Guerrero, revolutionary hero, on February 14, 1831.

14 Fjortende Februar (Fourteenth of February) is the traditional day for the exchange of tokens and gifts among schoolchildren in Denmark.

14 Literacy Day, a holiday in Liberia established to honor the worldwide campaign to wipe out illiteracy and to encourage adult education in that republic.

14 Oregon Statehood Day, commemorates Oregon's entry into the Union on February 14, 1859, as the thirty-third state. 741.

14 Valentine's Day, a folk festival, bears the name of the saint and continues the customs of the pagan festival called "Lupercalia." The widespread custom of exchanging cards and gifts on this day has no connection with Saint Valentine but is enjoyed by children of all ages. England, France, and, more recently, the United States are among the countries that unofficially celebrate this holiday. 8, 790–95.

14 Viticulturists' Day, or Trifon Zarezan, a centuries-old festivity celebrated in Bulgaria with customs based on the cult of Dionysus, god of wine and merriment.

15 Birthday of Susan Brownell Anthony (February 15, 1820–March 13, 1906). American abolitionist; pioneer crusader for women's civil rights, temperance, and Negro suffrage; author and lecturer. Elected to the Hall of Fame for Great Americans in 1950. Her birthday is observed in Minnesota and in other sections of the United States. 237, 825, 837.

15 Birthday of Oswaldo Aranha (February 15, 1894–January 27, 1960). Brazilian lawyer and statesman who served as the president of the United Nations Assembly in 1947.

15 Birthday of Galileo Galilei (February 15, 1564–January 8, 1642). Italian astronomer, mathematician, and physicist, considered to be the founder of the experimental method. 977.

15 Birthday of Cyrus Hall McCormick (February 15, 1809–May 13, 1884). American inventor of the mechanical reaper, industrialist, and philanthropist who endowed the McCormick Theological Seminary.

15 Birthday of Elihu Root (February 15, 1845–February 7, 1937). American lawyer and statesman, secretary of war under President McKinley. Recipient of the 1912 Nobel Peace Prize. 241.

15 Birthday of Alfred North Whitehead (February 15, 1861–December 30, 1947). English mathematician and philosopher. His most distinguished work is *Principia Mathematica*, which he wrote with Bertrand Russell. 977.

15 Battleship Day, observed in Maine in honor of the United States battleship called the *Maine*, which was blown up in the Havana harbor on February 15, 1898; the fate of the ship created the slogan "Remember the Maine," which became a part of the vocabulary of American history.

15 Anniversary of the establishment of the city of Saint Louis, Missouri, by Auguste Chouteau in 1764.

15 Spanish-American War Memorial Day and *Maine* Memorial Day, commemorating the war and honoring the men of the *Maine*, is recognized in Massachusetts.

15 Anniversary of the February 15, 1971, adoption by Britain of decimal currency after 1,200 years of a system based on 12-penny shillings.

16 Birthday of Henry Adams (February 16, 1838–March 27, 1918). American historian and philosopher whose best-known works are *Mont-Saint-Michel and Chartres* and *The Education of Henry Adams*; recipient of the Pulitzer Prize in 1919. 229.

16 Birthday of Ernst Heinrich Haeckel (February 16, 1834–August 9, 1919). German naturalist and philosopher. Leading exponent of the biological theory of evolution. 977.

16 Lithuanian Independence Day, marks the proclamation of independence for Lithuania in 1918; commemorated by Lithuanian-American communities and organizations with special programs and group observances.

16 Anniversary of the founding of the Benevolent and Protective Order of Elks in New York on February 16, 1868.

c17 World Day of Prayer, sponsored by the United Church Women, National Council of Churches, is observed around February 17.

17 Birthday of Dorothy Canfield Fisher (February 17, 1879–November 9, 1958). American novelist of stories dealing with Vermont life, a member of the book selection committee of the Book-of-the-Month Club from 1926 to 1951. A Dorothy Canfield Fisher Library Award has been established by the Book-of-the-Month Club as a memorial, with funds to be used by small libraries for the purchase of books.

17 Birthday of René Théophile Laënnec (February 17, 1781–August 13, 1826). French physician who invented the stethoscope, called "the Father of Chest Medicine." 977.

17 Anniversary of the organization of the National Congress of Parents and Teachers in Washington, D.C., February 17, 1897. The founders are honored annually on this day.

18 Festival of Saint Bernadette and the anniversary of her third vision, celebrated at Lourdes. 125.

18 Birthday of George Peabody (February 18, 1795–November 4, 1869). American merchant, financier, and philanthropist. Elected to the Hall of Fame for Great Americans in 1900. 237.

18 Birthday of Solomon Rabinowitz (February 18, 1859–May 13, 1916). Russian author, best known under the pen name of Sholom Aleichem. A master of the short story, he is known as "the Yiddish Mark Twain." 986.

18 Birthday of Alessandro Volta (February 18, 1745–March 5, 1827). Italian physicist and pioneer in the science of electricity; inventor of the electric battery. 977.

18 Birthday of Wendell Lewis Willkie (February 18, 1892–October 8, 1944). American lawyer, public-utility executive, and presidential candidate whose book *One World* added a new phrase to the common language.

18 Gambia Independence Day, a public holiday commemorating February 18, 1965, when Gambia, a British West African colony, became a self-governing nation within the Commonwealth.

18 Nepal Constitution Day, the anniversary of the adoption of a constitution on February 18, 1952.

19 Birthday of Francis Preston Blair, Jr. (February 19, 1821–July 9, 1875). American congressman from Missouri. He represents Missouri in Statuary Hall in a sculpture done by Alexander Doyle. 242.

19 Birthday of Elie Ducommun (February 19, 1833–December 7, 1906). Swiss journalist and pacifist, leader in the organization of the International League of Peace and Freedom, corecipient of the Nobel Peace Prize in 1902. 241.

19 Birthday of Sven Anders Hedin (February 19, 1865–November 26, 1952). Swedish scientist and explorer whose explorations in central and eastern Asia determined the source of the Indus and the continuity of the Trans-Himalayan Range.

19 Constitution Day, a holiday in Gabon, on the west coast of Africa, commemorating the proclamation of the constitution on February 19, 1959.

19 Martyr's Day in Ethiopia, a public holiday honoring the memory of the many Ethiopians killed in the Italian invasion of the 1930s.

19 Anniversary of the founding of the Knights of Pythias on February 19, 1864.

20 Anniversary of the death of Klas Pontus Arnoldson on February 20, 1916. Swedish author, founder of the Swedish Society for Peace and Arbitration; corecipient of the Nobel Peace Prize in 1908. 241.

20 John Glenn Day, commemorating the first orbit of the earth by a United States astronaut; John Glenn orbited on February 20, 1962.

21 Birthday of Wystan Hugh Auden (February 21, 1907–September 27, 1973). English-born American poet known as a "Poet's Poet." Awarded the 1948 Pulitzer Prize for his long philosophical poem *The Age of Anxiety*. 229.

21 Birthday of Otto Hermann Kahn (February 21, 1867–March 29, 1934). American banker and philanthropist who organized the Metropolitan Opera Company in 1907.

21 Anniversary of the death of Malcolm Little, known as Malcolm X, on February 21, 1965. Black militant leader; organizer of Muslim Mosque, Inc.; founder of the Organization of Afro-American Unity; and author of an *Autobiography* of widespread interest and influence. 1.

21 Birthday of John Henry Newman (February 21, 1801–August 11, 1890). English cardinal-deacon; author of the hymn *Lead Kindly Light* and the autobiography *Apologia pro Vita Sua*; honored by Newman societies in the United States and Europe. 986.

21 Birthday of Alice Freeman Palmer (February 21, 1855–December 6, 1902). Pioneer American educator. Elected to the Hall of Fame for Great Americans in 1920. 237.

21 Bangladesh National Mourning Day, a national holiday and memorial day in Bangladesh.

21 Anniversary of the dedication on February 21, 1885, of the Washington Monument in Washington, D.C., designed by Robert Mills.

22 Birthday of Sir Robert Stephenson Smyth Baden-Powell (February 22, 1857–January 8, 1941). British major general, founder of the Boy Scouts, and, with his sister, of the Girl Guides.

22 Birthday of Eric Gill (February 22, 1882–November 17, 1940). English sculptor, engraver, and typographer who carved the stations of the cross at Westminster Cathedral, executed other important commissions, and illustrated *Canterbury Tales, The Four Gospels*, and other books. Notable among his own writings are *Christianity and Art* and his *Autobiography*.

22 Birthday of James Russell Lowell (February 22, 1819–August 12, 1891). American poet, essayist, and diplomat. Remembered for *The Vision of Sir Launfal*. He was elected to the Hall of Fame for Great Americans in 1905. 237, 986.

22 Birthday of Edna St. Vincent Millay (February 22, 1892–October 19, 1950). American poet who made her reputation with the publication of *Renascence* in 1917. She received the Pulitzer Prize for *The Harp Weaver* and wrote the libretto for an opera composed by Deems Taylor. 229, 837.

22 Birthday of Arthur Schopenhauer (February 22, 1788–September 21, 1860). German philosopher and man of letters whose greatest work is *The World as Will and Idea*. 986.

22 Birthday of George Washington (February 22, 1732–December 14, 1799). English ancestry; Virginia planter; surveyor; colonel in Virginia militia; member of the House of Burgesses; commander-in-chief of the Continental Army; first president of the United States, 1789–97; Episcopalian. Buried at Mount Vernon, Virginia. Elected to the Hall of Fame for Great Americans in 1900. Washington's Birthday is observed as a legal holiday in all states, the District of Columbia, Canal Zone, Guam, Puerto Rico, and the Virgin Islands. It has been observed since 1782, while the Revolution was still being fought. Since 1971, Washington's Birthday has been observed in most states on the third Monday of February. 806–16.

c22 Brotherhood Week always includes Washington's Birthday in honor of the first president, who is a symbol of the nation's dedication to freedom from religious and racial prejudice. Brotherhood Week has been proclaimed continuously by the president since 1934. The original idea came from a Roman Catholic priest, Monsignor Hugh McNenamin.

22 Day of national mourning in Mexico, a holiday commemorating the February 22, 1913, death of Francisco I. Madero, who led the campaign to overthrow the dictatorship of Porfirio Díaz.

22 Girl Guides Thinking Day, observed by the members of the Girl Guides of England and the British Commonwealth countries; commemorates the February 22, 1857, birthday of their founder, Sir Baden-Powell.

22 Mother's Day in India, established as a memorial to Mrs. Mohandas K. Gandhi, the wife of India's most famous citizen.

c22 Presidents' Day in Hawaii, honoring George Washington and other American presidents; celebrated since 1971 on the third Monday of February.

22 Unity Day, celebrating the cooperation among the Arab states; a public holiday in Egypt and in Syria; the day is celebrated in other Arab nations on varying dates.

22 Virgin Island Donkey Races Day, alternating between Frederiksted and Christiansted and featuring both cart and bareback riding for the sheer entertainment of the public.

23 Feast day of Saint Damian, patron saint of doctors.

23 Birthday of William Edward Burghardt Du Bois (February 23, 1868–August 27, 1963). American sociologist and author; awarded the 1920 Spingarn Medal for leadership in securing opportunities for blacks. 1, 993.

23 Birthday of George Frederic Handel (February 23, 1685–April 20, 1759). German-born English composer famous for oratorios and operas. Handel's *Messiah* is sung around the world during the Christmas season. 986.

23 Birthday of Jean-Baptiste Le Moyne, Sieur de Bienville, (February 23, 1680–March 7, 1767). French-Canadian explorer and colonizer; founder of New Orleans in 1718. 760.

23 Birthday of Samuel Pepys (February 23, 1633–May 26, 1703). English writer famous for the most frequently quoted diary in the English language. 986.

23 Anniversary of the death of Sir Joshua Reynolds on February 23, 1792. English portrait painter and first president of the Royal Academy. 986.

23 Birthday of Emma Willard (February 23, 1787–April 15, 1870). Pioneer American educator whose major concern was the education of girls and young women. Elected to the Hall of Fame for Great Americans in 1905. 237, 825.

23 Guyana Republic Day, commemorating the February 23, 1970, establishment of Guyana as a sovereign democratic state in South America and within the British Commonwealth.

23 Iwo Jima Day, anniversary of the raising of the American flag atop Mount Suribachi in Iwo Jima by United States Marines on February 23, 1945.

23 Anniversary of the founding of Rotary Club International on February 23, 1905.

24 Feast of Saint Matthias, apostle, patron saint of carpenters and tailors, who was chosen to take the place of Judas; prayers to him included in the liturgies of all rites. (In leap year the Feast of Matthias is kept on February 25, since any feast of the Church occurring from February 24 to the end of the month is postponed by one day.) 705.

24 Birthday of Mary Ellen Chase (February 24, 1887–July 28, 1973). American educator; author of *Mary Peters* and other novels, as well as books on the Bible, including *The Bible and the Common Reader* and *Life and Language in the Old Testament*.

24 Anniversary of the death of Auguste Chouteau on February 24, 1829. American fur trader and cofounder of the city of Saint Louis.

24 Birthday of Winslow Homer (February 24, 1836–September 29, 1910). American landscape and seascape painter elected to the National Academy of Design in 1865. 986.

24 Estonia National Day, honoring a peace treaty signed on February 24, 1920, confirming Estonian independence; Estonia has since been absorbed by the Union of Soviet Socialist Republics.

24 Ghana Liberation Day, a public holiday celebrating the overthrow of the Nkrumah government in 1966.

24 Vincennes Day, observed in Indiana in commemoration of George Rogers Clark's defeat of the British at Vincennes during the American Revolution.

25 Birthday of Benedetto Croce (February 25, 1866–November 20, 1952). Italian humanist, historian, and editor, the foremost Italian philosopher of the first half of the twentieth century. 986.

25 Birthday of John Foster Dulles (February 25, 1888–May 24, 1959). American statesman; secretary of state; the chief author of the Japanese peace treaty at the end of World War II.

25 Birthday of Charles Lang Freer (February 25, 1856–September 25, 1919). American art collector who specialized in Chinese and Japanese painting and Oriental pottery. His collections were presented to the nation, and he endowed the Freer Gallery in Washington, D.C., to house them.

25 Birthday of Carlo Goldoni (February 25, 1707–February 6, 1793). Italian author, founder of Italian realistic comedy. 986.

25 Birthday of José Francisco de San Martín (February 25, 1778–August 17, 1850). Latin American general, liberator of Chile from Spanish control, leader in the wars of independence in Argentina and Peru. Honored in Chile for moral grandeur, military genius, and statesmanship. 18.

25 Birthday of John Watson (February 25, 1847–January 27, 1939). Canadian philosopher who was the chief spokesman of the school of objective idealism.

25 Kuwait National Day, a holiday in Kuwait in southeastern Asia celebrating the accession of Shaykh Sir 'Abdallah Al-Salim al-Sabah.

c25 Coronado Day, honoring Francisco Vásquez de Coronado's search for the Seven Cities of Cibola in 1540 and his exploration of Mexico and what is now the American Southwest; commemorated with regional festivals.

26 Birthday of William Frederick Cody, "Buffalo Bill" (February 26, 1846–January 10, 1917). American plainsman and showman who personifies the romance of the Old West.

26 Birthday of Victor Hugo (February 26, 1802–May 22, 1885). French novelist and dramatist known universally for his novel *Les Misérables*. 986.

26 Birthday of John George Nicolay (February 26, 1832–September 26, 1901). American author, secretary to, and biographer of, Abraham Lincoln.

26 Birthday of Sir Benegal Narsing Rau (February 26, 1887–November 29, 1953). Indian jurist and diplomat, president of the United Nations Security Council in 1950.

27 Feast day of Saint Gabriel Possenti, patron saint of young seminarians. 705.

27 Birthday of Sveinn Björnsson (February 27, 1881–January 25, 1952). First president of Iceland upon its establishment as a republic in 1944.

27 Birthday of Henry Edwards Huntington (February 27, 1850–May 23, 1927). American railroad executive and philanthropist; founder of the Huntington Library at San Marino, California.

27 Birthday of Henry Wadsworth Longfellow (February 27, 1807–March 24, 1882). American poet famed for *Evangeline* and *The Song of Hiawatha*. He was elected to the Hall of Fame for Great Americans in 1900. 237, 867, 986.

27 Independence Day in the Dominican Republic, a public holiday of parades and political meetings honoring the independence secured through the withdrawal of the Haitians in 1844.

27 Saint Kitts and Antigua Independence Day, commemorating February 27, 1967, when the two countries of the Leeward Islands jointly achieved independence.

28 Birthday of Sir Wilfred Grenfell (February 28, 1865–October 9, 1940). English medical missionary in Labrador who fitted out the first hospital ship for North Sea fisheries.

28 Birthday of Mary Lyon (February 28, 1797–March 5, 1849). Pioneer American educator; founder and first principal of Mount Holyoke Seminary, which later became Mount Holyoke College. She was elected to the Hall of Fame for Great Americans in 1905. 237, 837.

28 Birthday of Michel Eyquem de Montaigne (February 28, 1533–September 13, 1592). French essayist who was the first to use the term *essay* to describe the literary form he so successfully executed. 986.

28 Birthday of Louis Joseph de Montcalm de Saint-Véran (February 28, 1712–September 14, 1759). French general who was mortally wounded in battle with General Wolfe on the Plains of Abraham near Quebec. 10.

28 Birthday of Sir John Tenniel (February 28, 1820–February 25, 1914). English cartoonist and illustrator remembered as the illustrator of Lewis Carroll's *Alice's Adventures in Wonderland.*

28 Burgsonndeg, celebrated in Luxembourg with bonfires to greet the sun and with the re-creation of ancient customs signifying the end of winter.

28 Kalevala Day, a national holiday in Finland, dedicated to the Finnish epic poem *Kalevala* by Dr. Elias Lönnrot; observed on the anniversary of the dating of the preface of the first edition on February 28, 1835. Parades and other ceremonies honor Dr. Lönnrot, who transcribed more than 22,000 verses from the memories of his countrymen.

29 Birthday of Gioacchino Antonio Rossini (February 29, 1792–November 13, 1868). Italian composer famous for the operas *The Barber of Seville* and *William Tell* and for the sacred composition *Stabat Mater.* 986.

29 Leap Year Day, from the name given to every year of 366 days; occurs every fourth year; sometimes called Bachelors' Day.

March

March, the third month of the year, was named for Mars, the Roman god of war. In the days of the Julian calendar, March included New Year's Day. New Year's was then March 25 and was the day on which annual leases for homes and farms were signed, a time schedule that has continued in many parts of the world, even though New Year's Day was moved to January with the adoption of the Gregorian calendar.

March was called the "loud or stormy month" by the early Britons. It is the month of the vernal equinox, the official beginning of spring. The young people in the canton of the Grisons in Switzerland are among the first to respond to the season, by wearing herdsmen's costumes with wide belts from which are hung countless cowbells to "ring out the winter."

The most popular March day is the seventeenth, Saint Patrick's Day. It is a major holiday in Ireland, but it is celebrated in New York City, too, with the "wearers of the green" of all nationalities joining in a spectacular Saint Patrick's Day parade, a tradition that began in 1762.

The flowers for the month of March are the jonquil or daffodil, and the birthstones are the bloodstone and the aquamarine.

The Fixed Days of March

1 Feast day of Saint David, patron saint of Wales and of poets. Saint David's Day is a national holiday in Wales in commemoration of the famous battle won by David in A.D. 640. Welshmen wear a leek, a plant of the lily family and the emblem of Wales, in their hats on their patron saint's day. 705.

1 Birthday of Frédéric Chopin (March 1, 1810–October 17, 1849). Polish pianist and composer of well-known preludes, études, nocturnes, songs, and concertos for piano and orchestra. His romance with the novelist George Sand has been the subject of many books. 986.

1 Birthday of Dimitri Mitropoulos (March 1, 1896–November 2, 1960). Symphony orchestra conductor and composer. Director of the Minneapolis Symphony, the New York Philharmonic Orchestra, and the Metropolitan Opera; known for his interpretations of twentieth-century musical works.

1 Birthday of Augustus Saint-Gaudens (March 1, 1848–August 3, 1907). American sculptor whose works include statues of Abraham Lincoln and General Sherman. Elected to the Hall of Fame for Great Americans in 1920. 237.

1 Independence Day in Dominica and Saint Lucia in the Caribbean, a holiday in commemoration of the achievement of independence on March 1, 1967.

1 Constitution Day, a holiday in Panama honoring a new constitution adopted on March 1, 1946.

1 Heroes' Day, a public holiday in Paraguay; also called National Defense Day.

1 Nebraska Admission Day, proclaimed annually by the governor as a day of patriotic observance by citizens and by the schools in honor of the state's admission to the Union in 1867 as the thirty-seventh state. 741.

1 Ohio Admission Day; Ohio entered the Union on March 1, 1803, as the seventeenth state. 741.

1 Sam Il Chul, Independence Movement Day, the anniversary of the March 1, 1919, passive revolution against Japan, is a public holiday in South Korea.

1 The Peace Corps was established on March 1, 1961, by President John Kennedy to provide youth with the opportunity to help underdeveloped countries.

1 Chalanda Marz, a day of announcing the coming of spring in Engadine, the picturesque valley of the Inn River in eastern Switzerland. Young people wear herdsmen's costumes with wide belts from which are suspended countless cow bells with which they "ring out the winter."

c 1 Cotton Carnival, the anniversary of the first of the annual Memphis Cotton Carnivals held on March 1, 1931; now observed for five days beginning the second Tuesday in May, with a program illustrating life in the Old South, cotton-fabric style shows, parades, and dances. 8.

1 Pinzon Day in Bayona, Spain, commemorating the arrival of Martin Pinzon, who brought to Europe the news of the discovery of the New World.

1 Whuppity Scoorie Day, a festival day in Lanark, Lanarkshire, Scotland, carrying on an ancient custom of noisemaking to drive away the evil spirits and thus protect the crops of the new season. 164.

1 Anniversary of the first United States census, which began on March 1, 1790.

1 Anniversary of the establishment of Yellowstone National Park as the first of the great national parks of the United States on March 1, 1872. 49.

2 Birthday of Sir Thomas Bodley (March 2, 1545–January 28, 1613). English diplomat and scholar; founder of the Bodleian Library, Oxford.

2 Birthday of DeWitt Clinton (March 2, 1769–February 11, 1828). American statesman; congressman from New York; governor of New York; a sponsor of the Erie Canal; and a founder of the New York Historical Society.

2 Birthday of Samuel Houston (March 2, 1793–July 26, 1863). American statesman; first president of the republic of Texas, governor of the state of Texas, and regional leader for whom the city of Houston is named. He represents the state of Texas in Statuary Hall in a sculpture done by Elisabet Ney. 242.

2 Birthday of Carl Schurz (March 2, 1829–May 14, 1906). German-American author; editor and publicist who as secretary of the interior introduced competitive examinations for positions in civil service.

2 Birthday of Bedřich Smetana (March 2, 1824–May 12, 1884). Czech composer and orchestral leader whose opera *The Bartered Bride* has become popular. The Smetana Society in Prague maintains a museum dedicated to his work. 986.

2 Battle of Aduwa Day, a public holiday in Abyssinia commemorating the defeat of Italian forces in the Italian-Ethiopian conflict of 1896, which resulted in the Treaty of Addis Ababa recognizing the independence of Ethiopia. 10.

2 Independence Day in Morocco, a holiday commemorating the termination of the Treaty of Fez and the establishment of sovereignty on March 2, 1956.

2 Texas Independence Day, celebrated in Texas as the anniversary of the declaration of independence from Mexico in 1836; a legal holiday and the first day of Texas Week.

3 Birthday of Alexander Graham Bell (March 3, 1847–August 2, 1922). Scotch-born American physicist, famous for the invention of the telephone. Elected to the Hall of Fame for Great Americans, 1950. 237.

3 Birthday of Ragnar Frisch (March 3, 1895–January 31, 1974). Norwegian economist; shared in 1969 the first Nobel Prize in economics for the development of mathematical models used in econometrics. 241.

3 Birthday of William Green (March 3, 1873–November 21, 1952). American labor leader and president of the American Federation of Labor from December 19, 1924, to his death in 1952. 563.

3 Bulgaria Liberation Day, a commemoration of the anniversary of Bulgaria's release from Ottoman domination, secured through the Treaty of San Stefano in 1878.

3 Florida Admission Day. Florida entered the Union as the twenty-seventh state on March 3, 1845. 741.

3 Grenada, one of the West Indies Associated States, achieved partial independence on March 3, 1967, in association with Britain for defense and external affairs.

3 Malawi Martyr's Day, a public holiday in Malawi, formerly the British protectorate of Nyasaland in the eastern part of southern Africa; honors the nation's heroes.

3 Morocco National Day, called the Festival of the Throne, marks the succession of King Hassan II to the throne on March 3, 1961.

3 Unity Day, a public holiday in Sudan honoring cooperation among the Arab nations.

3 Anniversary of the authorization of the Civil Service Commission on March 3, 1871.

3 Dolls' Festival, Hina Matsuri, an annual Japanese national festival, honors little girls and their dolls. It is also called the Peach Blossom Festival, since that flower symbolizes to the Japanese the attributes of little girls. Dolls are on display on this day, and the little girls are hostesses to their friends and are honored by their families.

3 Japanese Girls' day, observed on March 3 in Hawaii with special music and dances.

3 Anniversary of the adoption by Congress, on March 3, 1931, of *The Star Spangled Banner*, by Francis Scott Key, as the national anthem of the United States.

4 Feast day of Saint Casimir, patron saint of Poland and Lithuania.

4 Birthday of Count Casimir Pulaski (March 4, 1747–October 11, 1779). Polish soldier; hero of the American Revolution; organizer of a corps of cavalry and light infantry known as Pulaski's Legion; mortally wounded in the siege of Savannah. A Pulaski Memorial Day is observed on the day of his death, October 11. 681–84.

4 Birthday of Knute Kenneth Rockne (March 4, 1888–March 31, 1931). American football coach famed for his leadership in the sport and for the development of the "Fighting Irish" and the "Four Horsemen," which are a part of the Notre Dame football legend.

4 Birthday of Benjamin Waterhouse (March 4, 1754–October 2, 1846). American physician, pioneer in the application of Jenner's discovery of smallpox vaccine; an initiator of the scientific approach to vaccinations in the United States.

4 Birthday of Johann Rudolf Wyss (March 4, 1782–March 21, 1830). Swiss folklorist and editor of his father's *Swiss Family Robinson*, which has been translated into many languages.

4 Charter Day, honored in Pennsylvania in commemoration of the granting by Charles II of a charter on March 4, 1681, to William Penn, the founder of the state.

4 United States Constitution Day. The United States Constitution was declared in effect on March 4, 1789; the date is celebrated annually as the anniversary of the first meeting of Congress under the Constitution.

4 Vermont Admission Day is a holiday commemorating the admission of Vermont into the Union on March 4, 1791, as the fourteenth state. 741.

4 Anniversary of the establishment of the Government Printing Office by President Lincoln on March 4, 1861.

5 Crispus Attucks Day, anniversary of the March 5, 1770, death of Crispus Attucks, American Revolutionary leader who led the group whose anti-British defiance precipitated the Boston Massacre; honored as the first American black to die for freedom. 1, 797.

5 Birthday of Elisha Harris (March 5, 1824–January 31, 1884). American physician; pioneer in public health and one of the organizers of the American Public Health Association.

5 Birthday of James Merritt Ives (March 5, 1824–January 3, 1895). American lithographer; a partner in the firm of Currier & Ives, publishers of prints showing the historic events, manners, and customs of nineteenth-century America.

5 Birthday of Howard Pyle (March 5, 1853–November 9, 1911). Illustrator, painter, and author, best known for his children's books.

5 Boston Massacre Day, the anniversary of the attack by British troops on colonial citizens on March 5, 1770, an event that lives in history as the Boston Massacre.

5 Mother-in-law Day, first celebrated on March 5, 1934, in Amarillo, Texas; initiated by the editor of the local paper; observed by individuals and families.

c5 Town Meeting Day, held in Vermont on the first Tuesday of March; a day of citizen participation in governmental affairs.

6 Birthday of Elizabeth Barrett Browning (March 6, 1806–June 29, 1861). English poet and wife of the poet Robert Browning. Her best-known work is *Sonnets from the Portuguese*. 825, 992.

6 Birthday of Michelangelo Buonarroti (March 6, 1475–February 18, 1564). Italian sculptor, painter, architect, and poet, famous for his statues of David and of Moses, the paintings of the Sistine Chapel, and the famous cupola of Saint Peter's basilica. 986.

6 Birthday of Philip Henry Sheridan (March 6, 1831–August 5, 1888). American soldier who made the famous ride to Cedar Creek and turned a Union defeat into a great victory of the Civil War; known as "Little Phil" because of his size.

6 Alamo Day, commemorates one of the great days in Texas and American history, the end of the siege of the Alamo by the Mexicans on March 6, 1836.

6 Ghana Independence Day, a public holiday in honor of the establishment of the former British Crown Colony of the Gold Coast as a sovereign nation on March 6, 1957.

6 Magellan Day, or Discovery Day, observed in Guam to commemorate the landing of Magellan on the island on March 6, 1521.

6 Anniversary of the establishment on March 6, 1858, of the Missionary Society of Saint Paul, the Apostle, known as the Paulists.

7 Feast of Saint Thomas Aquinas, patron saint of all universities and centers of study, honoring the "Angelic Doctor" whose greatest work is *Summa Theologica*. 80, 705, 707.

7 Birthday of Alessandro Manzoni (March 7, 1785–May 22, 1873). Italian novelist and poet whose novel *The Betrothed* is considered a model of Italian prose. 986.

7 Birthday of Tomáš G. Masaryk (March 7, 1850–September 14, 1937). Czech patriot called "the Father of Czechoslovakia."

7 Birthday of Maurice Joseph Ravel (March 7, 1875–December 28, 1937). French composer whose *Bolero* has been one of the most popular concert selections of the twentieth century. 986.

7 Burbank Day, commemorating the birth of Luther Burbank on March 7, 1849. American naturalist and plant breeder who introduced over six hundred varieties of plants to America, many of which form the basis of fruit industries. His birthday is observed in California; in some regions Burbank Day is combined with Bird or Arbor Day. 977.

8 Feast day of Saint John of God, patron saint of hospitals; patron saint of book- and printsellers. 5, 705.

8 Birthday of Frederick William Goudy (March 8, 1865–May 11, 1947). American printer and type designer; honored by printer's guilds and publishing associations.

8 Birthday of Kenneth Grahame (March 8, 1859–July 6, 1932). English banker and author of *The Wind in the Willows*, a children's classic. The book was dramatized by A. A. Milne as *Toad of Toad Hall* and became a popular play for Christmas-tide presentations. 986.

8 Birthday of Oliver Wendell Holmes, Jr. (March 8, 1841–March 6, 1935). American jurist and one of the most famous and revered justices of the United States Supreme Court; known as "the Great Dissenter." Elected to the Hall of Fame for Great Americans in 1965. 237, 986.

8 Birthday of Joseph Lee (March 8, 1862–July 28, 1937). Pioneer in the development of playgrounds for children; longtime president of the National Recreation Association.

8 International Women's Day, a public holiday in the Union of Soviet Socialist Republics.

8 Syrian Independence Day, a public holiday in Syria, honoring the assumption of political power by the National Council of Revolution on March 8, 1963.

9 Feast day of Saint Catherine of Bologna, patron saint of artists.

9 Feast day of Saint Frances of Rome, model for housewives and widows; patron saint of motorists; observed by Italian motorists, who drive to the Colosseum in Rome for the blessing of their cars. 705.

9 Birthday of George Hayward (March 9, 1791–October 7, 1863). American surgeon, the first to use ether in a major operation.

9 Birthday of Leland Stanford (March 9, 1824–June 21, 1893). American capitalist, politician; one of the builders of the first transcontinental railroad in the United States; the founder of Stanford University, a memorial to his son.

9 Amerigo Vespucci day, honoring the fifteenth-century Italian navigator for whom the Americas were named.

9 Baron Bliss Day, a public holiday in Belize, formerly British Honduras, honoring Baron Bliss, an Englishman, who left his entire fortune, for unknown reasons, to the city of Belize.

9 Anniversary of the Battle of Hampton Roads, the engagement between the *Monitor* and the *Merrimac* on March 9, 1862.

9 Taras Shevchenko day, Ukrainian public holiday honoring the great national poet of the Ukraine born on March 9, 1814.

10 Birthday of Ina Donna Coolbrith (March 10, 1842–February 29, 1928). American poet named poet laureate of California in 1915 by act of the state legislature.

10 Birthday of John McCloskey (March 10, 1810–October 10, 1885). American Roman Catholic prelate; the first president of St. John's College (later Fordham University), and the first United States cardinal of the Roman Catholic church.

10 Birthday of Mary Mills Patrick (March 10, 1850–February 25, 1940). American educator who devoted her life to lifting the educational level of women in the Far East; first president of the Istanbul Woman's College.

10 Birthday of Lillian D. Wald (March 10, 1867–September 1, 1940). American sociologist; founder of the Henry Street Settlement and the organizer of the first nonsectarian public-health nursing system in the world. Elected to the Hall of Fame for Great Americans in 1970. 237, 825.

c10 Arbor Day in New Mexico; observed on the second Friday of March.

10 Anniversary of the arrival of the Salvation Army in the United States on March 10, 1880; officially organized on March 28, 1885.

11 Birthday of Vannevar Bush (March 11, 1890–June 28, 1974). Electrical engineer; developer of the first electronic analogue computer.

11 Johnny Appleseed Day; anniversary of the death on March 11, 1845, of John Chapman, known as Johnny Appleseed, the "patron saint" of American orchards.

11 Birthday of Thomas Hastings (March 11, 1860–October 22, 1929). American architect of the firm of Carrère & Hastings, designer of the New York Public Library and the Frick mansion, which houses the Frick Collection.

11 Birthday of Torquato Tasso (March 11, 1544–April 25, 1595). Italian epic poet of the late Renaissance whose masterpiece is *Jerusalem Delivered*. 986.

11 Anniversary of the incorporation on March 11, 1850, of the Woman's Medical College of Pennsylvania, the first medical school for women in the world.

12 Feast day of Saint Gregory the Great; fourth doctor of the Latin church; strengthener of the Latin see; patron saint of musicians, schoolchildren, and scholars. 705.

12 Birthday of Kemal Atatürk (March 12, 1880–November 10, 1938). Turkish military commander and first president of the Turkish Republic.

12 Birthday of Gabriele D'Annunzio (March 12, 1863–March 1, 1938). Italian author and soldier who vigorously promoted Italian patriotism. 986.

12 Birthday of Simon Newcomb (March 12, 1835–July 11, 1909). American scientist; one of the greatest mathematical astronomers. He was elected to the Hall of Fame for Great Americans in 1935. 237, 977.

12 Anniversary of the death of Sun Yat-sen on March 12, 1925. Chinese physician and first president of the Chinese Republic; the day is observed in Taiwan and in Chinese-American communities.

12 The King's Birthday, a holiday in Libya.

12 Mauritius Independence Day, a public holiday in Mauritius honoring the attainment of independence from Britain on March 12, 1968.

12 Moshoeshoe's Day, a public holiday in Lesotho honoring the nineteenth-century tribal leader who consolidated the Basotho nation, now called Lesotho.

12 Girl Scout Day, the anniversary of the founding of the Girl Scouts on March 12, 1912; observed with special ceremonies by the Girl Scouts and their leaders.

12 Jane Delano Day, sponsored by the American Red Cross; recognizes the anniversary of the January 12, 1862, birth of Jane Delano, founder of the American Red Cross Nursing Service.

13 Feast day of Saint Ansovinus, protector and patron saint of crops. 705.

13 Birthday of Percival Lowell (March 13, 1855–November 12, 1916). American astronomer who laid the groundwork for the discovery of the planet Pluto. 977.

13 Birthday of Joseph Priestley (March 13, 1733–February 6, 1804). English discoverer of oxygen. 977.

13 Decoration Day, a public holiday in Liberia.

13 Anniversary of the dedication of *Christ of the Andes*, the bronze statue of Christ on the Argentina-Chile border, on March 13, 1904.

13 Anniversary of the naming of Harvard University, oldest university in the United States, on March 13, 1639, for clergyman John Harvard.

14 Birthday of Thomas Hart Benton (March 14, 1782–April 10, 1858). American congressman known as "Old Bullion" because of his stand on gold and silver currency. Benton represents the state of Missouri in Statuary Hall in a sculpture done by Alexander Doyle. 242.

14 Birthday of Charles Ammi Cutter (March 14, 1837–September 6, 1903). American librarian; director of the Boston Athenaeum; cofounder of the American Library Association; editor of the *Library Journal*, and originator of the Cutter System, which classifies books by author initials and numbers.

14 Birthday of Paul Ehrlich (March 14, 1854–August 20, 1915). German bacteriologist famous for his experiments on the effects of various chemicals upon living tissue. Awarded the 1908 Nobel Prize in physiology or medicine for his work on immunity. 238.

14 Birthday of Albert Einstein (March 14, 1879–April 18, 1955). German-Swiss-American theoretical physicist noted for his theory of relativity. Awarded the Nobel Prize in physics in 1921 for his photoelectric law and work in theoretical physics. 977.

14 Birthday of Casey Jones (March 14, 1864–April 30, 1900). American railroad engineer immortalized in a ballad originally composed by Wallace Saunders.

14 Birthday of Isadore Gilbert Mudge (March 14, 1875–May 17, 1957). American librarian, author, and bibliographer. Since 1959, a citation has been given annually in her name through the American Library Association to a reference librarian for "a distinguished contribution to reference librarianship."

15 Feast of Saint Longinus, believed to be the "soldier with the spear" at the Crucifixion of Christ. 705.

15 Birthday of Alice Cunningham Fletcher (March 15, 1838–April 6, 1923). American ethnologist and author who pioneered in the notation of Indian music.

15 Birthday of Lady Augusta Gregory (March 15, 1852–May 22, 1932). Irish playwright; poet; leader in the Irish literary revival and the Irish National Theatre. 986.

15 Birthday of Andrew Jackson (March 15, 1767–June 8, 1845). Scotch-Irish ancestry; frontiersman and soldier; general in War of 1812; self-taught Tennessee lawyer; seventh president of the United States, 1829–37; a Presbyterian; buried at Hermitage, near Nashville, Tenn. He was elected to the Hall of Fame for Great Americans in 1910. He represents the state of Tennessee in Statuary Hall in a sculpture by Belle Kinney Scholtz. Andrew Jackson's birthday is observed as a holiday in Tennessee. 237, 242, 244–48, 667–72, 674–76, 678–79.

15 Birthday of Joseph Jenkins Roberts (March 15, 1809–February 24, 1876). First president of Liberia, and first president of the College of Liberia. His birthday is a public holiday in Liberia.

15 Birthday of Paul von Heyse (March 15, 1830–April 2, 1914). German poet who received the Nobel Prize in literature in 1910. 227.

15 Ides of March, commemorating the assassination of Julius Caesar in 44 B.C.

15 Maine Admission Day. Maine entered the Union on March 15, 1820, as the twenty-third state.

15 Thanksgiving Day in Honduras, observed through religious services and by families.

15 Buzzard Day, the traditional day for the annual return of the buzzards to Hinckley, Ohio, for the mating season.

15 Anniversary of the dedication on March 15, 1960, of the National Observatory at Kitt Peak, Arizona, which houses the world's largest solar telescope.

15 Anniversary of the riot in the Watts section of Los Angeles on March 15, 1966, which re-emphasized the problems of the black community unresolved by the riots of 1965.

16 Anniversary of the death of Nathaniel Bowditch on March 16, 1838. American mathematician and astronomer famous for *The New American Practical Navigator*, and for the discovery of the Bowditch curves, which had important applications for future developments in physics and astronomy.

16 Birthday of Caroline Lucretia Herschel (March 16, 1750–January 9, 1848). Anglo-German astronomer who received a gold medal from the Royal Astronomical Society in 1828 for her discoveries of eight comets and many nebulae. 977.

16 Birthday of James Madison (March 16, 1751–June 28, 1836). English ancestry; Virginia lawyer, known as "the Father of the Constitution." Fourth president of the United States, 1809–17; an Episcopalian. Buried at Montpelier, Orange County, Virginia. Elected to the Hall of Fame for Great Americans in 1905. 237, 667–72, 674–76, 678–79, 991.

16 Birthday of René Sully Prudhomme (March 16, 1839–September 7, 1907). French poet and critic, the first to receive the Nobel Prize in literature, which was awarded to him in 1901. 227.

16 Docking Day, anniversary of the first docking of one space ship with another, accomplished by United States astronauts Neil Armstrong and David Scott on March 16, 1966.

16 Goddard Day, recalls the March 16, 1926, flight of the first liquid-fueled rocket, developed by Robert Goddard.

16 Mylai Massacre Day, anniversary of the massive killing of noncombatant villagers at Mylai and Mykhe in Vietnam on March 16, 1968.

16 Anniversary of the first National Library Week, observed from March 16–22, 1958. Established by the National Book Committee in cooperation with the American Library Association. Since 1958, the week has been celebrated in March or April of each year.

16 Anniversary of the establishment of the United States Military Academy at West Point, New York, on March 16, 1802; observed by graduates throughout the country at ceremonial dinners.

17 Feast day of Saint Gertrude of Nivelles, patroness of travelers; invoked for protection and for outdoor garden work.

17 Feast day of Saint Joseph of Arimathea, the noble counselor who provided the tomb in which the Lord's body was laid after the Crucifixion; patron saint of funeral directors. 705.

17 Feast day of Saint Patrick, patron saint of Ireland, Ireland's greatest holy day and holiday; enjoyed by "wearers of the green" in many countries. The St. Patrick's Day parade in New York City has been a spectacular annual event since 1762. St. Patrick's Day in Rome is observed only by religious services of great solemnity and ceremony. The trefoil shamrock is the traditional symbol of the day. 697–703.

17 Birthday of Kate Greenaway (March 17, 1846–November 6, 1901). English watercolor artist whose drawings of children provided an exemplary model for book illustration.

17 Birthday of Roger Brooke Taney (March 17, 1777–October 12, 1864). American jurist; fifth chief justice of the United States Supreme Court; famous for the decision in the Dred Scott case denying the status of citizenship to slaves.

17 Birthday of Stephen Samuel Wise (March 17, 1874–April 19, 1949). American reform rabbi and Jewish leader; president of the Zionist Organization of America; founder of the Jewish Institute of Religion, and instrumental in the founding of the World Jewish Congress.

17 Evacuation Day, observed in Boston and Suffolk County, Massachusetts; commemorates the British withdrawal from Boston on March 17, 1776. It has been a legal holiday in Suffolk County since 1941.

17 Camp Fire Girls Founders Day, commemorating the establishment of the Camp Fire Girls on March 17, 1910.

17 Anniversary of the opening of the National Gallery of Art in Washington, D.C., on March 17, 1941.

18 Feast day of Saint Anselm, patron saint of Mantua. 705.

18 Birthday of John Caldwell Calhoun (March 18, 1782–March 31, 1850). American statesman; congressman from South Carolina; brilliant exponent of states' rights. He represents the state of South Carolina in Statuary Hall in a sculpture done by Frederic Wellington Ruckstull. 242.

18 Birthday of Grover Cleveland (March 18, 1837–June 24, 1908). English ancestry; New York lawyer; the twenty-second and the twenty-fourth president of the United States. Presbyterian; buried at Princeton, New Jersey. Elected to the Hall of Fame for Great Americans in 1935. 667–72, 674–76, 678–79.

18 Birthday of Rudolph Diesel (March 18, 1858–September 29, 1913). German engineer and developer of the diesel internal-combustion engine. 977.

18 Birthday of Robert Peter Tristram Coffin (March 18, 1892–January 20, 1955). American author descended from a Nantucket whaling family; recipient of the 1936 Pulitzer Prize for *Strange Holiness*, a book of poems. 229.

18 Birthday of Nikolai Rimski-Korsakov (March 18, 1844–June 21, 1908). Russian composer whose work is representative of the Russian nationalist school. 986.

c18 De Molay Day, observed each year by the Order of De Molay in commemoration of the martyrdom of Jacques De Molay, the last grand master of the Order of Knights Templar, on March 18 or 19, 1314.

18 Sheelah's Day, observed in Ireland with shamrocks saved from Saint Patrick's Day to honor Sheelah, who might have been Saint Patrick's wife or his mother.

18 Anniversary of first space walk by the Union of Soviet Socialist Republics' cosmonaut Alekeski Lenov on March 18, 1965.

19 Saint Joseph's Day, a prescribed holy day in most Roman Catholic countries; a holiday in the Latin American countries, in Italy, and in Liechtenstein. Saint Joseph is the patron saint of Belgium and Columbia; patron of carpenters and cabinetmakers; patron saint of a happy death, and of the universal church. 5, 705.

19 Birthday of William Bradford (March 19, 1589–May 9, 1657). American Pilgrim Father, author of the *History of Plymouth Plantation*, and governor of the Plymouth Colony for thirty years.

19 Birthday of William Jennings Bryan (March 19, 1860–July 26, 1925). American lawyer and political leader, known as "the Silver-Tongued Orator," whose career ended shortly after the famous Scopes trial involving the anti-evolution law. Bryan gave powerful support to woman suffrage. He represents the state of Nebraska in Statuary Hall in a sculpture done by Rudulph Evans. 242.

19 Birthday of David Livingstone (March 19, 1813–May 1, 1873). Scotch doctor, explorer, and medical missionary who taught the church to develop an overall Christian culture in foreign lands; discoverer of Victoria Falls; the subject of the famous search by Henry Stanley following reports of his death in Africa.

19 Birthday of Earl Warren (March 19, 1891–July 9, 1974). Fourteenth chief justice of the United States in a period of great change in constitutional law; head of the Warren Commission, which investigated the assassination of President John Kennedy.

19 Swallows Day, the date on which the swallows traditionally return to the San Juan Capistrano Mission in California.

20 Birthday of Charles William Eliot (March 20, 1834–August 22, 1926). American educator, president of Harvard, and editor of the famous "five-foot shelf of books," the fifty-volume *Harvard Classics*.

20 Birthday of Mathias Keller (March 20, 1813–October 12, 1875). German-American song and hymn writer who wrote the *American Hymn* (Speed Our Republic, O Father on High).

20 Lajos Kossuth Day, anniversary of the death on March 20, 1894, of Kossuth, the symbol of Hungarian nationalism; commemorated by Hungarians around the world.

20 Anniversary of the final ratification of the peace treaty and administrative pact restoring sovereignty to Japan on March 20, 1952.

20 Independence Day in Tunisia, a holiday honoring French recognition of the autonomy of Tunisia under the treaty of March 20, 1956.

20 Naw-Ruz, the first day of the Baha'i year, observed by the National Spiritual Assembly of the Baha'is from sunset on March 20 to sunset on March 21.

20 Anniversary of the founding of the General Federation of Women's Clubs, March 20, 1890.

21 Feast day of Saint Benedict, patriarch of Western monks, founder of the Benedictine order, patron saint of speleologists. 705.

21 Birthday of Johann Sebastian Bach (March 21, 1685–July 28, 1750). German composer and instrumentalist. A master of counterpoint, Bach is noted as one of the foremost composers of all time. 986.

21 Birthday of Benito Pablo Juárez (March 21, 1806–July 18, 1872). Mexican lawyer elected in 1861 as Mexico's first president of Indian descent. Juárez is a national hero, and his birthday is an honored day in Mexico. It is popularly called "the Day of the Indian Chief"; Juárez is sometimes called "the Mexican Washington." 536.

21 Birthday of Albert Kahn (March 21, 1869–December 8, 1942). American architect known as the originator of modern factory design.

21 Bird Day in the state of Iowa.

21 Earth Day, a day of international recognition of the critical need to preserve the earth's resources. 414–22.

21 Anniversary of the first presentation of the Sylvanus Thayer Award, named for the fifth superintendent of West Point, on March 21, 1958. This medal, given annually by the Association of Graduates of West Point, is bestowed on "the United States citizen whose record of service to his country exemplifies devotion to the principles expressed in the motto of West Point—Duty, Honor, Country." The first recipient was Dr. Ernest O. Lawrence of the University of California.

c21 Vernal Equinox Day, a holiday in Japan on either March 21 or 22. The vernal equinox marks the beginning of spring in the northern hemisphere.

22 Feast day of Saint Nicholas von Flüe, patron saint of Switzerland.

22 Birthday of Randolph Caldecott (March 22, 1846–February 12, 1886). English artist and illustrator for whom the Caldecott Medal is named; the medal is awarded annually to the artist who has illustrated the most distinguished picture book for American children published in the preceding year. 234, 235.

22 Birthday of Robert Andrews Millikan (March 22, 1868–December 19, 1953). American physicist; specialist in research on cosmic rays. He received the 1923 Nobel Prize for isolating the electron, and the Presidential Medal of Merit for his work on rockets and jet propulsion during World War II. 241.

22 Birthday of Sir Anthony Van Dyck (March 22, 1599–December 9, 1641). Flemish painter of society portraits. One of his most famous is the portrait of Charles I. 986.

22 Arab League Day, commemorating the formation of the Arab League on March 22, 1945, a holiday for all signatories including Egypt, Iraq, Saudi Arabia, Lebanon, Syria, and Yemen.

22 Puerto Rican Emancipation Day, or Emancipation of the Slaves Day; a holiday in Puerto Rico marking the abolishment of slavery on the island on March 22, 1873.

22 Anniversary of the passage of the Equal Rights Amendment by the United States Congress on March 22, 1972, subject to ratification by the fifty states.

23 Birthday of John Bartram (March 23, 1699–September 22, 1777). American botanist who founded the first botanical garden in the United States. Known as the "Father of American Botany."

23 Birthday of Sidney Hillman (March 23, 1887–July 10, 1946). American labor leader and union official in whose name the Sidney Hillman Foundation presents an annual award for a book dealing with race relations, civil liberties, trade-union development, or world understanding. 234, 563.

23 Memorial Day in Bolivia, a public holiday.

23 Pakistan Republic Day, a holiday commemorating the establishment of Pakistan on March 23, 1956. Popularly known as Pakistan Day.

23 Anniversary of the establishment of the World Meteorological Organization, a specialized agency of the United Nations, on March 23, 1950, to facilitate an international system of standardizing and coordinating weather observations and collaborating data.

24 Feast day of Saint Gabriel, archangel of the Annunciation; patron saint of postmen, messengers, radio, telegraph and telephone workers. 705.

24 Birthday of Galen Clark (March 24, 1814–March 24, 1910). American naturalist who discovered the Mariposa Grove of giant sequoias or redwood trees in 1857. Mount Clark in Yosemite is named in his honor.

24 Birthday of Andrew William Mellon (March 24, 1855–August 26, 1937). American financier, public official who gave his art collection to the nation in 1937 for the establishment of the National Gallery of Art.

24 Birthday of William Morris (March 24, 1834–October 3, 1896). English poet, craftsman who designed fine furniture, wallpapers, and tapestries, and translator of Icelandic sagas. The William Morris Society was established in 1955 to revive interest in his ideas and works. 986.

24 Birthday of John Wesley Powell (March 24, 1834–September 23, 1902). American geologist and anthropologist who made the daring exploration of the Colorado and Green Rivers in 1869; published the first classification of American Indian languages; was the first director of the United States Bureau of Ethnology.

24 Agriculture Day, a day of recognition in the United States in tribute to farmers, ranchers, and growers; observed by farm bureaus and marketing associations.

c24 Laos Army Day, a holiday in Laos around March 24, honoring the armed forces.

25 Day of the Annunciation of the Blessed Virgin Mary, celebrating the Angel Gabriel's announcement to the Virgin Mary that she would be the mother of Jesus; a Church holy day since the seventh century. The Annunciation is celebrated by the Roman Catholic, Anglican, and Lutheran churches. The Feast of the Annunciation has had many popular names. It was once called Lady Day in England, and is known as Waffle Day in Sweden since it is a traditional day for serving waffles. 5, 125, 705.

25 Feast of Saint Dismas, "the Good Thief," patron saint of prisoners, persons condemned to death, and funeral directors. 705.

25 Birthday of Béla Bartók (March 25, 1881–September 26, 1945). Hungarian composer noted for the use of folk tunes in his concert works; famous for *Hungarian Folk Music*, a standard reference work in the field of music. 986.

25 Birthday of Gutzon Borglum (March 25, 1867–March 6, 1941). American sculptor and painter. Best known for his colossal head of Lincoln in the Capitol and for the Mount Rushmore Memorial figures of Washington, Jefferson, Lincoln, and Theodore Roosevelt.

25 Birthday of Arturo Toscanini (March 25, 1867–January 16, 1957). Italian musician considered by critics to be the greatest virtuoso conductor of the first half of the twentieth century.

25 Birthday of William Bell Wait (March 25, 1839–October 25, 1916). American educator, pioneer in the education of the blind, who devised an embossing machine for printing books for the blind and a typewriter for the blind.

25 Birthday of John Winebrenner (March 25, 1797–September 12, 1860). American clergyman who founded the denomination known as the Church of God.

25 Greek Independence Day, a holiday celebrated with parades and dances in Greece and Cyprus and with a parade in New York to honor the day in 1821 when the Greek flag was first raised in revolt against Ottoman domination.

25 Maryland Day, a legal holiday in Maryland celebrating the landing of the colonists sent to the New World in 1634 by Lord Baltimore under the leadership of his brother, Leonard Calvert.

25 Quarter Day, or Lady Day, a traditional day for paying rent in Ireland and England.

26 The Tichborne Dole, an annual event observed since the year 1150 in Alresford, Hampshire, in England. The head of the Tichborne family gives a gift of one gallon of flour for each adult and half a gallon for each child to every resident of the village to fulfill a deathbed promise and to avoid a curse on the house of Tichborne; special permission for allocation was given during World War II. 164.

26 Feast Day of Saint Braulio, patron saint of Aragon, one of the most popular saints in Spain. 705.

26 Birthday of Edward Bellamy (March 26, 1850–May 22, 1898). American author known for the novel *Looking Backward*.

26 Anniversary of the death of Sarah Bernhardt on March 26, 1923. French actress who has gone down in theatrical history as the "Divine Sarah."

26 Birthday of Robert Frost (March 26, 1874–January 29, 1963). American Pulitzer Prize winning poet especially known for his lyric poem *A Boy's Will* and the narrative poem *North of Boston*; poetry consultant at the Library of Congress. 867, 986, 1001.

26 Birthday of Louise Otto (March 26, 1819–March 13, 1895). German author and founder of the feminist movement in Germany.

26 Bangladesh Independence Day, a public holiday commemorating the proclamation of the establishment of Bangladesh on March 26, 1971.

26 Arbor Day in Spain, called Fiesta del Arbol, Fete of the Tree. It began on March 26, 1895, when King Alfonso planted a pine sapling at a ceremony near Madrid.

26 Prince Kuhio Day, the birthday of Prince Kuhio Kalanianole, Hawaii's second delegate to Congress. It is also called Regatta Day.

27 Birthday of Nathaniel Currier (March 27, 1813–November 20, 1888). American publisher and founder of the firm of Currier & Ives, printmakers who recorded American history from 1835 to the end of the century in famous prints which are now collector's items.

27 Birthday of Adolphus Washington Greely (March 27, 1844–October 20, 1935). American Arctic explorer and soldier who established Arctic observing stations in 1881; cofounder of the American Geographical Society.

27 Birthday of Wilhelm Konrad Röntgen (March 27, 1845–February 10, 1923). German scientist whose discovery of the x-ray made him the first recipient of the Nobel Prize in physics in 1901. 241.

27 Anniversary of the death of Constance Lindsay Skinner on March 27, 1939. American author and editor of the valuable Rivers of America series. The Constance Lindsay Skinner Award is presented annually in her honor by the Woman's National Book Association to an outstanding woman in the book world.

27 Birthday of Edward Steichen (March 27, 1879–March 25, 1973). World-known photographer and artist; associated for many years with the Museum of Modern Art; creator of such celebrated books of photographs as *The Family of Man*.

27 Birthday of Otto Wallach (March 27, 1847–February 26, 1931). German chemist whose research in ethereal oils and identification of alicyclic compounds was of importance to the modern perfume industry and won him a Nobel Prize in chemistry in 1910. 225.

27 Resistance Day, a public holiday in Burma, honoring the movement of guerrilla forces to oppose invaders during World War II.

27 Anniversary of the Alaska Earthquake of March 27, 1964.

27 Birthday of the United States Navy; anniversary of the signing by President Washington on March 27, 1794, of the act to officially establish the navy.

28 Birthday of Wade Hampton (March 28, 1818–April 11, 1902). American Confederate general, congressman, and governor of South Carolina. He represents South Carolina in Statuary Hall in a sculpture by Frederic Wellington Ruckstull. 242.

28 Teachers' Day in Czechoslovakia, commemorating the life and work of John Comenius, seventeenth-century Moravian educational reformer.

29 Birthday of Aleš Hrdlička (March 29, 1869–September 5, 1943). American anthropologist and author famous for his studies of American Indians; curator of the United States National Museum.

29 Birthday of John Tyler (March 29, 1790–January 18, 1862). English ancestry; Virginia lawyer; elected to vice-presidency; succeeded to presidency on death of President Harrison one month after inauguration. Tenth president of the United States, 1841–45; an Episcopalian; buried at Hollywood Cemetery, Richmond, Virginia. 667–72, 674–76, 678–79.

29 Birthday of Isaac Mayer Wise (March 29, 1819–March 26, 1900). American rabbi and educator, a principal founder of the Union of American Hebrew Congregations, and president of the Hebrew Union College.

29 Boganda Day, the anniversary of the March 29, 1959, death of Barthelemy Boganda; observed as a public holiday in the Central African Republic in tribute to the nation's first president.

29 Delaware Swedish Colonial Day, anniversary of the establishment of the first permanent settlement in 1638; a statewide observance.

29 Taiwan Martyr's Day and Youth Day, a day honoring the nation's martyrs and a day of tributes to young adults in the Republic of China.

29 Vietnam Veterans' Day, the anniversary of the March 29, 1973, withdrawal of American forces from the Vietnamese conflict.

29 Anniversary of the date of the chartering of the Knights of Columbus, a fraternal benefit society of Catholic men, on March 29, 1882.

30 Birthday of Clifford Whittingham Beers (March 30, 1876–July 9, 1943). American founder of the mental-hygiene movement; awarded the gold medal "for distinguished services for the benefit of mankind" by the National Institute of Social Sciences.

30 Birthday of Jo Davidson (March 30, 1883–January 2, 1952). American sculptor whose work includes sculptures of many prominent people, including Woodrow Wilson, Anatole France, Walt Whitman, and Robert La Follette.

30 Birthday of Vincent van Gogh (March 30, 1853–July 29, 1890). Dutch painter, lithographer, etcher, and a leader of the post-impressionist school. His letters to his brother, published under the title *Dear Theo*, are of continuing interest. 986.

30 Birthday of Francisco José de Goya (March 30, 1746–April 16, 1828). Spanish painter and etcher whose realism influenced nineteenth- and twentieth-century painters. 986.

30 Seward's Day in Alaska, a legal holiday honoring the purchase of Alaska from Russia by Secretary of State Seward in 1867.

31 Birthday of René Descartes (March 31, 1596–February 1, 1650). French mathematician and philosopher who made contributions to theories of algebra and geometry and to the field of philosophy of pure reason. Called "the Father of Modern Philosophy." 977.

31 Birthday of Edward FitzGerald (March 31, 1809–June 14, 1883). English poet celebrated for his translation of the *Rubáiyát of Omar Khayyám*. 986.

31 Birthday of Franz Joseph Haydn (March 31, 1732–May 31, 1809). Austrian composer, sometimes called "Papa" Haydn in recognition of his influence on instrumental music and on the development of the modern symphony. 986.

31 Birthday of Andrew Lang (March 31, 1844–July 20, 1912). Scottish author famous for Homeric translations and studies, fairy tales, children's books, folklore, history, biography, and fiction.

31 Birthday of Robert Ross McBurney (March 31, 1837–December 27, 1898). American YMCA leader; first paid secretary of the YMCA in New York in 1862; responsible for the centralized system of leadership in effect in the YMCA.

c31 Transfer Day, a holiday in the Virgin Islands on the last Monday of March commemorating the purchase of the islands by the United States from Denmark on March 31, 1917.

April

The name for April, the fourth month of the year, comes either from *Aprilis*, the Roman derivation of Aphrodite, the Greek name for Venus, or from the Latin verb *aperire*, meaning "to open." The month begins with a day and ends with a night that are linked in many lands with age-old customs.

The first day is April Fools' Day, or All Fools' Day, which is a day at one time popular for pranks and harmless practical jokes. The origin of this day is not positively known. Records show that it has been going on at least since 1564, when January 1 was re-established in France as the first day of the year. The change confused many people, but in time it led to the fun of exchanging false greetings for the first of the year on the old day. April 1 coincides with the Zodiac sign of the fish, so the French call it Fooling the April Fish Day. A one-time April Fools' prank of the Scots was "hunting the gowk," which sent the victim on false errands; anyone who fell for this prank was called a gowk, or cuckoo.

The last hours of the month of April are observed as Walpurgis Night in some parts of Europe. It is the custom in Scandinavian countries and in the mountains of Germany to light huge bonfires and hold gay events on the night of April 30 in remembrance of an old folkway that defended man and beast from witches and demons. In Sweden and Finland, university students start wearing their white velvet caps on that night and join together to sing spring songs. In some parts of Switzerland, a bachelor, if he observes old traditions, may plant a pine tree on the last day of April at the home of a girl he admires.

The sweet pea and the daisy are the flowers for April. The gem is the diamond.

The Fixed Days of April

1 Birthday of Edwin Austin Abbey (April 1, 1852–August 1, 1911). American painter and illustrator of editions of Shakespeare and Goldsmith. He painted the *Quest of the Holy Grail* murals in the Boston Public Library.

1 Birthday of William Harvey (April 1, 1578–June 3, 1657). English physician, anatomist, and physiologist known for his discovery of the circulation of the blood. 977.

1 Birthday of Sergei Rachmaninoff (April 1, 1873–March 28, 1943). Russian pianist and composer; last of the leading proponents of the musical tradition of Russian romanticism. 986.

1 Birthday of Edmond Rostand (April 1, 1868–December 2, 1918). French poet and playwright whose most frequently revived drama is *Cyrano de Bergerac*. 986.

1 Birthday of Richard Zsigmondy (April 1, 1865–September 23, 1929). German chemist; awarded the 1925 Nobel Prize in chemistry in recognition of his achievements in the field of colloid chemistry. 225.

1 San Marino National Day, the traditional date for the installation of the *Capitani Regginti* or government officials; a holiday in San Marino.

1 April Fools' Day, or All Fools' Day, a day of practical jokes and high humor. It has various names. In Scotland it is Huntigowok day, in the north of England it is April Noddy. In France it is called "Fooling the April Fish Day."

c1 Hebrew University Day in Israel; observes the inauguration of the university in Jerusalem in 1925.

43

1   Intolerance Day, established to confine intolerance to the most appropriate day of the year, April Fools' Day.

2   Feast day of Saint Francis of Paola, patron saint of sailors.

2   Birthday of Hans Christian Andersen (April 2, 1805–August 4, 1875). Danish poet and novelist best known for fairy and folk tales. A literary award, the Hans Christian Andersen Prize, is presented biennially at each Congress of the International Board on Books for Young People, in honor of Hans Christian Andersen. International Children's Book Day is celebrated on Andersen's birthday. 234, 986.

2   Birthday of Frédéric Auguste Bartholdi (April 2, 1834–October 4, 1904). French sculptor whose work includes the Statue of Liberty in New York harbor, presented to the United States by the people of France in 1885 and dedicated in 1886. 481.

2   Birthday of Nicholas Murray Butler (April 2, 1862–December 7, 1947). American educator; statesman; president of Columbia University. He was awarded the Nobel Peace Prize in 1931. 241, 986, 987.

2   Birthday of Emile Zola (April 2, 1840–September 28, 1902). French novelist who became the leader of the school of naturalism in French literature. 986.

2   Creation of the Union of Central African States Day, a public holiday in Chad commemorating the establishment of the Union on April 2, 1968.

2   Pascua Florida Day, observed in Florida on the anniversary of Juan Ponce de Leon's discovery of Florida, claiming it for the king of Spain on April 2, 1513.

2   Anniversary of the establishment of the United States mint on April 2, 1792.

2   Mildred L. Batchelder Award Announcement Day; established by the Children's Services Division of the American Library Association in 1966 to honor their former executive secretary with an annual award to an American publisher of an outstanding children's book originally published in a foreign language in a foreign country.

3   Birthday of John Burroughs (April 3, 1837–March 29, 1921). American essayist and literary naturalist. A Burroughs Medal is presented annually in his memory by the John Burroughs Association for the year's best book in the field of natural history; the first recipient of this award was William Beebe. 234.

3   Birthday of Edward Everett Hale (April 3, 1822–June 10, 1909). American clergyman and author of *The Man without a Country.*

3   Birthday of Washington Irving (April 3, 1783–November 28, 1859). American historian, essayist, and storyteller famous for the legends of Rip Van Winkle and Ichabod Crane. He was elected to the Hall of Fame for Great Americans in 1900. 237, 986.

3   American Creed Day, anniversary of the acceptance by the United States House of Representatives, on April 3, 1918, of *The American Creed*, written by William Tyler Page in 1917.

3   Anniversary of the beginning of the Pony Express on April 3, 1860.

4   Feast day of Saint Benedict the Moor; patron saint of North American Negroes; patron of the city of Palermo. 705.

4   Birthday of Dorothea Lynde Dix (April 4, 1802–July 17, 1887). American philanthropist, author, and pioneer in the establishment or improvement of asylums for the mentally ill. 825, 837, 843, 992.

4   Liberation Day, a holiday in Hungary, the Magyar People's Republic, commemorating April 4, 1945, when the last German soldier was driven from Hungarian soil.

4 Senegalese National Day, a public holiday in Senegal commemorating April 4, 1960, when agreements were completed to give sovereignty to Senegal, the oldest French colony in Black Africa.

4 Anniversary of the establishment of the North Atlantic Treaty Organization (NATO) on April 4, 1949.

c4 Student Government Day; observed in Massachusetts on the first Friday of April, to provide students with an insight into practical government.

5 Birthday of Joseph Lister (April 5, 1827–February 10, 1912). English physician, founder of aseptic surgery. 977.

5 Birthday of Algernon Charles Swinburne (April 5, 1837–April 10, 1909). English poet famous for his elegies and monographs on Shakespeare. 986.

5 Birthday of Booker Taliaferro Washington (April 5, 1856–November 14, 1915). American educator, author, and lecturer. The first Negro to be depicted on a United States postage stamp. He was elected to the Hall of Fame for Great Americans in 1945. 237.

5 Birthday of Elihu Yale (April 5, 1649–July 8, 1721). English philanthropist for whom Yale University is named.

5 Tomb-sweeping Day, a national holiday in Taiwan, the Republic of China; a day of cleaning tombs and participating in rites for the dead.

6 Birthday of Raphael (April 6, 1483–April 6, 1520). Italian painter noted for his idealized madonnas and great frescoes; one of the masters of the Italian High Renaissance style. 986.

6 Birthday of Joseph Lincoln Steffens (April 6, 1866–August 9, 1936). American journalist and foremost figure among the muckrakers who exposed political and business corruption in the United States. *The Autobiography of Lincoln Steffens* is the story of his career.

6 Anniversary of the death of William Strickland on April 6, 1854. American architect, the outstanding exponent of the Greek revival in the United States. He designed the first United States customhouse and the marble sarcophagus of Washington at Mount Vernon.

6 Chakri Day, a public holiday in Thailand, commemorating the foundation of the ruling dynasty by King Rama I.

6 Van Riebeeck Day, a holiday in the Union of South Africa honoring Jan Van Riebeeck, the seventeenth-century explorer and founder of Cape Town.

6 Anniversary of the launching of the first communication satellite, the *Early Bird*, on April 6, 1965.

6 Anniversary of the founding of the Mormon church, the Church of Jesus Christ of Latter-Day Saints, by Joseph C. Smith and Oliver Crowdy on April 6, 1830.

6 Anniversary of the formal opening of the first of the modern Olympic games at Athens, Greece, on April 6, 1896.

7 Birthday of Walter Camp (April 7, 1859–March 14, 1925). American coach who did more than anyone else to develop the game of football; originator of the annual All-American selections.

7 Birthday of William Ellery Channing (April 7, 1780–October 2, 1842). American Unitarian clergyman and author who played an influential role in the intellectual life of New England. Elected to the Hall of Fame for Great Americans in 1900. 237.

7 Birthday of David Grandison Fairchild (April 7, 1869–August 6, 1954). American botanist and explorer who traveled the globe in search of useful plants for introduction into the United States. The Fairchild Tropical Garden at Coral Gables is named for him.

7 Birthday of Gabriela Mistral (April 7, 1899–January 10, 1957). Chilean poet and educator who rose to important posts in the Chilean educational system and helped to reorganize the rural schools in Mexico. Her real name was Lucila Godoy de Alcayaga, but she is known by the pseudonym that combines the names of the poets D'Annunzio of Italy and Mistral of France. Winner of the 1945 Nobel Prize in literature. 227, 986.

7 Birthday of William Wordsworth (April 7, 1770–April 23, 1850). English poet laureate famous for *I Wandered Lonely as a Cloud* and *Ode: Intimations of Immortality*; greatest poet of the English Romantic movement. 986.

7 Yugoslav Republic Day, the anniversary of the proclamation of the formation of the Socialist Federal Republic of Yugoslavia on April 7, 1963.

7 World Health Day, anniversary of the establishment of the World Health Organization on April 7, 1948, with the objective of attaining the highest possible level of health for all peoples in the world.

8 Feast day of Saint Walter, patron saint of prisoners of war.

c8 Buddha's birthday is celebrated in Hawaii, Japan, and Korea with the embellishment of temples to honor the Infant Buddha. The day is called Kambutse in Japan. The Wesak flower festival commemorates Buddha's birthday in Hawaii on the first Sunday in April. It is a movable festival in the Far East.

8 Birthday of Harvey Cushing (April 8, 1869–October 7, 1939). American neurosurgeon, the leading brain specialist of his time; introduced blood-pressure determinations in the United States; author of the Pulitzer Prize winning biography of Sir William Osler. 229.

8 Anniversary of the death of El Greco on April 8, 1614. The most influential master of Spanish painting, who reflected the zeal of Spain and set new patterns for artistic expression. 986.

8 Birthday of William Henry Welch (April 8, 1850–April 30, 1934). American pathologist who established the first pathology laboratory in the United States; a founder of the Johns Hopkins School of Medicine.

9 Birthday of Charles Pierre Baudelaire (April 9, 1821–August 31, 1867). French poet and critic whose *Les Fleurs du Mal* was an important influence on French symbolists and modern poets. 986.

9 Birthday of Helene Lange (April 9, 1848–May 13, 1930). German educator and pioneer in the movement for higher education for women; organizer of a women's teachers' association.

9 Bataan Day, commemorating the surrender of the American and Philippine defenders of the Bataan peninsula on April 9, 1942. Observed in the Philippines on April 10.

9 Bolivian National Day, a public holiday commemorating a popular uprising and the reestablishment of the National Revolutionary Movement on April 9, 1952.

c9 The Glarus Festival is the anniversary of the defeat of the Austrians by the men of Glarus in Switzerland on April 9, 1388. It is commemorated as a patriotic holiday on the first Thursday in April, with a pilgrimage to Näfels during which the procession visits the eleven memorial stones that mark the Austrians' eleven unsuccessful attacks.

9 Tunisia Martyr's Day, a public holiday in Tunisia.

9 Churchill Day; anniversary of the April 9, 1963, proclamation granting honorary United States citizenship to Sir Winston Churchill.

9 Anniversary of the establishment of the Golf Hall of Fame by the Professional Golfers' Association on April 9, 1941.

10 Birthday of Hugo Grotius (April 10, 1583–August 28, 1645). Dutch jurist and statesman; founder of the science of international law.

10 Birthday of Matthew Calbraith Perry (April 10, 1794–March 4, 1858). American naval officer who reached Tokyo Bay on July 8, 1853, and later opened up diplomatic and trade relations between Japan and the United States.

10 Birthday of Joseph Pulitzer (April 10, 1847–October 29, 1911). American journalist and publisher who founded through his will the Columbia University Graduate School of Journalism and the Pulitzer Prizes in journalism, letters, and music. 229.

10 Anniversary of the founding of the American Boccaccio Association, April 10, 1974, for the encouragement of Boccaccio studies among scholars of all disciplines.

10 Humane Day, anniversary of the incorporation of the American Society for the Prevention of Cruelty to Animals on April 10, 1866. 514–18.

10 Salvation Army Founder's Day, commemorating the birth of General William Booth on April 10, 1829.

11 Birthday of Charles Evans Hughes (April 11, 1862–August 27, 1948). American jurist, statesman, and eleventh chief justice of the United States Supreme Court.

11 Battle of Rivas Day, a public holiday in Costa Rica commemorating the Costa Rican triumph over the foreign invaders of Nicaragua on April 11, 1856.

11 Fast and Prayer Day, a holiday and day of religious dedication in Liberia.

11 Resistance Movement Day, observed in Czechoslovakia in honor of the formal liberation of Buchenwald on April 11, 1945.

11 Anniversary of the authorization by Congress of the Distinguished Service Medal for the Merchant Marine on April 11, 1942. The first recipient was Edwin Fox Cheney, Jr.

12 Birthday of John Shaw Billings (April 12, 1838–March 11, 1913). American army surgeon and librarian; director of the New York Public Library, who consolidated the separately endowed units of the library and organized the city's system of branch libraries.

12 Birthday of Henry Clay (April 12, 1777–June 29, 1852). American statesman known as "the Great Compromiser" in the effort to preserve the Union. Elected to the Hall of Fame for Great Americans in 1900. He represents the state of Kentucky in a Statuary Hall sculpture done by Charles Henry Niehaus. 237, 242.

12 Birthday of Frederick G. Melcher (April 12, 1879–March 9, 1963). American publisher, editor, and a founder of Children's Book Week in 1919. Donor of the Newbery and Caldecott medals awarded annually for outstanding children's books. 235, 236.

12 Birthday of Otto Meyerhof (April 12, 1884–October 6, 1951). German-American physiologist and biochemist who won the 1922 Nobel Prize in medicine for research on chemical reactions in muscle metabolism. 238.

12 Halifax Resolutions Day, or Halifax Independence Day, a legal holiday in North Carolina. It commemorates the Halifax Resolutions of Independence adopted in North Carolina on April 12, 1776, which were influential in bringing about the adoption of the Declaration of Independence.

12 Space Probe Day, anniversary of the first manned orbit around the earth achieved by Russian astronaut Yuri Gagarin on April 12, 1961.

12 Fort Sumter Day, anniversary of the bombardment of Fort Sumter on April 12, 1861, the beginning of the American Civil War.

13 Birthday of John Hanson (April 13, 1721–November 22, 1783). American Revolutionary political leader. First president of the Congress of the Confederacy. He represents the state of Maryland in Statuary Hall in a sculpture by Richard Edwin Brooks. 242.

13 Birthday of Thomas Jefferson (April 13, 1743–July 4, 1826). Welsh ancestry; Virginia lawyer; third president of the United States, 1801–9. No formal religious affiliation. Buried at Monticello, Albemarle County, Virginia. Elected to Hall of Fame for Great Americans in 1900. Thomas Jefferson's birthday is a holiday in Alabama, Missouri, and Virginia and is proclaimed in several other states. The University of Virginia Founders Day celebration at Charlottesville is held annually on Jefferson's birthday. 237, 538–45, 667–72, 674–76, 678–79.

13 Songkran Day, a public holiday in Thailand in which two days of tribute are paid to monks, elders, and monasteries.

13 John Hanson Day, observed in Maryland to honor the state's outstanding leader of the period of the American Revolution.

13 Huguenot Day, the anniversary of the signing of the Edict of Nantes, on April 13, 1598, is observed by the Huguenot Society of America.

13 The Jefferson Memorial at Washington, D.C., was dedicated on the two-hundredth anniversary of Jefferson's birth, April 13, 1943.

14 Feast day of Saint Justin, patron saint of philosophers. 705.

14 Birthday of Junius Spencer Morgan (April 14, 1813–April 8, 1890). American merchant and philanthropist who was a benefactor of the Hartford Public Library, Trinity College, the Metropolitan Museum of Art, and other institutions.

14 Birthday of Anne Mansfield Sullivan (April 14, 1866–October 20, 1936). American educator famous as the teacher and companion of Helen Keller. 837, 992.

14 Pan American Day, established in 1931, honors the first International Conference of American States held on April 14, 1890, in Washington; observed in schools with special programs interpreting the folk songs, dances, and customs of the countries of this continent. Pan American Day is a public holiday in Haiti and in Honduras. 624–37.

14 Anniversary of the dedication of the Taft Memorial Bell Tower in Washington, D.C., on April 14, 1959; a memorial to Robert Alphonso Taft, senator from Ohio.

15 Birthday of John Lothrop Motley (April 15, 1814–May 29, 1877). American historian and diplomat. Author of *The Rise of the Dutch Republic*. He was elected to the Hall of Fame for Great Americans in 1910. 237.

15 Birthday of Charles Willson Peale (April 15, 1741–February 22, 1827). American painter famous for his many portraits of George Washington. 986.

15 Birthday of Leonardo da Vinci (April 15, 1452–May 2, 1519). Italian painter, sculptor, scientist, and inventor; one of the greatest minds of all time. 986.

16 Feast day of Saint Bernadette, celebrated throughout the Roman Catholic world and particularly at Lourdes, France, the site of the healing waters revealed to Bernadette and the focal point of one of the major pilgrimages of the modern world. 5, 705.

16 Birthday of Herbert Baxter Adams (April 16, 1850–July 30, 1901). American historian; a founder and first secretary of the American Historical Association, in whose name the association offers an annual award for a book in history. 234.

16 Birthday of Anatole France (April 16, 1844–October 13, 1924). French novelist, poet, playwright, and critic who received the Nobel Prize in literature in 1921. 227, 986.

16 Birthday of Wilbur Wright (April 16, 1867–May 30, 1912). American pioneer aviator who, with his brother Orville, invented the airplane. He was elected to the Hall of Fame for Great Americans in 1955. 237.

16 De Diego Day, a public holiday in Puerto Rico commemorating the April 16, 1867, birth of the patriot José de Diego.

16 Queen Margrethe's birthday, observed in Denmark by schoolchildren and the Royal Guard.

16 Anniversary of the beginning of the Book-of-the-Month Club on April 16, 1926.

17 Birthday of Ray Stannard Baker (April 17, 1870–July 12, 1946). American journalist of the muckraking era; author of boys' books and the authorized biographer of Woodrow Wilson; wrote essays under the pseudonym of David Grayson.

17 Birthday of Isabel Barrows (April 17, 1845–October 25, 1913). American editor and pioneer penologist.

17 Birthday of Charles Henry Parkhurst (April 17, 1842–September 8, 1933). American clergyman who is remembered for sermons denouncing crime in New York City government; president of the Society for the Prevention of Crime.

17 Children's Protection Day, observed annually in Japan as a day commemorating the passage of laws protecting juvenile delinquents.

17 Flag Day in American Samoa, commemorating April 17, 1900, when the seven high chiefs voluntarily signed the Instrument of Cession at the invitation of President Theodore Roosevelt. It also commemorates the establishment of Samoan constitutional government on April 17, 1960.

17 Syria Independence Day, a holiday in the Syrian Arab Republic commemorating the withdrawal of French troops on April 17, 1946; sometimes called Evacuation Day.

17 Verrazano Day, observed in New York State to commemorate the discovery of New York harbor by Giovanni da Verrazano on April 17, 1524.

18 Birthday of Clarence Seward Darrow (April 18, 1857–March 13, 1938). American lawyer associated with the Scopes trial and other dramatic court cases of the early twentieth century. His career is the subject of *The Story of My Life.*

18 Birthday of Richard Harding Davis (April 18, 1864–April 11, 1916). American journalist and author, one of the first of the roving foreign correspondents.

c18 First day of summer, a public holiday in Iceland.

18 Anniversary of the famous midnight ride of Paul Revere on April 18, 1775, which warned the colonists that "the British are coming." 650.

18 Anniversary of the San Francisco earthquake and fire of April 18, 1906; periodically commemorated with special events in California.

c18 89'ers Day, observed in Oklahoma around April 18 to commemorate the opening up of lands for settlement in 1889; a festival of parades and rodeos.

19 Feast day of Blessed James Duckett, patron saint of booksellers and publishers. 705.

19 Birthday of José Echegaray y Eizaguirre (April 19, 1832–September 4, 1916). Spanish dramatist, mathematician, and statesman; recipient of the 1904 Nobel Prize in literature; often called "the Spanish Ibsen."

19 Anniversary of the death of Simon Fraser on April 19, 1862. Canadian explorer and fur trader who explored the upper course of the Fraser River.

19 Birthday of Roger Sherman (April 19, 1721–July 23, 1793). American patriot and statesman. The only man to sign all four of the major documents of American independence—the Articles of Association, the Declaration of Independence, the Articles of Confederation, and the Constitution. He represents the state of Connecticut in Statuary Hall in a sculpture done by Chauncey B. Ives. 242.

19 Declaration of Independence and Day of the Indian, observed as a joint holiday in Venezuela.

19 Landing of the 33 Patriots Day, a public holiday in Uruguay commemorating the landing of thirty-three patriotic exiles on April 19, 1825, to begin the campaign that ultimately resulted in the independence of Uruguay.

c19 Patriots' Day, or Battles of Lexington and Concord Day, commemorating the first battle of the Revolutionary War, which occurred on April 19, 1775; observed in Maine and Massachusetts on the third Monday of April. 646–53.

19 Parker Day, or John Parker Day, a remembrance day in tribute to John Parker, a captain of the minutemen, who gave the order on April 19, 1775, at Lexington not to fire unless fired upon; remembered for the words "if they mean to have a war, let it begin here."

20 Birthday of Daniel Chester French (April 20, 1850–October 7, 1931). American sculptor who was commissioned to create many statues of prominent Americans. His best-known work includes the seated figure of Abraham Lincoln in the Lincoln Memorial in Washington and the *Minute Man* at Concord.

21 Birthday of Alexander Anderson (April 21, 1775–January 17, 1870). American engraver and illustrator who made the first wood engravings completed in the United States; his best-known work includes engravings for an edition of the plays of Shakespeare.

21 Birthday of Fredrik Bajer (April 21, 1837–January 22, 1922). Danish statesman and author; founder of the Danish Peace Society and the International Peace Bureau; recipient of the 1908 Nobel Peace Prize. 241.

21 Birthday of Charlotte Brontë (April 21, 1816–March 31, 1855). English novelist famous for *Jane Eyre* and other novels interpreting women in conflict with their individual needs and social conditions. 986.

21 Birthday of Friedrich Froebel (April 21, 1782–June 21, 1852). German educator; founder of kindergarten system.

21 Birthday of John Muir (April 21, 1838–December 24, 1914). American naturalist; advocate of forest conservation who discovered the glaciers in the High Sierras. The only stand of redwoods in the United States National Park System is named the Muir Woods National Monument in his honor. 986.

21 Brasilia Day, a Brazilian national holiday; anniversary of the proclamation naming Brasilia as the national capital of Brazil on April 21, 1960.

21 Kartini Day in Indonesia, a tribute to Raden Adjeng Kartini, leader in the emancipation of Indonesian women.

21 Natale di Roma, traditional day for observing the founding of Rome in 753 B.C., celebrated with parades and public speeches.

21 San Jacinto Day, a legal holiday in Texas commemorating the 1836 Battle of San Jacinto through which the Texans won independence from Mexico.

21 Tiradentes Day in Brazil, commemorates the execution of the dentist Jose da Silva Xavier, a conspirator in the 1789 revolt against the Portuguese.

22 Birthday of Alphonse Bertillon (April 22, 1853–February 13, 1914). French anthropologist; chief of the department of identification in the prefecture of police in Paris who devised the Bertillon system for identifying criminals.

22 Birthday of Henry Fielding (April 22, 1707–October 8, 1754). English novelist remembered for such novels as *The History of Tom Jones, a Foundling.* 986.

22 Birthday of Ellen Glasgow (April 22, 1873–November 21, 1945). American novelist credited with being the first to write honestly of the South. Her novel *In This Our Life* received the 1942 Pulitzer Prize. 986.

22 Birthday of Immanuel Kant (April 22, 1724–February 12, 1804). German philosopher who influenced such schools of philosophy as Kantianism and idealism; author of *The Critique of Pure Reason.* 977.

22 Birthday of Henri Lafontaine (April 22, 1854–May 14, 1943). Belgian jurist who was the corecipient with Elihu Root of the 1913 Nobel Peace Prize. 241.

22 Birthday of Nikolai Lenin (Vladimir Ilich Ulyanov); April 22, 1870–January 21, 1924. Russian revolutionary leader and writer whose ideas and career laid the foundations for Soviet totalitarianism; first head of the Russian state. His birthday is observed in the Union of Soviet Socialist Republics. 15.

22 Birthday of Julius Sterling Morton (April 22, 1832–April 27, 1902). American politician who started Arbor Day in Nebraska in 1872. He represents Nebraska in Statuary Hall in a sculpture made by Rudolph Evans; his birthday is recognized annually by arboretum societies and observed as Arbor Day in Nebraska. 184, 242.

22 Birthday of J. Robert Oppenheimer (April 22, 1904–February 18, 1967). Theoretical physicist, director of the Los Alamos laboratory during the development of the atomic bomb. Received the Enrico Fermi Award of the Atomic Energy Commission in 1963. 977.

22 Arbor Day, a legal holiday in Nebraska commemorating the birthday of J. Sterling Morton, April 22, 1832, founder of Arbor Day and former governor of the state. Arbor Day was first celebrated in Nebraska on April 10, 1872, but was later changed to Morton's birth date. 184–93.

22 Brazil Discovery Day, a public holiday commemorating the discovery of Brazil by Pedro Alvarez Cabral on April 22, 1500.

c22 Fast day in New Hampshire; a commemorative day dating from seventeenth-century New England; observed on the fourth Monday of April.

22 Oklahoma Day, a holiday celebrating the anniversary of the opening of the Oklahoma Territory for settlement on April 22, 1889.

22 Queen Isabella Day, honoring the April 22, 1451, birth of the Spanish queen who financed Christopher Columbus; the day is observed in Spain and frequently proclaimed by the governors of a number of states in the United States.

22 Earth Day, first observed internationally on April 22, 1970, to emphasize the necessity for the conservation of the natural resources of the world. 414–22.

23 Feast day of Saint George, patron saint of chivalry, of England, Canada, Portugal, Germany, Genoa, and Venice, and the protector of Ferrara and of scouts. 125, 705.

23 Birthday of James Buchanan (April 23, 1791–June 1, 1868). Scotch-Irish ancestry; Pennsylvania lawyer; fifteenth president of the United States, 1857–61. A Presbyterian and the only bachelor president. Buried at Woodward Hill Cemetery, Lancaster, Pennsylvania. 667–72, 674–76, 678, 679.

23 Anniversary of the death of Miguel de Cervantes Saavedra on April 23, 1616. Leading Spanish novelist, playwright, and poet famed for the writing of *Don Quixote.* 986.

23 Birthday of Edwin Markham (April 23, 1852–March 7, 1940). American poet who wrote *The Man with the Hoe* and *Lincoln, the Man of the People*. Markham has been called the Dean of American Poets.

23 Birthday of Lester Bowles Pearson (April 23, 1897–December 27, 1972). Prime minister of Canada and ambassador to the United States; awarded the Nobel Peace Prize for his success in averting war at the time of the 1957 Suez crisis. 241.

23 Birthday of William Shakespeare (April 23, 1564–April 23, 1616). Traditional date for the commemoration of the birth of William Shakespeare, who was baptized on April 26, 1564; universally acknowledged to be the greatest dramatist and poet the world has known. His birthday is a festival day at Stratford-upon-Avon, his birthplace, and is observed by Shakespeare societies in many nations. 715–26, 986.

23 Birthday of Joseph Mallord Turner (April 23, 1775–December 19, 1851). English landscape painter, admired for unusual use of light and color. 986.

23 National Sovereignty Day and Children's Day in Turkey, a patriotic holiday honoring children as the symbol of modern Turkey and commemorating the inauguration of the Grand National Assembly on April 23, 1923.

23 Anniversary of the founding of the American Academy of Arts and Letters on April 23, 1904.

23 Anniversary of the establishment of the Order of the Garter, the oldest and most illustrious of British orders of knighthood, on April 23, 1348. 228.

23 Peppercorn Day, an observance in Bermuda carrying out the Peppercorn ceremony, in which officials collect the annual rent of one peppercorn for the use of the Old State House in Saint George.

24 Anniversary of the death of Daniel Defoe on April 24, 1731. English novelist renowned for *Robinson Crusoe*. 986.

24 Birthday of John Russell Pope (April 24, 1874–August 27, 1937). American architect whose work includes the National Gallery of Art and the Jefferson Memorial.

24 Birthday of Carl Spitteler, "Felix Tandem" (April 24, 1845–December 29, 1924). Swiss poet who was awarded the Nobel Prize in literature in 1919. 227.

24 Armenian Martyrs' Day, memorializing the Armenian victims of the Turkish massacres of 1915–16; observed by groups with Armenian backgrounds throughout the world.

24 Secretaries' Day, honoring women in the secretarial field, a part of Secretaries' Week.

24 Anniversary of the establishment of the Library of Congress by authority of an Act of Congress on April 24, 1800.

25 Feast day of Saint Mark the Evangelist, patron saint of notaries, celebrated in the Roman Catholic, Anglican, and Lutheran churches. San Marcós Day is celebrated by all Mexican towns named San Marcós or in which San Marcós is the patron saint. 705.

25 Birthday of Charles Ferdinand Dowd (April 25, 1825–November 12, 1904). American educator and proponent of uniform time zones to replace the individual system whereby each city and railroad had its own time system. Dowd's ideas on standard time were adopted by most cities of the United States and by the railroads on November 18, 1883.

25 Birthday of Guglielmo Marconi (April 25, 1874–July 20, 1937). Italian electrician who perfected wireless telegraphy and experiments with short-waves and ultrashort waves. He was a co-winner of the 1909 Nobel Prize in physics. 241.

25 Birthday of Wolfgang Pauli (April 25, 1900–December 15, 1958). Austrian physicist; winner of the 1945 Nobel Prize in physics. 241.

25 Anzac Day, an Australian and New Zealand holiday of veterans parades and church services, commemorating the courageous but sacrificial landing of the Australian and New Zealand Army Corps troops at Gallipoli in World War I. The word *Anzac* is made up of the initials of the Australian and New Zealand Army Corps.

25 Liberation Day, observed in Italy as a holiday to honor the freedom that came with the Allied victory in World War II.

25 Swaziland National Flag Day, a public holiday in Swaziland, honoring the nation's flag and the responsibilities of citizenship.

25 Anniversary of the opening of the Saint Lawrence Seaway for lake traffic to the Midwest on April 25, 1959.

25 Anniversary of the opening of the United Nations Conference on International Organization in San Francisco on April 25, 1945. The San Francisco conference, called to work on the charter of a United Nations, was held from April 25 to June 26, 1945. 784.

26 Birthday of John James Audubon (April 26, 1785–January 27, 1851). American ornithologist and artist. His book *Birds of America* is recognized as the finest example of ornithological illustration; elected to the Hall of Fame for Great Americans in 1900. 237, 977.

26 Birthday of Michel Fokine (April 26, 1880–August 22, 1942). Russian-American dancer and choreographer; created *The Dying Swan* for Anna Pavlova; a major influence on twentieth-century classical ballet repertoire.

26 Birthday of Esek Hopkins (April 26, 1718–February 26, 1802). American commodore; first commander-in-chief of the American navy. 739.

26 Birthday of Frederick Law Olmsted (April 26, 1822–August 28, 1903). American landscape architect, noted for his design of Central Park in New York City and for the planning for Yosemite National Park and the Niagara Falls Park project. 986.

26 Birthday of Erminnie Adelle Platt (April 26, 1836–June 9, 1886). American ethnologist who lived with the Iroquois Indians and prepared an Iroquois-English dictionary.

26 Birthday of Sir Owen Willans Richardson (April 26, 1879–February 15, 1959). English physicist who won the 1928 Nobel Prize in physics for his work on dynamics. 241.

26 Union Day, a public holiday in Tanzania, commemorating the unification of Zanzibar and Tanganyika on April 26, 1964.

26 Cape Henry Day, designated annually by proclamation of the governor of Virginia as a commemoration of the first landing on American soil of the expedition that founded Jamestown.

c26 Confederate Memorial Day, observed in Alabama, Florida, and Mississippi on the last Monday of April.

c26 National Arbor Day in the United States, designated by presidential proclamation for observation on the last Friday of April; scheduled on varying dates throughout the country. 184–93.

27 Birthday of Norman Bel Geddes (April 27, 1893–May 8, 1958). American theatrical and industrial designer noted for his stage designs and for pioneering in the application of functionalism in the design of airplane interiors, trains, and automobiles.

27 Birthday of Mary Wollstonecraft Godwin (April 27, 1759–September 10, 1797). English writer whose major work was *Vindication of the Rights of Women*. 986.

27 Birthday of Ulysses Simpson Grant (April 27, 1822–July 23, 1885). Scottish ancestry; Illinois tanner; general-in-chief of the Union forces in the Civil War; eighteenth president of the United States. Methodist. Buried on Riverside Drive, New York City. Elected to the Hall of Fame for Great Americans in 1900. 237, 667–72, 674–76, 678, 679.

27 Anniversary of the death of Ferdinand Magellan on April 27, 1521. Portuguese navigator; often called the first circumnavigator of the earth; honored on Discoverers' Day.

27 Birthday of Samuel Finley Breece Morse (April 27, 1791–April 2, 1872). American artist and inventor of the electric telegraph and the Morse code. He was elected to the Hall of Fame for Great Americans in 1900. 237, 977.

27 Austrian Second Republic Day, a public holiday commemorating the foundation of the Second Republic of Austria on April 27, 1945.

27 Sierra Leone Independence Day, commemorating the achievement of independence by Sierra Leone on April 27, 1961.

27 Togo Independence Day, a public holiday in Togo, on the west coast of Africa, commemorating its establishment as a sovereign nation on April 27, 1960.

c27 National Christian College Day, established in 1941 to emphasize the importance of religion to higher education. The last Sunday in April was designated for its observance.

28 Birthday of Tobias Michael Carel (April 28, 1838–July 29, 1913). Dutch jurist and statesman, founder of the Institute of International Law, corecipient of the Nobel Peace Prize in 1911.

28 Birthday of James Monroe (April 28, 1758–July 4, 1831). Scottish ancestry; Virginia lawyer; fifth president of the United States, 1817–25. Episcopalian. Buried in Hollywood Cemetery, Richmond, Virginia. Elected to the Hall of Fame for Great Americans in 1930. 237, 667–72, 674–79.

28 Maryland Admission Day. Maryland entered the Union on April 28, 1788, as the seventh state of the original thirteen to be admitted.

c28 Arbor Day, a legal holiday in Utah, observed on the last Friday in April.

29 Birthday of Sir Thomas Beecham (April 29, 1879–March 8, 1961). English conductor; founder of the London Philharmonic Orchestra in 1932; champion of the music of Frederick Delius.

29 Birthday of Oliver Ellsworth (April 29, 1745–November 26, 1807). American jurist; third chief justice of the United States Supreme Court; major author of the Judiciary Act of 1789 establishing the federal court system.

29 Birthday of Lorado Taft (April 29, 1860–October 30, 1936). American sculptor whose notable works include *Black Hawk*, at Oregon, Illinois, and *Solitude of the Soul*, at the Chicago Art Institute.

29 Emperor's Birthday, honoring the birth of Emperor Hirohito on April 29, 1901; a national holiday in Japan.

30 Feast day of Saint Catherine of Siena, patron saint of Italy, author of many famous letters and a great mystical work entitled *Dialogue*. 705.

30 Birthday of H.M. Queen Juliana, April 30, 1909, is a holiday in the Netherlands, Aruba, Curaçao, Netherlands Antilles, and Surinam.

30 Louisiana Admission Day. Louisiana entered the Union on April 30, 1812, as the eighteenth state. 741.

30 May Day Eve, Maitag Vorabend, celebrated in various cantons of Switzerland carrying on the ancient traditions of lovers.

30 Walpurgis Night, an ancient festival to ward off witches, warlocks, and demons, is observed in the towns of the Harz Mountains of Germany, and in Finland and the Scandinavian countries, with bonfires and gala events.

30 Anniversary of George Washington's first oath of office as president of the United States, administered on April 30, 1789, by Robert Livingstone, chancellor of New York State.

May

May, the fifth month of the year, may have been named for Maia, the Roman goddess of spring and growth, or for the *Majores*, a branch of the Roman senate. It is a month that is associated with flowers and mild weather in the northern hemisphere, but it is a winter month in the southern hemisphere.

The first day, called May Day, was once a popular festival honoring Flora, the goddess of flowers. It was a day of maypole dancing and other charming customs, many of which disappeared with the fast pace of progress in the Western world. In the last half of the twentieth century, May 1 has been celebrated as a favorite international holiday for workers of all kinds. At least sixty-six nations in the world celebrate Labor Day on May 1 with parades, speeches, and civic gatherings. In a few European countries such as Finland, the day is also a special spring festival for students.

May is "the month of Mary" for Roman Catholics throughout the world. The Virgin Mary is honored during the entire month with pilgrimages and observances at great cathedrals and at special shrines. In the United States it is the month when the Protestant, Roman Catholic, and Jewish faiths, each in its own way, observe National Family Week, which leads up to the most popular of May observances, Mother's Day.

The special flowers for the month of May are the hawthorn and the lily of the valley. The birthstone is the emerald.

The Fixed Days of May

1 First day of the "Month of Mary," which includes special devotions to the Blessed Virgin throughout the Roman Catholic world.

1 The Feast of Saint Philip and Saint James, apostles, is celebrated on May 1 in the Roman Catholic, Anglican, and Lutheran churches. The Greek church commemorates the two apostles separately.

1 Birthday of Joseph Addison (May 1, 1672–June 17, 1719). English essayist. 986.

1 Birthday of Benjamin Henry Latrobe (May 1, 1764–September 3, 1820). American architect who designed the Roman Catholic cathedral in Baltimore, the first cathedral to be constructed in the United States, and rebuilt the Capitol after it was burned by the British in 1814. 986.

1 Dewey Day, honors Admiral George Dewey and the anniversary of the Battle of Manila Bay of May 1, 1898. It is observed primarily by veterans organizations.

1 Labour Day, or International Workers' Day, is a public holiday in sixty-six nations of the world. The major exceptions are the United States and Canada, where Labor Day is celebrated on the first Monday of September; Spain, where it is celebrated on July 18; New Zealand, October 22; and Jamaica, May 23. The May 1 Labour Day has various names. It is sometimes called May Day, Eight Hours Day, International Day of Solidarity of the Working People, or Saint Joseph the Worker Day.

1 Law Day, sponsored by the American Bar Association, is recognized by presidential proclamation; its aim is to further public knowledge, appreciation, and respect for law and its benefits to the citizen; observed by legal societies, schools, and the media. 572–79.

1 Lei Day, a Hawaiian flower festival, the only fete of its kind; dedicated to the lei as a symbol of Hawaiian beauty and friendship.

1 Loyalty Day, observed in the United States by presidential proclamation. Special ceremonies are presented by the Veterans of Foreign Wars, on or near May 1, at Cooch's Bridge, Delaware, where the Stars and Stripes were first displayed in battle.

1 May Day, the traditional day of flower festivals, is a spring festival in Turkey. The age-old rituals of hanging May baskets and dancing around the maypole are carried on by students and neighborhood groups in England and in some parts of the United States.

1 Senior Citizens Day, the beginning of Senior Citizens Month, which is observed in Massachusetts and other states; the month has honored senior citizens with annual presidential proclamations since 1963.

1 Vappu Day, a May Day continuation of Walpurgis Night in Finland; a student festival. In Finland, May 1 is also a holiday for organized workers.

2 Feast day of Saint Athanasius, champion of the faith, who held out against Arian heresy; one of the four great Greek Doctors of the Church. 705.

2 Birthday of Elias Boudinot (May 2, 1740–October 24, 1821). American lawyer, patriot-philanthropist; leader in the organization of the American Bible Society and its first president.

2 Birthday of Theodor Herzl (May 2, 1860–July 3, 1904). Founder of modern Zionism; honored in Israel and in Jewish communities throughout the world.

2 Birthday of Henry Martyn Robert (May 2, 1837–May 11, 1923). American military engineer and parliamentarian who is famous for the codification of the rules of parliamentary procedure under the familiar title *Robert's Rules of Order Revised.*

2 Burma Peasants' Day, a holiday for Burmese agricultural workers following the May 1 Labor, or Workers', Day; both are correlated with week-long seminars and training programs.

3 Feast of the Inventio, the finding of the Holy Cross, commemorates Saint Helena's discovery of the Cross on which the Lord was crucified; called the Day of the Holy Cross in Mexico and especially honored by construction tradesmen.

3 Feast of Our Lady of Czestochowa, Queen of the Crown of Poland, is celebrated at the Polish National Shrine of Czestochowa in honor of the Virgin of Czestochowa. The shrine holds the venerated picture of the mother of Christ which was found by Saint Helena. Pilgrimages are, for the most part, prohibited by the Communists.

3 Birthday of Niccoló Machiavelli (May 3, 1469–June 21, 1527). Italian political statesman and author whose fame is based on the books *The Prince* and *The Discourses.* 986.

3 Japanese Constitution Day, a national holiday in Japan which celebrates the establishment, on May 3, 1947, of a democratic form of government under parliamentary rule.

3 Polish Constitution Day, Swieto Trzeciego Majo, commemorates the nation's first constitution, adopted in 1794.

3 Anniversary of the issuance of the "Freedom to Read" statement prepared by the Westchester Conference of the American Library Association and the American Book Publishers Council on May 2–3, 1953. This important statement has been reprinted in many forms, but it is easily accessible in *The First Freedom: Liberty and Justice in the World of Books and Reading,* edited by Robert B. Downs.

c3 May Fellowship Day, sponsored by the Church Women United and observed on the first Friday in May.

3 Anniversary of the establishment of the Society for the Propagation of the Faith at Lyon, France, on May 3, 1822.

4 Feast day of Saint Florian, patron saint of firemen.

4 Feast day of Saint Monica, patron saint of wives and mothers. 705.

4 Birthday of Johann Friedrich Herbart (May 4, 1776–August 14, 1841). German philosopher, psychologist, and pioneer in a scientific pedagogy known as the Herbartian system.

4 Birthday of Thomas Henry Huxley (May 4, 1825–June 29, 1895). English biologist, educator, and writer; champion of the Darwinian theory of evolution. 986.

4 Birthday of Horace Mann (May 4, 1796–August 2, 1859). American educator and crusading champion of educational reforms; known as the "Father of the Public School System." He was elected to the Hall of Fame for Great Americans in 1900. 237.

c4 Humane Sunday, a day dedicated to the prevention of child abuse and cruelty to animals; sponsored by the American Humane Society, usually on the first Sunday of May. 514–18.

4 Rhode Island Declaration of Independence Day, a bank holiday commemorating through public meetings and school programs the Declaration of Independence proclaimed by the colony on May 4, 1776, two months before the Continental Congress made its declaration.

c4 McDonogh Day, a day of commemoration by New Orleans schoolchildren honoring John McDonogh, who died on October 26, 1850, leaving half of his fortune to found public schools in New Orleans; a request that children occasionally place flowers on his grave is honored on the first Friday in May by a march to his statue and appropriate ceremonies.

4 Students' Memorial Day, observed in memory of four students killed during anti-war demonstrations at Kent State University on May 4, 1970; pays tribute also to students martyred elsewhere.

4 Anniversary of the chartering of the American Academy of Arts and Sciences on May 4, 1780.

5 Birthday of Sören Aabye Kierkegaard (May 5, 1813–November 11, 1855). Danish philosopher whose writings influenced such modern schools of thought as existentialism. 986.

5 Birthday of Karl Marx (May 5, 1818–March 14, 1883). German socialist whose best-known work is *Das Kapital.*

5 Birthday of Henryk Sienkiewicz (May 5, 1846–November 15, 1916). Polish novelist who wrote a patriotic trilogy dealing with Poland's struggle for freedom in the seventeenth century. He received the 1905 Nobel Prize in literature. 227.

5 Liberation Day in Denmark, marking the end on May 5, 1945, of five years of Nazi occupation during World War II.

5 Ethiopian Liberation Day, a public holiday commemorating May 5, 1941, when the emperor regained Addis Ababa after five years of Italian occupation of the capital city.

5 Boys' Festival or Children's Day, Tango-no-sekku, a public holiday in Japan honoring children; features festivities and customs symbolizing strength.

5 Cinco de Mayo, a holiday in Mexico, celebrating the defeat of the French at the Battle of Puebla in 1867. The day is also celebrated on Olvera Street in Los Angeles and in other cities of the United States with large Mexican-American populations.

5 Coronation Day in Thailand, a public holiday honoring the king, who is the titular chief of state.

5 Dutch Liberation Day, a holiday in the Netherlands, commemorating May 5, 1945, when the Nazi forces were driven out of Holland by the Allies.

c5 Zambia Labour Day, observed in Zambia on the first Monday of May; a day dedicated to the principle of maximum productivity.

c5 Anniversary of the organization of the American Bible Society in New York in May of 1816.

6 Birthday of Phoebe Ann Coffin (May 6, 1829–June 2, 1921). American Universalist minister; first woman ordained as a minister in New England.

6 Birthday of Martin Robinson Delaney (May 6, 1812–January 24, 1885). American physician; first Negro to be commissioned a major in the United States Army Medical Corps. 797.

6 Birthday of Sigmund Freud (May 6, 1856–September 23, 1939). Austrian physician and psychoanalyst, who is called the "Father of Psychoanalysis." 977, 986.

6 Birthday of Chapin Aaron Harris (May 6, 1806–September 29, 1860). American dentist; a founder of *The American Journal of Dental Science* and the American Society of Dental Surgeons.

6 Birthday of William Daniel Leahy (May 6, 1875–July 20, 1959). American naval officer and diplomat; one of the first three officers to be promoted to the five-star rank of admiral of the fleet in December 1944; author of *I Was There*.

6 Birthday of John McCutcheon (May 6, 1870–June 10, 1949). American cartoonist who was awarded a Pulitzer Prize in 1931 for his cartoons on political events and everyday life; creator of the cartoon *Injun Summer*, an annual fall reprint in the *Chicago Tribune*.

6 Birthday of Rear Admiral Robert Edwin Peary (May 6, 1856–February 20, 1920). American Arctic explorer; first to reach the North Pole, on April 6, 1909.

6 Birthday of Wladyslaw Stanislaw Reymont (May 6, 1868–December 5, 1925). Polish novelist who won the Nobel Prize in literature in 1924 for his four-volume masterpiece *The Peasants*.

6 Martyr's Day in Lebanon, a public holiday honoring the martyrs of ancient and modern times.

6 Shepherd's and Herdsman's day, an old folk festival day in Bulgaria.

7 Feast day of San Nicola; the people of Bari, in the Italian province of Apulia, celebrate the feast of San Nicola (Saint Nicholas) in May rather than on his regular feast day on December 6. May 7 and 8 is the anniversary of the transfer of the saint's relics from Myra, Asia Minor, to Bari.

7 Birthday of Johannes Brahms (May 7, 1833–April 3, 1897). German composer, considered one of the foremost musicians of all times; honored by annual music festivals throughout the world. 986.

7 Birthday of Robert Browning (May 7, 1812–December 12, 1889). English poet who climaxed his career with the writing of *The Ring and the Book*. 986.

7 Birthday of Sir Rabindranath Tagore (May 7, 1861–August 7, 1941). Hindu poet, philosopher, and artist. Author of *Gitanjali*, *The Religion of Man*, and other books. Awarded the Nobel Prize in literature in 1913. 227.

7 Birthday of Peter Ilich Tchaikovsky (May 7, 1840–November 6, 1893). Russian composer famous for his symphonies, orchestral works, and the familiar song *None but the Lonely Heart*. 986.

7 Spring Day, a public holiday in Scotland established to honor the season and provide a free day for the benefit of the citizens.

c7 State Ploughing Ceremony Day, a public holiday in Thailand celebrating the beginning of the rice-growing season.

7   Anniversary of the organization of the American Medical Association on May 7, 1847, at Philadelphia, with Dr. Jonathan Knight as the first president.

7   Anniversary of the sinking of the liner *Lusitania* on May 7, 1915.

8   Feast day of Saint Michael the Archangel, patron saint of policemen and grocers. 705.

c8   The Holy Blood Procession takes place on the streets of Bruges, Belgium, on the first Monday following May 2 to celebrate the spring day of 1150 when Count Thierry d'Alsace returned from the Crusades with the relic of the Holy Blood. The Passion play, *Sanguis Christi*, based on the story of the Holy Blood, is presented every five years.

8   Anniversary of the death of Helena Petrovna Blavatsky on May 8, 1891. Russian theosophist who founded the Theosophical Society in New York and whose book *Isis Unveiled* became a classic in theosophical literature; the day is commemorated by theosophical societies throughout the world.

8   Birthday of Jean Henri Dunant (May 8, 1828–October 30, 1910). Swiss philanthropist and founder of the Red Cross Society who shared the Nobel Peace Prize in 1901; World Red Cross Day is celebrated on his birthday.

8   Birthday of Edward Gibbon (May 8, 1737–January 16, 1794). English historian; author of *The History of the Decline and Fall of the Roman Empire*. 986.

8   Birthday of Oscar Hammerstein (May 8, 1846–August 1, 1919). German-American opera impresario, playwright, and inventor who established the Manhattan Opera House for the presentation of popular musical events.

8   Birthday of Miguel Hidalgo (May 8, 1753–July 31, 1811). Roman Catholic priest; organizer of a movement that became a social and economic revolution; known as "the Father of Mexican Independence."

8   Birthday of Harry S. Truman (May 8, 1884–December 26, 1972). English-Scotch-Irish ancestry; Missouri senator; vice-president who succeeded to the presidency on the death of President Roosevelt; thirty-third president of the United States, 1945–53. Baptist. Devoted his retirement to building up the archives in the Truman Library at Independence, Missouri. Author of *Years of Decisions* and *Years of Trial and Hope*. Buried in the rear courtyard of the Truman Library in Independence, Missouri. 667–80.

c8   Czechoslovakia National Holiday, a two-day civic celebration honoring the end of World War II.

8   V-E (Victory in Europe) Day, commemorating the end of World War II in Europe with the signing of the unconditional surrender by the Germans in May of 1945. It is called Armistice Day in France.

8   Furry Day, a Helston, England, celebration originally honoring Saint Michael's victory over Satan, now a spring festival with the entire town in movement; men in top hats and women in fancy dresses dance in the streets to the "Furry Dance" that is as old as the custom itself. 164.

8   Stork Day, the traditional day for the arrival of the storks at Ribe, Denmark, to repair their nests on the tops of old houses; the stork population is reported to be diminishing in the 1970s.

8   World Red Cross Day, honoring Henri Dunant, the originator of the Red Cross movement. 871–74.

9   Birthday of Sir James Matthew Barrie (May 9, 1860–June 9, 1937). Scottish playwright and novelist with a gift for whimsy. His most famous work is *Peter Pan*, which has provided a celebrated role for generations of famous actresses. 989.

9   Birthday of Belle Boyd (May 9, 1843–June 11, 1900). American actress who was, before her theatrical career, one of the most successful Confederate spies during the Civil War.

9 Birthday of James Pollard Espy (May 9, 1785–January 24, 1860). American meteorologist who laid the foundation for scientific weather prediction.

9 Birthday of José Ortega y Gasset (May 9, 1883–October 18, 1955). Spanish philosopher and humanist; known for *The Revolt of the Masses*, which advocates rule by the creative minority. 986.

9 Birthday of Alexander Ross (May 9, 1783–October 23, 1856). Canadian pioneer, fur trader, and author who is associated with the Northwest Company and the Red River settlement.

c9 Saint Joan's Day, observed in New Orleans in honor of Joan of Arc, who forced the English to raise the siege on Orleans, France in May 1429.

9 Victory Day, observed in the Union of Soviet Socialist Republics in honor of the end of World War II.

9 North Pole Flight Day, anniversary of the first flight over the North Pole, achieved by Commander Richard E. Byrd of the United States Navy and Floyd Bennett on May 9, 1926.

c10 Common Prayer Day, a public holiday in Denmark.

10 Commemoration of National Institutions Day, a special day in Cameroon; the anniversary of the first meeting of the Legislative Assembly on May 10, 1957.

10 Confederate Memorial Day, a statewide holiday in both North and South Carolina honoring the memory of the Confederate soldiers and civilians lost during the Civil War.

10 Fort Ticonderoga Day, observed at Ticonderoga, New York, marking the capture of the fort by Ethan Allen on May 10, 1775.

10 Golden Spike Day, commemorating the completion of the railroads and the driving of a golden spike on May 10, 1869, to symbolize the unification of the East and the West by railroad; observed at the Golden Spike Historical Monument at Corrine, Utah.

c10 Mother's Day. The first Mother's Day was held in Philadelphia on May 10, 1908, following suggestions made by Julia Ward Howe in 1872 and Anne Jarvis in 1907. The day received national recognition on May 9, 1914, when President Woodrow Wilson issued a proclamation asking American citizens to give a public expression of reverence to mothers. The selection of carnations as a symbol of the day, pink for a living mother and white for remembrance, was made in memory of President William McKinley, who always wore a white carnation, his own mother's favorite flower. In the United States, Mother's Day is now observed on the second Sunday in May. 611–17.

11 Birthday of Ottmar Mergenthaler (May 11, 1854–October 28, 1899). American inventor who developed the first Linotype machine in 1884.

11 Birthday of Mari Sandoz (May 11, 1901–March 10, 1966). Author of *Old Jules* and other books on the American pioneer period; Mari Sandoz Day was proclaimed by the Nebraska State Legislature to honor her birthday and work.

11 Laos Constitution Day, a public holiday honoring the proclamation of the 1947 constitution providing for a parliamentary democracy with a king as nominal chief executive.

11 Minnesota Admission Day. Minnesota entered the Union on May 11, 1858, as the thirty-second state. 741.

11 International Mother's Day, observed on May 11, unites mothers of the world in an action program for peace.

12 Birthday of Robert Baldwin (May 12, 1804–December 9, 1858). Canadian statesman, exponent of representative government. 995.

12 Birthday of Lincoln Ellsworth (May 12, 1880–May 26, 1951). American engineer and polar explorer who led the first transarctic flights in 1926 and the first transanarctic flights in 1935.

12 Birthday of Edward Lear (May 12, 1812–January 29, 1888). English author and painter; popularizer of the limerick; best known for his nonsense verse. 986.

12 Birthday of Florence Nightingale (May 12, 1820–August 13, 1910). English nurse and the founder of modern nursing; called the "Lady with the Lamp" during the Crimean War. She was the first woman to receive the Order of Merit. 825, 843, 992.

12 Birthday of Gabriel Dante Rossetti (May 12, 1828–April 9, 1882). English poet and painter who was the most important member of the Pre-Raphaelites. 986.

12 Birthday of Halsey William Wilson (May 12, 1868–March 1, 1954). American publisher of reference and bibliographic tools.

12 Khmer Republic (Cambodia) Constitution Day, a public holiday honoring the constitution adopted in April of 1972.

12 Garland Day in Abbotsbury, Dorsetshire, England; a ceremony left over from the old May Day festivities; observed by children who carry garlands from door to door and receive gifts for the welcoming of May; the garlands are later laid in front of the War Memorial.

12 National Hospital Day has been observed annually on May 12 since 1921; observed by many hospitals and hospital associations with special programs honoring Florence Nightingale.

12 Snellman Day, observed in Finland to honor the birth on May 12, 1806, of J. V. Snellman, journalist, statesman, and leader of the Nationalist movement; ceremonies are held at his statue in Helsinki.

12 Anniversary of the public presentation of the idea of Book Week made by Franklin K. Mathiews in a May 12, 1915, convention speech.

13 Feast day of Saint Robert Bellarmine; Doctor of the Church; patron saint of religious instruction. 705.

13 Birthday of Sir Ronald Ross (May 13, 1857–September 16, 1932). British pathologist noted for his malarial studies; awarded the 1902 Nobel Prize in physiology and medicine. 238.

13 Birthday of Sir Arthur Sullivan (May 13, 1842–November 22, 1900). British composer who with William Gilbert created the unique and perennially popular Gilbert and Sullivan operettas. 978, 986.

c13 Indian Day, first observed on May 13, 1916, was sponsored by the Society of American Indians to honor the American Indian and to improve his situation. Indian Day is now generally observed on the second Saturday in May, although the dates and months vary in states having large Indian populations. 170–83.

13 Jamestown Day, observed in Virginia in commemoration of the settlement of Jamestown on May 13, 1607.

13 Anniversary of the establishment of the first Episcopal church in the United States at Jamestown on May 13, 1607.

14 Anniversary of the baptism of Thomas Gainsborough (May 14, 1727–August 2, 1788). English portrait and landscape painter known for such paintings as *The Blue Boy*. 986.

14 Birthday of Robert Owen (May 14, 1771–November 17, 1858). Welsh manufacturer and educator, founder of British socialism, and founder of the utopian colony at New Harmony, Indiana.

c14 Israeli National Day, a holiday honoring the proclamation of the independence of Israel adopted on May 14, 1948; observed on or near the day of proclamation; the observance dates vary in accordance with the lunar calendar. 534.

14 Kamuzu Day, a public holiday in Malawi, formerly Nyasaland, bearing the first name of the republic's first president, Dr. Kamuzu Banda.

14 Liberian Unification and Integration Day, honors the beginning of the National Unification Party, which is dedicated to a unified Liberia.

14 Paraguay Independence Day, beginning a two-day holiday celebrating the nation's separation from Spain on May 14, 1811.

14 Philippine Islands Constitution Day, honoring the ratification of the constitution on May 14, 1935.

14 Anniversary of the orbiting of *Skylab I*, the first United States manned space station on May 14, 1973; remained in space twenty-eight days.

15 Feast day of Saint Dympna, patron saint of the insane, particularly observed in Geel in Belgium, where the townspeople take care of the mentally or emotionally disturbed through a "boarding out" system. Pilgrimages are made to Saint Dympna's tomb in Geel. 5, 705.

15 Feast of Saint Isidore the Husbandman (or Farmer), patron saint of Madrid and of farmers, celebrated annually in Spain with religious services in chapels in the fields followed by local fairs; it is an integral part of the "Week of Bull Fights." The feast is also celebrated in all Mexican towns that have San Isidro as a patron saint. 5, 705.

15 Feast day of Saint John Baptist de la Salle, patron saint of all teachers.

15 Birthday of Lyman Frank Baum (May 15, 1856–May 6, 1919). American writer and playwright remembered chiefly for a series of books about the imaginary land of Oz; observed by the International Wizard of Oz Clubs.

15 Anniversary of the signing of the Austrian State Treaty on May 15, 1955, a holiday in Austria.

15 Peace Officers Memorial Day, observed in the United States by presidential proclamation since 1963.

16 Birthday of Edmund Kirby-Smith (May 16, 1824–March 28, 1893). American soldier and educator. West Point graduate who served with the Confederate Army in the Civil War. He represents the state of Florida in Statuary Hall in a sculpture by C. Adrian Pillars. 242.

16 Birthday of Elizabeth Palmer Peabody (May 16, 1804–January 3, 1894). American educator and author; one of the famous Peabody sisters; a pioneer in championing the study of history in public schools and the founder of the first kindergarten in the United States in 1860.

16 Birthday of William Henry Seward (May 16, 1801–October 10, 1872). American statesman; secretary of state under Abraham Lincoln; negotiator of the purchase of Alaska from Russia.

17 Norwegian Independence Day, marks the adoption of the constitution in 1814; a popular holiday in Norway. A highlight of the day is a spectacular parade in which all schoolchildren participate, each wearing national costume and waving a Norwegian flag. Syttende Mai is also observed by Norwegian-American communities in Minnesota, Montana, North Dakota, and other American states.

c17 National Defense Transportation Day, observed in the United States by presidential proclamation on the third Friday in May.

c17 Anniversary of the first Kentucky Derby Day held on May 17, 1875; now scheduled annually on varying days in May.

17 Anniversary of the banning by the United States Supreme Court of racial segregation in the public schools on May 17, 1954.

18 Feast day of Saint Eric of Sweden; martyr and lawgiver; patron saint of Sweden. 705.

c18 Armed Forces Day, the third Saturday in May, combines Army Day, once celebrated in April, Air Forces Day, formerly observed in September, and Navy Day, originally observed on Theodore Roosevelt's birthday; authorized for observance by a presidential proclamation of May 7, 1965, covering all succeeding years. 194–205.

18 Battle of Las Piedras, the anniversary of the end of the 1828 conflict between Uruguayan patriots and Brazil; a public holiday in Uruguay.

18 Haitian Flag Day, a public holiday in Haiti.

18 Anniversary of the incorporation of the Antiquarian Booksellers Association of America on May 18, 1949.

c18 Feis Ceoil, an Irish music festival, was first held in Dublin on May 18, 1897; now held regularly during the week of the second Monday in May to promote Irish music.

19 Feast day of Saint Dunstan, patron saint of goldsmiths. 705.

19 Feast day of Saint Peter Celestine, patron saint of book-industry workers. 705.

19 Pardon of Saint Ives, a French religious pilgrimage notable for pious devotion and displays of regional costumes and music; dedicated to Saint Ives, patron saint of lawyers; attracts lawyers from many nations.

19 Birthday of Carl Ethan Akeley (May 19, 1864–November 17, 1926). American naturalist who developed the museum technique of mounting animals in habitat groups.

19 Birthday of Ho Chi Minh (May 19, 1890–September 3, 1969). President of the Democratic Republic of Vietnam (North Vietnam) from 1945 to 1969; one of the most powerful Communist leaders of the twentieth century. 15.

19 Birthday of Johns Hopkins (May 19, 1795–December 24, 1873). American merchant and philanthropist; founder of Johns Hopkins University, incorporated on August 24, 1867.

19 Flag Day of the Army, observed as a patriotic celebration in Finland honoring those who died to preserve their country's freedom. It is comparable to Memorial Day in the United States, with memorial services and the placing of wreaths on the graves of the war dead.

19 Youth and Sports Day, a public holiday in Turkey, commemorating the day Mustafa Kemal Atatürk landed in Samsun and began the national movement for independence.

19 Anniversary of the organization of the Federated Boys' Clubs on May 19, 1906, now known as the Boys' Clubs of America, Inc.

19 Anniversary of the founding of the National Society of Colonial Dames of America on May 19, 1892.

20 Feast day of Saint Bernardino of Siena, patron saint of publicity agents. 705.

20 Birthday of Honoré de Balzac (May 20, 1799–August 18, 1850). French novelist famous for the series *La Comédie Humaine*, which presents a panorama of French society covering the first half of the twentieth century. 986.

20 Birthday of Rose Hawthorne Lathrop (May 20, 1851–July 9, 1926). American nun; daughter of Nathaniel Hawthorne, who dedicated her life to the care of people incurably ill with cancer.

20 Birthday of John Stuart Mill (May 20, 1806–May 8, 1873). English economist, logician, and philosophical writer noted for his *Essay on Liberty*. 986.

20 Birthday of Sara Louisa Oberholtzer (May 20, 1841–February 2, 1930). American author and social reformer; organized the Anti-Tobacco Society and was a leader in establishing the school-savings movement in the United States.

20 Birthday of Frédéric Passy (May 20, 1822–June 12, 1912). French economist and pacifist; founder of the International and Permanent League of Peace. Shared the first Nobel Peace Prize with Jean Henri Dunant in 1901. 241.

20 Birthday of Sigrid Undset (May 20, 1882–June 10, 1949). Norwegian novelist famous for *Kristin Lavransdatter*. She was awarded the 1928 Nobel Prize in literature. 227.

20 Botev Day, anniversary of the May 20, 1876, death of Khristo Botev, Bulgarian poet and hero in the revolutionary movement against the Turks; observed in Bulgaria with poetry festivals and concerts.

20 Cameroon Constitution Day, a public holiday in Cameroon, on the west coast of Africa, commemorating the ratification of the constitution on May 20, 1972.

20 Cuban Independence Day, commemorates the transfer of government from Spain to Cuba on May 20, 1902.

20 Independence Day in Saudi Arabia, a holiday commemorating a May 20, 1927, treaty with Great Britain acknowledging the independence of the kingdom.

20 Lafayette Day, commemorating the May 20, 1834, death of the Marquis de Lafayette, French general who aided the armies of the American Revolution; observed in Massachusetts.

20 Mecklenburg Day, the anniversary of the signing of the Mecklenburg Declaration of Independence on May 20, 1775, by citizens of Mecklenburg County, North Carolina; a holiday in North Carolina.

20 Eliza Doolittle Day, established in honor of the heroine of Bernard Shaw's *Pygmalion* to encourage the proper use of language.

21 Birthday of Glenn Hammond Curtiss (May 21, 1878–July 23, 1930). American aviator and aeronautical inventor who set many pioneer flying records, established the first flying school, and invented the flying boat and the first heavier-than-air craft intended for transatlantic flight.

21 Birthday of Albrecht Dürer (May 21, 1471–April 6, 1528). German painter and printmaker; the major artist of German Renaissance altarpieces, religious works, and engravings. 986.

21 Birthday of Elizabeth Gurney Fry (May 21, 1780–October 12, 1845). English prison reformer who founded an association to improve conditions for women prisoners at Newgate.

21 Birthday of Alexander Pope (May 21, 1688–May 30, 1744). English poet and essayist known for his *Essay of Man*; outstanding satirist of the English Augustan period. 986.

21 Chilean Navy Day, a public holiday in Chile commemorating the Battle of Iquique in 1879.

21 Anniversary of the organization of the American Red Cross, on May 21, 1881, by Clara Barton, who became its first president.

21 The Anastenarides Feast, celebrated at Macedonia in Greece in accordance with classic and Byzantine traditions, including the old barefoot dance on beds of coals.

21 Lindbergh Flight Day, commemorating the landing of Charles A. Lindbergh in Paris on May 21, 1927, which concluded the first successful nonstop transatlantic flight.

22 Feast day of Saint Rita of Cascia, called La Abogada de Impossibles, the saint of desperate cases, in Spanish-speaking countries.

22 Birthday of Mary Cassatt (May 22, 1844–June 14, 1926). American artist noted for her pictures of mothers and children at home. 825, 837.

22 Birthday of Sir Arthur Conan Doyle (May 22, 1859–July 7, 1930). British novelist known as the creator of the fictional detective Sherlock Holmes of Baker Street; observed by the Baker Street Irregulars and other Sherlock Holmes societies. 986.

22 Birthday of Richard Wagner (May 22, 1813–February 13, 1883). German composer famous for *Tannhäuser, Lohengrin, Parsifal,* and *The Ring of the Nibelungs.* 986.

22 Haitian National Sovereignty Day, a public holiday in Haiti honoring the head of state and the Haitian culture.

22 National Maritime Day, proclaimed in 1933 to honor the SS *Savannah,* which made the first transatlantic voyage under steam propulsion in 1819.

22 Sri Lanka Republic Day, a holiday in Sri Lanka, formerly Ceylon, honoring the ratification of the constitution on May 22, 1972.

22 Anniversary of the organization of the Associated Press on May 22, 1900.

c22 Jumping Frog Jubilee Day, an event featuring a frog-jumping contest inspired by a Mark Twain short story; observed around May 22 at Angel's Camp, California.

23 Feast day of Saint Ives of Chartres, patron saint of lawyers. 705.

23 Birthday of James Buchanan Eads (May 23, 1820–March 8, 1887). American engineer and inventor. One of his major achievements was the construction of the Eads Bridge at Saint Louis, Missouri. He was elected to the Hall of Fame for Great Americans in 1920. 237.

23 Birthday of Margaret Fuller (May 23, 1810–July 19, 1850). American writer and critic who is credited as being the first professional book-review editor, with columns running in the *New York Tribune* beginning in 1844. 825, 837.

23 Birthday of Carolus Linnaeus (May 23, 1707–January 10, 1778). Swedish naturalist who developed new methods of classifying plants; his *Species Plantarum* is the official bible of botanical nomenclature. His home and gardens in Uppsala are maintained as a monument and memorial.

23 Anniversary of the establishment of the German Federal Republic (West Germany) on May 23, 1949.

23 South Carolina Admission Day. South Carolina entered the Union on May 23, 1788, as the eighth state.

23 Anniversary of the first performance of Anne Nichols' *Abie's Irish Rose* on May 23, 1922, which ran for over twenty-five hundred performances.

c23 Mayoring Day in Rye, Sussex, England, a ceremonial day in late May that carries on the old custom of the hot-penny scramble in which the new mayor tosses hot pennies to children; a ritual that may go back to the time when Rye minted its own coins and they were distributed hot from the molds.

23 Anniversary of the dedication by President William Howard Taft of the New York Public Library's Central Building at Fifth Avenue at 42nd Street on May 23, 1911.

23 Jamaican Labour Day, a public holiday in Jamaica in tribute to the Jamaican worker.

24 Birthday of Lillian M. Gilbreth (May 24, 1878–January 2, 1972). Engineer and pioneer in time-motion studies. Mother of twelve children, who became a part of the American literary scene with the publication of *Cheaper by the Dozen* by Frank B. Gilbreth, Jr., and Ernestine Gilbreth Carey. 837.

24 Birthday of Jan Christian Smuts (May 24, 1870–September 11, 1950). South African soldier and statesman, originator of the concept of the British Commonwealth of Nations, leader in the establishment of the League of Nations and the United Nations. 15.

c24 La Fête des Saintes Maries (Festival of the Holy Maries) on May 24–25 attracts thousands of gypsies for a holiday at Les Saintes-Maries-de-la-Mer in France honoring their patron Sara and Saints Marie Jacobe and Marie Salome.

24 Battle of Pichincha Day, a public holiday in Ecuador celebrating a crucial defeat of the Spaniards by independence forces on May 24, 1822.

24 Bulgarian Day of Slavonic Letters, observed on May 24 in tribute to Bulgarian culture, education, and communications; also called Education Day.

c24 Victoria Day, or Empire Day, is celebrated in England to commemorate the birth of Queen Victoria on May 24, 1819; ceremonies and customs reflect life in far-flung posts of the British Commonwealth. It is a public holiday in the countries of the British Commonwealth on varying days in May. It is observed in Canada on the first Monday preceding May 25 to honor Victoria and to pay tribute to the reigning monarch's "official" birthday.

25 Birthday of Ralph Waldo Emerson (May 25, 1803–April 27, 1882). American essayist, poet, and lecturer. Elected to the Hall of Fame for Great Americans in 1900. 237, 386, 986, 987, 1001.

25 Birthday of John Raleigh Mott (May 25, 1865–January 31, 1955). American religious and social worker; general secretary of the International Committee of the Young Men's Christian Association; organizer of the World's Student Christian Federation. Received the Nobel Peace Prize in 1946 with Emily Greene Balch. 241.

25 African Freedom Day, or Liberation of Africa Day, a public holiday dedicated to freedom, labor, and national productivity in Chad, Mauritania, and Zambia; observed in some African nations in tribute to the May 25, 1963, formation of the Organization of African Unity.

25 Revolución de Mayo, the anniversary of the 1810 revolution, a public holiday in Argentina.

25 Jordan Independence Day and Arab Renaissance Day, a combined holiday in Jordan honoring a treaty of 1946 that gave Jordan autonomy and set up a monarchy.

25 Sudan National Day, a public holiday in Sudan honoring the May 1969 assumption of governmental power by the revolutionary council.

25 Yugoslavian Day of Youth, a children's and young people's holiday celebrated in Yugoslavia on Marshall Tito's birthday; a day combining exhibits of children's work with other festivities.

26 Guyana Independence Day, a public holiday in Guyana commemorating the agreement that gave independence on May 26, 1966, to the former British colony of British Guiana; the new name means "Land of Waters."

26 Anniversary of the transfer of the American Flag House, the Betsy Ross home, to the city of Philadelphia on May 26, 1941; a gift from the Betsy Ross Memorial Association.

27 Feast day of Saint Bede ("the Venerable"), author of the *Ecclesiastical History of the English Nation*. 125.

27 Birthday of Arnold Bennett (May 27, 1867–March 27, 1931). English novelist best known for *The Old Wives' Tale* and his "Five Towns" novels, set in the towns which make up the county borough of Stoke-on-Trent, England. 986.

27 Birthday of Amelia Jenks Bloomer (May 27, 1818–December 30, 1894). American social reformer who fought for temperance and women's rights but is remembered chiefly for her advocacy of "sensible" dress, which she demonstrated by the wearing of full trousers that came to be known as "bloomers." 825.

27 Birthday of Rachel Louise Carson (May 27, 1907–April 14, 1964). American biologist whose book *Silent Spring* published in 1962 aroused worldwide concern for the dangers of environmental pollution. 415.

27 Birthday of Isadora Duncan (May 27, 1878–September 14, 1927). American dancer who developed interpretive dancing through adaptations of the classical dances of Greece.

27 Birthday of Julia Ward Howe (May 27, 1819–October 17, 1910). American author, social reformer, author of *The Battle Hymn of the Republic*, and first woman member of the American Academy of Arts and Letters.

27 Afghanistan Independence Day, a holiday honoring May 27, 1921, when Afghanistan achieved sovereignty after eighty-four years of dependence upon British influence.

27 Children's Day in Nigeria, honoring boys and girls of the more than one hundred distinct tribal communities that are a part of the Federation of Nigeria.

c27 Confederate Memorial Day, observed in Virginia on the last Monday of May; observed in other southern states on varying dates during April and May.

27 Nicaraguan Army Day, a national holiday in Nicaragua.

27 Turkish Freedom and Constitution Day, a public holiday in Turkey honoring the movement toward national unity in 1960 and the constitution adopted in 1961.

c27 American Merchant Marine Book Week, held around May 27 to "replenish the book supply to provide seagoing library units for the American Merchant Marine."

28 Feast day of Saint Augustine of Canterbury, apostle to the English. 125, 705.

28 Feast day of Saint Bernard of Menthon, patron saint of all mountain climbers and skiers. 705.

28 Birthday of Louis Agassiz (May 28, 1807–December 14, 1873). Swiss-born American teacher, naturalist, biologist, geologist, and ichthyologist. His bibliography consists of more than 425 published books and papers. Established the Museum of Comparative Zoology at Harvard, the model of all American natural-history museums, and founded the Anderson School of Natural History on Penikese Island, Buzzards Bay, Massachusetts, the forerunner of all marine and lacustral stations. Elected to the Hall of Fame for Great Americans in 1915. 237.

28 Puerto Rican Memorial Day, a public holiday in Puerto Rico.

29 Birthday of Gilbert Keith Chesterton (May 29, 1874–June 14, 1936). English journalist, novelist, poet, and critic; creator of the fictional priest-detective, Father Brown. 986, 987.

29 Birthday of Patrick Henry (May 29, 1736–June 6, 1799). American Revolutionary statesman who said, "Give me Liberty or give me Death." He was elected to the Hall of Fame for Great Americans in 1920. 237, 739.

29 Birthday of John Fitzgerald Kennedy (May 29, 1917–November 22, 1963). Irish ancestry; World War II hero; Roman Catholic; Massachusetts senator; thirty-fifth president of the United States, 1961–63; author of *Profiles in Courage* and *A Nation of Immigrants*; assassinated in Dallas, Texas; buried in Arlington National Cemetery. 667–76, 678–80, 996.

29 Rhode Island Admission Day. Rhode Island entered the Union on May 29, 1790, as the thirteenth state, the last of the thirteen original colonies to ratify the United States Constitution.

29 Wisconsin Day, the anniversary of statehood is a statewide observance of the anniversary of Wisconsin's becoming the thirtieth state of the Union on May 29, 1848.

29 Oak Apple Day, or Royal Oak Day, or Nettle Day, observed in parts of England in honor of the May 29, 1660, restoration of King Charles II, saved from his pursuers in the Battle of Worcester by an oak apple tree.

29 Royal Hospital Founders Day, observed annually since 1692 by the Chelsea Pensioners at the Royal Hospital, Chelsea, London in honor of the birthday of Charles II, the founder of the hospital.

29 Anniversary of the adoption on May 29, 1916, of the official flag of the president of the United States.

30 Feast day of Saint Ferdinand III, patron saint of engineers.

30 Feast day of Saint Joan of Arc, patron saint of France, observed throughout the world as the major festival of the day, except in New Orleans, which has a special Saint Joan's Day on May 9.

30 Birthday of Countee Cullen (May 30, 1903–January 9, 1946). American poet; a leader of the Harlem Renaissance; author of *The Black Christ and Other Poems* and *The Ballad of the Brown Girl*. 9.

30 Birthday of Alice Sophia Stopford Green (May 30, 1847–May 28, 1929). Irish historian, champion of Irish independence who served in the first Irish senate from 1922 to her death; author of *The Making of Ireland and Its Undoing*.

30 Birthday of Pierre Marie Felix Janet (May 30, 1859–February 24, 1947). French psychologist and neurologist who is noted for research in mental pathology and for investigations of hysteria.

c30 Memorial Day, or Decoration Day, was first observed on May 30, 1868, when two women of Columbus, Mississippi, placed flowers on the graves of both Union and Confederate soldiers. It is now a legal holiday in every state; observed by forty-eight states on the last Monday of May. 598–602.

30 Anniversary of the dedication of the Hall of Fame for Great Americans on the campus of New York University on May 30, 1901.

30 Anniversary of the dedication on May 30, 1922, of the Lincoln Memorial, designed by Henry Bacon and housing the seated Lincoln statue done by Daniel Chester French, in Washington, D.C.

31 Feast day of Saint Angela Merici, founder of the Ursuline Order. 705.

31 Anniversary of the death of Tintoretto on May 31, 1594. Italian painter of the late Renaissance famous for *The Last Supper*. 986.

31 Birthday of Walt Whitman (May 31, 1819–March 26, 1892). American poet, author of the great elegy *When Lilacs Last in the Dooryard Bloom'd* and the famous *Leaves of Grass*. Known as the "Good Gray Poet," Whitman was elected to the Hall of Fame for Great Americans in 1930. 237, 757.

31 Brunei National Day, a public holiday commemorating the Royal Brunei Malay Regiment.

31 South African Republic Day, or Union Day, celebrated in the Union of South Africa as a public statutory holiday honoring the unification of the South African colonies in 1910 and the establishment of the republic in 1961.

June

June, the sixth month in the Gregorian calendar, was named according to legend for Juno, the goddess of women and of marriage. If this is true, it is an appropriate name since June is a favored month for weddings, although modern brides no longer necessarily cling to tradition. Some authorities, however, claim that the month was named for *Juniores*, the lower branch of the Roman senate, or that it was associated with the consulate of Junius Brutus.

Many traditional events are associated with the month of June. Among the most famous are the great flower festivals of the world. June has long been commencement time, when young people are graduated from schools and colleges. It is also the month when the British celebrate the official, not the real, birthday of Queen Elizabeth in order to assure favorable weather for the public ceremonies. The most ancient of June festivals are those associated with Midsummer Eve in northern countries where bonfires have added to the merrymaking and festivities from time immemorial.

The special flower for the month of June is the rose, and the gems are the moonstone, the pearl, and the alexandrite.

The Fixed Days of June

1 Birthday of Philip Kearny (June 1, 1814–September 1, 1862). American general; leader of the New Jersey Volunteers in the Civil War. He represents New Jersey in Statuary Hall in a sculpture by Henry Kirke Brown. 242.

1 Birthday of Jacques Marquette (June 1, 1637–May 18, 1675). French Jesuit missionary and explorer of the territory of the Wisconsin, Mississippi, and Illinois rivers. He represents the state of Wisconsin in a Statuary Hall sculpture by Gaetano Trentanove. 242.

1 Birthday of John Masefield (June 1, 1878–May 12, 1967). Fifteenth British poet laureate; best known for poems of the sea such as *Salt Water Ballads*; awarded the Order of Merit in 1935.

1 Birthday of Brigham Young (June 1, 1801–August 29, 1877). American Mormon leader; president of the Mormon church; founder of Salt Lake City.

1 Children's Festival Day, a public holiday in the People's Republic of China.

1 Kentucky Statehood Day is observed in many ways, from mountain laurel festivals to patriotic programs, in commemoration of the entrance of Kentucky into the Union as the fifteenth state on June 1, 1792.

1 Labour Day, a public holiday in the Bahama Islands.

1 Madaraka Day, a public holiday in Kenya; also called Responsibility Day, or Self-Government Day, designed as a day for rejoicing in freedom.

1 Tennessee Statehood Day is a holiday commemorating the admission on June 1, 1796, of Tennessee as the sixteenth state in the Union on June 1, 1796.

1 Tunisia Constitution Day, a national public holiday in Tunisia, on the southern shore of the Mediterranean Sea; commemorates the promulgation of the constitution on June 1, 1959.

1 Elfreth's Alley Day, observed in Philadelphia with an open house on the oldest residential street in the United States.

2 Feast day of Saint Erasmus, patron saint of sailors. It is frequently called Saint Elmo's Day. 705.

2 Birthday of Thomas Hardy (June 2, 1840–January 11, 1928). English novelist and poet, author of *The Return of the Native* and other novels. 986.

2 Italian National Day, a public holiday commemorating the proclamation of the republic established by the referendum of June 2, 1946, in which a majority vote was cast for the republic as opposed to the retention of the monarchy.

2 Seaman's Day, celebrated in Iceland to honor the nation's sailors and fishermen who represent the lifeline of the country's economy.

c2 Teachers' Day, observed in Massachusetts on the first Sunday in June.

2 Youth Day, a holiday in Tunisia, honoring the young people of the nation.

2 Anniversary of the Coronation of Elizabeth II on June 2, 1953.

c3 Jefferson Davis Day. Birthday of Jefferson Davis (June 3, 1808–December 6, 1889). American soldier, legislator, and president of the Confederate States of America. His birthday is celebrated in Alabama, Florida, Georgia, Louisiana, Mississippi, and South Carolina. Alabama and Mississippi observe the day on the first Monday in June. In Arkansas, Jefferson Davis' birthday is a memorial day. Jefferson Davis represents the state of Mississippi in Statuary Hall in a sculpture done by Augustus Lukeman. 242, 404–9.

c3 Jack Jouett Day, observed in Virginia to honor the anniversary of the June 3, 1781, ride of Jack Jouett from Cuckoo Tavern to Charlottesville to warn Thomas Jefferson of the approach of the British and to allow for his escape.

3 Memorial to Broken Dolls Day, a Buddhist ceremony in Japan attended by little girls and their mothers, at which time all broken dolls are enshrined by a priest.

c4 Commonwealth Day, a public holiday in Botswana in southern Africa, formerly Bechuanaland, celebrating the government's affiliation with the British Commonwealth of Nations.

4 Flag Day of the Finnish Armed Forces, commemorating the June 4, 1867, birth of Marshall Carl Gustaf Mannerheim, Finland's great military leader.

5 Feast day of Saint Boniface, patron saint of Germany, celebrated in the Roman Catholic and the Anglican churches in honor of the missionary who is known as "the Apostle of Germany." 705.

5 Birthday of John Couch Adams (June 5, 1819–January 21, 1892). English astronomer who first observed the planet Neptune. The Adams Prize, awarded biannually at Cambridge University, commemorates his discovery.

5 Birthday of George Thorndike Angell (June 5, 1823–March 16, 1909). American lawyer; pioneer reformer in crime prevention; one of the founders of the American Humane Education Society.

5 Birthday of Ruth Fulton Benedict (June 5, 1887–September 17, 1948). American anthropologist and humanist whose book *Chrysanthemum and the Sword* aided in the determination of American policy toward the Japanese following World War II.

5 Birthday of Jabez Lamar Monroe Curry (June 5, 1825–February 12, 1903). American educator and statesman; president of the Southern Educational Board; the founder of grade schools and normal schools throughout the South. He represents the state of Alabama in Statuary Hall in a sculpture by Dante Sodini. 242.

5 Birthday of John Maynard Keynes (June 5, 1883–April 21, 1946). English economist, financial expert, and author of *The General Theory of Employment, Interest and Money*.

5 Anniversary of the baptism of Adam Smith (June 5, 1723–July 17, 1790). Scottish economist and philosopher celebrated for his *Inquiry into the Nature and Causes of the Wealth of Nations*.

5 Denmark Constitution Day, a holiday honoring the constitution signed on June 5, 1849, and the new constitution adopted on June 5, 1953.

5 Thanksgiving Day in Colombia, a public holiday.

c5 Dragon Boat Festival Day, a holiday in the Republic of China (Taiwan) commemorating the attempt of boatmen of 221 B.C. to rescue China's great poet, Chu Yuan, from drowning; observed in Singapore and mainland China on varying dates in early June.

c5 Irish Bank Day, a midyear holiday in Ireland, observed on the first Monday of June.

5 Anniversary of the beginning of the Six-Day War, June 5–10, 1967, between Israel and the forces of Egypt, Syria, and Jordan.

5 World Environment Day, observed by the members of the United Nations in accordance with a resolution of the June 1972 Stockholm Conference on the Human Environment supporting a day on which all people may undertake activities reaffirming the worldwide need for the preservation of the environment.

6 Birthday of Pierre Corneille (June 6, 1606–October 1, 1684). French dramatist whose masterful plays are frequently revived on the modern stage. 986.

6 Birthday of Nathan Hale (June 6, 1755–September 22, 1776). American soldier, known as the "Martyr Spy" of the American Revolution, who spoke the words "I only regret that I have but one life to lose for my country." 739.

6 Birthday of Thomas Mann (June 6, 1875–August 12, 1955). German novelist famous for *Buddenbrooks*, for four novels about the biblical Joseph, and *The Magic Mountain*; awarded the Nobel Prize in literature in 1929. 226.

6 Birthday of Aleksandr Sergeyevich Pushkin (June 6, 1799–February 10, 1837). Russian poet frequently called "the Founder of Modern Russian Literature." 986.

6 Birthday of John Trumbull (June 6, 1756–November 10, 1843). American painter known for the historical paintings in the rotunda of the Capitol in Washington and for portraits of Washington, Adams, and Jefferson. 242.

6 Anniversary of the baptism of Diego Velásquez on cJune 6, 1599. Spanish painter famous for portraits of Philip IV, and of princes, admirals, jesters, and dwarfs. 986.

6 Constitution and Flag Day in Sweden, recognizing the adoption of the Swedish constitution of June 6, 1809, and honoring June 6, 1523, when Gustavus I ascended the throne.

6 The King's Birthday, a public holiday in Malaysia, at the southern end of the Malay Peninsula.

6 Korean Memorial Day, a public holiday in the Republic of Korea (South Korea).

6 Allied Landing Observances Day at Normandy, France, honoring D Day, June 6, 1944, when the Allies invaded Europe under the command of Dwight Eisenhower. 401–3.

c6 The annual Sibelius festival is held in Helsinki, Finland, around June 6 in tribute to the nation's greatest composer.

7 Birthday of Susan Elizabeth Blow (June 7, 1843–March 26, 1916). American educator who pioneered in the establishment of public kindergartens and training schools for kindergarten teachers; called the "mother of the kindergarten in the public schools of the United States."

7 Birthday of Paul Gauguin (June 7, 1848–May 8, 1903). French painter and author who described his life in Tahiti in *Noa Noa* and in *Intimate Journals*. 986.

7 Birthday of Sir James Young Simpson (June 7, 1811–May 6, 1870). Scottish obstetrician and developer of anesthesia. 977.

7 Foundation Day, a public holiday in Western Australia commemorating the 1838 creation of the colony that became a part of the Commonwealth of Australia in 1900.

8 Anniversary of the death of Mohammed on June 8, 632. Founder of Islam who established Mecca as the sacred religious city of the Mohammedans. The Koran is the revered record of his philosophy. 82–83, 86.

8 Birthday of Frank Lloyd Wright (June 8, 1867–April 9, 1959). American architect famous for the Imperial Hotel in Japan, the Solomon R. Guggenheim Museum in New York, and other buildings. Wright established the Taliesin Fellowship for experiment in the arts. 979.

c8 Commonwealth Day, a public holiday in Swaziland, in honor of membership in the British Commonwealth of Nations.

9 Feast day of Saint Columba, Abbot of Iona, secondary patron of Ireland, who is associated with the story of how the robin got its red breast by pulling out the thorns piercing the Lord's forehead on the day of the Crucifixion. 705.

9 Birthday of John Howard Payne (June 9, 1791–April 9, 1852). American songwriter, playwright, and actor, remembered for writing _Home, Sweet Home_.

9 Birthday of George Stephenson (June 9, 1781–August 12, 1848). English inventor who perfected the locomotive.

c9 Children's Day, observed in Massachusetts on the second Sunday of June; observed on varying dates by many nations throughout the world, with activities ranging from religious services to educational activities and projects.

9 Senior Citizens Day, observed in Oklahoma, to honor older Americans and their contributions to society.

10 Birthday of John Morgan (June 10, 1735–October 15, 1789). American physician-in-chief of the Continental armies; foremost medical educator of the pre-Revolutionary period.

10 Portugal National Day, or Camões Memorial Day, a national fete day in Portugal and its territories commemorating the death on June 10, 1580, of Luiz Vaz de Camões, Portugal's immortal poet.

10 Anniversary of the establishment of Alcoholics Anonymous, founded by William G. Wilson and Dr. Robert Smith on June 10, 1935.

10 Lidice Day, anniversary of the razing of the village of Lidice in Czechoslovakia and the massacre of its people by the Nazis on June 10, 1942. 13.

c10 Rose Day at Manheim, Pennsylvania, observed on the second Sunday of June; an annual ritual fulfilling the terms of the deed for the Lutheran church from Baron William Stiegel, which requires that the church pay "Therefor unto the said Henry William Stiegel, his heirs or assigns . . . the rent of one red rose if demanded." 8.

11 Birthday of Ben Jonson (cJune 11, 1572–August 6, 1637). English playwright and poet famous for _Volpone_, or _The Fox_, and other important plays of the Elizabethan period. 986.

11 Birthday of Jeannette Rankin (June 11, 1880–May 18, 1973). American pacifist, crusader for social and election reform, first woman member of the Congress of the United States. 822.

11 Kamehameha Day is an important and gay holiday in Hawaii commemorating the victories of Kamehameha I, who unified the islands in the eighteenth century. 997.

11 The King's Birthday, a national holiday in Nepal, a kingdom on the southern slopes of the Himalayas.

12 Birthday of Anne Frank (June 12, 1929–March [?], 1945). German-Dutch adolescent of sensitivity and talent whose diary of two years of hiding from the Germans was published under the title *The Diary of a Young Girl*; the exact day of her death is unknown. 998.

12 Birthday of Charles Kingsley (June 12, 1819–January 23, 1875). English clergyman, novelist, and poet remembered for the novels *Westward Ho!* and *Hereward the Wake*. 986.

12 Peace of Chaco Day, a public holiday in Paraguay celebrating the end of the Chaco War between Bolivia and Paraguay in 1935.

12 Helsinki Day, celebrated in Finland since 1959 to commemorate the founding of the city of Helsinki in 1550.

12 Philippine Independence Day, a public holiday since 1962, commemorating June 12, 1898, when independence from Spain was declared.

13 Feast day of Saint Anthony of Padua, patron saint of the illiterate; special advocate of the poor and the downtrodden. His feast day is of particular importance in the city of Lisbon, where the saint was born, and is celebrated as a public holiday. 705.

13 Birthday of Fanny Burney (June 13, 1752–January 6, 1840). English novelist whose *Diary* and *Letters* are an excellent source of background material on manners, customs, and personalities of the mid-nineteenth century. 986.

13 Birthday of Paavo Johannes Nurmi (June 13, 1897–October 2, 1973). Finnish Olympic track star whose 1925 record for the two-mile race was not broken until 1941.

13 Birthday of William Butler Yeats (June 13, 1865–January 29, 1939). Irish poet, dramatist and leader of the Irish literary revival; received the Nobel Prize in literature in 1923. 231.

14 Birthday of Robert Marion La Follette (June 14, 1855–June 18, 1925). American statesman, reform leader, presidential candidate for the Progressive party; exponent of the "Wisconsin idea." He represents the state of Wisconsin in Statuary Hall in a sculpture done by Jo Davidson. 242, 976.

14 Birthday of Karl Landsteiner (June 14, 1868–June 26, 1943). Austro-American pathologist whose blood-group discoveries won him the 1930 Nobel Prize in medicine. 238.

14 Birthday of Harriet Elizabeth Beecher Stowe (June 14, 1811–July 1, 1896). American novelist and humanitarian; author of *Uncle Tom's Cabin*. Elected to the Hall of Fame for Great Americans in 1910. 237, 825, 837.

14 Flag Day is observed in the United States to commemorate the adoption of the Stars and Stripes by the Continental Congress on June 14, 1777. Flag Day has been a legal holiday in Pennsylvania since 1937; observed by all other states through the display of the flag on public buildings and homes or special programs. 453–59, 461–63.

14 Independence Day in the Republic of Vietnam (South Vietnam) honoring June 14, 1949, when the French granted the nation its freedom.

14 Mother's Day in Afghanistan, a public holiday.

14 Anniversary of the first presentation of the Caldecott Medal; awarded annually to the artist of the most distinguished American picture book for children published in the United States during the preceding year; first presented on June 14, 1938, to Dorothy P. Lathrop for *Animals of the Bible*. 235.

14 Anniversary of the establishment of the Canadian Library Association (Association Canadienne des Bibliothèques) on June 14, 1946.

14 Anniversary of the day, June 14, 1954, when the pledge of allegiance to the flag of the United States was amended by Congress and approved by President Eisenhower to add the words "under God," so that the last line of the pledge now reads "One Nation under God indivisible, with liberty and justice for all."

15 Feast day of Saint Vitus, patron saint of dancers, actors, comedians, and epilepsy sufferers. 125, 705.

15 Birthday of Edvard Grieg (June 15, 1843–September 4, 1907). Norwegian composer who established a new musical image for his country; famous for the *Peer Gynt* suites and arrangements of songs and Norwegian dances; commemorated annually by the Grieg music festivals in Norway. 986.

15 Arkansas Admission Day. Arkansas was admitted to the Union as the twenty-fifth state on June 15, 1836. 741.

15 Farmer's Day, observed in Korea, an official day for the transplanting of rice seedlings.

15 Idaho Pioneer Day has been a legal holiday since 1910 and commemorates with picnics, pioneer reunions, and other festivities the founding of the first permanent white settlement at Franklin on June 15, 1860.

c15 Queen Elizabeth of England's official or public birthday; the second Thursday of June is the traditional date for the celebration of the birthday of England's sovereign to assure favorable weather for the ceremonies held at the parade ground behind Saint James Park. The ceremony includes the trooping of the color, the most brilliant and imposing of all British military parades. The birthday is now set by annual proclamation.

15 Valdemar's Day, commemorating the victory of King Valdemar's troops on June 15, 1219, observed throughout Denmark. It is also the Danish Flag Day, honoring the oldest flag in the world, one which, according to legend, came down from heaven to bring victory to King Valdemar.

15 Magna Charta Day, anniversary of the day, June 15, 1215, when King John signed the Magna Charta, the first important document in the history of human freedom. 254, 256.

15 Oregon Treaty Day, anniversary of the signing of the Oregon Treaty on June 15, 1846, by the United States and Great Britain, to fix the northwest boundary at the 49th parallel extending to the Pacific.

16 Feast day of the Madonna of Carmine, a Neapolitan saint said to heal ailments in various parts of the body; observed in Italy and by Italian-Americans.

17 Birthday of Charles Gounod (June 17, 1818–October 18, 1893). French composer whose Marguerite in the opera *Faust* was the first operatic role for a lyric soprano. 986.

17 Birthday of John Robert Gregg (June 17, 1867–February 23, 1948). Irish-American inventor of the Gregg shorthand system. A John Robert Gregg Award in Business Education is presented annually for the best contribution to business education in the preceding year. 234.

17 Birthday of James Weldon Johnson (June 17, 1871–June 26, 1938). American poet and anthologist; first Negro to be admitted to the Florida bar; founder and secretary of the National Association for the Advancement of Colored People; awarded the Spingarn Medal in 1925. 1, 589.

17 Birthday of John Wesley (June 17, 1703–March 2, 1791). English evangelical preacher; founder of Methodism; influential leader in the eighteenth-century revival movement in North America. 986.

17 Bunker Hill Day, celebrated in Boston and Suffolk County, Massachusetts, in honor of the Battle of Bunker Hill, June 17, 1775.

17 Day of German Unity, or Remembrance Day, observed in the Federal Republic of Germany and in West Berlin; recalls the public emotion that led to a riot of workers in the Russian section of Berlin on June 17, 1953, and spread throughout Germany; a day of prayer for national unity.

17 National Day in Iceland, a holiday commemorating the reestablishment of an independent republic in 1944, and honoring the birth on June 17, 1811, of Jon Sigurdsson, the nation's outstanding nineteenth-century leader.

17 Anniversary of the establishment of the Union of Kalmar, created by Queen Margaret of Denmark on June 17, 1397, for the purpose of unifying Denmark, Norway, and Sweden in the interest of lasting and unbroken peace.

17 Watergate Day, anniversary of the June 17, 1972, break-in at the Democratic National Headquarters in Washington; occasioned the congressional investigations of 1972–74.

18 Birthday of Henry Clay Folger (June 18, 1857–June 11, 1930). American industrialist; collector of Shakespeareana, now bequeathed to the American people in the Folger Shakespeare Library in Washington, D.C.

18 Evacuation Day, a holiday in the United Arab Republic (Egypt) celebrating the 1956 departure of the last of foreign troops.

18 Waterloo Day, anniversary of the Battle of Waterloo, lost by Napoleon in 1815.

18 Anniversary of the adoption of the Library Bill of Rights by the Council of the American Library Association, June 18, 1948.

19 Birthday of Sir John Barrow (June 19, 1764–November 23, 1848). English geographer; chief founder of the Royal Geographical Society in 1830.

19 Birthday of Blaise Pascal (June 19, 1623–August 19, 1662). French philosopher, mathematician, and scientist whose work on the pressure of liquids resulted in Pascal's law. 977, 986.

19 Algeria National Day, a public holiday in Algeria commemorating the deposition of Mohammed Ben Bella in a bloodless coup d'état on June 19, 1965.

19 Artigas Day, the anniversary of the June 19, 1764, birth of General José Gervasio Artigas, father of Uruguayan independence; a public holiday in Uruguay.

19 Independence Day in the state of Kuwait, honoring the establishment of sovereignty on June 19, 1961, the termination of an 1899 treaty with Britain.

c19 Father's Day. The first Father's Day was held on June 19, 1910. The idea originated with Mrs. John Bruce Dodd and was promoted by the Ministerial Association and the YMCA of Spokane, Washington. Father's Day was officially approved by President Calvin Coolidge in 1924. The rose is the official Father's Day flower—a white rose for remembrance, a red rose for the living. Father's Day is now observed on the third Sunday in June.

19 Juneteenth, or Emancipation Day, observed in parts of Texas in honor of the June 19, 1865, proclamation declaring emancipation for Texan slaves.

20 Birthday of Helen Miller Shepard (June 20, 1868–December 21, 1938). American philanthropist whose many gifts included the establishment of a Hall of Fame for Great Americans at New York University in 1900.

20 Argentina Flag Day, a national holiday.

20 Senegal Independence Day, honors the sovereignty achieved by the former French colony on June 20, 1960.

20 West Virginia Admission Day. West Virginia entered the Union on June 20, 1863, as the thirty-fifth state; a legal holiday. 741.

20 Anniversary of the establishment of the Lifesaving Medal of the United States, awarded by the Treasury Department, authorized by an act of Congress on June 20, 1874. The first award was presented to Lucian M. Clemons, keeper of the United States Lifesaving Service Station, on June 19, 1876, for saving the men of the schooner *Consuelo* on May 1, 1875.

c20 Anniversary of the first of the famous Portland rose festivals on June 20, 1907, in Portland, Oregon, with exhibitions of roses and a "human rosebud" parade. It has been held ever since during the rose season in June.

21 Feast day of Saint Aloysius Gonzoga, patron saint of youth.

21 Birthday of Daniel Carter Beard (June 21, 1850–June 11, 1941). American naturalist, writer, and illustrator who organized the first Boy Scout troop in the United States.

21 Birthday of Rockwell Kent (June 21, 1882–March 13, 1971). American painter and illustrator of the American scene; one of the most popular artists of the first half of the twentieth century.

21 New Hampshire Admission Day. New Hampshire entered the Union on June 21, 1788, the ninth of the thirteen original United States. 741.

c21 Summer solstice, first day of summer.

22 Feast day of Saint Alban, early Christian martyr of Britain, celebrated with an annual rose festival at Saint Alban's Cathedral, Hertfordshire, England.

22 Feast day of Saint Paulinus, celebrated with the Lilies of Nola spectacle in Nola, Italy. 125.

22 Birthday of Frank Heino Damrosch (June 22, 1859–October 22, 1937). American musician, author, and teacher whose career stimulated popular appreciation of music.

22 Haitian President's Day, a public holiday in Haiti; sometimes called Oath of the President's Day.

c22 Organic Act Day, a holiday in the Virgin Islands in honor of the Organic Act or constitution which was granted the islands by the United States on June 22, 1936; celebrated on or near June 22.

22 Schoolteachers Day in El Salvador, a public holiday.

22 Anniversary of the creation of the United States Department of Justice by an Act of Congress on June 22, 1870.

23 Feast day of Saint Joseph Cafasso, patron saint of prisons. 705.

23 Birthday of Irvin Shrewsbury Cobb (June 23, 1876–March 10, 1944). American author, actor, and humorist; the first winner of the O. Henry Award for the best short story of the year in 1922.

23 Birthday of Carl Milles (June 23, 1875–September 19, 1955). Swedish-American sculptor whose monumental sculpture is to be found in Europe and the United States. The *Meeting of the Waters* at St. Louis is a good example of his work.

23 Luxembourg National Day, a public holiday with major celebrations in Luxembourg City celebrating the grand duke's birthday.

23 Anniversary of the first regatta held on the Thames in England on June 23, 1775, patterned after the water fetes of Venice.

23 Midsummer Eve, or Saint John's Eve, the opening of major holiday festivities in Finland, Latvia, and the Scandinavian countries to celebrate the beginning of summer.

24 The Nativity of Saint John, the Baptist, is celebrated on June 24 in the Roman Catholic, Anglican, and Lutheran churches and commemorates the actual birth date of Saint John. The feast day of Saint John, the Baptist, patron saint of missionaries and tailors, prophet and forerunner of Christ is observed with special events in Mexico, Montreal, Quebec City, and San Juan. 80.

24 Birthday of Henry Ward Beecher (June 24, 1813–March 8, 1887). American Congregational clergyman, reformer, lecturer, and author. Elected to Hall of Fame for Great Americans in 1900. 237.

24 Birthday of Horatio Herbert Kitchener (June 24, 1850–June 5, 1916). British military leader who avenged the death of General Gordon and became a national hero in 1898; one of the twelve original members of the Order of Merit.

24 Bannockburn Day in Scotland, commemorates June 24, 1314, when Robert Bruce won independence for Scotland by expelling the English.

24 Battle of Carabobo Day, a public holiday in Venezuela commemorating Bolivar's victory at Carabobo on June 24, 1823. It is also Venezuelan Army Day.

24 Day of the Indian, or Dia del Indio, celebrated in Peru and other Latin American countries to preserve and enjoy native customs, musical contests, folklore, and poetry, horsemanship exhibits, sports, and general feasting.

c24 Discovery Day, celebrated in Newfoundland on the Monday nearest June 24 to commemorate the discovery by John Cabot of the coastal area of North America in June 1497.

c24 Midsummer Day, a holiday on varying June days in Iceland, Latvia, Sweden, and other northern regions celebrating the beginning of the summer season. Svenskarnas Dag is observed in Minnesota and other sections of the United States on the Sunday nearest Midsummer Day.

24 San Juan Day, a holiday in Puerto Rico commemorating, in addition to the religious observances of Saint John's Day, the Battle of San Juan, which ended in victory for the Americans over the Spanish. The island was ceded to the United States at the end of the Spanish-American War.

25 Birthday of Prince Bernhard of the Netherlands, celebrated in Curaçao.

25 Spring Bank Holiday, a holiday in Gibraltar; a traditional day of relaxation for the public.

25 Virginia Ratification Day. Virginia entered the Union on June 25, 1788, the tenth of the thirteen original United States to do so. 741.

25 Custer Day, anniversary of "Custer's Last Stand" at the Battle of Little Big Horn, Montana, on June 25, 1876.

26 Birthday of Bernard Berenson (June 26, 1865–October 6, 1959). American art critic whose *Italian Painters of the Renaissance* was the most influential book in its field in the twentieth century.

26 Birthday of Pearl Buck (June 26, 1892–March 6, 1973). American author noted for *The Good Earth* and other novels of life in China; recipient of the Nobel Prize in literature in 1938. 226, 227, 616.

26 Independence Day, observed in the Malagasy Republic occupying Madagascar, the fourth largest island in the world; the day commemorates the transfer of power from France to Malagasy on June 26, 1960.

26 Somalia Independence Day, a public holiday in the African east coast republic, commemorating the June 26, 1960, agreement on Somali self-government.

26 Anniversary of the dedication of the Mackinac Straits Bridge connecting Lower and Upper Michigan on June 26, 1958.

26 Anniversary of the creation of the Order of Merit, a British order designed as a special distinction for eminent men and women, on June 26, 1902. Florence Nightingale is the only woman to have received this honor.

26 Anniversary of the official dedication of the Saint Lawrence Seaway on June 26, 1959, at Saint Lambert Lock near Montreal, Canada, with Queen Elizabeth II of Great Britain and President Dwight Eisenhower of the United States officiating.

26 United Nations Charter Day, commemorates the signing of the charter in five official languages, Chinese, English, French, Russian, and Spanish, on June 26, 1945. 784.

27 Birthday of Lafcadio Hearn (June 27, 1850–September 26, 1904). American author famous for his interpretation of the history of Japanese life. 986.

27 Birthday of Helen Adams Keller (June 27, 1880–June 1, 1968). The most accomplished blind woman of the twentieth century; author of *The Story of My Life*, *Helen Keller's Journal*, and other books and articles; her birthday is honored annually by many associations for the blind. 825, 837, 992.

27 Birthday of Charles Stewart Parnell (June 27, 1846–October 6, 1891). Irish political leader active in the Home Rule party, which opposed British control.

27 Anniversary of the death of Joseph Smith, founder and leader of Mormonism, at the hands of a mob at Carthage, Illinois, on June 27, 1844.

27 Anniversary of the death of James Smithson, June 27, 1829. English scientist whose will established the Smithsonian Institution in Washington, D.C.

27 Anniversary of the first presentation on June 27, 1922, of the Newbery Medal, awarded annually to the author of the most distinguished contribution to American literature for children published during the preceding year; the first recipient was Hendrik van Loon for *The Story of Mankind*. 232, 236.

28 Birthday of Luigi Pirandello (June 28, 1867–December 10, 1936). Italian dramatist and novelist whose plays have been translated into thirty-three languages; awarded the Nobel Prize in literature in 1934. 986.

28 Birthday of Jean-Jacques Rousseau (June 28, 1712–July 2, 1778). French philosopher and author of great influence; author of the celebrated *Confessions* and other works. 986.

28 Birthday of Peter Paul Rubens (June 28, 1577–May 30, 1640). Flemish painter famous for historical and religious scenes and portraits of kings, clergymen, and scholars. 986.

28 Mnarja Folk Festival Day, celebrated in Malta with the re-creating of customs dating from the Middle Ages.

28 Anniversary of the signing on June 28, 1919, of the Treaty of Versailles ending World War I.

29 The Feast of Saint Peter and Saint Paul, apostles, June 29, celebrated in the Roman Catholic, Anglican, and Lutheran churches. It is one of the oldest saints' days and commemorates two apostles who have been associated in Christian thought since the early centuries. 73.

29 Birthday of William E. Borah (June 29, 1865–January 19, 1940). American statesman and lawyer, opponent of America's affiliation with the League of Nations. He represents the state of Idaho in Statuary Hall in a sculpture done by Bryant Baker. 242.

29 Birthday of William James Mayo (June 29, 1861–July 28, 1939). American surgeon, specialist in cancer and gallstones, a member of the medical family who developed the world-famous Mayo Clinic.

29 Birthday of James Harvey Robinson (June 29, 1863–February 16, 1936). American historian and educator who believed that history and its teaching should include accounts of scientific, artistic, and intellectual progress as well as political developments; author of *The Mind in the Making*.

c30 Independence Sunday, observed in Iowa on the Sunday preceding July 4 as a tribute to the Declaration of Independence and its meaning for all Americans.

30 Revolution Day, a holiday in Guatemala commemorating the revolution for agrarian reform of 1871.

c30 Troop Withdrawal Day, a holiday in the Libyan Arab Republic honoring the departure of foreign troops from Libya.

30 Zaire Independence Day, commemorating the establishment of the nation, formerly the Democratic Republic of the Congo, on June 30, 1960.

30 Anniversary of the establishment of the United States Fish and Wild Life Service on June 30, 1940.

30 Anniversary of the passage of the Pure Food and Drug Act on June 30, 1906.

July

The month of July, the seventh month in the Gregorian calendar, was named for Julius Caesar, the Roman who reformed the calendar in 44 B.C.

July is an important month in the United States because of July 4, the birthday of the nation. It was on July 4, 1776, that the Continental Congress, meeting in Philadelphia, adopted the Declaration of Independence. July 4 is now a legal holiday for all Americans. The United States Independence Day is also observed with ceremonies in England, Norway, Sweden, Denmark, Guatemala, the Philippines, Canal Zone, and Guam, and at all American embassies in foreign lands.

July is one of the most important months for bullfights and the continuance of old customs. An example is the Fiesta de San Fermen at Pamplona in Spain, which is dangerously exciting because the bulls are still allowed to run wild on the streets just before the bullfights, as they did in olden times.

Japan also observes an ancient July festival associated with four-footed animals. This is a Japanese horse festival that has been held for over six hundred years. It lasts for three days, during which a thousand horsemen clad in ancient armor and helmets joust and compete in archery and horsemanship.

The July flowers are the water lily and the larkspur, and the birthstone is the ruby.

The Fixed Days of July

1 Feast of the Most Precious Blood celebrated by the Roman Catholic Church.

1 Pilgrimage to the shrine of the Blessed Oliver Plunkett, the martyred Catholic Primate of Ireland, an annual event in Drogheda, County Louth, Ireland.

1 Birthday of James Sloan Gibbons (July 1, 1810–October 17, 1892). American banker; abolitionist; remembered for the refrain of the patriotic song *We Are Coming, Father Abra'am, Three Hundred Thousand More.*

1 Birthday of Walter White (July 1, 1893–March 21, 1955). American author; longtime secretary of the National Association for the Advancement of Colored People; awarded the Spingarn Medal in 1937 for his fight against lynching. 1.

1 Bank Employees' Day, a public holiday in Guatemala.

1 Burundi Independence Day, a public holiday commemorating the proclamation of sovereignty for the African nation on July 1, 1962.

1 Dominion Day, or Canada Day, a national holiday commemorating the confederation of the provinces of Canada into the Dominion of Canada under the terms of the British North America Act of July 1, 1867.

1 Ghana Republic Day, commemorating the change from dominion status to that of a republic in the British Commonwealth on July 1, 1960.

1 Half-Year Day, a public holiday in Hong Kong providing a midyear day of relaxation for all citizens.

1 Rwanda Independence Day, a public holiday in the Central African republic, commemorating the granting of sovereignty on July 1, 1962, to the former Belgian trust territory.

1 Somalian Foundation of the Republic Day, a holiday commemorating the union on July 1, 1960, of the former British and Italian protectorates into the Somali Republic on the east coast of Africa.

1 Surinam Labour Day, a public holiday in Surinam, on the north-central coast of South America, formerly Dutch Guiana.

1 Turkish Navy and Merchant Marine Day, a holiday in Istanbul and other cities in Turkey in honor of the national fleets.

c1 Zambia Heroes' Day, a public holiday in the south-central African nation of Zambia, formerly Northern Rhodesia; observed on the first Monday in July.

1 Gettysburg Day, anniversary of the beginning of the Battle of Gettysburg on July 1, 1863, one of the most decisive conflicts of the American Civil War; observed with annual commemorative services at Gettysburg.

1 Anniversary of the establishment of the Gideons on July 1, 1899. One of the oldest interdenominational laymen's evangelistic associations in the world, familiar to all travelers for the Gideon Bibles placed in hotel rooms throughout the world.

1 Anniversary of the beginning on July 1, 1957, of a coordinated, worldwide scientific research program called the International Geophysical Year, in which sixty-seven nations joined in measurements and studies at over two thousand stations.

c1 The Strážnice folk festival, celebrated in Czechoslovakia during the first two weeks in July, with hundreds of folk singers and dancers participating.

1 American Stamp Day, anniversary of the issuance of the first United States postage stamps on July 1, 1847; observed by philatelic societies.

2 The Visitation of Blessed Virgin Mary, commemorates the Gospel account of the visit of Mary to her cousin Elizabeth, who was overjoyed at the coming of "the mother of my Lord"; celebrated by Roman Catholic, Anglican, and Lutheran churches.

2 Birthday of Thomas Cranmer (July 2, 1489–March 21, 1556). Archbishop of Canterbury and chief author of *The English Book of Common Prayer.*

2 Corso del Palio (Race for the Palio) Day, a festival horse-racing day in Siena, Italy, in honor of the armless Madonna di Provenzano.

c2 Unity Day, a public holiday in Zambia, formerly Northern Rhodesia, observed on the first Tuesday of July to honor the goals of all African people.

2 Anniversary of the authorization on July 2, 1926, of the Distinguished Flying Cross of the United States "for heroism or extraordinary achievement while participating in an aerial flight." The first recipient was Charles Augustus Lindbergh, who received the medal on June 11, 1927, for his solo Atlantic flight.

2 Anniversary of the official establishment of the national Statuary Hall in the United States Capitol on July 2, 1864, when Congress approved an act authorizing the president "to invite each and all the states to provide and furnish statues, in marble or bronze, not exceeding two in number for each state, of deceased persons who have been citizens thereof, and illustrious for their historic renown or for distinguished civic or military services." 242.

3 Birthday of Franz Kafka (July 3, 1883–June 3, 1924). Austrian novelist and essayist whose work expresses the frustrations and anxieties of modern man. 986.

3 Birthday of Alfred Korzybski (July 3, 1879–March 1, 1950). Polish-born American scientist, author, pioneer in semantics, founder of general semantics. His best-known book is *Science and Sanity.*

3 Algerian Independence Day, commemorating the passage of a self-determination referendum on July 3, 1962, ending 130 years of French rule and establishing permanent independence for the African nation.

3 Idaho Admission Day. Idaho became the forty-third state on July 3, 1890.

3 Anniversary of the assumption of command of the Continental Army by George Washington at Cambridge, Massachusetts, on July 3, 1775.

4 Anniversary of the death of Chaim Nachman Bialik on July 4, 1934. Hebrew poet famous for his elegiac poem *In the City of Slaughter* and for his support of the Zionist movement.

4 Birthday of Calvin Coolidge (July 4, 1872–January 5, 1933). English ancestry; Massachusetts lawyer; vice-president who succeeded to the office of the presidency upon the death of President Harding; thirtieth president of the United States, 1923–29. Congregationalist. Buried at Plymouth, Vermont. 667–72, 674–76, 678–79.

4 Birthday of Stephen Collins Foster (July 4, 1826–January 13, 1864). American composer and writer of songs that reflect the sentiment of pre-Civil War America. Elected to the Hall of Fame for Great Americans in 1940. Memorial and commemorative observances are held in Foster's honor on or near January 13, the anniversary of his death. 237, 986.

4 Birthday of Nathaniel Hawthorne (July 4, 1804–May 19, 1864). American novelist whose home was the "Old Manse" in Concord, Massachusetts. His most famous book is *The Scarlet Letter*. He was elected to the Hall of Fame for Great Americans in 1900. 237.

4 Alaska's F-Day, or Flag Day, is the anniversary of July 4, 1959, when the forty-ninth star was officially added to the field of blue of the United States.

4 Fighter's Day, a holiday in Yugoslavia honoring the patriots who lost their lives in defending their country.

4 Garibaldi Day in Italy, commemorates the July 4, 1807, birthday of Giuseppi Garibaldi, the most forceful figure in the unification of Italy in the nineteenth century.

4 Hawaii's F-Day, or Flag Day, is the anniversary of July 4, 1960, when the fiftieth star was officially added to the American flag as a symbol of Hawaii's statehood.

4 Independence Day, or the Fourth of July, the birthday of the United States. It celebrates the signing of the Declaration of Independence on July 4, 1776; a holiday in each of the fifty states, the District of Columbia, Canal Zone, Guam, Puerto Rico, and the Virgin Islands. It is also observed in Denmark, Norway, Sweden, and England. 476–89.

4 Philippine-American Friendship Day, a public holiday in the Philippine Islands, with floral ceremonies at the American battle monuments and other observances honoring American freedom.

4 Providence Day, anniversary of the founding of the city of Providence on July 4, 1636; observed in Rhode Island.

4 Anniversary of the authorization of the fifty-star flag as the official flag of the United States on July 4, 1960.

4 Anniversary of the establishment on July 4, 1956, of Independence National Historical Park in Philadelphia; includes seventeen sites and buildings that have historical associations with the American Revolution.

4 Tom Sawyer Fence-painting Day, a contest based on the famous episode in *Tom Sawyer* by Mark Twain; observed in Hannibal, Missouri, on the Fourth of July.

5 Birthday of Phineas Taylor Barnum (July 5, 1810–April 7, 1891). American showman; pioneer advertiser; manager of Jenny Lind's concert tour; and author.

5 Birthday of Dwight Filley Davis (July 5, 1879–November 28, 1945). American public official; donor in 1900 of the Davis Cup, the most prized team trophy in international tennis.

5 Birthday of David Glasgow Farragut (July 5, 1801–August 14, 1870). American naval officer, Civil War hero of the Battles of New Orleans and Mobile Bay. Elected to the Hall of Fame for Great Americans in 1900. 237.

5 Birthday of Wanda Landowska (July 5, 1879–August 16, 1959). Polish pianist and harpsichordist responsible for a revival of interest in early musical instruments.

5 Birthday of Cecil John Rhodes (July 5, 1853–March 26, 1902). English colonial statesman; developer of Rhodesia; founder of the coveted Rhodes Scholarships at Oxford University.

c5 Family Day, a public holiday in Lesotho, a former British High Commission Territory in Africa; celebrated on the first Monday of July.

5 Peace and Unity Day, observed in the African republic of Rwanda to honor the peaceful objectives of its citizens.

5 Venezuela Independence Day, a holiday in Venezuela honoring the declaration of independence by the Congress of Cabildos on July 5, 1811. Venezuela was the first South American country to declare its independence from Spain.

5 Anniversary of the founding of the Salvation Army in London by William Booth on July 5, 1865.

6 Birthday of Verner von Heidenstam (July 6, 1859–May 20, 1940). Swedish author and winner of the 1916 Nobel Prize in literature. 227.

6 Anniversary of the death of Jan Huss on July 6, 1415. Czech religious reformer who was burned at the stake; his death is commemorated in Czechoslovakia.

6 Birthday of John Paul Jones (July 6, 1747–July 18, 1792). American naval officer of the Revolutionary period and founder of the American navy. A national monument was erected in his honor in Potomac Park in Washington. He was elected to the Hall of Fame for Great Americans in 1925. 237.

6 Birthday of Eino Leino (July 6, 1878–January 10, 1926). Finnish poet, playwright, and novelist who expressed the aspirations of the Finnish people.

6 Malawi Republic Day, a national holiday commemorating the proclamation of July 6, 1965, changing the former British Protectorate of Nyasaland into the Republic of Malawi.

6 Anniversary of the establishment of the United States Medal of Freedom on July 6, 1945, awarded to civilians for meritorious acts or service against the enemy on or after December 7, 1941.

6 Anniversary of the presentation of the Harry S. Truman Library at Independence, Missouri, to the National Archives, July 6, 1957.

7 Feast day of Saints Cyril and Methodius, patron saints of the Danubian countries, patrons of Eastern and Western church unity. 705.

7 Anniversary of the ceremonies of canonization, on July 7, 1946, of Mother Frances Xavier Cabrini, the first citizen of the United States to be proclaimed a saint by the Roman Catholic church.

7 Anniversary of the death of Thomas Hooker on July 7, 1647. American colonial clergyman whose interpretation of the theory that the people have the right to choose their public officials gave him the name "the Father of American Democracy."

7 Birthday of Lillien Jane Martin (July 7, 1851–March 26, 1943). American psychologist; pioneer in child guidance; founder in 1929 of a clinic for the aged, thus becoming one of the first pioneers in gerontology.

7 The Fiesta de San Fermin, celebrated at Pamplona, Spain, during the week that includes July 7. It is the festival at which the bulls are allowed to run in the streets prior to the bullfights.

7 Saba Saba Day, a public holiday and festival in Tanzania, commemorating the 1954 founding of the Tanganyika African National Union.

7 The Star Festival, or Tanabata, a Japanese festival based on a legend about two stars who meet only on the seventh night of the seventh month.

7 Anniversary of the opening of King's College on July 7, 1754. The name was changed to Columbia College in 1784, and to Columbia University in 1896.

8 Birthday of John Davison Rockefeller (July 8, 1839–May 23, 1937). American industrialist and philanthropist, head of the Standard Oil Company, and benefactor of the University of Chicago, the Rockefeller Foundation, and other important institutions.

8 Anniversary of the issuance on July 8, 1796, of the first passport for foreign travel granted to a citizen of the United States.

9 Feast day of Saint Thomas More, English humanist and martyr. A medal is presented annually in his name by the Thomas More Association for the most distinguished contribution to Catholic publishing during the year. 234.

9 Birthday of Elias Howe (July 9, 1819–October 3, 1867). American inventor and manufacturer who invented the sewing machine. He was elected to the Hall of Fame for Great Americans in 1915. 237.

9 Independence Day, a holiday in Argentina commemorating the formal proclamation of independence from Spain on July 9, 1816, which was forecast by the May revolution of 1810.

9 Anniversary of the July 9, 1918, authorization of the Distinguished Service Cross of the United States Army to honor extraordinary heroism on the part of persons serving the army in any capacity.

10 Feast of the Virgin of Begoña at Bilbao, Spain, a river festival featuring the carrying of the Virgin along the coast at the head of a procession of gaily decked ships.

10 Birthday of Mary McLeod Bethune (July 10, 1875–May 18, 1955). American educator, founder of Bethune-Cookman College, and founder and president of the National Council of Negro Women. 837, 993.

10 Birthday of Sir William Blackstone (July 10, 1723–February 14, 1780). English jurist whose fame rests on his influential *Commentaries on the Laws of England*. 986.

10 Birthday of John Calvin (July 10, 1509–May 27, 1564). Protestant theologian and reformer, author of *Institutes of the Christian Religion*.

10 Birthday of Toyohiko Kagawa (July 10, 1888–April 23, 1960). Japanese social reformer and evangelist, a leader in the Japanese labor movement and in the establishment of cooperatives.

10 Birthday of Nikola Tesla (July 10, 1856–January 7, 1943). Croatian scientist; discoverer of the rotating magnetic field.

10 Albanian Army Day, a public holiday honoring the armed forces.

10 Independence Day, a public holiday in the Bahama Islands commemorating the proclamation of sovereignty on July 10, 1973.

10 Wyoming Statehood Day, commemorating its admission to the Union on July 10, 1890, as the forty-fourth state; the first state to grant the vote to women through its original constitution. 741.

11 Birthday of John Quincy Adams (July 11, 1767–February 23, 1848). English ancestry; Massachusetts lawyer; secretary of state to Monroe; sixth president of the United States, 1825–29; a Unitarian; died in the Hall of Congress; buried in Unitarian Church, Quincy, Massachusetts. Elected to the Hall of Fame for Great Americans in 1905. 237, 667–72, 674–76, 678, 679.

11 Birthday of Colin Purdie Kelly (July 11, 1915–December 10, 1941). American army captain and aviator, first United States air hero of World War II, posthumously awarded the Distinguished Service Cross.

11 Birthday of George William Norris (July 11, 1861–September 2, 1944). American statesman and congressman from Nebraska who was instrumental in the establishment of the Tennessee Valley Authority. The first TVA dam was named in his honor. Author of the Twentieth Amendment, known as the "Lame Duck" amendment, which provided for inauguration of a newly elected president on January 20 instead of March 4.

11 Mongolian National Day, a holiday in the Mongolian People's Republic, commemorating the Communist revolution of 1921.

11 Bawming the Thorn Day, a generations-old tradition in Appleton, Cheshire, England, based on the ancient worship of trees; primarily a festival in which children garland and dance around a hawthorn tree. 164.

11 Anniversary of the dedication of the United States Air Force Academy at Lowry Air Base, Colorado, on July 11, 1955.

12 Feast day of Saint John Gualbert, patron saint of forest workers.

12 Birthday of George Eastman (July 12, 1854–March 14, 1932). American inventor of cameras and camera equipment; philanthropist who gave funds to the University of Rochester, the Massachusetts Institute of Technology, and Hampton and Tuskegee Institutes.

12 Birthday of Sir William Osler (July 12, 1849–December 29, 1919). Canadian physician and teacher noted for his research on the circulatory system.

12 Birthday of Henry David Thoreau (July 12, 1817–May 6, 1862). American author most famous for the book *Walden, or Life in the Woods*. Elected to the Hall of Fame for Great Americans in 1960. 237, 990, 1001.

c12 Family Day, a holiday in South Africa; celebrated on the second Monday of July.

12 Orangeman's Day, or Orange Day, dedicated to the anniversary of the Battle of the Boyne of 1690; a statutory public holiday in Northern Ireland.

12 Anniversary of the authorization of the Medal of Honor by Congress on July 12, 1862, to honor noncommissioned officers and privates who distinguish themselves in actual conflict by gallantry and intrepidity at the risk of life beyond the call of duty. The first award was made to six members of a Union army raiding party.

13 Festival of Our Lady of Fátima, commemorating the vision of the Virgin Mary to the dos Santos children in the village of Fátima in Portugal in 1917.

13 Birthday of Nathan Bedford Forrest (July 13, 1821–October 29, 1877). American cavalry commander in the Confederate army whose famous motto was "Get thar fastest with the mostest." His birthday is observed annually in Tennessee as a legal holiday.

13 Night Watch, or La Retraite aux Flambeaux, a French half-day holiday celebrating the eve of the fall of the Bastille and followed by Bastille Day, a full holiday.

c13 Reed Dance Day, a festival day in Swaziland, celebrated on the second Monday in July as a tribute from the Swazi girls to the Queen Mother, known as "Ndlovukazi" or she-elephant.

13 Rhodes' and Founders' Day, a two-day holiday in Southern Rhodesia honoring Rhodesian pioneers and settlers.

14 Birthday of Florence Bascom (July 14, 1862–June 18, 1945). American geologist. First woman to receive a degree from Johns Hopkins and the first woman to receive a Ph.D. degree from any American university.

14 Birthday of Jules Mazarin (July 14, 1602–March 9, 1661). French statesman, Roman Catholic cardinal, and founder of the Mazarin Library.

14 Birthday of Emmeline Pankhurst (July 14, 1858–June 14, 1928). English woman-suffrage leader who used militant methods of campaigning and was sentenced to prison. She lived to see the passage of the Representation of the People Act on June 9, 1928, which gave full and equal suffrage to women. A memorial statue to her was erected near the Houses of Parliament in London. 836.

14 Birthday of James Abbott McNeill Whistler (July 14, 1834–July 17, 1903). American artist and wit. Elected to the Hall of Fame for Great Americans in 1930. 237, 986.

14 Bastille Day, or Fête Nationale, the national festival of France, commemorating the storming of the Bastille in 1789 and the release of political prisoners. Also called the "Holiday of all Free Men," Bastille Day is observed in all French territories and provinces and in Guatemala, and by French societies throughout the world. 527.

14 African Community Day, or Day of Association, a public holiday in Senegal on the west coast of Africa; a tribute to African goals and culture.

14 Republic Day in Iraq, a public holiday marking the overthrow of the monarchy on July 14, 1958; considered by the Iraqis to be the "real day of independence."

14 Anniversary of the first industrial exposition in the United States, opened by President Franklin Pierce in New York on July 14, 1853.

15 Feast day of Saint Swithin, known as a weather prophet. If it rains on this day, according to folklore, it will continue for forty days.

15 Feast day of Saint Vladimir of Kiev, honored by Russian and Ukrainian Christians.

15 Anniversary of the baptism of Inigo Jones (July 15, 1573–June 21, 1652). English architect whose restoration of Saint Paul's Cathedral in London, and other buildings, revived classic architecture. 986.

15 Birthday of Clement Clarke Moore (July 15, 1779–July 10, 1863). American scholar and poet. Best known for the poem called *A Visit from Saint Nicholas.* 346.

15 Birthday of Rembrandt van Rijn (July 15, 1606–October 4, 1669). Dutch painter and etcher, foremost member of the Dutch school of painting. 986.

c15 Black Ship Day, a festival observed in Yokosuka, Shimoda, and other ports of Japan around July 15 to commemorate the arrival of Commodore Perry in 1853; observed in other ports on varying days.

c15 Feast of Lanterns, or Bon Festival, a Japanese tribute to deceased ancestors; observed around July 15 in Japan and Japanese communities throughout the world.

16 Feast day of Our Lady of Mount Carmel, patron saint of fishermen; a special day for the Carmelite order, for Roman Catholic churches in Italy, Italian sections of American cities, and the fishing villages of Puerto Rico. It is also observed in Trastevere, one of the oldest quarters of Rome, with a special festival called "Festival of We Others," in which the entire population takes part. 705.

16 Birthday of Mary Baker Eddy (July 16, 1821–December 3, 1910). Founder of the Church of Christ, Scientist and author of *Science and Health with Key to the Scriptures* and other books. 825, 837.

16 District of Columbia Day, the anniversary of the establishment on July 16, 1790, of the District of Columbia and the authorization of Washington as the permanent capital of the United States.

c16 Gion Matsuri, a traditional many-day festival observed around July 16 to carry on supplications begun in ancient Japan for divine protection against an epidemic.

16 La Paz Day, the anniversary of the founding of the capital of Bolivia on July 16, 1548.

17 Constitution Day, a holiday in the Republic of Korea (South Korea) commemorating the constitution adopted in 1963.

17 July Revolution Day, a public holiday in Iraq commemorating the revolts of 1968.

17 Day of National Mourning, observed in Mexico to commemorate the death on July 17, 1928, of Alvaro Obregón, supporter of the 1910 revolution and president of Mexico in 1920.

17 Muñoz Rivera day, celebrated in Puerto Rico to honor the July 17, 1859, birth of Luis Muñoz Rivera, patriot and journalist.

18 Feast day of Saint Camillus de Lellis, patron saint of the sick, of nurses, and of nurses' associations. 705.

18 Birthday of Laurence Housman (July 18, 1865–February 20, 1959). English illustrator, author, and playwright remembered particularly for the play *Victoria Regina*. 986.

18 Birthday of William Makepeace Thackeray (July 18, 1811–December 24, 1863). English novelist and satirical humorist famous for *Vanity Fair* and *The History of Henry Esmond*. 986.

18 Day of National Mourning in Mexico, commemorating the July 18, 1872, death of Benito Juárez, patriot-soldier who destroyed the Maximillian empire.

18 Spanish Labor Day, a public holiday in Spain.

18 Uruguay Constitution Day, a public holiday commemorating the adoption of the 1951 constitution providing for a collegiate form of government.

18 International Railroad Day, marking the completion of the Grand Trunk line, the first international railroad on the American continent, on July 18, 1853.

19 Feast day of Saint Vincent de Paul, French priest and founder of the Sisters of Charity; patron saint of all charitable societies. 705.

19 Birthday of Mary Ann Ball Bickerdyke (July 19, 1817–November 8, 1901). American nurse known as "Mother Bickerdyke" for her services to the Union armies in the West during the Civil War.

19 Birthday of Charles Horace Mayo (July 19, 1865–May 26, 1939). American surgeon, specialist in goiters and preventive medicine; cofounder of the Mayo Clinic.

19 Burma Martyrs' Day, a holiday honoring the heroes and martyrs of the Burmese nation.

19 Laos Independence Day, a holiday commemorating the treaty of July 19, 1949, through which Laos became a sovereign state within the French union, with full sovereignty achieved on December 24, 1954.

20 Feast day of Saint Margaret; patron saint of all women in childbirth. 705.

20 Birthday of Erik Axel Karlfeldt (July 20, 1864–April 8, 1931). Swedish poet who was posthumously awarded the Nobel Prize in literature in 1931. 227.

20 Birthday of Francesco Petrarch (July 20, 1304–July 18, 1374). Italian lyric poet and scholar. Major figure in the Renaissance. 986.

20 Tunisia Independence Recognition Day, recording the French acknowledgement of Tunisian independence on July 20, 1956; celebrations are associated with Republic Day on July 25.

20 Anniversary of the establishment of the Legion of Merit Medal by Act of Congress on July 20, 1942, for meritorious service performed by individuals in the armed services of the United States or by citizens of other nations.

20 Moon Day, the anniversary of the historic landing on the moon on July 20, 1969, of the United States *Apollo II*, manned by astronauts Neil A. Armstrong and Edwin Aldrin, Jr., who became the first men to engage in explorations of the moon's surface.

21 Feast day of Saint Victor, patron saint of cabinetmakers.

21 Birthday of Ernest Hemingway (July 21, 1899–July 2, 1961). American novelist, short-story writer, and world traveler. His book *The Old Man and the Sea* won the Pulitzer Prize in 1953. He was awarded the Nobel Prize in literature in 1954. 226, 227, 988.

21 Birthday of Paul Julius Reuter (July 21, 1816–February 25, 1899). German journalist and founder of Reuter's News Agency, which pioneered in gathering news from all over the world.

21 Belgium Independence Day, a holiday commemorating the accession of the first Belgian king, Leopold I, following separation from the Netherlands on July 21, 1831.

21 Martyrs' Day in Bolivia, a holiday-memorial to the nation's heroes.

21 Liberation Day, a holiday in Guam in honor of July 21, 1944, when forces of the United States Army and Marines freed the island from the Japanese, who had seized it in December 1941.

21 Anniversary of the establishment of the United States Veterans Administration on July 21, 1930.

22 Birthday of Stephen Vincent Benét (July 22, 1898–March 13, 1943). American poet and novelist who received the Pulitzer Prize in poetry in 1929 for *John Brown's Body* and in 1944 for the posthumously published *Western Star*.

22 Birthday of Emma Lazarus (July 22, 1849–November 19, 1887). American poet and essayist who wrote *The New Colossus*, the closing lines of which are engraved on the pedestal of the Statue of Liberty. 481.

c22 Hurricane Supplication Day, observed on the fourth Monday of July in the Virgin Islands; a day of prayer for safety in the hurricane season.

22 Polish National Liberation Day, a holiday in Poland honoring the end of the war in 1944, and a constitution enacted on July 22, 1952.

23 Birthday of Charlotte Saunders Cushman (July 23, 1816–February 17, 1876). American actress known for her portrayal of Lady Macbeth. She was elected to the Hall of Fame for Great Americans in 1915. 237, 825.

23 Birthday of James Gibbons (July 23, 1834–March 24, 1921). American Roman Catholic cardinal, author of *The Faith of Our Fathers*.

23 Day of the Republic, or Revolution Day, a holiday in Egypt (The United Arab Republic) and in Libya, commemorating July 23, 1952, when the revolutionary command terminated the Egyptian royal government and declared the nation to be a republic.

23 Ethiopian National Day, a holiday in Ethiopia which honored the birthday of Emperor Haile Selassie until his deposition in 1974.

23 Oman National Day, a holiday in Oman, at the far end of the Arabian peninsula; a tribute to the accession of the sultan.

24 Birthday of John Middleton Clayton (July 24, 1796–November 9, 1856). American statesman, senator from Delaware, and Secretary of State under Zachary Taylor. He represents the state of Delaware in Statuary Hall in a sculpture done by Bryant Baker. 242.

24 Birthday of Amelia Earhart (Putnam) (July 24, 1898–July 2, 1937). American aviatrix. The first woman to fly an airplane across the Atlantic and winner of many aviation "firsts." The first woman to receive the Distinguished Flying Cross. 837, 992.

24 Birthday of Henrik Pontoppidan (July 24, 1857–August 21, 1943). Danish novelist whose works describe peasant life in rural Denmark; shared the Nobel Prize in literature with Karl Gjellerup in 1917.

24 Bolivar Day, a holiday in Ecuador and Venezuela honoring the July 24, 1783, birth of Simon Bolivar, known as the "George Washington of South America."

c24 Pioneer Day in Utah, a legal holiday celebrating the entry of Brigham Young and the Mormon pioneers into the valley of the Salt Lake in 1847 and the establishment of the first settlement in the area. It has been observed every year since 1849 on varying dates near July 24.

24 Valencia Fair Days, begin on July 24 in Valencia, Spain. As a celebration of the Battle of Flowers, carnations are thrown in mock battles and festivities.

25 Saint Christopher's Day, honoring the popular patron of motorists, bus drivers, and travelers, who is invoked against perils from water, tempests, and plagues.

25 Feast day of Saint James the Great, patron saint of Spain and of Chile.

25 Birthday of Davidson Black (July 25, 1884–March 15, 1934). Canadian doctor and professor of anatomy whose contributions to anthropology in studying protohuman remains and in identifying the "Peking Man" brought him international fame.

25 Birthday of Flora Adams Darling (July 25, 1840–January 6, 1910). American author and founder of patriotic societies of which the most important is the Daughters of the American Revolution, which she founded with Mary S. Lockwood on October 11, 1890.

25 Guanacaste Day, anniversary of the annexation of Guanacaste province; a public holiday in Costa Rica.

25 Netherlands Independence Day, recognizes the events of the nineteenth century which assured autonomy under a constitutional monarchy to the kingdom of the Netherlands.

25 Puerto Rico Constitution, or Commonwealth, Day, a holiday in Puerto Rico honoring the proclamation of the constitution on July 25, 1952; also called "Occupation Day," commemorating the landing of United States troops in Puerto Rico on July 25, 1898.

25 Tunisian Republic Day, anniversary of the proclamation of July 25, 1957, which abolished the monarchy and established the republic; a national holiday in Tunisia.

26 Feast day of Saint Anne, patron saint of Canada, patroness of housewives and of miners, mother of the Virgin Mary, wife of Joachim; celebrated throughout the world. The pilgrimage to the Basilica of Sainte Anne de Beaupré in the province of Quebec is one of the major pilgrimages on the North American continent. The shrine at Beaupré has been called the "Lourdes of the New World." 5, 705.

26 Birthday of George Louis Beer (July 26, 1872–March 15, 1920). American historian, an authority on the British colonial system in whose name the American Historical Association presents a prize for an outstanding book on history.

26 Birthday of Auguste Beernaert (July 26, 1829–October 6, 1912). Belgian statesman, prominent member of the International Peace Conference, corecipient of the 1909 Nobel Peace Prize. 241.

26 Birthday of Constantino Brumidi (July 26, 1805–February 19, 1880). Italian-American painter whose lifework was the painting of portraits and frescoes for the Capitol building in Washington, D.C.

26 Birthday of George Catlin (July 26, 1796–December 23, 1872). American artist who made special studies and portraits of American Indians. His work is displayed in the Catlin Gallery of the United States National Museum and at the American Museum of Natural History in New York.

26 Birthday of George Clinton (July 26, 1739–April 20, 1812). American Revolutionary War soldier; first governor of the state of New York; twice vice-president of the United States; lawyer. He represents the state of New York in Statuary Hall in a sculpture done by Henry Kirke Brown. 242.

26 Birthday of Serge Koussevitzky (July 26, 1874–June 4, 1951). Russian-American bass player, conductor of the Boston Symphony Orchestra, and founder of the Berkshire Music Center.

26 Birthday of George Bernard Shaw (July 26, 1856–November 2, 1950). Irish-English dramatist, critic, novelist, and pamphleteer. Recipient of the Nobel Prize in literature in 1925, using the money to establish an institution for the study of Scandinavian literature in Great Britain, since, in his case, the money was "a life belt thrown to a man who had already reached shore." A Bernard Shaw Day is observed on his birthday by Shaw societies throughout the United States. 231, 986, 987.

26 Cuban Revolution Day, a holiday in Cuba commemorating Fidel Castro's "26th of July movement" of 1953 against the Batista military dictatorship. 528.

26 Liberian Independence Day, a holiday commemorating the establishment of the Free and Independent Republic of Liberia on July 26, 1847, following its founding by the American Colonization Society, as a place to send free Negroes from the United States, by authority of a charter granted by the Congress of the United States in 1816.

26 Maldives Independence Day, commemorating July 26, 1965, when the British recognized the full independence of the Sultanate of the Maldives, the group of islands in the Indian Ocean that became the Republic of the Maldives.

26 New York Ratification Day. New York entered the Union on July 26, 1788, the eleventh of the thirteen original United States to do so. 741.

26 Bellman Day, celebrated annually in Stockholm in memory of Carl Michael Bellman, eighteenth-century troubadour whose songs and poems are enjoyed in twentieth-century Sweden.

27 Feast day of Saint Pantaleon, patron saint of physicians.

27 Barbosa Day, observed in Puerto Rico in honor of the July 27, 1857, birth of José Celso Barbosa, black physician and political hero of the nineteenth century.

28 Birthday of Beatrix Potter (July 28, 1866–December 22, 1943). English author and illustrator, famous for *The Tale of Peter Rabbit*, which has been translated into many languages.

28 Anniversary of the death of John Peter Zenger on July 28, 1746. American printer and journalist tried for seditious libels. His acquittal is considered the first important victory for the freedom of the press in the colonies.

28 Fall of Fascism Day, a public holiday in San Marino commemorating the resignation of Mussolini as dictator of Italy in 1943; San Marino has been under the protection of Italy since 1862.

c28 Independence Day in Peru, a holiday commemorating the declaration of independence from Spain on July 28, 1821, which led to war and complete freedom in 1824. This holiday is celebrated for two days.

28 Somers Day, observed in Bermuda in commemoration of the settlement of Bermuda by Admiral Sir George Somers in 1609.

28 Joseph Lee Day, sponsored by the National Recreation Association to commemorate the July 28, 1937, death of the "Father of the Playground Movement."

28 Founder's Day for the Volunteers of America, honors the birth of Ballington Booth on July 28, 1859.

29 Feast day of Saint Martha, patron saint of housewives, cooks, innkeepers, and laundresses.

29 Feast day of Saint Olaf, patron saint of Norway since 1164; ceremonies commemorate the death of King Olaf in battle and honor his support of the Christian faith.

29 Birthday of Dag Hammarskjöld (July 29, 1905–September 18, 1961). Swedish economist; second secretary-general of the United Nations; posthumously awarded the Nobel Peace Prize in 1961.

29 Birthday of Don Marquis (July 29, 1878–December 30, 1937). American journalist, poet, and playwright; creator of Archy, the cockroach, and Mehitabel, the cat, the newspaper philosophers of the 1920s.

29 Birthday of Booth Tarkington (July 29, 1869–May 19, 1946). American author who won the Pulitzer Prize in 1919 for *The Magnificent Ambersons* and in 1922 for *Alice Adams*. Perhaps best known for *Penrod*. 986.

29 Birthday of Alexis de Tocqueville (July 29, 1805–April 16, 1859). French statesman and author of a famous four-volume work called *Democracy in America*, which won the Montyon Prize of the French Academy in 1836. 986.

29 Olsok Eve Festival, a Norwegian holiday celebrated with bonfires and folk dancing in honor of Saint Olaf, the martyr king Olav Haraldsson who brought Christianity to Norway and was killed in the first Battle of Stiklestad, July 29, 1030; frequently called Norway Day in the United States and observed in Norwegian-American communities.

29 Anniversary of the ratification of the International Atomic Agency on July 29, 1957. Its purpose is to insure peaceful benefits of atomic research to peoples throughout the world.

30 Birthday of Emily Brontë (July 30, 1818–December 19, 1848). English author, famous for the novel *Wuthering Heights*. 986.

30 Birthday of Henry Ford (July 30, 1863–April 7, 1947). American inventor, automobile manufacturer, and philanthropist whose fortune and family established the Ford Foundation.

30 Birthday of James Edward Kelly (July 30, 1855–May 25, 1933). American sculptor who chose subjects from American history for his work and became known as the "Sculptor of American History."

30 Birthday of Robert Rutherford McCormick (July 30, 1880–April 1, 1955). American newspaperman, editor and publisher of the *Chicago Tribune*, and philanthropist.

30 Crater Day in Virginia, commemorates July 30, 1864, the occasion of an unsuccessful attempt of the Union forces to take Petersburg by blowing up the forts, causing craters in the earth; observed by veterans and civic organizations.

30 Marseillaise Day. The *Marseillaise*, the national anthem of France, was sung in Paris for the first time on July 30, 1792, by five hundred men from the port city of Marseilles, which gave its name to the French national anthem.

30 Anniversary of the organization of the WAVES, women's reserve unit of the United States Naval Reserves, on July 30, 1942.

31 Feast day of Saint Ignatius of Loyola; founder and patron of the Society of Jesus; patron saint of retreats and retreatants. Ignatius was the author of the classic book *Spiritual Exercises*.

31 Birthday of John Ericsson (July 31, 1803–March 8, 1889). American inventor of the screw propeller, pioneer in modern naval construction, builder of the famous *Monitor*; memorials to him have been built in New York; Worcester, Massachusetts; and in Sweden.

31 Birthday of James Kent (July 31, 1763–December 12, 1847). American lawyer, jurist, and famous legal commentator. He was elected to the Hall of Fame for Great Americans in 1900. 237.

31 Day of national mourning in Mexico, commemorating the 1811 death of Miguel Hidalgo y Costilla, priest and revolutionary hero in the 1810 revolt against Spain.

August

August, the eighth month of the year, was named for the Roman emperor Augustus. In many countries it is a traditional time for music festivals, fairs, expositions, and family holidays.

The one religious day in August that is observed around the world is August 15, the Feast of the Assumption of Mary, a holy day and a holiday in many Roman Catholic countries. On this day the Italian, Spanish, and Latin American peoples cherish age-old religious processions often followed by fiesta activities.

The flowers for August are the gladiolus and the poppy. The birthstones are the sardonyx and the peridot.

The Fixed Days of August

1 Feast of Saint Peter's Chains, commemorating the miraculous release of the Apostle Paul from prison.

1 Birthday of William Clark (August 1, 1770–September 1, 1838). American soldier and explorer; a leader of the Lewis and Clark expedition, which set up a route to the Pacific and stimulated the westward expansion of the American nation.

1 Birthday of Richard Henry Dana (August 1, 1815–January 6, 1882). American author, lawyer, and sailor, best known for his book *Two Years before the Mast.*

1 Birthday of Francis Scott Key (August 1, 1779–January 11, 1843). American lawyer and author of the national anthem *The Star-Spangled Banner*; honored on Defenders' Day. 410, 411, 413.

1 Birthday of Herman Melville (August 1, 1819–September 28, 1891). American author; his major book, *Moby Dick*, won Melville a permanent place in world literature. 986.

1 Birthday of Maria Mitchell (August 1, 1818–June 28, 1889). American astronomer and first woman to be elected to the American Academy of Arts and Sciences. She was elected to the Hall of Fame for Great Americans in 1905. 237, 837.

1 Army Day, a public holiday in the People's Republic of China; observed on or near August 1; also called the National Liberation Army festival.

c1 Bahamas Emancipation Day, a holiday in the West Indian Bahamas group, commemorating the emancipation of British slaves in 1838; now celebrated on the first Monday of August.

1 Colorado Day, a legal holiday in Colorado in honor of the admission of Colorado to the Union in 1876 as the thirty-eighth state.

1 Dahomey National Day, a public holiday in the African nation of Dahomey celebrated with parades and folklore dances; commemorates the proclamation of independence of August 1, 1960.

1 Nicaragua Fiesta Day, a public holiday honoring the republic's patron saint, Saint Domingo.

1 Swiss Confederation Day, anniversary of the foundation of the Swiss Confederation on August 1, 1291; a nationally celebrated holiday in Switzerland and one that has a significance comparable to the Fourth of July in the United States.

1 Lammas Day, once an important British festival day, historically important as the forerunner of America's Thanksgiving and Canada's Harvest Festival.

1 Sports Day, a day promoting sportsmanship in the United States in all fields, from business to politics, race relations, and sports.

2 Feast day of Saint Alphonsus Liguori, patron saint of confessors and lawyers.

c2 Feast day of Saint Wilfred, a day of processions and ceremonials in Ripon, Yorkshire, England, recalling the return from exile of the seventh-century bishop, later saint, Wilfred of York; observed on the first Saturday of August.

2 Feast day of the Virgin of the Angels, the patroness of Costa Rica; a national holiday and a day of pilgrimage to the basilica in Cartago, the site of the black stone statue of the Virgin called "La Negrita."

2 Birthday of Pierre Charles L'Enfant (August 2, 1754–June 14, 1825). French army engineer and an officer in the American Revolutionary army; honored as the designer of the plans for the city of Washington, D.C. 986.

2 Birthday of Henry Steel Olcott (August 2, 1832–February 17, 1907). American spiritualist and first president of the Theosophical Society.

c2 Jamaican Independence Day, a holiday commemorating the achievement of independence for Jamaica on August 6, 1962; observed on the first Monday in August.

2 Lesotho National Tree-Planting Day, a day of citizen participation in the planting of trees to combat soil erosion in the landlocked African nation of Lesotho.

3 Birthday of Vernon Louis Parrington (August 3, 1871–June 16, 1929). American critic and educator, author of the classic *Main Currents in American Thought*.

3 Birthday of Ernest (Ernie) Taylor Pyle (August 3, 1900–April 18, 1945). American journalist and spokesman of the American soldier; the most famous American correspondent in World War II.

3 Birthday of Lady Isabella Caroline Somerset (August 3, 1851–March 12, 1921). English philanthropist; temperance worker; successor to Frances Willard as president of the world WCTU; founder of a pioneer farm colony for alcoholic women in 1895, the first institution of its kind in England.

c3 August Bank Holiday, a free day observed on the first Monday of August in the countries of the British Commonwealth; established to give workers a long weekend during the summer season.

3 Bourguiba's Day, a public holiday in Tunisia celebrating the August 3, 1902, birth of Habib Bourguiba, the nation's first president and the leader in the struggle for peace.

3 Niger Independence Day, a holiday commemorating the August 3, 1960, declaration of independence for Niger, a landlocked country in Africa.

4 Feast day of Saint Dominic, founder of the Dominican order; patron saint of preachers and of astronomers.

4 Birthday of Knut Hamsun (August 4, 1859–February 19, 1952). Norwegian author of *Growth of the Soil* and *Hunger*; recipient of the Nobel Prize in literature in 1920. 986.

4 Birthday of Oliver Perry Morton (August 4, 1823–November 1, 1877). Indiana's Civil War governor who represents his state in Statuary Hall in a sculpture made by Charles Henry Niehaus. 242.

4 Birthday of Gaspar Núñez de Arce (August 4, 1832–June 9, 1903). Spanish poet known as the "Spanish Tennyson."

4 Birthday of Percy Bysshe Shelley (August 4, 1792–July 8, 1822). English poet in whose honor the Poetry Society of America presents the annual Shelley Memorial Award to a living American poet. 986.

4 Coast Guard Day, anniversary of the establishment on August 4, 1790, of the Revenue Cutter Service, which merged with the Life Saving Service in 1915 to become the United States Coast Guard.

c4 Peer Gynt Festival Days, observed in Norway beginning about August 4 to re-create the folklore and pageantry of the historical Peer Gynt, known to the world through the dramatic play of Ibsen.

5 The Feast of the Dedication of Our Lady of the Snows of the Church of Saint Mary Major in Rome. A feast of thanksgiving that includes a shower of white blossoms commemorating the August 5 snowfall of the third century that outlined the shape of a basilica.

5 Birthday of Conrad Aiken (August 5, 1899–August 17, 1973). American short-story writer; poet and critic; awarded the Pulitzer Prize in poetry in 1916.

5 Birthday of Mary Ritter Beard (August 5, 1876–August 14, 1958). American historian who in numerous books concentrated on women's roles in society; collaborated with her husband Charles in the writing of American history.

5 Birthday of John Eliot (August 5, 1604–May 21, 1690). American clergyman, "the Apostle to the Indians"; author of a catechism which was the first book printed in an American Indian language; his translation of the Bible into the Pequot language, completed in 1663, was the first Bible printed on the American continent.

5 Birthday of Guy de Maupassant (August 5, 1850–July 6, 1893). French novelist and one of the greatest short-story writers of the nineteenth century. 986.

5 Iran Constitution Day, a public holiday in Iran honoring the document that provides that country with a constitutional monarchy.

5 Upper Volta Independence Day, a holiday in Upper Volta commemorating its establishment as an independent nation on the African continent on August 5, 1960.

c5 Rush-Bearing Day, observed at Grasmere, England, on the Saturday nearest Saint Oswald's Day, August 5; a ceremony in which children carry garlands and rushes to the churchyard where Wordsworth is buried.

6 The Feast of the Transfiguration of Our Lord is observed in Roman and Anglican churches on August 6. It is observed in the Lutheran church on the sixth Sunday after Epiphany. This feast commemorates the revelation to Peter, James, and John of Christ's role as the fulfillment of the Law and the Prophets.

6 Birthday of Paul Claudel (August 6, 1868–February 23, 1955). French diplomat and author of poems and plays that combine traditional Catholicism with French symbolist techniques. 986.

6 Birthday of Sir Alexander Fleming (August 6, 1881–March 11, 1955). Scottish bacteriologist who discovered penicillin; corecipient of the Nobel Prize in medicine in 1945. 238.

6 August Bank Holiday, a public, late-summer free day in Ireland.

6 August Holiday, a public holiday in Malawi.

6 Bolivian Independence Day, a public holiday in Bolivia commemorating the proclamation of independence from Peru declared at the Congress of Chuquisaca on August 6, 1825; the day is a part of two-day national festival.

6 Iceland Bank Holiday, a public holiday in Iceland.

6 Hiroshima Day, anniversary of the dropping of the first atomic bomb on Hiroshima, from a B-29 Superfortress on August 5 (U.S. time), August 6 (Japan time), 1945. Hiroshima is now a city dedicated to world peace and the site of the Atomic Bomb Casualty Commission, which is dedicated to medical and biological research.

7   Feast of the Holy Name of Jesus, observed by the Church of England and the American Episcopal churches.

7   Birthday of Ralph Johnson Bunche (August 7, 1904–December 9, 1971). A founder and leader of the United Nations. Winner of the 1950 Nobel Peace Prize for the negotiation of an Arab-Israel truce. The first black man to receive the Nobel Prize. 241.

7   Birthday of Nathanael Greene (August 7, 1742–June 19, 1786). American Revolutionary War general who represents Rhode Island in Statuary Hall in a sculpture done by Henry Kirke Brown. 242, 739.

7   Battle of Boyacá Day, a public holiday in Colombia commemorating the victory of the South American insurgents over the Spanish forces on August 7, 1819.

7   Ivory Coast Independence Day, a public holiday commemorating the establishment on August 7, 1960, of Ivory Coast as an independent nation on the west coast of Africa.

7   Discovery Day in Trinidad and Tobago, a public holiday commemorating the arrival of Columbus in the Caribbean in 1498.

7   Anniversary of the dedication on August 7, 1927, of the International Peace Bridge honoring the peace that exists between Canada and the United States.

7   The anniversary of the establishment of the Order of the Purple Heart, a United States decoration for military merit created by George Washington on August 7, 1782, for enlisted men and noncommissioned officers. The first recipients were Sergeants Daniel Bissel, Daniel Brown, and Elijah Churchill of the Connecticut regiment, who were honored on May 9, 1783.

8   Birthday of Charles Bulfinch (August 8, 1763–April 4, 1844). American architect who introduced the styles of Christopher Wren and Robert Adam into American architecture; the first professional architect in the United States. 986.

8   Birthday of Ernest Orlando Lawrence (August 8, 1901–August 27, 1958). American physicist, inventor of the cyclotron, recipient of the 1939 Nobel Prize in physics; recipient of the first Sylvanus Thayer Award from West Point. 241.

8   Birthday of Henry Fairfield Osborn (August 8, 1857–November 6, 1935). American paleontologist and author who broadened public understanding of paleontology through instructive museum displays.

8   Bhutan, a Himalayan kingdom known as the "Land of Dragons," became an independent monarchy on August 8, 1949.

8   Tij Day, or Woman's Holiday, celebrated by the women of Nepal.

9   Birthday of William Thomas Green Morton (August 9, 1819–July 15, 1868). American dentist who received an award from the French Academy of Science in 1852 for the application of the discovery of etherization to surgical operation. He was elected to the Hall of Fame for Great Americans in 1920. 237.

9   Birthday of Izaak Walton (August 9, 1593–December 15, 1683). English biographer and author famous for *The Compleat Angler*. 986.

9   Sanusi Army Day, a holiday in the Libyan Arab Republic honoring the forces responsible for internal security.

9   Singapore National Day; a public holiday honoring separation, on August 9, 1965, from Malaysia and the establishment of independent sovereignty.

9   Nagasaki Memorial Day, a memorial observance in Nagasaki, Japan, for the victims of the second atomic bombing on August 9, 1945; also called the Moment of Silence.

9   Resignation Day, anniversary of the resignation of Richard M. Nixon on August 9, 1974; the first president of the United States to resign from executive office.

10 Feast day of Saint Lawrence of Rome for whom the Saint Lawrence River is named; patron saint of cooks, invoked against rheumatism and fire and for the protection of vineyards; a notable festival in his honor is held at the Escorial in Madrid.

10 Birthday of Camillo Benso di Cavour (August 10, 1810–June 6, 1861). Italian statesman, premier of Italy, major leader in Italian unification.

10 Birthday of Herbert Clark Hoover (August 10, 1874–October 20, 1964). German-Swiss ancestry; Iowa-born mining engineer; administrator and humanitarian; thirty-first president of the United States, 1929–33. Chairman, Commission on Organization of the Executive Branch. Society of Friends. Founded the Hoover Library on War, Revolution, and Peace at Stanford University. Buried at West Branch, Iowa. 667–72, 674–76, 678, 679.

10 Ecuador Independence Day, a holiday commemorating the August 10, 1809, proclamation of independence; celebrated throughout Ecuador with patriotic events.

10 Missouri Admission Day. Missouri entered the Union as the twenty-fourth state on August 10, 1821. 741.

10 The anniversary of the signing by President James K. Polk of the act establishing the Smithsonian Institution on August 10, 1846.

c11 Independence Day in the Central African Republic, a holiday honoring the achievement of full independence on August 11, 1960, following a colonial status dating from 1894; celebrated on or near August 11.

11 Independence Day in Chad, which became a free nation on August 11, 1960; celebrated nationally on January 11 to avoid the rainy season of August.

11 Coronation Day, the anniversary of the accession of King Hussein; celebrated in Jordan as a holiday.

12 Feast day of Saint Clare, founder of the Franciscan order of nuns known as the Poor Clares; patron saint of laundresses; patron saint of television. 705.

12 Birthday of Katharine Lee Bates (August 12, 1859–March 28, 1929). American educator and writer, author of the text for the national hymn *America the Beautiful*.

12 Birthday of Jacinto Benavente y Martínez (August 12, 1866–July 14, 1954). Spanish dramatist remembered for *The Banquet of Wild Beasts* and *The Passion Flower*. He was awarded the Nobel Prize in literature in 1922.

12 Birthday of Robert Mills (August 12, 1781–March 3, 1855). American architect, the first to study exclusively in the United States; his most memorable work is the Washington Monument.

12 Indian Day, observed in Massachusetts; the beginning of American Indian Exposition Week in Oklahoma.

12 Ponce de Leon Day, a festival day in Puerto Rico honoring the arrival of Ponce de Leon in 1508.

c12 Texas Pioneers' Day, honoring the first settlers on or near this date.

12 Thailand National Day, a holiday honoring the queen's birthday with ceremonials and festivities.

c12 Zambia Youth Day, a public holiday in Zambia that focuses on the interests and activities of young people; observed on the second Monday of August.

13 Birthday of John Logie Baird (August 13, 1888–June 14, 1946). Scottish inventor known as "the Father of Television."

13 Birthday of Sir George Grove (August 13, 1820–May 28, 1900). English engineer, biblical scholar and editor of the famous *Dictionary of Music and Musicians*.

13 Birthday of Annie Oakley (August 13, 1860–November 3, 1926). American markswoman whose personality and exploits are re-created in pageants of the American West.

13 Birthday of Lucy Stone (August 13, 1818–October 18, 1893). American social worker and pioneer for women's rights. 825, 992.

13 William Caxton Day, anniversary of the birth on August 13, c1422, of William Caxton, who, in 1477, printed the first book in English; a day of recognition observed by collectors and literary organizations.

13 Women's Day, a public holiday in Tunisia.

14 Birthday of John Galsworthy (August 14, 1867–January 31, 1933). English author famous for *The Forsyte Saga*. He received the Order of Merit in 1929 and was the recipient of the Nobel Prize in literature in 1932.

14 Birthday of Hans Christian Oersted (August 14, 1777–March 9, 1851). Danish physicist who discovered electromagnetism in 1819.

14 Bahrain proclaimed its status as an independent emirate on August 14, 1971, ending 110 years of formal British protection.

14 Pakistan Independence Day, a holiday commemorating the establishment of Pakistan as a free nation on August 14, 1947.

14 V-J Day, or Victory Day, honoring the end of fighting in World War II, August 14, 1945; a holiday in Rhode Island and in Michigan.

14 World War II Memorial Day in Arkansas.

14 Atlantic Charter Day, observed in the United States by presidential proclamation; honors the Atlantic Charter, signed by President Franklin Roosevelt and Winston Churchill on August 14, 1941, on which the signatories based their "hopes for a better future for the world" and outlined the eight points that were later incorporated in the United Nations declaration.

c14 Bud Billiken Day, a children's day observed in Chicago on or near August 14 in honor of Bud Billiken, the mythical godfather of Chicago's black children, created in 1923 by Robert S. Abbott, founder of the *Chicago Defender* newspaper.

14 Liberty Tree Day, observed in Massachusetts to memorialize the American colonists' challenge to the British governor in placing, on August 14, 1765, two effigies in a Boston elm tree, soon to be known as the Liberty Tree.

15 The Feast of the Assumption of Mary, a prescribed holy day in Roman Catholic countries, is also observed by the Eastern Orthodox churches. Mary, under the name Immaculate Conception, is the patron saint of the Roman Catholic Church of the United States. On the day of the Assumption, Italy, Spain, and some American cities have colorful processionals; the day is a holiday in most Roman Catholic countries. 80.

15 Birthday of Walter Crane (August 15, 1845–March 15, 1915). English painter and illustrator remembered for his illustrations of *Beauty and the Beast, Cinderella*, and other books.

15 Birthday of Thomas Edward Lawrence (August 15, 1888–May 19, 1935). British soldier and author known as "Lawrence of Arabia." 986.

15 Birthday of Sir Walter Scott (August 15, 1771–September 21, 1832). Scottish novelist and poet famous for such books as *Ivanhoe, Rob Roy*, and *Quentin Durward*. 986.

15 Congo Independence Day, a holiday in the People's Republic of the Congo (Brazzaville) honoring August 15, 1960, when the country achieved its sovereignty.

15 Independence Day in India, a holiday commemorating August 15, 1947, when the Indian Independence Act went into effect.

15 Korean Liberation Day, or Republic Day, a holiday in the Democratic People's Republic of Korea celebrating the 1945 liberation from Japan and the August 15, 1948, inauguration of the republic.

15 Laotian Memorial Day, a public holiday in Laos.

15 Liechtenstein National Day, a holiday of festivities honoring both the Day of the Assumption and associations with the royal family.

15 Mother's Day, a holiday combined with the Day of the Assumption in Costa Rica.

15 Napoleon's Day, a holiday in Corsica, a department of France, celebrating the birth of Napoleon I on August 15, 1769.

15 Anniversary of the organization of the United Lutheran Church in the United States on August 15, 1748, by Henry Melchior Mühlenberg, the "Father of Lutheranism in America."

16 Anniversary of the death of Duncan Phyfe on August 16, 1854. American cabinetmaker famous for fine furniture; honored in museum collections.

16 Bennington Battle Day, August 16, a legal holiday in Vermont honoring the Green Mountain Boys' victory over the British in 1777.

16 Cyprus Independence Day, the anniversary of the August 16, 1960, agreement between the British and the Greek and Turkish Cypriots to provide independence for Cyprus.

16 Political Restitution Day, or Dominican Restoration Day, commemorating the restoration of independence in 1963; a public holiday in the Dominican Republic.

16 Birthday of H.S.H. Prince Franz-Josef II, observed as a national day in Liechtenstein.

17 Gabon Independence Day, a public holiday in the equatorial nation on the west coast of Africa, commemorating independence secured on August 17, 1960.

17 Indonesia Independence Day, a holiday honoring the proclamation of independence made by the Indonesian Revolutionaries on August 17, 1945, the decisive day for full independence achieved on December 27, 1949.

17 San Martín Day, a holiday in Argentina, commemorates the death of José Francisco de San Martín on August 17, 1850, with special events honoring the most famous Argentine of all time.

18 Feast day of Saint Helena, discoverer of the True Cross, mother of the Emperor Constantine.

18 Birthday of Meriwether Lewis (August 18, 1774–October 11, 1809). American explorer and coleader of the Lewis and Clark expedition into the American Northwest.

c18 Klondike Gold Discovery Day, a holiday in the Yukon commemorating the discovery of gold on August 17, 1896; observed on the Friday immediately preceding the 18th of August.

19 Birthday of Edith Nesbit (August 19, 1858–May 4, 1924). English author, cofounder of the Fabian Society, who is remembered for her lively stories of the adventures of the Bastable children. 986.

19 Birthday of Manuel Luis Quezon (August 19, 1878–August 1, 1944). Philippine statesman; first president of the Philippine Commonwealth.

19 Birthday of Orville Wright (August 19, 1871–January 30, 1948). American aviator and inventor who made the first self-powered airplane flight in history on December 17, 1903. 222.

19 National Aviation Day, honoring the Wright brothers and other pioneer aviators.

20 Feast day of Saint Bernard, "Doctor Mellifluous," the Honeysweet Doctor; author of the injunction "Love me, love my dog."

20 Birthday of Benjamin Harrison (August 20, 1833–March 13, 1901). English ancestry; Indiana lawyer and soldier; twenty-third president of the United States, 1889–93. Presbyterian. Buried at Indianapolis, Indiana. 667–72.

20 Birthday of Bernardo O'Higgins (August 20, 1778–October 24, 1842). Chilean general and statesman called "the Liberator of Chile."

20 Birthday of Oliver Hazard Perry August 20, 1785–August 23, 1819). American naval officer famous for the statement "We have met the enemy and they are ours."

20 Constitution Day, a holiday in Hungary, the Magyar People's Republic, commemorating the institution of a constitution in 1949.

21 Birthday of Roark Bradford (August 21, 1896–November 13, 1948). American writer and humorist whose short-story collection *Ol' Man Adam an' His Chillun* was adapted by Marc Connelly for the play *Green Pastures*.

21 Hawaii Statehood Day, a holiday honoring Hawaii's admission to the Union as the fiftieth state on August 21, 1959.

21 The anniversary of the organization of the American Bar Association, one of the chief sponsors of Law Day, on August 21, 1878, at Saratoga, New York.

21 Anniversary of the Lincoln-Douglas debates of 1858, a major political event of the nineteenth century.

22 The Festival of the Immaculate Heart of Mary, celebrated by the Roman Catholic church.

22 King Richard III Day, anniversary of the death of the last of the Plantagenets, slain in battle on August 22, 1485; observed by Richard III societies in the United States and England.

23 Birthday of Edgar Lee Masters (August 23, 1869–March 5, 1950). American poet and author of the *Spoon River Anthology*. 986.

23 Romanian Liberation Day, a public holiday commemorating the coup that deposed the Fascist Iron Guard dictatorship in Romania on August 23, 1944.

24 The Feast of Saint Bartholomew, apostle, celebrated by the Roman Catholic, Anglican, Lutheran, and Eastern churches.

24 Birthday of Sir Max Beerbohm (August 24, 1872–May 20, 1956). English caricaturist and critic, best known for his caricature portraits of literary and political figures. 986.

24 Birthday of William Wilberforce (August 24, 1759–July 29, 1833). Crusader against oppression and slavery in the British Empire. His name was given to Wilberforce College in Ohio.

24 Liberian Flag Day, observed in Liberia to honor the flag and the 1847 convention that approved the flag design with eleven stripes representing the eleven men who signed the declaration of independence and the first constitution.

25 Feast day of Saint Genesius, patron saint of secretaries, actors, and lawyers.

25 Feast day of Saint Louis, patron saint of hairdressers, barbers, builders, and of France.

25 Birthday of Bret Harte (August 25, 1836–May 5, 1902). American poet and novelist, best known for his short stories *The Luck of Roaring Camp* and *The Outcasts of Poker Flat.* 986.

25 French Liberation Day, celebrating the end of the Nazi occupation of Paris with the arrival of the Allied forces on August 25, 1944; observed with special ceremonials in Paris despite the general population exodus that takes place in August, the favorite month for holidays in France.

25 Paraguay Constitution Day, a public holiday commemorating the revision of the constitution adopted on August 25, 1967.

25 Uruguayan Independence Day, a holiday in Uruguay commemorating the declaration of independence from Brazil proclaimed on August 25, 1825.

26 Birthday of Sir John Buchan (August 26, 1875–February 11, 1940). Scottish statesman and author; governor-general of Canada. 995.

26 Birthday of Lee De Forest (August 26, 1873–June 30, 1961). American inventor, known as "the Father of Radio" for his 1906 invention of the three-electrode vacuum tube.

26 Birthday of James Harlan (August 26, 1820–October 5, 1899). American congressman and secretary of the interior. Represents the state of Iowa in Statuary Hall in a sculpture by Nellie V. Walker. 242.

26 Birthday of Jules Romains (August 26, 1885–August 14, 1972). French novelist; best known for the many-volumed epic *Men of Good Will*, a portrayal of an entire society in decline.

26 The Sultan's Birthday, a public holiday in Zanzibar.

26 Woman's Equality Day, or Susan B. Anthony Day, the anniversary of the proclamation of final approval of the Nineteenth Amendment, on August 26, 1920, which gave voting privileges to women; observed by presidential proclamation in the United States. 822–38.

27 Birthday of Theodore Herman Dreiser (August 27, 1871–December 28, 1945). American author who made his reputation with such naturalistic novels as *Sister Carrie* and *An American Tragedy*; awarded the Merit Medal of the American Academy of Arts and Letters in 1944. 986.

27 Birthday of Hannibal Hamlin (August 27, 1809–July 4, 1891). American statesman; vice-president in Lincoln's first administration; United States minister to Spain. He represents the state of Maine in Statuary Hall in a sculpture by Charles E. Tefft. 242.

27 Birthday of Lyndon Baines Johnson (August 27, 1908–January 22, 1973). Thirty-sixth president of the United States; promulgator of legislation for the "Great Society" program; member of the Church of the Disciples of Christ; author of *The Vantage Point*, an interpretation of the Johnson administration. Buried at the Johnson ranch near Johnson City, Texas. 667–76, 678–80.

27 Anniversary of the death of Titian on August 27, 1576. Italian painter famous for the altarpiece *The Assumption of the Virgin* and other great religious paintings. 986.

c27 Late Summer Bank Holiday, a holiday in Gibraltar for public relaxation and enjoyment.

28 Feast day of Saint Augustine of Hippo; Doctor of Grace; patron saint of students for the priesthood. Saint Augustine is remembered as the man whose worldly background caused him to pray "Make me pure—but not yet"; he became one of the greatest figures in the Christian church; author of *Confessions* and *The City of God.* 125, 705.

28 Birthday of Johann Wolfgang von Goethe (August 28, 1749–March 22, 1832). German poet, dramatist, novelist, philosopher, statesman, and scientist. *Faust*, one of Goethe's major works, has been translated into all of the major languages of the world. 986, 987.

c28 Afghanistan's Jeshyn-Afghan Days, celebrated during the last three days in August to commemorate the peace treaty of August 1920; also called Independence Days.

28 Anniversary of the Spanish landing in 1565 at the site of present-day Saint Augustine, Florida.

29 The Martyrdom of Saint John, beheaded by King Herod at the insistence of Salome, commemorated on August 29 in honor of one of the greatest and most popular of saints; called "the Feast of the Beheading" in the Greek Orthodox church.

29 Birthday of Henry Bergh (August 29, 1811–March 12, 1888). American philanthropist; founder and first president of the Society for the Prevention of Cruelty to Animals; commemorated through the observance of Humane Days.

29 Birthday of Oliver Wendell Holmes (August 29, 1809–October 7, 1894). American poet, essayist, and novelist. His best-known poems include *The Chambered Nautilus* and *The Wonderful One-Hoss Shay*. He was elected to the Hall of Fame for Great Americans in 1910. 237.

29 Birthday of John Locke (August 29, 1632–October 28, 1704). English philosopher who wrote the famous work *An Essay Concerning Human Understanding*. 986.

29 Birthday of Maurice Maeterlinck (August 29, 1862–May 6, 1949). Belgian dramatist, poet, and essayist, author of such dramas as *Pelléas et Mélisande*, the basis of an opera by Claude Debussy, and *L'Oiseau Bleu*. Awarded the 1911 Nobel Prize in literature for his contributions to drama. 227.

29 Slovak National Uprising Day, a public holiday in parts of Czechoslovakia honoring the nation's heroes who fought for independence.

30 Feast day of Saint Fiacre, patron saint of gardeners and of cab drivers.

30 Feast day of Saint Rose of Lima, patron saint of South America and the Philippines; a native of Peru and the first South American to be canonized. Her feast day is a holiday in Peru. 5, 705.

30 Birthday of Huey Pierce Long (August 30, 1893–September 10, 1935). Louisiana politician and lawyer; governor of the state and exponent of a "share-the-wealth" plan. He represents the state of Louisiana in Statuary Hall in a sculpture by Charles Keck. His birthday is a holiday in Louisiana. 242.

30 Children's Day, a public holiday in Afghanistan, honoring the children of the nation.

c30 Liberation Day, a holiday in Hong Kong commemorating the end of Japanese occupation on August 30, 1945; observed on the last Monday in August.

30 Victory Day, a holiday in Turkey in tribute to the memory of warriors who died in the 1922 Battle of Dumlupinar, the final battle for Turkish independence.

31 Feast day of Saint Raymund Nonnatus, patron saint of the falsely accused.

31 Anniversary of the death of John Bunyan on August 31, 1688. English preacher renowned for *Pilgrim's Progress*.

31 Birthday of DuBose Heyward (August 31, 1885–June 16, 1940). American novelist whose novel *Porgy* was used as the basis for George Gershwin's opera *Porgy and Bess*.

31 Birthday of Ramón Magsaysay (August 31, 1907–March 17, 1957). Philippine statesman; recipient of the United States Legion of Merit in 1952; president of the Philippines.

31 Birthday of Maria Montessori (August 31, 1870–May 6, 1952). Italian educator, founder of the "Montessori method."

31   Malaysia Day, a holiday in Malaysia celebrating its achievement of status as an independent member of the British Commonwealth, reached on August 31, 1957. Malaysia achieved full independence on September 16, 1963.

31   Trinidad and Tobago Independence Day, a public holiday commemorating the independence achieved on August 31, 1962, within the British Commonwealth of Nations.

31   Anniversary of the chartering on August 31, 1960, of the Agricultural Hall of Fame to honor farm men and women who have contributed to America's greatness.

31   Festal Day, observed by the Order of the Eastern Star on August 31, the birthday of Robert Morris, who was one of the founders of the Order of the Eastern Star in the United States.

September

September, the ninth month in our calendar, received its name from the Latin numeral *septem*, meaning "seven," because it was the seventh month in the old Roman calendar. It became the ninth month when Julius Caesar changed the calendar to make January the first month. The middle of September brings autumn to the northern hemisphere and the beginning of spring to the southern hemisphere.

September is an important month in military history since it marks the official end of World War II, the signing of the unconditional surrender papers by Japan on September 2, 1945. Battle of Britain Week, which honors the British airmen who drove back the German planes on September 15, 1940, the most decisive air battle of World War II, is observed in September in Britain. September is also a special month for veterans who belong to the American Legion because their organization was chartered on September 16, 1919. September also honors the mothers who lost their sons and daughters in military service with a day called "Gold Star Mother's Day," which is observed in late September.

The flowers for September are the morning glory and the aster, and the birthstone is the sapphire.

The Fixed Days of September

1 Saint Adjutor Day, patron saint of of yachtsmen. His feast day is April 30.

1 Feast day of Saint Giles, patron saint of cripples, beggars, and blacksmiths.

1 Birthday of Sir Roger David Casement (September 1, 1864–August 3, 1916). Irish martyr patriot.

1 Birthday of Elizabeth Harrison (September 1, 1849–October 31, 1927). American educator, leader in the kindergarten movement, and one of the founders of the organization that became the National Congress of Parents and Teachers.

1 Libyan Revolution Day, a public holiday in Libya commemorating the assumption of governmental control by the revolutionary council in 1969.

1 Mackinac Bridge Walk Day, the one day of the year during which pedestrians may walk the five-mile span from Mackinaw City to Saint Ignace, Michigan.

1 Presidential Message Day, the opening of the Mexican Congress on September 1; a public holiday in Mexico.

c1 Settlers' Day, a public holiday in South Africa honoring the pioneers of the southernmost part of Africa; observed on the first Monday in September.

1 Tanzania Heroes' Day, a holiday in honor of the founding of the Tanzania Defense Force and in tribute to heroes in their fight against colonialism.

2 Birthday of Eugene Field (September 2, 1850–November 4, 1895). American journalist; author of children's verses, of which the most familiar are *Little Boy Blue* and *Wynken, Blynken, and Nod*.

2 Birthday of Henry George (September 2, 1839–October 29, 1897). American economist best known for his book *Progress and Poverty*.

2 Birthday of Lydia Kamekeha Liliuokalani (September 2, 1838–November 11, 1917). Queen of the Hawaiian Islands, overthrown in 1893 but remembered as the author of several songs including *Aloha Oe* (Farewell to Thee).

2 Independence Day in the Democratic Republic of Vietnam (North Vietnam) honoring September 2, 1945, when Ho Chi Minh declared the nation's independence from France and the revolts began.

2 Anniversary of the historic London fire that began on September 2, 1666, leaving four-fifths of London in ashes.

2 Anniversary of the signing of the unconditional surrender by Japan on September 2, 1945, which officially ended World War II in the Pacific.

3 Feast day of Saint Pius X, canonized in 1954.

3 Birthday of John Humphrey Noyes (September 3, 1811–April 13, 1886). American social reformer and author; founder of the Oneida Community.

3 Birthday of Louis Henri Sullivan (September 3, 1856–April 4, 1924). American architect who established the principle that form should follow function.

3 Commemoration of September 3, 1934, Day, a public holiday in Tunisia honoring the beginning of the independence movement.

c3 Labor Day, a public holiday, celebrated in the United States and Canada on the first Monday in September. Labor Day in the United States was founded by Peter J. Maguire in tribute to American industry. The day became a holiday for federal employees in 1894, and was quickly approved as a holiday in the individual states. 560–71.

3 Qatar Independence Day, a public holiday in the state of Qatar, situated on a peninsula on the west coast of the Arabian Gulf, commemorating the declaration of independence from Great Britain in September 1971.

3 Saint Marino Day, a public holiday in San Marino, honoring Saint Marinus the Deacon.

3 Treaty of Paris Day, the anniversary of the signing on September 3, 1783, of the treaty between the United States and England ending the Revolutionary War.

4 Birthday of Daniel Hudson Burnham (September 4, 1846–June 1, 1912). American architect; pioneer in fireproof skyscraper construction; developer of the Burnham Plan, the "think big" plan, used for many years as the basis for city planning in Chicago.

4 Birthday of Dadabhai Naoroji (September 4, 1825–June 30, 1917). Indian statesman; first Indian member of the British Parliament.

4 Birthday of Robert Raikes (September 4, 1736–April 5, 1811). English Sunday-school pioneer who was a major force in the development of the religious-education movement.

4 Birthday of Marcus Whitman (September 4, 1802–November 29, 1847). American pioneer and missionary physician whose faith in the future of the state of Oregon and representations to the federal government led to the securing of Oregon for the United States.

4 Birthday of the city of Los Angeles, celebrated with a variety of observances, especially on Olvera Street, the oldest street in the city, to honor the September 4, 1781, founding of the city.

5 Anniversary of the first meeting of the Continental Congress in Philadelphia on September 5, 1774.

5 Anniversary of the first Labor Day holiday parade held on September 5, 1882, in New York City.

6 Feast of Saint Zachariah, Old Testament prophet.

6 Birthday of Jane Addams (September 6, 1860–May 21, 1935). American social worker, advocate of international peace, founder of Hull House in Chicago. She shared the Nobel Peace Prize with Nicholas Murray Butler in 1931. A Jane Addams Children's Book Award, given annually to the children's book that "best combines literary worth with a strong statement of faith in people," is presented by the Women's International League for Peace and Freedom and the Jane Addams Peace Association. Observance of her birthday occurs at Hull House in Chicago and in programs of social agencies and peace organizations. 234, 241, 837.

6 Lafayette's Birthday, a day of recognition honoring the September 6, 1757, birth of the Marquis de Lafayette, who served in Washington's army during the American Revolution. 739, 992.

6 Birthday of Heinrich Melchior Mühlenberg (September 6, 1711–October 7, 1787). American Lutheran clergyman, chief founder of the Lutheran church in the United States, known as the "Patriarch of the Lutheran Church in America."

6 Pakistan Defense Day, a public holiday in Pakistan.

6 Somhlolo Day, a public holiday in Swaziland, commemorating the nation's independence, achieved on September 6, 1968.

7 Birthday of Ferdinand Vandiveer Hayden (September 7, 1829–December 22, 1887). American geologist who participated in the 1859–86 geological and geographical surveys of the United States; a leader in the movement to preserve Yellowstone as a federal park.

7 Brazil Independence Day, a holiday honoring Dom Pedro's proclamation of independence from Portugal, declared on September 7, 1822.

7 Granddad's Day, a day of tribute to grandfathers.

8 Feast of the Nativity of the Blessed Virgin Mary, honoring Mary's birthday as a Jewish child and as a lineal descendant of the royal family of David; observed by the Roman Catholic countries of the world.

8 Birthday of Lodovico Ariosto (September 8, 1474–July 6, 1533). Italian poet; author of *Orlando Furioso*, an epic of Roland recognized as a classic example of Renaissance literature. 986.

8 Birthday of Anton Dvořák (September 8, 1841–May 1, 1904). Czech composer famous for the *New World Symphony*, which was composed in Iowa.

8 Birthday of Frédéric Mistral (September 8, 1830–March 25, 1914). French poet who used Provencal, the dialect of southern France, as his medium; a corecipient of the 1904 Nobel Prize in literature. 227, 986.

8 Birthday of Robert Taft (September 8, 1889–July 31, 1953). American congressman; drafter of the Taft-Hartley Act of 1947; known as "Mr. Republican."

8 Andorra National Day, a holiday in the Andorran coprincipality of the eastern Pyrenees honoring the Notre Dame of Meritxell; a folklore event and pilgrimage based on the finding of an unusual figure under an almond tree blooming out of season.

8 Guinea-Bissau Independence Day, the anniversary of the establishment, on September 8, 1974, of Guinea-Bissau as a sovereign nation; terminating five centuries of colonial rule for the former territory of Portuguese Guinea.

8 Korean National Day, celebrated in North Korea, the Democratic People's Republic of Korea, in commemoration of the September 8, 1948, establishment of the government.

8 Uganda Republic Day, a public holiday in Uganda honoring the establishment of the republic on September 8, 1967.

8 Anniversary of the establishment on September 8, 1565, of the parish of Saint Augustine, Florida, the first Roman Catholic parish in the United States.

8 The Sheriff's Ride Ceremony, an annual event at Lichfield, England, observed on the day of the Feast of the Nativity of the Blessed Virgin Mary to fulfill the terms of Queen Mary's Charter of 1553, which created the city.

9 Birthday of Armand Jean du Plessis de Richelieu (September 9, 1585– December 4, 1642). Cardinal of the Roman Catholic church and French statesman of tremendous political power; founder of the French Academy and the Jardin des Plantes.

9 Birthday of Count Leo Tolstoy (September 9, 1828–November 20, 1910). Russian novelist, moral philosopher, and social reformer, famous for *War and Peace* and *Anna Karenina*. 986.

9 Bulgarian Liberation, or Freedom, Day, a public holiday in Bulgaria memorializing September 9, 1944, when Bulgarian partisans and Soviet troops joined to drive out the Nazis.

9 California Admission Day, a legal holiday in California commemorating the day in 1850 when California was admitted to the Union.

9 Luxembourg Liberation Day, a holiday commemorating the liberation of the grand duchy by the Allied forces in World War II.

c9 National Assembly Foundation Day, a public holiday in Afghanistan honoring the ratification of a new constitution by the Grand National Assembly in September 1964; observed on the second Wednesday in September.

9 Salerno Day, anniversary of the Allied landing at Salerno, Italy, on September 9, 1943; observed by veterans associations.

10 Birthday of Sir John Soane (September 10, 1753–January 20, 1837). English architect whose art collection and fortune formed the basis of the Soane Museum in London. 987.

10 Birthday of Franz Werfel (September 10, 1890–August 26, 1945). Austrian novelist, dramatist, and poet whose most popular novel was *The Song of Bernadette.*

10 Belize National Day, a holiday in Belize, formerly British Honduras, commemorating the 1798 Battle of Saint George's Cay, won by a few local baymen over a superior Spanish force.

11 Birthday of Erastus Flaval Beadle (September 11, 1821–December 18, 1894). American publisher of dime novels of interest to collectors as authentic Americana.

11 Birthday of David Herbert Lawrence (September 11, 1885–March 2, 1930). English writer whose most famous novel is *Lady Chatterley's Lover.* 986.

11 Birthday of William Sidney Porter, "O. Henry" (September 11, 1862– June 5, 1910). American short-story writer and journalist; author of the most deftly plotted stories in American literature. 986.

11 Jinnah Day, anniversary of the September 11, 1948, death of Quaid-i-Azam Mohammed Ali Jinnah, the founder of a free and independent Pakistan; a public holiday in Pakistan.

12 Birthday of Alexander Campbell (September 12, 1788–March 4, 1866). American religious leader, a founder of the Disciples of Christ.

12 Defenders' Day, a legal holiday in Maryland commemorating the Battle of Fort McHenry and the defense of Baltimore in the War of 1812. 410–13.

12 Occupation Day, a holiday in Southern Rhodesia commemorating the British annexation on September 12, 1923, of Mashonaland, under the title Colony of Southern Rhodesia, after twenty-three years of occupation.

c12 Fisherman's Walk Day, a harvest holiday festival for the fisherfolk of Musselburgh and other villages in Scotland; observed on the second Friday in September with garlands, doll processions, games, and sporting events.

12 Respect for the Aged Day, a public holiday in Japan; a day of honor and ceremonials for senior citizens.

13 Birthday of Adolf Meyer (September 13, 1866–March 17, 1950). American psychiatrist and neurologist who, with Clifford Beers, began the mental-hygiene movement.

13 Birthday of John Joseph Pershing (September 13, 1860–July 15, 1948). American general; commander-in-chief of the Allied Expeditionary Force in World War I; United States Army Chief of Staff; winner of the 1932 Pulitzer Prize in history for *My Experiences in the World War*.

13 Birthday of Walter Reed (September 13, 1851–November 22, 1902). American physician and surgeon who made important studies in the causes of typhoid and yellow fever. Walter Reed Hospital in Washington, D.C., is named in his honor. Dr. Reed was elected to the Hall of Fame for Great Americans in 1945. 237.

13 Birthday of Arnold Schönberg (September 13, 1874–July 13, 1951). Austrian-American composer who had a revolutionary influence on modern music through his use of the twelve-tone scale. 986.

13 Barry Day, anniversary of the September 13, 1803, death of John Barry, first American commodore; observed in Pennsylvania in tribute to his contributions to the nation.

13 Battle of Quebec, anniversary of the decisive battle of the French and Indian War won on the Plains of Abraham near the city of Quebec on September 13, 1759. The victory of Montcalm's forces assured the dominance of English influence on the North American continent.

14 The Feast of the Exaltation of the Holy Cross, a high-ranking day in the church calendar, is observed with special pilgrimages to Jerusalem.

14 Birthday of Karl Taylor Compton (September 14, 1887–June 22, 1954). American physicist, atomic-bomb scientist; recipient of many awards, including the French Legion of Honor.

14 Anniversary of the death of Dante Alighieri on September 14, 1321. The greatest of all Italian poets, known throughout the world for his *Divine Comedy*. 986.

14 Birthday of Jan Garrigue Masaryk (September 14, 1886–March 10, 1948). Czechoslovak statesman.

14 Birthday of Margaret Sanger (September 14, 1883–September 6, 1966). Founder and international leader of the birth-control movement; first president of both the American Birth Control League and the International Planned Parenthood Federation; her birthday is commemorated by Planned Parenthood associations and groups. 837, 976.

14 Battle of San Jacinto Day, a national holiday in Nicaragua commemorating the defeat of foreign invaders on September 14, 1856.

14 National Anthem Day, observed in the United States, and particularly in Maryland, to honor Francis Scott Key and the writing of the verses of *The Star-Spangled Banner* on the morning of September 14, 1814, following the bombardment of Fort McHenry. 410, 411, 413, 461.

14 Anniversary of the opening of the first school of journalism on September 14, 1908, at the University of Missouri.

15 Birthday of James Fenimore Cooper (September 15, 1789–September 14, 1851). American novelist famous for "the Leather Stocking Tales," which include *The Last of the Mohicans* and *The Deerslayer*. He was elected to the Hall of Fame for Great Americans in 1910. 237, 986.

15 Birthday of Francois de La Rochefoucauld (September 15, 1613–March 17, 1680). French moralist, famous for his *Maxims*.

15 Birthday of William Howard Taft (September 15, 1857–March 8, 1930). English ancestry; Ohio lawyer; governor of the Philippines, 1901–4; secretary of war under Theodore Roosevelt; twenty-seventh president of the United States, 1909–13. Chief justice of the Supreme Court, 1921–30. Unitarian. Buried in Arlington National Cemetery. 667–72, 674–76, 678, 679.

15 Battle of Britain Day, celebrated annually in England in honor of September 15, 1940, when British airmen drove back the invading German planes in the most decisive air battle of World War II.

15 Central American Republics Independence Day, observed by Costa Rica, El Salvador, Guatemala, Honduras, and Nicaragua in commemoration of the overthrow of Spanish rule in 1821.

16 Anniversary of the death of Anne Bradstreet on September 16, 1672. American poet, first woman of letters in America. 825.

16 Birthday of Alfred Noyes (September 16, 1880–June 28, 1958). English poet whose work has been set to music by Edward Elgar and others. Noyes's best known single poem is *The Highwayman*.

16 Birthday of Sir Anthony Panizzi (September 16, 1797–April 8, 1879). Librarian of the British Museum, who designed its reading room and was responsible for the acquisition of some of its first treasures.

16 Birthday of Francis Parkman (September 16, 1823–November 8, 1893). Distinguished American historian and author. Elected to the Hall of Fame for Great Americans in 1915. 237, 986.

16 Cherokee Strip Day, a holiday in Oklahoma in commemoration of the great land rush of September 16, 1893, when the Cherokee territory in northcentral Oklahoma was opened for settlement.

16 Malaysia Independence Day, a holiday in Malaysia celebrating the achievement of sovereignty on September 16, 1963.

c16 Mexican Declaration of Independence Day, a legal holiday in Mexico comparable in significance to July 4 in the United States, with celebrations beginning on September 15; the president of Mexico gives the famed *grito*, the cry of independence, during the major ceremonies.

16 Singapore Independence Day, a holiday in Singapore honoring the sovereignty that was achieved on September 16, 1963.

16 American Legion Charter Day, anniversary of the chartering by Congress on September 16, 1919, of the American Legion, composed of honorably discharged veterans. It was founded during a caucus of members of the First Expeditionary Force held from March 15–17, 1919.

16 Anniversary of the sailing of the Pilgrims on the *Mayflower* from Plymouth, England, on September 16, 1620, bound for the New World.

17 Citizenship Day, honoring new Americans, replaced "I Am an American Day" and Constitution Day in the United States in 1952; proclaimed annually by the president of the United States; it is the beginning of Constitution Week. 382–92.

17 Steuben Day, commemorating the birth, on September 17, 1730, of Friedrich von Steuben, a German officer charged with training the Continental forces in the American Revolution; observed in the major cities of the United States. 764–69.

18 Feast day of Saint Joseph of Cupertino, patron saint of aviators.

18 Birthday of Samuel Johnson (September 18, 1709–December 13, 1784). English poet, essayist, critic, and dictionary maker, author of the *Rambler* and *Lives of the Poets*; his birthday is celebrated annually in his hometown of Lichfield, England. 986, 987.

18 Birthday of Joseph Story (September 18, 1779–September 10, 1845). American jurist, associate justice of the United States Supreme Court whose writings helped to form American legal thought. Elected to the Hall of Fame for Great Americans in 1900. 237.

18 Birthday of Clark Wissler (September 18, 1870–August 25, 1947). American anthropologist, the first to develop a systematic concept of culture areas, which he used in studying and writing many fine books about the American Indian.

c18 Chile Independence Day, a holiday extending over several days; Fiestas de la Patria celebrate the termination of allegiance to Spain on September 18, 1810, and the achievement of independence in 1818.

19 Feast day of Saint Januarius, patron saint of blood banks; patron saint of Naples.

19 Birthday of Charles Carroll (September 19, 1737–November 14, 1832). American Revolutionary leader; signer of the Declaration of Independence. He represents the state of Maryland in Statuary Hall in a sculpture done by Richard Edwin Brooks. 242, 478, 479, 487.

19 Birthday of Arthur Rackham (September 19, 1867–September 6, 1939). English artist whose illustrations of literary classics, such as *Grimm's Fairy Tales*, have attracted worldwide appreciation.

19 Chilean Army Day, a public holiday in Chile, celebrated as a part of the Independence Day honors and festivities of September 18.

20 Anniversary of the founding of the Equal Rights party in San Francisco on September 20, 1884.

c20 Harvest-Moon Days, the period of the full moon closest to the autumn equinox; a time for traditional harvest festivals.

21 The Feast of Saint Matthew, apostle and evangelist, celebrated in the Roman Catholic, Anglican, and Lutheran churches, honors the tax collector who became an apostle. Saint Matthew, author of the First Gospel is the patron saint of bankers, tax collectors, and customs officers.

21 Birthday of Charles Jean Henri Nicolle (September 21, 1866–February 28, 1936). French physician and bacteriologist; awarded the 1928 Nobel Prize in physiology and medicine for his work on typhus. 238.

21 Birthday of Kwame Nkrumah (September 21, 1909–April 27, 1972). President of Ghana; first to lead an African country to independence; author of *Toward Colonial Freedom*, and *Africa Must Unite*.

21 Birthday of Girolamo Savonarola (September 21, 1452–May 23, 1498). Italian religious reformer.

21 Birthday of Herbert George Wells (September 21, 1866–August 13, 1946). English novelist, sociological writer, and historian whose most important work of nonfiction is the *Outline of History*. 986.

21 Malta Independence Day, a public holiday in Malta honoring the achievement of independence on September 21, 1964.

21 Press Sunday, a day of tribute to the freedom of the press and to the first newspapers published in the United States.

21 World Peace Day, sponsored by the Spiritual Assembly of the Baha'is of the United States to encourage American leadership in world peace.

22 Birthday of Michael Faraday (September 22, 1791–August 25, 1867). English scientist who made the greatest electrical discovery of all time, the generation of electricity by means of magnetism.

22 Mali Independence, or National Festival of the Republic, Day, celebrated to honor September 22, 1960, when Mali achieved independence, replacing its earlier status as the territory of French Sudan.

23 Birthday of John Lomax (September 23, 1870–January 26, 1948). American folklorist; collector of folk songs; founder of the American Folklore Society and its first president.

23 Birthday of William Holmes McGuffey (September 23, 1800–May 4, 1873). American educator; author of the *Eclectic Readers*, which are collector's items.

23 Birthday of John Sevier (September 23, 1745–September 24, 1815). American pioneer and soldier who was famous as an Indian fighter. He represents the state of Tennessee in Statuary Hall in a sculpture done by Belle Kinney Scholz and Lee F. Scholz. 242.

c23 Autumnal Equinox Day, a holiday in Japan that is observed either on September 23 or 24 to celebrate the first day of autumn and to memorialize family ancestors.

23 Saudi Arabia Unification Day, a holiday in Saudi Arabia celebrating the uniting on September 23, 1932, of the political units that now make up the nation.

23 Frontier Day, anniversary of the first frontier celebration, held in Cheyenne, Wyoming, on September 23, 1897, later extended to a week-long event. Frontier Days are now observed in many communities and counties in the United States on varying dates or weeks.

24 Feast day of Nuestra Señora de las Mercedes, a holiday in the Dominican Republic and in Peru; known as Mercedes Day.

24 Birthday of Francis Scott Key Fitzgerald (September 24, 1896–December 21, 1940). American novelist, identified with the "lost-generation school," whose novel *This Side of Paradise* was one of the most famous books in the 1920s. 986.

24 Birthday of John Marshall (September 24, 1755–July 6, 1835). American lawyer, jurist, fourth chief justice of the Supreme Court, founder of the American system of constitutional law. He was elected to the Hall of Fame for Great Americans in 1900. 237.

24 Schwenkenfelder Thanksgiving Day, observed by the members of the Schwenkenfelder Society in the Pennsylvania Dutch country in commemoration of the safe arrival of its first members in 1733 and 1734.

25 Birthday of William Faulkner (September 25, 1897–July 6, 1962). American novelist; author of the series known as the "Yoknapatawpha cycle"; awarded the Nobel Prize in literature in 1955. 226, 986.

25 Birthday of Thomas Hunt Morgan (September 25, 1866–December 4, 1945). American biologist; one of the chief founders of modern genetics; awarded the 1933 Nobel Prize in physiology and medicine. 238.

25 Government Day, or National Assembly Day, a public holiday in Rwanda marking the opening of sessions of the National Assembly.

25 Pacific Ocean Day, the anniversary of the discovery of the Pacific Ocean by Vasco Nuñez de Balboa on September 25, 1513.

26 Feast of Martyrs of North America, honors eight priests who lost their lives trying to bring the Christian faith to the American Indians.

26 Birthday of Edith Abbott (September 26, 1876–July 28, 1957). American social worker, dean of the University of Chicago School of Social Service Administration, authority on public assistance and immigration problems.

26 Birthday of Thomas Stearns Eliot (September 26, 1888–January 4, 1965). Poet and playwright renowned for *The Waste Land*; awarded the Nobel Prize in literature in 1948. 226, 227.

26 Birthday of George Gershwin (September 26, 1898–July 11, 1937). American composer famed for such compositions as *Rhapsody in Blue* and *Porgy and Bess*. 983, 1002.

26 Bandaranaike Day, a tribute to Solomon Bandaranaike, prime minister of Ceylon, who was assassinated on September 26, 1959; a public holiday in Sri Lanka, formerly Ceylon.

c26 Ceremony of the Dead, a two-day public holiday in the Khmer Republic, formerly Cambodia.

26 Proclamation of the Republic Day, a public holiday in the Yemen Arab Republic, commemorating the declaration of the republic on September 26, 1962.

26 Anniversary of the dedication on September 26, 1972, of the American Museum of Immigration, housed in the base of the Statue of Liberty in the New York harbor.

27 Feast day of Saint Cosmas, patron saint of barbers and druggists. 705.

27 Birthday of Samuel Adams (September 27, 1722–October 2, 1803). American patriot, signer of the Declaration of Independence, governor of Massachusetts. Represents Massachusetts in Statuary Hall in a sculpture done by Anne Whitney. 242, 976.

27 Birthday of Sándor Kisfaludy (September 27, 1772–October 28, 1844). Hungarian poet who is considered the founder of the Hungarian school of lyric poetry.

27 Birthday of Alfred Thayer Mahan (September 27, 1840–December 1, 1914). American naval officer and historian whose major work is *The Influence of Sea Power upon History.*

27 Birthday of Thomas Nast (September 27, 1840–December 7, 1902). American illustrator and cartoonist whose work so influenced politics, and public opinion that Abraham Lincoln called him "our best recruiting sergeant"; creator of the donkey and elephant emblems of the Democratic and Republican parties.

c27 American Indian Day, observed on the fourth Friday of September in many regions of the United States; first proclaimed in 1916. 170–83.

28 The Fiesta of San Miguel, celebrated in San Miguel de Allende, Mexico, a four-day fete lasting from September 28 to October 1.

28 Birthday of Georges Clemenceau (September 28, 1841–November 24, 1929). French editor and statesman who presided at the Versailles Peace Conference; called "le Tigre" and "le Pere de la Victoire" by his fellow Frenchmen.

28 Birthday of Francis Turner Palgrave (September 28, 1824–October 24, 1897). English poet and critic best known for his classic anthology the *Golden Treasury of the Best Songs and Lyrical Poems in the English Language.*

28 Birthday of Kate Douglas Wiggin (September 28, 1856–August 24, 1923). American educator and author; cofounder of the first free kindergarten in the Far West, who started to write books for children in her own school. She is remembered for *The Birds' Christmas Carol* and for *Rebecca of Sunnybrook Farm.*

28 Birthday of Frances Elizabeth Caroline Willard (September 28, 1839–February 18, 1898). American temperance reformer, editor, author, and president of the Woman's Christian Temperance Union. Elected to the Hall of Fame for Great Americans in 1910. 237.

28 Confucius' Birthday, or Teachers' Day, a public holiday in Taiwan (Republic of China).

28 Referendum Day, a public holiday in Guinea, on the west coast of Africa, commemorating the public vote, on September 28, 1958, for complete independence.

c28 Cabrillo Day, observed in California as part of a six-day festival honoring Juan Rodriguez Cabrillo, Portuguese navigator, who discovered California on September 28, 1542.

c28 Good Neighbor Day, observed on the fourth Sunday of September in the United States to promote understanding and good relationships.

28 Kiwanis Kid Day, observed by the clubs of Kiwanis International in tribute to children and youth as the promise of the future.

29 Michaelmas Day, the Feast of Saint Michael, honoring Michael "the Warrior Saint" as representative of all angels, is celebrated in the Roman Catholic, Anglican, and Lutheran churches on the day, September 29, in the fifth century when the first church in Italy was dedicated in honor of Michael. Saint Michael is the patron saint of policemen, grocers, paratroopers, and radiologists.

29 Birthday of Enrico Fermi (September 29, 1901–November 28, 1954). Italian physicist, noted for his studies in nuclear physics, his work on the atomic-bomb project, and his teaching at the Institute of Nuclear Studies at the University of Chicago. He was awarded the 1938 Nobel Prize in physics for his research in radioactive substances. 241.

29 Birthday of Horatio Nelson (September 29, 1758–October 21, 1805). English admiral who is remembered for his battle-signal "England expects that every man will do his duty"; the monument to Nelson in Trafalgar Square is one of the best-known monuments in the world.

29 Battle of Boquerón Day, a public holiday in Paraguay commemorating the end of a 1930 border conflict.

29 Brunei Constitution Day, a public holiday in Brunei, a British-protected sultanate on the northeast coast of Borneo; honors the promulgation of the constitution on September 29, 1959.

c29 Gold Star Mothers Day, observed on the last Sunday of September by presidential proclamation to honor the mothers "whose sons and daughters died in line of duty in the Armed Forces of the United States."

30 Feast day of Saint Jerome, patron saint of students of Scripture, and of librarians. Jerome, whose translation of the Bible into Latin is known as the "Vulgate," is venerated as a Doctor of the Church. 705.

30 Botswana Day, a holiday commemorating September 30, 1966, when the Bechuanaland Protectorate became the thirtieth African nation to receive full independence as the Republic of Botswana.

October

October, the tenth month in the Gregorian calendar, received its name from the Latin numeral *octo*, meaning "eight," because in the days of the old Roman calendar it was the eighth month.

One of the notable days in October is Columbus Day, October 12, honoring the discovery of America by the Italian map-maker and explorer, Christopher Columbus. It is celebrated as Discovery Day in Central and South America and was set aside as a holiday in the United States in 1892 by President Harrison.

Hawaii has a special October event called "the Aloha Festival," sometimes described as the "Mardi Gras of the Pacific." It is observed with pageantry, street dancing, hula festivals, luaus, parades, and fancy balls.

October gave its name to one of the best-known German fall festivals. Oktoberfest started on October 17, 1810, the wedding day of King Ludwig I. It still retains the name, even though the festivities may start in September, with October having only a partial share of the time schedule.

An important October day for the entire world is October 24, United Nations Day, which commemorates the founding of the United Nations on October 24, 1945. It is a holiday for many of the member nations and is generally observed by all nations as a way of publicizing the aims and achievements of the world organization.

The month ends with Halloween or All Hallow's Eve. It is a religious festival in some countries but a trick-or-treat night in the United States, when small children in costume roam through their neighborhoods to solicit candy or cookies.

The flowers for October are the calendula and the cosmos. The birthstones are the opal and the tourmaline.

The Fixed Days of October

1 Birthday of Annie Besant (October 1, 1847–September 20, 1933). English theosophist and philosophical writer who, through long residence in India, was instrumental in acquainting Europeans with Hindu thought.

1 Birthday of Rufus Choate (October 1, 1799–July 13, 1859). American lawyer, author, and statesman; preeminent among American advocates. Elected to the Hall of Fame for Great Americans in 1915. 237.

1 Birthday of John Peter Gabriel Muhlenberg (October 1, 1746–October 1, 1807). American revolutionary general, Lutheran pastor, and congressman. He represents the state of Pennsylvania in Statuary Hall in a sculpture done by Blanche Nevin. 242.

1 Cameroon Unification Day, commemorating the joining of East and West Cameroon into the United Republic of Cameroon on October 1, 1961.

1 Day of the Caudillo, observed in Spain to mark the establishment of the Spanish state by General Francisco Franco on October 1, 1936.

1 Korean Armed Forces Day, a public holiday in South Korea honoring the armed forces of the Republic of Korea.

1 Nigerian Independence Day, a public holiday in Nigeria honoring the achievement of independence on October 1, 1960, and the achievement of republic status on October 1, 1963.

c1 The People's Republic of China National Day, a public holiday in mainland China on October 1 and 2, commemorating the establishment of Communist China on October 1, 1949.

1 Agricultural Fair Day, the anniversary of the first agricultural fair in the United States, the Berkshire Cattle Show, held at Pittsfield, Massachusetts, on October 1, 1810. Launched with a quotation from George Washington that "the multiplication of useful animals is a common blessing to mankind," it became the forerunner of the state fairs of today.

c1 The Ak-Sar-Ben Days are celebrated annually at Omaha, Nebraska, during the first part of October by the Knights of Ak-Sar-Ben, a civic organization founded in 1894 to promote patriotism among citizens.

2 Feast of the Guardian Angels, celebrated in the Roman Catholic Church in honor of the guardian angels of individuals, cities, and provinces.

2 Birthday of Mohandas Karamchand Gandhi (October 2, 1869–January 30, 1948). Hindu statesman and spiritual leader whose anniversaries are commemorated by his countrymen and honored throughout the world. 986.

2 Birthday of Cordell Hull (October 2, 1871–July 23, 1955). American statesman, United States secretary of state, contributor to "good-neighbor" policies, planner of a postwar world organization, known as the "Father of the United Nations"; recipient of the Nobel Peace Prize in 1945. 241.

2 Birthday of Ruth Bryan Rohde (October 2, 1885–July 26, 1954). American public official, congresswoman, and first woman ever appointed to head a United States diplomatic post, serving as minister to Denmark for three years.

2 Gandhi Jayanti, a public holiday celebrated in India in honor of the birthday of Mahatma Gandhi.

2 Guinea Republic Day, a public holiday, anniversary of the proclamation of the Republic of Guinea on October 2, 1958.

c2 Missouri Day, observed throughout the state of Missouri on the first Monday in October to commemorate the state's history with special programs and exercises. 741.

3 Feast day of Saint Thérèse de Lisieux, patron saint of foreign missions and of aviators; secondary patron of France; known as the "Little Flower."

3 Birthday of George Bancroft (October 3, 1800–January 17, 1891). American diplomat, historian, and public official. Author of *History of the United States*, which he treated as an illustration of a divine plan for democracy, freedom, and equality. Served as United States minister to Great Britain, to Prussia, and to the German empire. Elected to the Hall of Fame for Great Americans in 1910. 237.

3 Birthday of William Crawford Gorgas (October 3, 1854–July 4, 1920). American sanitarian, surgeon-general of the United States Army, famous for his success in controlling yellow fever, an achievement that permitted the completion of the Panama Canal. He was elected to the Hall of Fame for Great Americans in 1950. 237.

3 Birthday of John Gorrie (October 3, 1803–June 16, 1855). American physician and inventor; an innovator in artificial cooling for hospitals and mechanical refrigeration. He represents the state of Florida in Statuary Hall in a sculpture done by C. Adrian Pillars. 242.

3 Birthday of Sir Patrick Manson (October 3, 1844–April 9, 1922). British physician and parasitologist who is known as "the Father of Tropical Medicine."

3 Anniversary of the death of Myles Standish on October 3, 1656. English colonist in America whose memory has been perpetuated by Longfellow's *The Courtship of Miles Standish.*

3 Independence Day in Iraq, a public holiday commemorating the termination on October 3, 1932, of a ten-year training period in self-government.

3 Korean National Foundation Day, a special day in South Korea commemorating the mythical founding of Korea by Gangun in 2333 B.C.

3 Morazán Day, a holiday in Honduras in honor of Francisco Morazán, early nineteenth-century Honduran statesman whose dream was a unified Central America.

3 Leyden Day, observed in the Netherlands and by the Holland Society of New York to commemorate the lifting of the Siege of Leyden in 1573–74, through a tempest that carried the Spanish fleet out into the ocean.

4 Feast day of Saint Francis of Assisi, patron saint of Italy, of Catholic action, and of merchants. Saint Francis, brother to men, animals, and birds, and founder of the Franciscan order, is universally honored. Pilgrimages to Assisi are particularly popular.

4 Birthday of Rutherford Birchard Hayes (October 4, 1822–January 17, 1893). Scottish ancestry; Ohio lawyer; Civil War soldier; governor of Ohio; nineteenth president of the United States, 1877–81. Methodist. Buried at Fremont, Ohio. 667–72, 674–76, 678, 679.

4 Birthday of Frederic Remington (October 4, 1861–December 26, 1909). American artist and author famous for his on-site drawings and paintings of frontier life, Indians, and horses. 986.

4 Lesotho Independence Day, a public holiday honoring October 4, 1966, when Basutoland became a sovereign member of the British Commonwealth under the name of the Kingdom of Lesotho.

4 Anniversary of the launching of *Sputnik I*, the first artificial satellite, sent into orbit by the Russians on October 4, 1957, an event that stimulated widespread concern for scientific education.

5 Birthday of Chester Alan Arthur (October 5, 1831–November 18, 1886). Scotch-Irish ancestry; New York teacher and lawyer; vice-president succeeding the assassinated President Garfield; twenty-first president of the United States, 1881–85. Episcopalian. Buried at Albany, New York. 667–72, 674–76, 678, 679.

5 Birthday of Jonathan Edwards (October 5, 1703–March 22, 1758). American theologian, philosopher, and college president who has been called "the greatest American mind of the Colonial Period." He was elected to the Hall of Fame for Great Americans in 1900. 237.

5 Army Day, a holiday in Indonesia.

5 National Sports Day, a public holiday in Lesotho, formerly Basutoland.

5 Portuguese Republic Day, a public holiday in Portugal, honoring the proclamation of the republic on October 5, 1910.

6 Birthday of Albert Jeremiah Beveridge (October 6, 1862–April 27, 1927). American politician and author, best known for *The Life of John Marshall*. An Albert J. Beveridge Award is given by the American Historical Association for an outstanding book in history.

6 Birthday of George Westinghouse (October 6, 1846–March 12, 1914). American inventor who invented the air brake. Elected to the Hall of Fame for Great Americans in 1955. 237.

c6 Grandparents' Day, observed in Massachusetts on the first Sunday in October.

6 Universal Children's Day, a day of happiness for children in Malaysia, featuring bands, acrobatics, and awards to the most gallant children of the year.

6 Anniversary of the organization of the American Library Association on October 6, 1876, in Philadelphia.

7 Feast of the Most Holy Rosary and the commemoration of the Greek naval victory over the Turks at Lepanto on October 7, 1571, a day of commemoration in Greece.

7 Birthday of Martha McChesney Berry (October 7, 1866–February 27, 1942). American educator and founder of the Berry schools for children in the mountain districts around Georgia. The recipient of many awards; voted in 1931 one of the twelve greatest American women.

7 Birthday of James Whitcomb Riley (October 7, 1849–July 22, 1916). Known as "the Hoosier Poet"; considered by some critics as "the Burns of America." Among his many popular poems is *When the Frost is on the Punkin.* His birthday is an occasion for annual tributes in schools and communities in Indiana.

7 Birthday of Caesar Rodney (October 7, 1728–June 29, 1784). American patriot, signer of the Declaration of Independence who represents Delaware in Statuary Hall in a sculpture done by Bryant Baker. 242.

7 Constitution Day, a holiday in the German Democratic Republic (East Germany) commemorating the enactment of a constitution on October 7, 1949.

c7 Deed of Cession, a holiday in Fiji marking the ceding of Fiji to the British crown in 1874; celebrated around October 7.

c7 Child Health Day, observed on the first Monday of October by presidential proclamation; proclaimed for the first time in the United States on May 1, 1928.

8 Feast day of Saint Bridget, patron saint of Sweden, known for her heroic virtues; foundress of the Order of the Most Holy Saviour. 705.

8 Birthday of Eddie Rickenbacker (October 8, 1890–July 23, 1973). American aviator known as the "Ace of Aces" of World War I. Author of *Fighting the Flying Circus, Seven Came Through,* and an autobiography.

8 Peshtigo Fire Day, anniversary of the beginning on October 8, 1871, of the forest fire at Peshtigo, Wisconsin; considered to be one of the most disastrous fires in history.

9 Feast day of Saint Denis, patron saint of Paris and of France.

9 Birthday of Lewis Cass (October 9, 1782–June 17, 1866). American statesman, soldier, and author. Governor of the Michigan territory who improved relations with the Indians. He represents the state of Michigan in Statuary Hall in a sculpture done by Daniel Chester French. 242.

9 Birthday of Martin Elmer Johnson (October 9, 1884–January 13, 1937). American explorer and photographer of savage tribes and wild-animal life for the American Museum of Natural History.

9 Day of National Dignity, a public holiday in Peru observing the October 9, 1968, governmental seizure of the oil fields on behalf of the Peruvian nation; the day is regarded as a second Independence Day.

9 Guayaquil's Independence Day, a national holiday in Ecuador, honoring October 9, 1820, when the city declared itself free from Spain.

9 Hangul Day, anniversary of the proclamation of the Korean alphabet devised by King Sejong in 1446; a public holiday in South Korea.

c9 Husain Day, commemorated by the Shiites, a branch of Islam, as a memorial to the martyrdom of Husain, grandson and third successor of Mohammed, on October 9, 680. The story of the martyrdom is recited in Moslem halls and is reenacted in religious dramas on succeeding days.

9 Khmer Republic Day, a public holiday commemorating the October 9, 1970, proclamation of the Khmer Republic, formerly Cambodia.

9 Leif Ericson Day, a holiday celebrated in Iceland and Norway to honor the landing of Norsemen in Vinland, New England, about A.D. 1000. Leif Ericson Day is observed by communities in Wisconsin, Minnesota, and other states in the United States. 439–43.

117

9 Uganda Independence Day, a national holiday commemorating the achievement of autonomy for the African nation of Uganda on October 9, 1962, after nearly seventy years of British rule.

c9 Fire Prevention Day, anniversary of the Chicago Fire of October 8–9, 1871; observed in the United States as a part of a week including October 9 dedicated to public information and fire-prevention education; by presidential proclamation.

9 Mission Dolores Founding Day, anniversary of the founding of the Mission San Francisco de Asis on October 9, 1776, a historic survivor of the 1906 San Francisco, California, earthquake and fire.

10 Birthday of Fridtjof Nansen (October 10, 1861–May 13, 1930). Norwegian Arctic explorer; awarded the 1922 Nobel Peace Prize. 241.

10 Birthday of Giuseppe Verdi (October 10, 1813–January 27, 1901). Italian operatic composer famous for *Aïda*, *Rigoletto*, *Il Trovatore*, and *La Traviata*. 986.

10 Birthday of Benjamin West (October 10, 1738–March 11, 1820). Anglo-American painter famous for historical paintings; one of the first to paint his subjects in contemporary dress rather than in Greek or Roman togas. 750, 986.

10 Aleksis Kivi Day, a school holiday in Finland commemorating the October 10, 1834, birth of the author of the greatest play (*Kullervo*) and the greatest novel (*Seitsemän veljestä*) in the Finnish language.

10 Double Tenth Day, a public holiday in Taiwan (Republic of China); commemorates the anniversary of the Proclamation of the Republic of Sun Yat-sen on October 10, 1911, and the anniversary of the revolts that overthrew the Manchu dynasty in 1911.

10 Kruger Day, a holiday in South Africa, honoring the October 10, 1825, birth of Paulus Kruger, South African statesman known as "Oom Paul."

10 Oklahoma Historical Day, honoring the first non-Indian settlement in Oklahoma, established in 1802.

10 Physical Education Day, or Sports Day, a public holiday in Japan, commemorating the Tokyo Olympics of 1964.

10 The Proclamation of Yara Day, a Cuban holiday commemorating a revolt stimulated by the declaration of the Plan of Yara on October 10, 1868.

10 Samuel Fraunces Memorial Day, established in memory of the first White House steward and the proprietor of the eighteenth-century inn that is one of New York's historic preservations.

10 Anniversary of the founding of the United States Naval Academy on October 10, 1845, at Annapolis, Maryland.

11 Birthday of Eleanor Roosevelt (October 11, 1884–November 7, 1962). American humanitarian; official United States delegate to the United Nations; wife of the thirty-second president of the United States; author of *This Is My Story* and other books. 825, 837, 992.

11 Birthday of Sir George Williams (October 11, 1821–November 6, 1905). English founder of the Young Men's Christian Association.

11 Panama Revolution Day, a public holiday in Panama commemorating the 1968 revolt.

11 Pulaski Memorial Day, a presidential proclamation day observed in Georgia, Illinois, Nebraska, and Wisconsin to commemorate the October 11, 1779, death of General Casimir Pulaski, native of Poland and hero of the American Revolution. 681–84.

11 Anniversary of the founding of the Daughters of the American Revolution on October 11, 1890.

11 Anniversary of the opening of the Second Vatican Council by Pope John XXIII on October 11, 1962.

12 Birthday of Helena Modjeska (October 12, 1840–April 9, 1909). Polish-American actress noted for Shakespearean roles who was barred from Poland because of her anti-Russian speeches.

12 Columbus Day, a public holiday in Spain, Central and South America, and forty-three states in the United States, has several names. It is called Discovery of America Day in the nations of the southern hemisphere and in Indiana, North Dakota, and Ohio. It is Fraternal Day in Alabama, Landing Day in Wisconsin, and Pioneers' Day in South Dakota. It is observed in the United States on the second Monday of October. 393–400.

12 Dia de la Raza, or the Day of the Race, a legal holiday in Mexico and Latin American countries in which tribute is paid to the contributions of Spanish civilization to the American continent.

c12 Discoverers' Day, a holiday in Hawaii honoring Pacific and Polynesian navigators and all other discoverers; observed on the second Monday of October.

12 Equatorial Guinea Independence Day, a public holiday in Equatorial Guinea in honor of the achievement of sovereignty on October 12, 1968, which ended its status as a Spanish colony.

c12 Farmers' Day in Florida, a legal holiday since 1915 in tribute to Florida agriculture; coincides with Columbus Day. The observances are those of a typical legal holiday.

c12 Thanksgiving Day in Canada, a public holiday celebrated on the second Monday of October.

c12 Virgin Islands-Puerto Rico Friendship Day, a holiday on the second Monday of October honoring the longstanding friendship between the two nations.

13 Feast day of Saint Edward, patron saint of England; observed with an impressive pilgrimage to his tomb in Westminster Abbey.

13 Assassination of the Hero of the Nation Day, a public holiday in Burundi commemorating the death of a popular twentieth-century leader and prime-minister elect, Prince Louis Rwagasore.

14 Birthday of Joseph Duveen (October 14, 1869–May 25, 1939). English art connoisseur who gave the British Museum the gallery in which the Elgin marbles are housed.

14 Birthday of Dwight David Eisenhower (October 14, 1890–March 28, 1969). Pennsylvania German ancestry; World War II general; statesman; Columbia University president; man of letters; thirty-fourth president of the United States, 1953–61; Presbyterian. Author of *The White House Years*. Buried at Abilene, Kansas. President Eisenhower's birthday has been designated as National Friendship Day in the United States. 667–76, 678–80, 996.

14 Birthday of William Penn (October 14, 1644–July 30, 1718). Founder of Pennsylvania and famed leader of the Society of Friends. Elected to the Hall of Fame for Great Americans in 1935. His birthday is observed in Pennsylvania on or near October 14, with events honoring him and the state that is named for him. 237.

14 Malagasy Republic Independence Day, honoring October 14, 1958, when Madagascar became an independent nation.

14 Peggy Stewart Day, observed in Maryland to honor the sinking of the tea-laden brig *Peggy Stewart* in Annapolis harbor on October 14, 1774, a protest against the stamp taxes.

14 Yemen National Day, a public holiday for the People's Democratic Republic of Yemen in honor of the revolts of 1962.

15 Feast day of Saint Teresa of Avila, patron saint of Spain, noted for her devotion to discipline and for her spiritual writings.

15 Birthday of Helen Maria Hunt Jackson (October 15, 1831–August 12, 1885). American author who is remembered for *Ramona*, a romance of Old California. A Ramona Pageant, a theatrical presentation of the novel, is presented at Hemet, California, in April and May.

15 Birthday of Friedrich Nietzsche (October 15, 1844–August 25, 1900). German philosopher whose most influential work is *Thus Spoke Zarathustra*. 986.

15 Birthday of Virgil (October 15, 70 B.C.–September 21, 19 B.C.). Roman poet, author of *The Aeneid*, the national epic of Rome. 986.

c15 Ether Day, commemorates the first public use of ether to deaden pain in a surgical operation, administered by Dr. William Thomas Green Morton in 1846. The day is observed periodically by the Massachusetts General Hospital in Boston.

15 White Cane Safety Day, dedicated to the visually handicapped by presidential proclamation.

15 World Poetry Day, a day of tribute established "to unite the nations of the world by the invisible ties of poetry." 850–70.

16 Feast day of Saint Gerard Majella, patron saint of mothers; saint of "happy delivery."

16 Birthday of David Ben-Gurion (October 16, 1886–December 6, 1973). Israel's first prime minister and leading statesman in the struggle to make Palestine a refuge for the Jewish people and an independent nation.

16 Birthday of Eugene Gladstone O'Neill (October 16, 1888–November 27, 1953). American playwright, the first to win the Nobel Prize in literature; a three-time recipient of the Pulitzer Prize in drama. 226, 986.

16 Birthday of Noah Webster (October 16, 1758–May 28, 1843). American lexicographer whose name is synonymous with *dictionary*.

16 National Heroes' Day, a public holiday in Jamaica.

16 National Boss Day, a day of tribute to employers; observed by women employees.

c16 National Day of Prayer, set aside by presidential proclamation for a day other than Sunday; observed around the third Wednesday of October.

17 Black Poetry Day, the anniversary of the birth on October 17, 1711, of Jupiter Hammon, the first Negro in the United States to publish his own poetry.

17 Burgoyne's Surrender Day, anniversary of the October 17, 1777, surrender at Saratoga, the turning point in the American Revolutionary War; observed in New York State.

17 Dessalines Day, a special day in Haiti commemorating the death on October 17, 1806, of Jean Jacques Dessalines, revolutionist who was proclaimed emperor of Haiti in 1805.

17 Mother's Day, a day of tribute in Malawi, formerly Nyasaland, with events and ceremonials for mothers.

18 Feast day of Saint Luke, evangelist, "the beloved physician," and author of the Third Gospel and the Acts of the Apostles; patron saint of doctors, painters, and artists in general, supposedly because he painted a portrait of the Virgin Mary from life, and/or because of his style of writing. His feast is observed by the Roman Catholic, Anglican, and Lutheran churches. 80, 705.

18 Birthday of Henri Louis Bergson (October 18, 1859–January 4, 1941). French philosopher whose book *Creative Evolution* became one of the classics of the twentieth century. Bergson received the 1927 Nobel Prize in literature. 227, 986.

18 Birthday of Florence Dahl Walrath (October 18, 1877–November 7, 1958). American humanitarian, founder of the Cradle Society, organized in 1923 to prepare children for adoption.

c18 Alaska Day, celebrated as a holiday in the forty-ninth state, to commemorate the formal transfer of Alaska to the United States on October 18, 1867; observed on the third Monday of October.

c18 Sweetest Day, observed on the third Saturday in October; originating as a day for spreading cheer among the unfortunate, it is now an occasion to remember any one with a kind act or remembrance.

19 Feast day of Saint Peter of Alcantara, patron saint of night watchmen.

19 Birthday of John McLoughlin (October 19, 1784–September 3, 1857). American pioneer in the Oregon territory. He represents the state of Oregon in Statuary Hall in a sculpture by Gifford MacGregor Proctor. 242.

19 Yorktown Day, observed at Yorktown, Virginia, in commemoration of the surrender of Cornwallis on October 19, 1781.

20 Feast day of Saint Irene, patron saint of young girls.

20 Birthday of John Dewey (October 20, 1859–June 1, 1952). American educator and philosopher whose watchword was "learning by doing."

20 Birthday of Sir Christopher Wren (October 20, 1632–February 25, 1723). English architect whose great public buildings include Saint Paul's Cathedral. 986.

20 Guatemala Revolution Day, a public holiday commemorating the revolution of October 20, 1944.

20 Kenyatta Day, a public holiday in Kenya, honoring Jomo Kenyatta, the nation's first prime minister, affectionately called the "Grand Old Man." 519.

21 Feast day of Saint Ursula, patron saint of teachers and young people in general; observed in many Roman Catholic countries, particularly El Salvador.

21 Birthday of Samuel Taylor Coleridge (October 21, 1772–July 25, 1834). English poet, critic, and philosopher. 986.

21 Birthday of Alfred Bernhard Nobel (October 21, 1833–December 10, 1896). Swedish chemist and engineer who invented dynamite and other explosives and left his fortune for the Nobel Prizes. *See also* Nobel Prize Presentation Day, December 10. 238, 241.

21 Honduras Army Day, observed in Honduras, sometimes called "Ousting of Lozano Diaz Day," commemorating an October 1956 revolt.

21 Sudan Revolution Day, a public holiday in the Sudan, celebrates the people's revolution of 1964.

22 Anniversary of the death of Jean Grolier de Servières on October 22, 1565. French bibliophile for whom the Grolier Society in New York is named and who is honored annually by the society on the anniversary of his death.

22 Birthday of Franz Liszt (October 22, 1811–July 31, 1886). Hungarian composer and pianist, famous for the *Hungarian Rhapsodies*, symphonic poems for orchestra, and many piano compositions. 986.

22 Jidai Matsuri, or Festival of the Eras, observed in Kyoto, Japan, since 1895 as a ceremonial day reviewing the main periods of Kyoto's and Japan's history from the eighth to the nineteenth centuries.

c22 Labour Day, a public holiday in New Zealand, observed on the last Monday in October.

22 Veterans' Day, a public holiday in Puerto Rico.

22 Anniversary of the Revocation of the Edict of Nantes by Louis XIV on October 22, 1685, which deprived the French Protestants of religious freedom and resulted in the Huguenot emigration to Holland and England and eventually to the United States.

22 Anniversary of the organization of the first chapter of the Sons of the American Revolution on October 22, 1875.

23 Birthday of Robert Bridges (October 23, 1844–April 21, 1930). Poet laureate of England, remembered especially for his work *The Testament of Beauty*. 986.

23 Chulalongkorn Day, a holiday in Thailand which commemorates the birthday of Rama V, a progressive ruler who lived from 1868–1910.

23 Swallows of Capistrano Day, the traditional day for swallows to leave the San Juan Capistrano Mission in California. *See also* Swallows Day, March 19.

24 Feast day of Saint Raphael the Archangel, patron saint of travelers and of the blind.

24 Birthday of Sarah Josepha Hale (October 24, 1788–April 30, 1879). American author and pioneer woman editor of *Godey's Lady's Book*. The Friends of the Richards Free Library at Newport, New Hampshire, present an annual award in her name to an individual who has made a lifetime contribution to literature associated with New England. 234, 825.

24 Birthday of Anton van Leeuwenhoek (October 24, 1632–August 26, 1723). Dutch microscopist and biologist; known as "the Father of Microscopy" and the first biological scientist. 977.

24 United Nations Day, commemorating the founding of the United Nations on October 24, 1945; a holiday in many of the member nations and generally observed in some way by all nations to inform the people of the world of the aims and achievements of United Nations. The day is a part of United Nations Week. The permanent United Nations headquarters building in New York City was dedicated on October 24, 1949. 782–88.

24 Zambia Independence Day, a public holiday of two-day's duration, celebrating October 24, 1964, when Northern Rhodesia became the independent Republic of Zambia.

24 Black Thursday, October 24, 1929, the day of the disastrous stock-market crash that was the starting point of the great depression of the 1930s.

25 Feast day of Saint Crispin, patron saint of shoemakers.

25 Birthday of Georges Bizet (October 25, 1838–June 3, 1875). French composer whose most famous work is the opera *Carmen*. 986.

25 Birthday of Richard Evelyn Byrd (October 25, 1888–March 11, 1957). American naval officer and polar explorer who made five important expeditions to the Antarctic. He received the Congressional Medal of Honor in 1926.

25 Birthday of Thomas Babington Macaulay (October 25, 1800–December 28, 1859). English essayist, poet, historian, and statesman, famous for *Horatius at the Bridge* and his *History of England*. 986.

25 Birthday of Pablo Ruiz Picasso (October 25, 1881–April 8, 1973). Spanish-born painter and sculptor; founder of the Cubist school and leader in the surrealistic movement in France.

25 Taiwan Restoration Day, commemorates the return of Taiwan to the Chinese Nationalists in 1945 after fifty years of Japanese occupation.

25 Thanksgiving Day in the Virgin Islands, celebrating the end of the hurricane season.

26 Feast day of Saint Demetrios, patron saint of Salonika, Greece, honored by the Greeks with annual ceremonials that had their origin in the Middle Ages.

26 South Vietnam Constitution and Republic Day, a holiday in South Vietnam commemorating the declaration of Vietnam as a republic on October 26, 1955, and the October 26, 1956, promulgation of a constitution.

26 International Red Cross Day, anniversary of the establishment of the worldwide Red Cross organization at an October 26, 1863, meeting of nations in Geneva.

27 Birthday of Theodore Roosevelt (October 27, 1858–January 6, 1919). Dutch ancestry; New York assemblyman; naturalist; conservationist; explorer; man of letters; twenty-sixth president of the United States, 1901–9. Awarded Nobel Peace Prize in 1906. Member of the Reformed Dutch church. Buried at Oyster Bay, New York. Elected to the Hall of Fame for Great Americans in 1950. 237, 667–72, 674–76, 678, 679.

27 Birthday of Dylan Marlais Thomas (October 27, 1914–November 9, 1953). British poet whose verse has been compared to surrealist painting. 986.

c27 Frances E. Willard Day, observed by temperance associations and schools on the fourth Friday in October to honor the American temperance leader.

27 Cuba Discovery Day, anniversary of the discovery of Cuba by Columbus on October 27, 1492.

27 Navy Day, anniversary of establishment of the American navy on October 27, 1775; observed as Navy Day since 1922.

28 Feast day of Saint Jude, patron saint of desperate cases.

28 The Feast of Saint Simon and Saint Jude, apostles, is celebrated in the Roman Catholic, Anglican, and Lutheran churches.

28 Birthday of Anna Elizabeth Dickinson (October 28, 1842–October 22, 1932). American orator known as the "Joan of Arc" of the Civil War.

28 Czechoslovakia Foundation of the Republic Day, a public holiday in Czechoslovakia, honoring the birth of the Czechoslovak state on October 28, 1918.

28 Ochi Day, a national day in Greece, commemorating the anniversary of the successful resistance to the Italian attack in 1940.

c28 Veterans' Day, a holiday, by presidential proclamation, observed by some states in the United States on the fourth Monday in October; observed by others on November 11. 796–805.

28 Statue of Liberty Dedication Day, anniversary of the dedication of the Statue of Liberty on October 28, 1886. 481.

29 Birthday of James Boswell (October 29, 1740–May 19, 1795). English author, famous as a diarist and as the biographer of Dr. Samuel Johnson. 986.

29 Anniversary of the death of Sir Walter Raleigh on October 29, 1618. English military and naval commander of expeditions to North America. A Sir Walter Raleigh Award is presented annually by the Historical Book Club of North Carolina for the best work of fiction by a North Carolinian. 234.

29 Turkish Republic Days, observed on October 29 and 30 in Turkey in honor of the proclamation of the republic in 1923.

29 Anniversary of the formation of the National Organization for Women (NOW), organized on October 29, 1966, "to press for true equality for all women in America."

30 Birthday of John Adams (October 30, 1735–July 4, 1826). English ancestry; Massachusetts teacher, lawyer, diarist, and letter writer; second president of the United States, 1797–1801. A Unitarian. Buried in First Unitarian Church at Quincy, Massachusetts. Elected to the Hall of Fame for Great Americans in 1900. 237, 667–72, 674–76, 678, 679.

31 Birthday of John Keats (October 31, 1795–February 23, 1821). English poet trained as a surgeon but turned to poetry. *The Eve of St. Agnes* and other poems assure him a permanent place in world literature. Keats, known as the "Poet's Poet," is buried in the Protestant cemetery in Rome. 986.

31 Birthday of Juliette Gordon Low (October 31, 1860–January 17, 1927). American youth leader and founder of the Girl Scouts in America.

31 Birthday of Sir George Hubert Wilkins (October 31, 1888–Nov. 30/ Dec. 1, 1958). Australian polar explorer; the first to fly an airplane in the Antarctic and to fly over both polar regions.

31 Nevada Admission Day, a legal holiday, celebrating Nevada's admission to the Union on October 31, 1864, as the thirty-sixth state.

31 Halloween, All Hallows' Eve, or Beggars' Night, a festival for children, known in the United States as Trickor-Treat night, when costumed youngsters roam their neighborhoods with open bags for treats and with soap for the windows of their absent or ungiving neighbors. 490–504.

31 National Magic Day, honoring the skills of magicians and commemorating the death of the great magician Harry Houdini on October 31, 1926.

c31 Reformation Day, commemorating Luther's signing of the theses. The Sunday preceding October 31 is usually observed as Reformation Sunday in Lutheran churches. Called "Luther's Theses Day" in some parts of Germany in memory of October 31, 1517, when Martin Luther posted his ninety-five theses in Wittenberg. 73.

31 UNICEF Day, a day set aside by presidential proclamation in the United States and observed in many nations for the purpose of aiding the United Nations International Children's Fund.

31 Youth Honor Day, observed in Iowa and in Massachusetts to honor young people.

November

November, the eleventh month in the Gregorian calendar, received its name from the Latin numeral *novem* because it was the ninth month in the Julian calendar.

The month of November includes the oldest special day to have originated in the United States. In 1621, Governor William Bradford of Massachusetts proclaimed a day for feasting, prayer, and thanksgiving. It had its forerunner in the harvest-home celebrations of England, but it was a very special day for the Pilgrims. The idea spread throughout the states but was not universally celebrated until Sarah Josepha Hale, the editor of *Godey's Lady's Book*, persuaded President Lincoln to issue a general proclamation in 1863. Since then, Thanksgiving Day has been observed as a holiday by all states and territories of the United States.

November also has a traditional day for revelry. It is Guy Fawkes Day, the anniversary of the November 5, 1605, gunpowder plot to blow up the English Parliament and the king. It is observed throughout England and in many parts of the British Commonwealth. It is a popular festival for children and students. It is said that the undergraduates at Oxford University fill the streets on Guy Fawkes night lighting fireworks. The students who get into trouble on this night are eligible to join the Bowler Hat Club, whose members vow to promote the use of the Bowler hat. In other parts of England, the celebration centers around big bonfires. In Nassau and in the Caribbean, Guy Fawkes parades are accompanied by calypso bands.

The chrysanthemum is the November flower, and the gem is the topaz.

The Fixed Days of November

1 All Saints Day, a prescribed holy day in Roman Catholic churches and a holiday in many Roman Catholic countries.

1 Birthday of Sholem Asch (November 1, 1880–July 10, 1957). American novelist famous for novels and plays in English and in Yiddish.

1 Birthday of Charles Brantley Aycock (November 1, 1859–April 4, 1912). American politician and educational reformer. Governor of North Carolina, best known for the establishment of a rural high-school system in that state. He represents North Carolina in Statuary Hall in a sculpture done by Charles Keck. 242.

1 Birthday of Stephen Crane (November 1, 1871–June 5, 1900). American author who is famous for the novel *The Red Badge of Courage.* 986.

1 Birthday of Crawford Williamson Long (November 1, 1815–June 16, 1878). American surgeon who pioneered in the use of ether for anesthesia. He represents the state of Georgia in Statuary Hall in a sculpture by J. Massey Rhind. 242.

1 Birthday of Carlos Saavedra Lamas (November 1, 1878–May 5, 1959). Argentine lawyer and statesman, president of the League of Nations Assembly, winner of the Nobel Peace Prize in 1936. 241.

1 Algerian Revolution Day, a public holiday in Algeria, commemorating the revolution begun by the National Liberation Front on November 1, 1954, against the French administration and armed forces.

c1 Commemoration of the Dead, a public holiday in San Marino, with ceremonies of respect for the dead.

1 Memorial Day in the Republic of Togo on the west coast of Africa; a public holiday.

1 Vietnam Revolution Day, anniversary of the November 1, 1963, revolt against the Diem regime, observed in the Republic of Vietnam (South Vietnam).

1 Author's Day, observed since November 1, 1928, by study clubs to honor the work of writers who have developed American literature and to encourage authors "to lend their talents to making a better America." 206–12.

2 All Souls' Day, a religious day of commemoration of all the souls of the faithful departed, observed in the Roman Catholic and Episcopal churches.

2 Día de Muertos, Day of the Dead, a memorial holiday in Mexico dedicated to the *difuntos mayores,* or adult dead; observed by family gatherings and graveside offerings and with traditional drama at theaters.

2 Birthday of Daniel Boone (November 2, 1734–September 26, 1820). American pioneer explorer, settler, and surveyor, subject of many books, honored particularly in the state of Kentucky. Elected to the Hall of Fame for Great Americans in 1915. 237.

2 Birthday of Warren Gamaliel Harding (November 2, 1865–August 2, 1923). Scotch-Dutch descent; Ohio newspaper editor and publisher; twenty-ninth president of the United States, 1921–23. Baptist. Buried at Marion, Ohio. 667–72, 674–76, 678, 679.

2 Birthday of James Knox Polk (November 2, 1795–June 15, 1849). Scotch-Irish ancestry; Tennessee lawyer; eleventh president of the United States, 1845–49; Methodist. Buried at Nashville, Tennessee. 667–72, 674–76, 678, 679.

2 Balfour Declaration Day, a semiholiday in Israel in commemoration of the establishment of a Jewish national home on November 2, 1917.

2 North Dakota Admission Day. North Dakota entered the Union on November 2, 1889, as the thirty-ninth state. 741.

2 South Dakota Admission Day. South Dakota entered the Union on November 2, 1889, as the fortieth state. 741.

2 Portugal's Dia de Finados, "Day of the Dead"; observed with special masses and processions to cemeteries, followed by open-air feasts of wine and chestnuts.

3 Feast day of Saint Hubert of Liége, patron saint of hunters, of the hunt, of dogs, and of victims of hydrophobia; especially honored at the Church of Saint Hubert in Luxembourg; Saint Hubert's mass officially opens the hunting season in Belgium.

3 Birthday of Stephen Fuller Austin (November 3, 1793–December 27, 1836). American pioneer and Texas colonizer. Represents the state of Texas in Statuary Hall in a sculpture done by Elisabet Ney. 242.

3 Birthday of William Cullen Bryant (November 3, 1794–June 12, 1878). American poet; one of the most influential newspaper editors of the mid-nineteenth century. His best-known poem is *Thanatopsis,* first published in 1817. Bryant was elected to the Hall of Fame for Great Americans in 1910. 237.

3 Cuenca Independence Day, a holiday in Ecuador honoring the declaration of independence for the city declared on November 3, 1820.

3 Culture Day, a national holiday in Japan established to encourage public interest in freedom and in cultural activities; prior to World War II, November 3 was reserved for the Emperor Meiji's birthday, honoring the man who led his country out of feudalism; the tribute to the emperor is still observed by older citizens in Tokyo.

3 Father of Texas Day, or Austin Day, observed in Austin, Texas, to honor Stephen Austin's birth in 1793.

3 Panamanian Independence Day, a public holiday in Panama commemorating separation from Colombia on November 3, 1903.

4 Feast day of Saint Charles Borromeo, patron saint of religious instruction; patron saint of libraries.

4 Birthday of James Fraser (November 4, 1876–October 11, 1953). American sculptor who designed the Indian head and buffalo on the pre-1938 United States five-cent coins and whose sculpture includes statues of Alexander Hamilton, General George Patton, Jr., and other famous Americans.

4 Birthday of Will Rogers (November 4, 1879–August 15, 1935). American humorist and author. Honored by Oklahoma, his native state, since 1947, with a legal holiday on his birthday that is officially called Will Rogers Day. He represents the state of Oklahoma in Statuary Hall in a sculpture done by Jo Davidson. 242, 689–92.

c4 Liberty Day, a holiday in the Virgin Islands, observed on the first Monday of November to honor the establishment in 1915 of the first press in the Virgin Islands.

4 Panama Flag Day, a holiday in Panama celebrated in conjunction with the nation's Independence Day on November 3.

4 Anniversary of the establishment on November 4, 1946, of the United Nations Educational, Scientific and Cultural Organization (UNESCO), an autonomous organization affiliated with the United Nations to enlist educational, scientific, and cultural institutions in the service of peace and the ennoblement of man. 784.

4 Victory of Vittorio Veneto, a day honoring the Italian Unknown Soldier, observed in Rome at the tomb in the monument to Victor Emmanuel II.

5 Feast day of Blessed Martin de Porres, patron saint of interracial understanding.

5 Birthday of Rui Barbosa (November 5, 1849–March 1, 1923). Brazilian statesman, jurist, essayist, and strong advocate of human and civil liberties whose private library has become a national shrine.

5 Birthday of Ida Minerva Tarbell (November 5, 1857–January 6, 1944). American biographer of Lincoln and author of the influential *History of the Standard Oil Company.* 982, 990.

c5 Election Day in the United States, the first Tuesday after the first Monday in November; a legal holiday in some states of the United States in years of general and presidential elections.

5 First Call for Independence Day, a holiday in El Salvador, commemorating the first battle for freedom from Spain led by Padre José Matias Delgado on November 5, 1811.

5 Guy Fawkes Day, the anniversary of the November 5, 1605, "Gunpowder Plot" to blow up Parliament and the king; observed in England and in other parts of the British Commonwealth with bonfires, fireworks, and revelries.

c5 Thanksgiving Day, a public holiday in Liberia, observed on the first Thursday of November.

6 Birthday of James Naismith (November 6, 1861–November 28, 1939). Canadian-American educator and physical-education leader who invented the game of basketball as a class assignment in 1891.

6 Birthday of Ignace Jan Paderewski (November 6, 1860–June 29, 1941). Polish pianist, composer, and statesman.

6 Gustavus Adolphus Day, a commemorative day in Sweden, honoring the great Swedish king who died in battle on November 6, 1632.

7 Feast day of Saint Willibrord, patron saint of Holland.

7 Birthday of Albert Camus (November 7, 1913–January 4, 1960). French author; recipient of the 1957 Nobel Prize in literature. 227.

7 Birthday of Marie Sklodowska Curie (November 7, 1867–July 4, 1934). Polish-French chemist and physicist, the only person whose name appears twice on the Nobel Prize list. 225, 843.

7 Birthday of Andrew Dickson White (November 7, 1832–November 4, 1918). American educator and diplomat; first president of Cornell University; cofounder and first president of the American Historical Association.

7 Soviet Revolution Day, a holiday in Russia and the member countries of the Union of Soviet Socialist Republics; celebrated on November 7 and 8 to honor the "Great October Revolution" of 1917.

8 Feast day of Saint Claude, patron saint of sculptors.

8 Saints, Doctors, Missionaries, and Martyrs Day, observed by the Church of England in memory and commemoration of the "unnamed saints of the nation."

8 Birthday of Edmund Halley (November 8, 1656–January 14, 1742). English astronomer who won lasting fame for his studies of comets.

8 Birthday of Margaret Mitchell (November 8, 1900–August 16, 1949). American novelist famous for *Gone with the Wind*, which was awarded the 1937 Pulitzer Prize in fiction.

8 Montana Admission Day. Montana entered the Union on November 8, 1889, as the forty-first state. 741.

8 Dunce Day, the anniversary of the November 8, 1308, death of Duns Scotus, medieval scholastic, responsible for the introduction of the word *dunce* into the language; a day of recognition of the folly of being a dunce.

9 Birthday of Elijah Parish Lovejoy (November 9, 1802–November 7, 1837). American newspaperman killed in a mob attack on his presses; known as "the martyr abolitionist" of the Civil War period.

9 Crystal Night, the anniversary of the street riots of November 9 and 10, 1938, when Nazi storm troopers raided Jewish homes and synagogues; the name came from the shattering of glass in Jewish homes and stores.

c9 The Lord Mayor's Day, held annually on the second Saturday of November; dates from 1215; a day of civic pageantry in which the lord mayor of London drives in state to the Guildhall for ceremonials and on to the law courts to take the oath of office. 164.

9 Sadie Hawkins Day, a fun day created in the mind of Alfred Gerald Caplin, cartoonist popularly known as Al Capp, for his comic strip *Li'l Abner*; introduced on November 9, 1938, as an occasion upon which the spinsters of Dogpatch might rightfully pursue the unattached males; observed on occasion by students and social groups.

9 Tree Festival Day, an Arbor Day and national agricultural festival in Tunisia.

10 Anniversary of the death of Kemal Atatürk on November 10, 1938. Turkish patriot, founder and first president of the Turkish Republic; known as "the Father of the Turks."

10 Birthday of Sir Jacob Epstein (November 10, 1880–August 21, 1959). Anglo-American sculptor who gained fame with his controversial bronze figures and unidealized portraits. 986.

10 Birthday of Oliver Goldsmith (November 10, 1730–April 4, 1774). Irish author remembered for *The Vicar of Wakefield, She Stoops to Conquer*, and *The Deserted Village*. 986.

10 Birthday of Nicholas Vachel Lindsay (November 10, 1879–December 5, 1931). American poet remembered as the vagabond poet who wrote *General William Booth Enters into Heaven* and *The Congo*. He was the first American poet invited to appear at Oxford University. 986.

10 Birthday of Martin Luther (November 10, 1483–February 18, 1546). German religious reformer and translator of the Bible whose stand led to the establishment of the Lutheran church. Also famous for the writing of hymns, of which *A Mighty Fortress Is Our God* is the most familiar. Luther Day is observed by the Protestants of Germany and commemorated by Lutheran churches on November 10.

10 Death of Iman Ali Day, a public holiday in Iran, a day of commemoration for a spiritual leader considered by some followers to be the only true successor to the Prophet.

c10 Guru Nanak's Day, a public holiday in India honoring the contributions of a fifteenth-century spiritual leader, first teacher of the Sikhs.

10 Hero Day, also called Youth Day, celebrated as a holiday in Indonesia honoring both the nation's patriots and the youth of the nation.

10 Anniversary of the first nationwide observance of Book Week on November 10, 1919; observed continually ever since during a selected week in November. Originally proposed by Franklin K. Mathiews, librarian, Boy Scouts of America, in a convention speech.

10 Birthday of the United States Marine Corps, celebrated annually by the Marines to commemorate the founding of the corps on November 10, 1775.

11 Feast day of Saint Martin of Tours, patron saint of soldiers, horsemen, tailors, beggars, and reformed drunkards. Saint Martin is the special guardian of vine growers, tavern keepers, harvest foods, and festivals; Saint Martin's Day is Beggar's Day in the Netherlands, with children pretending to be beggars as they go from door to door.

11 Birthday of Fyodor Dostoyevsky (November 11, 1821–February 9, 1881). Russian novelist famed for such books as *The Brothers Karamazov* and *Crime and Punishment*. 986.

11 Birthday of Ephraim McDowell (November 11, 1771–June 25, 1830). American surgeon; pioneer in abdominal surgery who performed the first recorded ovariotomy in the United States. He represents the state of Kentucky in Statuary Hall in a sculpture by Charles Henry Niehaus. 242.

11 Armistice Day, a public holiday in Belgium and in France commemorating the end of World War I. *See also* Remembrance Day; Veterans Day.

11 Cartagena Day, a holiday in Colombia honoring the proclamation of November 11, 1811, declaring the separation of the city of Cartagena from Spain.

11 Concordia Day, a day of commemoration in the island of Saint Maarten in the Caribbean honoring the 1648 agreement to divide the island between the Dutch and the French.

11 Remembrance Day, a public holiday in Canada commemorating the end of World Wars I and II.

11 Rhodesia Independence Day, a holiday commemorating the unilateral declaration of independence proclaimed on November 11, 1965, on behalf of the African nation.

c11 Veterans' Day, formerly called Armistice Day in the United States, honors the members of the Armed Forces who saw service in World Wars I and II and in Korea; some states observe the holiday on November 11; the majority of the states celebrate it on the fourth Monday of October. 796–805.

11 Washington State Day, a holiday in commemoration of Washington's admission to the Union as the forty-second state on November 11, 1889. 741.

11 Anniversary of the entombment of the Unknown Soldier of World War I in the Tomb of the Unknowns at Arlington, Virginia, on November 11, 1921. An Unknown Soldier of World War II and one from the Korean conflict were interred in crypts on either side of the Tomb of the Unknown Soldier on Memorial Day, 1958. 800.

12 Birthday of Bahaullah (Mirza Husayn Ali), November 12, 1817–May 29, 1892. Persian-born teacher and leader of the Baha'i faith.

12 Birthday of Juana Inés de La Cruz (November 12, 1651–April 12, 1695). Mexican poet-nun considered to be the greatest woman of the colonial period of Spanish America, next to Rose of Lima; known as "the first feminist of Spanish America."

129

12 Birthday of Elizabeth Cady Stanton (November 12, 1815–October 26, 1902). American woman-suffrage reformer. Her birthday is observed by women's organizations as Elizabeth Cady Stanton Day. 823, 825, 976.

12 Birthday of Sun Yat-sen (November 12, 1866–March 12, 1925). Leader of the Chinese Nationalist party; his birthday is a national holiday in Taiwan, the Republic of China.

12 Austrian Republic Day, observed in Austria in honor of November 12, 1918, when Austria declared itself a republic.

12 Bermuda Remembrance Day, a public holiday in Bermuda.

13 Birthday of Edwin Thomas Booth (November 13, 1833–June 7, 1893). American tragedian famous for his interpretation of *Hamlet.* Founded the Players in 1888, a famous club for actors. Elected to the Hall of Fame for Great Americans in 1925. 237.

13 Birthday of Louis Dembitz Brandeis (November 13, 1856–October 5, 1941). American associate justice of the United States Supreme Court, for whom Brandeis University, inaugurated in 1948, was named. 572, 825.

13 Birthday of Robert Louis Stevenson (November 13, 1850–December 3, 1894). Scottish novelist, poet, and essayist famous for *Treasure Island, A Child's Garden of Verses,* and many other books. Known as "Tusitala," or "teller of tales," in Samoa, where he died at "Vailema," the destination of a literary pilgrimage for travelers in the area. 986.

13 The King's Birthday, a public holiday in Laos.

13 Anniversary of the publication on November 13, 1830, of *Old Ironsides* by Oliver Wendell Holmes, which prevented the scrapping of the battleship *Constitution,* now a national memorial in the United States.

14 Birthday of Robert Fulton (November 14, 1765–February 24, 1815). American artist, civil engineer, and inventor famous for the development of the steamboat. He was elected to the Hall of Fame for Great Americans in 1900. He represents the state of Pennsylvania in Statuary Hall in a sculpture done by Howard Roberts. 237, 242.

14 Birthday of Claude Monet (November 14, 1840–December 5, 1926). French landscape and still-life painter who applied scientific principles of light to the art of painting; considered one of the greatest landscape painters in the world. 986.

14 Birthday of Jawaharlal Nehru (November 14, 1889–May 27, 1964). First prime minister of independent India. 976.

14 Birthday of Adam Gottlob Oehlenschläger (November 14, 1779–January 20, 1850). Danish poet and dramatist; acclaimed the Danish national poet in 1849.

14 Birthday of Frederick Jackson Turner (November 14, 1861–March 14, 1932). American historian best known for *The Frontier in American History.* His work *The Significance of Sections in American History* received the Pulitzer Prize in 1933. 229.

14 Prince Charles's Birthday, a public holiday in Belize, formerly British Honduras, honoring the heir apparent of the British throne.

c14 Repentance Day, in West Germany, the Federal Republic of Germany, observed on the Wednesday before the third Sunday in November.

15 Feast day of Saint Albertus Magnus, patron saint of scholars, students, medical technologists, and scientists; known in his day as "Doctor Universalis" because of his extensive knowledge.

15 Feast day of Saint Leopold, observed in particular in Vienna and at Klosterneuburg with a wine festival and a pilgrimage to Saint Leopold's shrine. The popular name for Saint Leopold's Day is *Fasslrutschen.*

15 Birthday of Sir William Herschel (November 15, 1738–August 25, 1822). Anglo-German astronomer who built his own telescope and discovered the planet Uranus. His work was carried on with distinction by his son, Sir John Frederick William Herschel. 977.

15 Birthday of August Krogh (November 15, 1874–September 13, 1949). Danish physiologist who received the 1920 Nobel Prize in physiology and medicine. 238.

15 Birthday of Marianne Craig Moore (November 15, 1887–February 5, 1972). American poet; winner of the Pulitzer Prize in poetry in 1951, the 1952 National Book Award, and the 1953 gold medal of the National Institute of Arts and Letters; decorated by France for her translation of *The Fables of La Fontaine*.

15 Birthday of William Pitt, the elder (November 15, 1708–May 11, 1778). British statesman, known as "the Great Commoner"; advocate of a conciliatory policy toward the American colonies.

15 Proclamation of the Republic Day in Brazil, a holiday with military parades and ceremonies honoring the proclamation of November 15, 1889, which dethroned Dom Pedro II.

15 Seven-Five-Three Festival Day, observed by parents in Japan as a day of thanksgiving for the safety of girls, aged seven and three, and boys, aged five and three; a tradition that is a legacy from old Japan.

16 Feast of Saint Matthew, apostle, is observed in the Greek church on November 16.

16 Feast of Saint Paul of the Cross, founder of the Passionist order.

16 Birthday of William Christopher Handy (November 16, 1873–March 28, 1958). American composer best known for his *St. Louis Blues* and called "the Father of the Blues." 1002.

16 Oklahoma Statehood Day, honoring admission of Oklahoma to the Union as the forty-sixth state on November 16, 1907.

17 Feast of Saint Hilda, patron saint of business and professional women.

17 Zaire Army Day, a public holiday in Zaire, a republic in Central Africa.

18 Birthday of Louis Jacques Daguerre (November 18, 1789–July 10, 1851). French inventor famous for the development of a method of producing permanent pictures called the "daguerreotype process."

18 Birthday of Clarence Shepard Day (November 18, 1874–December 28, 1935). American author of *Life with Father*. A Clarence Day Award for "outstanding work in encouraging the love of books and reading" was established in 1960 by the American Textbook Publishers Institute and is administered by the American Library Association; the first recipient was Lawrence Powell, librarian, bibliophile, and author. 234.

18 Birthday of Asa Gray (November 18, 1810–January 30, 1888). American botanist, one of the great creators of a systematic American flora. He was elected to the Hall of Fame for Great Americans in 1900. 237.

18 Birthday of Jacques Maritain (November 18, 1882–April 28, 1973). French philosopher, teacher, and man of letters; renowned for his study of Saint Thomas Aquinas, *The Angelic Doctor*, and for such books as *True Humanism* and *Art and Scholasticism*.

18 Birthday of Nils Adolf Erik Nordenskjöld (November 18, 1832–August 12, 1901). Swedish Arctic explorer and geologist who participated in many expeditions into the polar regions and into the interior of Greenland.

18 Haitian Army Day, a holiday in Haiti commemorating November 18, 1803, when the Haitians defeated the French in the Battle of Vertières.

c18 World Fellowship Day, sponsored by the Young Women's Christian Association as a part of World Fellowship Week, the climax of a year-round program of cooperation among the YWCA's of sixty-nine countries.

19 Feast of Saint Elizabeth of Hungary, patron saint of charities for the poor and of bakers. 705.

19 Birthday of George Rogers Clark (November 19, 1752–February 13, 1818). American soldier and surveyor; conqueror of the Old Northwest during the Revolutionary War. A memorial bridge over the Wabash River at Vincennes, Indiana, is named in his honor. 739.

19 Birthday of James Abram Garfield (November 19, 1831–September 19, 1881). English ancestry; Ohio educator and congressman; general in the Civil War; twentieth president of the United States, November 1880 to September 1881. Shot after six and a half months in office. Disciple of Christ. Buried in Lake View Cemetery, Cleveland, Ohio. He represents the state of Ohio in Statuary Hall in a sculpture done by Charles Henry Niehaus. 242, 667–72, 674–76, 678, 679.

19 Birthday of Ferdinand Marie de Lesseps (November 19, 1805–December 7, 1894). French engineer and diplomat remembered as the planner and engineer of the Suez Canal, which opened in 1869.

19 Birthday of Albert Bertel Thorvaldsen (November 19, 1770–March 24, 1844). Danish sculptor whose best-known work is *Night and Morning*. Buried in the Thorvaldsen Museum in Copenhagen.

19 Discovery Day, Puerto Rico, a holiday in honor of the day Puerto Rico was discovered by Columbus on his second voyage in 1493.

19 Monaco National Day, a public holiday, is the national fete day honoring the official birthday of Prince Rainier III. The anniversary of his coronation in 1949 is also recalled on this day.

19 Equal Opportunity Day, anniversary of Lincoln's Gettysburg Address of November 19, 1863; ceremonies commemorating Lincoln's address are held at the National Cemetery under the sponsorship of the Sons of Union Veterans and the Lincoln Fellowship of Pennsylvania.

20 Birthday of Selma Lagerlöf (November 20, 1858–March 16, 1940). Swedish novelist; the first woman to receive the Nobel Prize in literature, which she was awarded in 1909. In 1914 she was elected to the Swedish Academy, the first woman to be admitted.

20 Birthday of Peregrine White (November 20, 1620–July 22, 1704). First child born in New England of English parents.

20 Mexico Revolution Day, anniversary of the Mexican Revolution of 1910, a legal holiday throughout Mexico commemorating the revolt of the common people against poverty and the dictatorship of Porfirio Diaz.

20 Rights of the Child Day, anniversary of the adoption of the Declaration of the Rights of the Child by the General Assembly of the United Nations on November 20, 1959.

21 Birthday of William Beaumont (November 21, 1785–April 25, 1853). American surgeon whose distinct contribution was a study of digestion and digestive processes through observation of a patient whose stomach was exposed because of a gunshot wound.

21 Birthday of Jean François Marie Voltaire (November 21, 1694–May 30, 1778). French author and freethinker known for the romance *Candide* and for his social-philosophical articles. 986.

21 North Carolina entered the Union as the twelfth state on November 21, 1789. 741.

22 Feast Day of Saint Cecilia, patron saint of musicians, religious music, and of organ builders, for whom many choirs and musical societies have been named; special concerts are presented in Rome on this day.

22 Anniversary of the death of Ann Bailey on November 22, 1825. American pioneer woman who became the heroine of Fort Lee, Virginia, when she rode one hundred miles in 1791 to secure gunpowder to save the fort from an Indian attack.

22 Birthday of Charles de Gaulle (November 22, 1890–November 9, 1970). French general, statesman, president and leader of the Fifth Republic; author of *The Edge of the Sword.* 996.

22 Birthday of George Eliot (Mary Ann Evans) (November 22, 1819–December 22, 1880). English novelist famous for her books *Silas Marner, Mill on the Floss*, and others, for which she is considered one of the most distinguished English novelists of her time. 986.

23 Feast day of Saint Clement, patron saint of stonecutters.

23 Feast day of Saint Felicitas, patron saint of barren women.

23 Birthday of José Clemente Orozco (November 23, 1883–September 7, 1949). Mexican painter, modern master of fresco painting. 986.

23 Birthday of Franklin Pierce (November 23, 1804–October 8, 1869). English ancestry; New Hampshire lawyer; fourteenth president of the United States, 1853–57. Episcopalian. Buried at Minot Cemetery, Concord, New Hampshire. 667–72, 674–76, 678–79.

23 Labor-Thanksgiving Day, a national holiday in Japan, originally established as a day of thanks, now a special day of rest for the Japanese people.

23 Repudiation Day in Maryland, commemorates Frederick County's refusal to observe the Stamp Act in 1765; a partial holiday in the county.

23 The anniversary of the founding of the Horatio Alger Society on November 23, 1961, to further the Algerian philosophy of "Strive and Succeed."

24 Anniversary of the death of John Knox on November 24, 1572. Scottish preacher, leader of the Protestant Reformation in Scotland.

24 Birthday of Friar Junípero Serra (November 24, 1713–August 28, 1784). Spanish priest-missionary, founder of the California missions. He represents the state of California in Statuary Hall in a sculpture done by Ettore Cadorin. Since 1948, a Serra pageant reenacting Father Junípero Serra's arrival at San Diego has been presented annually at the old mission near Carmel, California. 242.

24 Birthday of Zachary Taylor (November 24, 1784–July 9, 1850). English ancestry; Louisiana-born soldier, known as "Old Rough and Ready"; twelfth president of the United States, 1849–50, died after one year and four months in office. Episcopalian. Died in the White House. Buried near Louisville, Kentucky. 667–72.

24 Anniversary of the New Regime, a public holiday in Zaire honoring the November 24, 1964, end of rebellion and conflict and the start of a new governmental structure.

c24 Bible Sunday, observed in Protestant churches in the United States on the last Sunday in November.

c24 John F. Kennedy Day, observed in Massachusetts on the last Sunday in November as a memorial to the thirty-fifth president of the United States, a native son of Massachusetts.

c24 Onion Market Day, an autumn festival held on the fourth Monday of November in Bern, Switzerland, to commemorate the granting of market privileges to the men of Fribourg for their assistance in rebuilding Bern after the great fire of 1405.

25 Feast day of Saint Catherine of Alexandria, patroness of philosophers, jurists, maidens, and women students. Saint Catherine's Day in France is a day of laughter, with parades of the midinettes, Parisian shopgirls, in which the participants are girls of over twenty-five who pay lighthearted homage to Saint Catherine, the patron saint of old maids; the midinettes get the afternoon off on this day.

25 Birthday of Andrew Carnegie (November 25, 1835–August 11, 1919). American iron and steel manufacturer; benefactor of libraries.

25 Birthday of Pope John XXIII (November 25, 1881–June 3, 1963). The so-called interim Pope who began a new era in the Roman Catholic church in convoking the second Vatican Council and working for Christian unity.

25 Birthday of Carrie Nation (November 25, 1846–June 9, 1911). American temperance leader who used a hatchet to implement her campaign against saloons. 828.

26 Feast day of Saint John Berchmans, patron saint of altar boys.

26 Feast of Saint Leonard of Port Maurice, patron saint of home missions.

26 Lebanese Independence Day, a holiday in Lebanon commemorating the independence achieved on November 26, 1941, after twenty years of French rule.

c26 John Harvard day, commemorating the birth in 1607 of John Harvard, chief founder of Harvard, honoring his bequest of a library and funds for the new college.

26 Sojourner Truth Day, the anniversary of the death on November 26, 1883, of a leading black abolitionist of the nineteenth century who adopted the name Sojourner as a symbol of her lecture tours, which espoused abolition and women's rights. 1, 825.

27 Feast of the Miraculous Medal, a Roman Catholic observance that owes its origin to the apparitions made by Mary to Saint Catharine Laboure in 1830, during which the form and the elements of the Miraculous Medal were revealed.

27 Birthday of Robert R. Livingston (November 27, 1746–February 26, 1813). American statesman and jurist; member of the Continental Congress and chancellor of New York State, who administered Washington's first oath of office as president. Robert Livingston represents New York state in Statuary Hall in a sculpture by Erastus Dow Palmer. 242.

27 Birthday of José Asunción Silva (November 27, 1865–May 24, 1896). Colombian poet famous for *Nocturno III* and for his flexibility in verse forms, which had great influence on Spanish-American poetry. 986.

27 Birthday of Chaim Weizmann (November 27, 1874–November 9, 1952). Israeli statesman and scientist who was instrumental in the British formulation of the Balfour Declaration that a national home for the Jews would be established in Palestine; Israel's first president. Weizmann Day is observed on his birthday at Tel Aviv.

28 Birthday of Henry Bacon (November 28, 1866–February 16, 1924). American architect who specialized in the classic Greek style. One of his most important works is the Lincoln Memorial in Washington, D.C., completed in 1920.

28 Accession of the Ruler of Abu Dhabi, a public holiday in the United Arab Emirates extending along the coast of the Arabian Gulf.

28 Albanian Independence Day, a public holiday in Albania commemorating the proclamation of independence of November 28, 1912, issued at the end of the Balkan War that terminated Turkish rule. The observance is followed with Liberation Day activities on November 29.

28 Burundi Republic Day, a national holiday honoring November 28, 1966, when Prime Minister Michel Micrombero declared Burundi to be a republic.

28 Chad Republic Day, a holiday commemorating the proclamation of the republic of November 28, 1958, which gave Chad the status of a member state in the French community.

28 Independence Day in Mauritania, honoring November 28, 1960, as the day when the country achieved sovereignty after being a French protectorate and colony.

c28 Thanksgiving Day, a legal holiday in the United States, by presidential proclamation; a day of thanksgiving and praise observed by all states and territories on the fourth Thursday of November. 770–81.

29 Birthday of Louisa May Alcott (November 29, 1832–March 6, 1888). American novelist and author of *Little Women* and other books that appeal to many generations of readers. 825, 837, 986.

29 Birthday of Andrés Bello (November 29, 1781–October 15, 1865). Chilean poet, journalist, and statesman. Author of some of the greatest poetry of South America, he also developed Bello's code, which put an end to juridical anarchy in Chile. 986.

29 Albanian Liberation Day, a public holiday in Albania, celebrating Liberty Day, which marks the November 29, 1944, withdrawal of foreign troops.

29 President Tubman's Birthday, a public holiday in Liberia honoring the November 29, 1895, birth of William Tubman, who served as the nation's president for twenty-seven years.

29 Yugoslavian Proclamation of the Republic Days are observed on November 29 and 30 as public holidays in commemoration of the proclamation of the Federal People's Republic of Yugoslavia in 1945.

29 Anniversary of the establishment of the National Council of the Churches of Christ in the United States of America on November 29, 1950.

30 Feast day of Saint Andrew, apostle, patron saint of Scotland, Russia, and Greece, and of fishermen, fish merchants, and golfers; celebrated in the Greek, Roman Catholic, Anglican, and Lutheran churches.

30 Birthday of Sir Winston Churchill (November 30, 1874–January 24, 1965). British statesman; prime minister; symbol of the British spirit during World War II; author of many books, including *The Second World War*; Churchill Day is observed on April 9 in the United States. 231, 996.

30 Birthday of Samuel Langhorne Clemens, "Mark Twain" (November 30, 1835–April 21, 1910). American author, humorist, and lecturer whose most famous books are *The Adventures of Tom Sawyer* and *The Adventures of Huckleberry Finn*. He was elected to the Hall of Fame for Great Americans in 1920. An annual birthday party honoring Samuel Clemens is held on November 30 in the Mark Twain Memorial House in Hartford, Connecticut, sometimes called "the birthplace of Tom Sawyer." 237, 986.

30 Birthday of Theodor Mommsen (November 30, 1817–November 1, 1903). German classical scholar and historian who wrote a *History of Rome* and many other books of pure scholarship. He was awarded the 1902 Nobel Prize in literature. 227.

30 Birthday of Jonathan Swift (November 30, 1667–October 19, 1745). English clergyman, poet, political writer, and satirist remembered particularly for *Gulliver's Travels*. 986.

30 Barbados Independence Day, a holiday commemorating November 30, 1966, when the West Indian island became an independent member of the British Commonwealth of Nations.

30 Bonifacio Day, or National Heroes' Day, a public holiday in the Philippines, commemorating the November 30, 1863, birth of Andres Bonifacio, the Philippine patriot who led the 1896 revolt against the Spanish.

30 Yemen Independence Day, a public holiday in Yemen, recognizing November 30, 1967, as a day of "new sovereignty."

December

December is the twelfth and last month in the Gregorian calendar. It was the tenth month in the ancient Roman calendar, and its name comes from the Latin word *decem*, meaning "ten."

December is the most festive month of the year. It is the month when Christians all over the world celebrate the birth of Christ, and many activities are carried out in preparation for that great day. The season of preparation, which is called "Advent" in the Christian calendar, begins on the fourth Sunday before Christmas.

December is a month of happy traditions. Many people keep up customs that have been in their families for generations. They cook special dishes that originated with their forefathers, such as the English plum pudding or the Swedish lutefisk and other delicacies. December is the month for the singing of Christmas carols, the trimming of the tree, the writing of Christmas cards, and the selection of gifts for Christmas giving.

December is the month of Santa Claus in the United States and the month of Saint Nicholas in the countries of Europe. This saint has a feast day on December 6, and on that day he brings fruit and cakes to children if they have been good.

The last day of December closes the year. In Japan it is a time of stocktaking and the payment of debts. December 31 is called "Hogmanay Day" in Scotland, and it is a day when adults exchange presents and give cakes to children. It is also Saint Sylvester's Day, which is observed in Germany and Belgium with customs that anticipate the New Year. In Belgium, the last child out of bed on the morning of December 31 is a "Sylvester," a lazy one who has to pay a tribute to early risers. In the United States, the last hours of December constitute New Year's Eve, a time of merrymaking for adults and Watch Night parties for young people.

The poinsettia has come to be the flower that is symbolic of December. Holly and mistletoe are also special December floral decorations used at Christmas time.

December has two birthstones. They are the turquoise and the zircon.

The Fixed Days of December

1 Feast day of the Blessed Edmund Campion in whose name the annual Campion Award is given by the Catholic Book Club to recognize eminence in the field of Catholic letters.

1 Feast day of Saint Eligius, patron saint of jewelers and metalworkers.

1 Central African Republic National Day, a holiday commemorating the proclamation of the republic on December 1, 1958.

1 Independence Day in Iceland, commemorating the achievement of freedom from Denmark on December 1, 1918; a special day of celebration for university students.

1 Matilda Newport Day, a holiday in Liberia honoring a pioneer widow who ignited a cannon with her pipe during the 1822 siege by African tribesmen and thus saved her country.

1 Mocidade Day, a holiday in Portuguese Guinea, honoring the youth of the country.

1 Mother Seton Day, observed by the Sisters of Charity of Saint Vincent de Paul as the anniversary of the founding of their order in the United States by Elizabeth Ann Bayley Seton.

2 Birthday of Henry Thacker Burleigh (December 2, 1866–September 12, 1949). American Negro composer and choir director widely known for arrangements of Negro spirituals, notably *Deep River*; awarded the Spingarn Medal in 1916. 1.

2 Birthday of George Richards Minot (December 2, 1885–February 25, 1950). American physician and hematologist who made important discoveries with William Parry Murphy on the control of pernicious anemia; a corecipient of the 1934 Nobel Prize in medicine. 238.

2 Pan American Health Day, observed by presidential proclamation in the United States to focus on hemispheric cooperation in the field of public health.

3 Feast day of Saint Cassian, patron saint of stenographers.

3 Feast day of Saint Francis Xavier, patron saint of all Christian missions; patron saint of Borneo, Australia, and China; patron of the Propogation of the Faith.

3 Birthday of Cleveland Abbe (December 3, 1838–October 28, 1916). American meteorologist known as "the Father of the Weather Bureau"; influential in establishing the use of standard time throughout the United States; initiated the publication of daily weather forecasts.

3 Birthday of Joseph Conrad (December 3, 1857–August 3, 1924). English novelist of Polish birth who wrote *Lord Jim*, *The Nigger of the "Narcissus,"* and other titles of lasting interest. 986.

3 Birthday of Ellen Henrietta Richards (December 3, 1842–March 30, 1911). American chemist; founder of the home-economics movement; first president of the American Home Economics Association.

3 Birthday of Gilbert Charles Stuart (December 3, 1755–July 9, 1828). American portrait painter who painted Washington, Jefferson, Madison, and other great Americans of his day. Elected to the Hall of Fame for Great Americans in 1900. 237.

3 Illinois Admission Day. Illinois entered the Union as the twenty-first state on December 3, 1818. 741.

3 Heart Transplant Day, the anniversary of the first human heart transplant performed by Dr. Christian Barnard in Cape Town, South Africa, on December 3, 1967.

3 Sir Rowland Hill Day, anniversary of the birth of Sir Rowland Hill, who introduced the first postage stamp in the world in England in 1840; observed by philatelic societies.

4 Feast day of Saint Barbara, patron saint of firemen, artillery men, architects, stonemasons, and mathematicians; protectress against lightning, fire, sudden death, and impenitence; the day is considered the beginning of the Christmas season in parts of France, Germany, and Syria.

4 Birthday of Thomas Carlyle (December 4, 1795–February 5, 1881). Scottish essayist and historian called "the Sage of Chelsea." His *French Revolution* established his reputation. 986.

4 Birthday of Edith Louisa Cavell (December 4, 1865–October 12, 1915). English nurse, heroine of World War I who was executed by the Germans. A monument to her memory stands in Saint Martin's Place, Trafalgar Square, London.

4 Birthday of Frances Power Cobbe (December 4, 1822–April 5, 1904). British feminist and author, champion of higher education for women, and one of the founders of the National Anti-Vivisection Society.

4 Birthday of John Cotton (December 4, 1584–December 23, 1652). American Puritan clergyman who had great influence in the Massachusetts Bay colony.

4 Day of the Artisans, observed in Mexico to honor the workers of the nation.

5   Birthday of Walt Disney (December 5, 1901–December 15, 1966). American motion-picture and television producer; pioneer in the creation of animated motion-picture cartoons; creator of such cartoon characters as Mickey Mouse and Donald Duck; organizer of the first Disneyland in 1955.

5   Birthday of Martin Van Buren (December 5, 1782–July 24, 1862). Dutch ancestry; New York lawyer and eighth president of the United States, 1837–41. Reformed Dutch churchman. Buried at Kinderhook, New York. 667–72.

5   Arbor Day in Beirut, Lebanon.

5   Discovery Day, a national holiday in Haiti, commemorating its discovery by Christopher Columbus in 1492.

5   Soviet Constitution Day, a public holiday in the Union of Soviet Socialist Republics commemorating the adoption of a new constitution by the eighth Congress of the Soviets on December 5, 1936.

5   Saint Nicholas' Eve is celebrated in European countries with families sharing stories of the life and works of Saint Nicholas, third-century Bishop of Myra, and preparing for the saint's feast day on December 6.

5   Anniversary of the founding of Phi Beta Kappa on December 5, 1776, at the College of William and Mary.

6   Feast day of Saint Nicholas, patron saint of Russia, of sailors, pilgrims, schoolboys, young girls, children, and pawnbrokers. Saint Nicholas, the prototype of the modern Santa Claus, brings fruits, cakes, and gifts to children on his feast day; celebrated widely in central and northern Europe.

6   Birthday of Warren Hastings (December 6, 1732–August 22, 1818). English statesman, colonial administrator, and first governor-general of British India.

6   Birthday of Joyce Kilmer (December 6, 1886–July 30, 1918). American poet and critic who is remembered especially for a single poem called *Trees*.

6   Birthday of John Singleton Mosby (December 6, 1833–May 30, 1916). American lawyer; Confederate soldier who organized Mosby's Partisan Rangers; credited with originating the phrase "the solid south."

6   Day of Quito, a holiday in Ecuador honoring the founding of Quito by the Spaniards in 1534.

6   Finnish Independence Day, a holiday in Finland commemorating the December 6, 1917, declaration of freedom from Russia.

6   Ruler's Accession Day, a public holiday in Bahrain, an island off the west coast of Africa.

7   Feast day of Saint Ambrose; one of the four great Latin Fathers; father of hymnology in the Western Church.

7   Birthday of Giovanni Lorenzo Bernini (December 7, 1598–November 28, 1680). Italian architect, sculptor, and painter; one of the architects of Saint Peter's Church in Rome. 987.

7   Birthday of Matthew Heywood Campbell Broun (December 7, 1888–December 18, 1939). American journalist and first president of the American Newspaper Guild.

7   Birthday of Willa Sibert Cather (December 7, 1873–April 24, 1947). American author considered to be one of the outstanding twentieth-century writers in the United States. She is particularly remembered for *A Lost Lady*, *O Pioneers*, and *Death Comes for the Archbishop*. *One of Ours* was awarded a Pulitzer Prize. 229, 837, 986.

7   Day of National Mourning, a public holiday in Cuba.

7 Delaware Day, a statewide holiday, celebrates the anniversary of the adoption of the Federal Constitution by Delaware on December 7, 1787, making Delaware the first state in rank among the thirteen original states of the United States. 741.

7 Pearl Harbor Day, anniversary of the Japanese attack on Pearl Harbor, the Philippines, and Guam on December 7, 1941. Civil Defense Day is observed on the anniversary of Pearl Harbor to emphasize the role of civil defense in the security of the United States. 654–58.

7 Anniversary of the first concert given by the Philharmonic Symphony Society of New York, oldest symphony orchestra in the United States, on December 7, 1842.

7 Anniversary of the founding on December 7, 1875, of the Native Sons of the West, an organization of native-born Californians.

8 Feast day of the Immaculate Conception of Mary, patron saint of the United States; a prescribed holy day in Roman Catholic countries; a holiday in many nations; Mother's Day in Panama City, Panama. 80.

8 Birthday of Björnstjerne Björnson (December 8, 1832–April 26, 1910). Norwegian novelist and dramatist and one of his nation's most ardent patriots. He received the 1903 Nobel Prize in literature. ·227.

8 Birthday of Padraic Colum (December 8, 1881–January 11, 1972). Irish poet, folklorist, dramatist, and essayist. His *Collected Poems* reveal his deep involvement with the lore and the legends of Ireland.

8 Birthday of Jean Sibelius (December 8, 1865–September 20, 1957). Finnish composer, famous for *Valse Triste*, *Finlandia*, and his symphonic music. 986.

8 Birthday of Eli Whitney (December 8, 1765–January 8, 1825). American inventor and manufacturer who invented the cotton gin. He was elected to the Hall of Fame for Great Americans in 1900. 237.

8 Beach Day, or Blessing of the Waters Day, a public holiday in Uruguay, marking the beginning of the beach season on the "Uruguayan Riviera"; sometimes called "Family Day."

8 Lady of Camarin Day, a legal holiday in Guam, honoring the Virgin as the nation's protector.

8 Mother's Day in Spain; has long been associated with the Feast of the Immaculate Conception; a day of joyful family celebrations throughout the country.

8 School Reunion Day, the traditional day of school celebrations and alumni reunions in Spain.

9 Birthday of Fritz Haber (December 9, 1868–January 29, 1934). German chemist who was awarded the 1918 Nobel Prize for his synthesis of ammonia. 241.

9 Birthday of John Milton (December 9, 1608–November 8, 1674). English poet best known for *Paradise Lost* and *Paradise Regained*. 986.

9 Tanzania Independence Day, a public holiday in Tanzania commemorating the complete sovereignty granted on December 9, 1961.

9 Zanzibar National Day, commemorating the sultan's accession.

9 The anniversary of the founding of the John Birch Society on December 9, 1958.

10 Birthday of Zachariah Chandler (December 10, 1813–November 1, 1879). American merchant and politician who was among those who signed the call for the Jackson, Michigan, meeting that is said to have founded the Republican party. He represents the state of Michigan in Statuary Hall in a sculpture done by Charles Henry Niehaus. 242.

10 Human Rights Day, the anniversary of the adoption of the Universal Declaration of Human Rights on December 10, 1948; an official United Nations holiday.

10 Mississippi entered the Union on December 10, 1817, as the twentieth state. 741.

10 Rights of Man Day, a public holiday in the Khmer Republic, formerly Cambodia.

10 Thailand Constitution Day, a public holiday commemorating the December 10, 1932, constitution, the first for the Thai people.

10 Wyoming Day, a holiday commemorating the adoption of woman's suffrage in the Wyoming Territory on December 10, 1869.

10 Nobel Prize Presentation Day, the anniversary of the 1896 death of Alfred Bernhard Nobel, founder of the annual Nobel Prizes. Awards are presented in Stockholm with the reigning monarch officiating. The Peace Prize is presented in Oslo, Norway.

11 Birthday of Hector Berlioz (December 11, 1803–March 8, 1869). French composer noted for his contributions to dramatic instrumental music. 986.

11 Birthday of Robert Koch (December 11, 1843–May 27, 1910). German bacteriologist awarded the 1905 Nobel Prize for his discovery of the bacilli of tuberculosis and cholera. 238.

11 Birthday of Fiorello Henry La Guardia (December 11, 1882–September 20, 1947). American lawyer, mayor of the city of New York, congressman, first director of the Federal Office of Civilian Defense; called "the Little Flower." 990.

11 Indiana Day, observed throughout the state with patriotic programs commemorating the admission of the state to the Union on December 11, 1816, as the nineteenth state. 741.

11 Scaling Day, or the Escalade, celebrated in Geneva, Switzerland; honors the night of December 11, 1602, when the citizens routed the Savoyards, who were scaling the walls of their city. Shops sell chocolate bonbons representing the soup pots the women used on that night to throw hot water on the invaders.

11 Upper Volta Republic Day, commemorates December 11, 1958, when Upper Volta's territorial assembly voted to become an autonomous state within the French community.

12 Fiesta of Our Lady of Guadalupe, Mexico's greatest religious festival, commemorates with religious ceremonies and pilgrimages the appearance of the Blessed Virgin to an Indian boy in 1531. Conchero dancers, processions, and fireworks honor Mexico's patroness, Our Lady of Guadalupe, who in 1945 was crowned "the Queen of Wisdom and of the Americas." This feast is also celebrated in the Southwest of the United States, where Spanish influence prevails, and on Olvera Street in Los Angeles. 5, 125.

12 Birthday of Gustave Flaubert (December 12, 1821–May 8, 1880). French writer and novelist of the school of naturalism, famous for *Madame Bovary*.

12 Birthday of John Jay (December 12, 1745–May 17, 1829). American lawyer, jurist, statesman, and diplomat; first chief justice of the United States Supreme Court. 991.

12 Day of the Indians, a special day in El Salvador with programs honoring the Virgin of Guadalupe, the patroness of the Indians.

12 Jamhuri Day, or Kenya Independence Day, a holiday in Kenya commemorating the proclamation of sovereignty for Kenya as declared on December 12, 1963.

12 Pennsylvania Admission Day. Pennsylvania entered the Union on December 12, 1787, as the second of the thirteen original states. 741.

12 Anniversary of the establishment of the United Nations Committee on the Peaceful Uses of Outer Space on December 12, 1959.

12 Washington, D.C., Birthday, anniversary of the decision on December 12, 1800, to establish Washington as the permanent capital of the United States government.

13 Feast day of Saint Lucy, patroness of writers, of people with eye trouble, and of lights.

13 Birthday of Phillips Brooks (December 13, 1835–January 23, 1893). American Episcopal bishop, remembered in the twentieth century as the author of the Christmas hymn *O Little Town of Bethlehem*. He was elected to the Hall of Fame for Great Americans in 1910. 237, 999.

13 Birthday of Clark Mills (December 13, 1810–January 12, 1883). American sculptor and bronze founder who made the equestrian statues of Andrew Jackson and George Washington, did the bronze casting of Thomas Crawford's *Freedom*, or *Armed Liberty*, for the dome of the Capitol, and took a life mask of Abraham Lincoln before his death.

13 Lucia Day, an important festival in Sweden, honoring Saint Lucia, "the Queen of Light," with a candlelight parade through Stockholm; the reigning queen wears a crown of lighted candles, receives the Lucia jewel, and is awarded a trip to the United States to visit Swedish-American communities that also celebrate the festival of lights.

14 Feast day of Saint Spyridon, honored by the people of Greece with a celebration at Corfu, including a procession in which the relic of the saint dressed in costly vestments is carried.

14 Birthday of John Mercer Langston (December 14, 1829–November 15, 1897). American lawyer and public official, probably the first Negro to be elected to public office in the United States; served as minister to Haiti and as a college president.

14 Alabama Admission Day. Alabama entered the Union as the twenty-second state on December 14, 1819. 741.

14 Death of Iman Ja'far Sadeq Day, a public holiday in Iran honoring an eighth-century spiritual leader.

15 Birthday of Maxwell Anderson (December 15, 1888–February 28, 1959). American playwright, famous for verse plays and such successful productions as *What Price Glory?*

15 Birthday of George Romney (December 15, 1734–November 15, 1802). English portrait painter whose celebrated model was Lady Hamilton.

15 Bill of Rights Day, honoring the ratification of the first ten amendments to the United States Constitution; observed in the United States by presidential proclamation. 249–56.

15 Kingdom Day, or Statute Day, celebrated in the Netherlands Antilles to honor the autonomy granted on December 15, 1954, which provided for equal status with the Netherlands and Surinam.

15 Zamenhof Day, sponsored by the Esperanto League for North America, commemorates the December 15, 1859, birthday of Dr. Ludwik Zamenhof, the founder of Esperanto, the international language.

16 Birthday of Jane Austen (December 16, 1775–July 18, 1817). English novelist, remembered for *Persuasion* and *Pride and Prejudice*.

16 Birthday of Ludwig van Beethoven (December 16, 1770–March 26, 1827). German composer considered to be one of the foremost musicians of all time. 986.

16 Birthday of Noel Peirce Coward (December 16, 1899–March 26, 1973). British playwright, director, songwriter, and actor. His plays include *Blithe Spirit*, *Private Lives*, and *This Happy Breed*. His songs include *Mad Dogs and Englishmen* and *Someday I'll Find You*.

16 Birthday of Ralph Adams Cram (December 16, 1863–September 22, 1942). American architect and authority on Gothic architecture whose firm designed the Cathedral of Saint John the Divine in New York City.

16 Birthday of George Santayana (December 16, 1863–September 26, 1952). Spanish poet and philosopher, author of the *Idea of Christ in the Gospels, Egotism in German Philosophy, The Last Puritan,* and an autobiography, *Persons and Places.* 986.

16 Bangladesh Victory Day, a public holiday commemorating the end of the 1971 conflict with Pakistan.

16 Dingaan's Day, proclaimed a national holiday by the 1910 constitution of the Union of South Africa in honor of the Sunday, December 16, 1838, when the Boers, under Andries Pretorius, defeated Dingaan, the Zulu chieftain.

16 Foretrekkers' Day, a holiday observed in Pretoria, South Africa, in salute to the pioneers.

16 Nepal Constitution Day, a public holiday honoring the adoption on December 16, 1962, of a constitution for the Kingdom of Nepal.

16 Boston Tea Party Day, anniversary of the Boston Tea Party of December 16, 1773, when the colonists boarded a British vessel and dumped a shipload of tea into the Boston Harbor; a prelude to the American Revolution.

16 Posadas Days, or the "Lodgings," begins on December 16 in the cities and villages of Mexico with a procession that recalls the journey of Mary and Joseph to Bethlehem. Posadas lasts nine days and includes religious ceremonies, festivities, and the popular ceremony of the breaking of the piñata. Las Posadas is also celebrated on Olvera Street in Los Angeles.

17 Birthday of Joseph Henry (December 17, 1797–May 13, 1878). American physicist noted for research in electromagnetism. He was elected to the Hall of Fame for Great Americans in 1915. 237.

17 Birthday of Thomas Starr King (December 17, 1824–March 4, 1864). American Unitarian clergyman and author. He represents the state of California in Statuary Hall in a sculpture done by Haig Patigian. 242.

17 Birthday of William Lyon Mackenzie King (December 17, 1874–July 22, 1950). Canadian statesman and prime minister of Canada who worked for the complete autonomy of Canada within the British Commonwealth of Nations.

17 Birthday of John Greenleaf Whittier (December 17, 1807–September 7, 1892). American poet, abolitionist, and journalist, known as "the Quaker Poet." Elected to the Hall of Fame for Great Americans in 1905. 237, 986.

17 Bolivar Day, a holiday in Venezuela commemorating the death of the soldier-statesman Simon Bolivar, on December 17, 1830. Venezuela also observes Bolivar's birthday on July 24.

17 Colombia Independence Day, a holiday in Colombia honoring the declaration of independence from Spain, which was proclaimed on December 17, 1819.

17 Wright Brothers Day, observed in the United States by presidential proclamation to honor the Wrights' first flight on December 17, 1903; special observances near Kill Devil Hills and Kitty Hawk in North Carolina. December 17 is also Pan American Aviation Day. 214, 219, 222, 752.

18 The Fiesta of the Virgin of the Lonely, celebrated by thousands of pilgrims at Oaxaca, Mexico, to honor the patroness of muleteers and sailors.

18 Birthday of William Allen (December 18, 1803–July 11, 1879). American politician, congressman, and governor of Ohio. Represents Ohio in Statuary Hall in a sculpture done by Charles Henry Niehaus. 242.

18 Birthday of Edward Alexander MacDowell (December 18, 1861–January 24, 1908). American pianist and composer. He was elected to the Hall of Fame for Great Americans in 1960. An Edward MacDowell Medal is awarded annually by the Edward MacDowell Association to recognize individuals whose work has enriched the arts. 237.

18 Birthday of Joseph John Thomson (December 18, 1856–August 30, 1940). English physicist whose experiments with the cathode ray opened up a new field of subatomic physics; awarded the Nobel Prize in physics in 1906. 241.

18 Birthday of Charles Wesley (December 18, 1707–March 29, 1788). English Methodist preacher and famous hymn-writer of such hymns as *Jesus, Lover of My Soul* and *Love Divine, All Love Excelling.*

18 Niger Republic Day, a civic holiday in the African nation named for the world's twelfth-largest river; commemorates the establishment of the constitutional government.

18 New Jersey Admission Day. New Jersey entered the Union on December 18, 1787, the third of the thirteen original United States to do so. 741.

18 Anniversary of the orbiting of the United States *Atlas* satellite on December 18, 1958, which broadcast a message from the president of the United States, expressing "America's wish for peace on earth and good will . . . everywhere."

19 Birthday of Henry Clay Frick (December 19, 1849–December 2, 1919). American industrialist who left his priceless art collection and his mansion to the public as a museum, now known as the Frick Collection.

19 Birthday of Albert Abraham Michelson (December 19, 1852–May 9, 1931). American physicist, the first American scientist to receive the Nobel Prize; awarded the Nobel Prize in physics in 1907. Elected to the Hall of Fame for Great Americans in 1970. 237.

19 Princess Bernice Pauahi Bishop's birthday anniversary, observed in Hawaii on December 19, with ceremonies at the Kamehameha schools and at the Royal Mausoleum.

20 Birthday of Samuel Jordan Kirkwood (December 20, 1813–September 1, 1894). American politician; United States secretary of the interior under President Garfield; governor of Iowa. He represents Iowa in Statuary Hall in a sculpture by Vinnie Ream Hoxie. 242.

20 Anniversary of the transfer on December 20, 1803, of the Louisiana Territory from France to the United States.

21 Feast day of Saint Thomas the Apostle, patron saint of the East Indies, of India, of architects and builders; depicted in Christian art with a square rule; celebrated by the Roman Catholic, Anglican, Lutheran, and Eastern churches.

21 Birthday of Kemal Bey (December 21, 1840–December 2, 1888). Turkish poet and author whose writing influenced the Young Turk movement.

21 Birthday of Jean Henri Fabre (December 21, 1823–October 11, 1915). French entomologist who devoted his life to studying and writing about the habits of insects.

21 Birthday of Joseph Stalin (December 21, 1879–March 5, 1953). Russian dictator in power from 1929 until his death in 1953; credited with ruthless development of the USSR as a major world power.

21 Birthday of Henrietta Szold (December 21, 1860–February 13, 1945). American teacher, Zionist leader, and founder of Hadassah; a founder of schools and hospitals in Palestine.

21 Forefather's Day, observed in Plymouth, Massachusetts, and by various New England societies to commemorate the landing of the Pilgrims on December 21, 1620. 464–75.

21 Independence Day, a holiday in Nepal honoring the change in status from British protectorate to independence on December 21, 1923.

22 Feast day of Saint Frances Xavier Cabrini, first United States saint; founder of the Missionary Sisters of the Sacred Heart; patron saint of immigrants and of hospital administrators. 705.

22 Anniversary of the death of Stephen Day on December 22, 1668. First printer in the British colonies in America; printed the famous *Bay Psalm Book* in 1640.

22 Anniversary of the death of John Newbery on December 22, 1767. English publisher and bookseller who made a specialty of children's books and in whose honor the annual Newbery Medal has been given since 1922 for the most distinguished contribution to children's literature published in the preceding year. 234, 236.

22 Birthday of James Edward Oglethorpe (December 22, 1696–July 1, 1785). English soldier and founder of the Georgia colony in the New World.

22 Birthday of Giacomo Puccini (December 22, 1858–November 29, 1924). Italian operatic composer perhaps best known for *Madame Butterfly*. 986.

22 Birthday of Luca della Robbia (December 22, 1400–September 22, 1482). Italian sculptor who created the famous della Robbia reliefs in terra cotta. 986.

22 Day of National Mourning in Mexico, commemorating the December 22, 1815, death of José Maria Morelos, revolutionary hero.

22 International Arbor Day, established to encourage winter tree planting and the celebration of Arbor Day activities throughout the world.

c22 The winter solstice occurs approximately on December 22, when the sun appears highest in the northern sky at any location south of the Tropic of Capricorn.

23 Birthday of Martin Opitz (December 23, 1597–August 20, 1639). German poet and critic known as "the Father of Modern German Poetry."

23 Birthday of Joseph Smith (December 23, 1805–June 27, 1844). American Mormon leader, founder of the Church of Jesus Christ of Latter-Day Saints.

c23 John Canoe Day, a traditional native fiesta of Jamaica, held at Montego Bay between December 23 and January 23.

24 Christmas Eve, the night before Christmas, is usually a partial or full holiday in the nations observing Christmas; observed with the midnight mass and traditional customs.

24 Birthday of Juan Ramón Jiménez (December 24, 1881–May 29, 1958). Spanish lyric poet who received the Nobel Prize in literature in 1956. 986.

24 Birthday of Benjamin Rush (December 24, 1745–April 19, 1813). American physician, signer of the Declaration of Independence, and medical pioneer for whom the Rush University in Chicago was named.

24 Laos Sovereignty Day, the anniversary of the achievement of autonomy by Laos on December 24, 1954; also called Independence Day.

24 Independence Day in Libya, the first country in the world created by the United Nations; the holiday commemorates December 24, 1951, the day the powers of government were turned over to the Libyans.

25 Christmas Day, the day of the Nativity of the Lord. The word *Christmas* can be traced back to 1038, to the Old English *Cristes Maesse*, meaning "the Mass of Christ." The Nativity of Christ was introduced as a special feast in Rome about the middle of the fourth century. The Church of the Annunciation at Nazareth is the focal point of the worldwide celebration; Christmas is a holiday in 105 nations of the world. 296–381.

25 Birthday of Clara Barton (December 25, 1821–April 12, 1912). American philanthropist, an organizer of the Red Cross.

25 Birthday of Evangeline Cory Booth (December 25, 1865–July 17, 1950). International Salvation Army general serving in London, Canada, and the United States; author and composer of Salvation Army songs.

25 Taiwan Constitution Day, a public holiday in Taiwan (Republic of China) honoring the adoption of the constitution on December 25, 1946.

25 The anniversary of the founding of the Lambs Club in New York on December 25, 1875.

26 Feast day of Saint Stephen, patron saint of Hungary and of stonecutters, and the first Christian martyr; celebrated by the Roman Catholic, Anglican, Lutheran, and Eastern churches; a holiday in Ireland, Austria, and Liechtenstein.

26 Boxing Day, a holiday throughout the British Commonwealth of Nations, excluding Scotland. It was once a day when boxes of gifts were given to those entitled to gratuities; now it is a legal holiday observed on the day following Christmas.

26 Second day of Christmas, a holiday in the Federal Republic of Germany (West Germany), providing a two-day Christmas holiday.

27 Feast of Saint John, apostle, evangelist, and "the Beloved" of the Lord, celebrated on December 27 in the Roman Catholic, Anglican, and Lutheran churches. Saint John the Evangelist's Day, the third day of Christmas in Scandinavia, is devoted to visiting among friends; in Norway cooking is reduced to the minimum on this day.

27 Birthday of Louis Pasteur (December 27, 1822–September 28, 1895). French chemist and founder of microbiological sciences and of preventive medicine.

27 Indonesia Independence Day, commemorating December 27, 1949, as the date of agreement with the Dutch on the independence of Indonesia; official and public observances of independence are held on August 17 in tribute to the proclamation by the Indonesian revolutionaries of the Republic of Indonesia on August 17, 1945.

28 Holy Innocents' Day, Feast of the Holy Innocents, or Childermas, commemorates the massacre of young children by Herod, who wished to be sure of killing the Infant Jesus; celebrated by the Western churches on December 28 and by the Eastern churches on December 29.

28 Birthday of Woodrow Wilson (December 28, 1856–February 3, 1924). Scotch-Irish ancestry; president of Princeton University; statesman; man of letters; advocate of the League of Nations; twenty-eighth president of the United States, 1913–21. Presbyterian. Awarded the Nobel Peace Prize in 1919. Buried in Washington Cathedral. Elected to the Hall of Fame for Great Americans in 1950. Woodrow Wilson's birthday is a legal holiday in South Carolina. 667–72, 674–76, 678, 679.

28 Iowa Admission Day. Iowa entered the Union on December 28, 1846, as the twenty-ninth state. 741.

28 King Birendra's Birthday, a public holiday in Nepal.

29 Feast of Saint Thomas of Canterbury, the anniversary of the day Thomas à Becket was murdered on the altar, December 29, 1170. His cathedral, Canterbury, became the mecca for pilgrims from all England and all Europe.

29 Birthday of Pablo Casals (December 29, 1876–October 22, 1973). The greatest cellist of the twentieth century. Received the United Nations Peace Prize for his *Hymn to the United Nations.*

29 Birthday of John James Ingalls (December 29, 1833–August 16, 1900). American congressman from Kansas. He represents the state of Kansas in Statuary Hall in a sculpture by Charles Henry Niehaus. 242.

29 Birthday of Andrew Johnson (December 29, 1808–July 31, 1875). English ancestry; Tennessee politician; seventh president of the United States, 1865–69. No formal religious affiliation. Buried at Greenville, Tennessee. Elected to the Hall of Fame for Great Americans in 1910. 237, 667–72, 674–76, 678, 679.

29 Texas Admission Day. Texas entered the Union as the twenty-eighth state on December 29, 1845. 741.

30 Birthday of Simon Guggenheim (December 30, 1867–November 2, 1941). American capitalist and philanthropist; founder, with his wife, of the John Simon Guggenheim Memorial Foundation, established as a memorial to their son. The Guggenheim Fellowships offer opportunities to further research and artistic creation for artists and scholars regardless of sex, color, creed, or marital status.

30 Birthday of Joseph Rudyard Kipling (December 30, 1865–January 18, 1936). English novelist, poet, and short-story writer famous for *Captains Courageous*, the *Jungle Books*, *Recessional*, and many other titles. He was awarded the 1907 Nobel Prize in literature. 231, 986.

30 Birthday of Stephen Butler Leacock (December 30, 1869–March 28, 1944). Canadian humorist and man of letters, political scientist, university professor, and lecturer, who ranked with Mark Twain in popular esteem.

30 Birthday of Iman Reza, a public holiday in Iran.

30 Rizal Day, a holiday in the Philippines commemorating the death of José Mercado Rizal on December 30, 1896. Philippine doctor and author whose books denouncing the Spanish administration were an inspiration to the Philippine nationalist movement.

30 Watch Night, or New Year's evening, a traditional time of merrymaking in which people gather to watch the old year out and the new year in.

31 Saint Sylvester's Day, dedicated to Pope Sylvester, is observed in Germany, Belgium, Switzerland, and other European countries, with ceremonies anticipating the New Year.

31 Birthday of George Catlett Marshall (December 31, 1880–October 16, 1959). American soldier and statesman who developed the principles of the European Recovery Program implemented in 1948 and known as "the Marshall Plan."

31 Anniversary of the death of John Wycliffe on December 31, 1384. English religious reformer called "the Morning Star of the Reformation"; first to translate the Bible into English.

31 Evacuation Day, a public holiday in Lebanon celebrating the withdrawal of French troops on December 31, 1946.

31 Hogmanay Day, observed in Scotland and northern England as a part of the New Year's festivities. The name comes from the Old French meaning "New Year."

31 Noche de Pedimento, a Wishing Night, during which the Indians at Mitla, Oaxaca, gather around a cross to pray for their wishes for the coming year and present small miniatures of their wishes at the cross.

31 Omisoka Day, the last day of the year, a traditional time for stocktaking and the payment of debts in Japan.

31 Watch Night, or New Year's evening, a traditional time of merrymaking in which people gather to watch the old year out and the new year in.

Calendars of Movable Days

The term *movable days* is used to encompass the holy days and festivals that are determined by lunar calculations. Movable days do not have a set place in the Gregorian calendar, since they are observed at different times in successive years. In a few nations of the Far East, the exact dates of movable holidays are announced at the beginning of each new year. In the Christian world, the forthcoming dates for Easter, which determines the observance of religious days for approximately one-third of the Christian church year, have been calculated in advance. Comparable projections have been made for the Islamic, Jewish, Chinese, and Vietnamese calendars. Dates for movable holidays in specific years may be found in the yearbooks listed in the section of the bibliography on Almanacs and Dictionaries of Days, which is found on pages 610–17.

This section on movable days covers the calendars and major days of the Christian church and those of the Islamic and Jewish faiths, followed by the religious and secular festivals of the Eastern and Western world.

Each category of movable days is arranged chronologically in parallel columns. The right-hand column identifies the days or events, arranged alphabetically, that occur within the time frame of the months in the Gregorian calendar that are indicated in the left-hand column.

The Christian Church Calendar

The focal point of the Christian church calendar is Easter, the day of the Resurrection of Christ. The death of Christ took place during the major Jewish feast, the Pesach, or Passover, which is celebrated at the full moon following the spring equinox. The Christians fixed the anniversary of the Resurrection on the first day of the week in which it took place. Consequently, Easter falls on the first day of the week after the first full moon following the spring equinox. It can be as early as March 22 and as late as April 25.

The Christian church calendar is thus dominated by the central event in Christianity and is regulated in part by the movement of the sun and the moon. It includes both fixed and movable feasts.

The first Christian church calendar was derived from the Hebrew calendar. At the beginning of the Christian era, many congregations developed their own calendars. The result was universal confusion. Finally, at the Council of Nicaea in A.D. 325, the Church accepted the Julian calendar as the basis for reckoning ecclesiastical dates. The inaccuracies in the Julian calendar led to the promulgation of calendar reform by Pope Gregory by 1582.

The Gregorian calendar, however, was not acceptable to all branches of the Christian church. The Orthodox church in the East continued to use the Julian calendar under the impact of the decisions at the Council of Nicaea. The sixteenth-century Protestant Reformation contributed to the reluctance to adopt the Gregorian calendar in the West. A number of factors, not exclusively religious, led to the adoption of the Gregorian calendar by England and her colonies in 1752 and by Germany in 1775. From the middle of the eighteenth century, the Gregorian calendar supplemented the calendar of movable dates for Roman Catholic, Anglican, and Protestant observances. The Orthodox churches of the twentieth century still utilize the Julian calendar. In the 1970s, the major calendar negotiations between the Eastern and Western churches are concerned with the proposal to set a date for Easter on a permanent specific Sunday, an action that would simplify the ecclesiastical calendar for the entire Christian world.

The following are the major movable Christian holy days and feasts matched with the Gregorian timetable. The pre-Lenten festivals, pilgrimages, and fiestas associated with saints' days are entered in The Festival Calendar in the Western World, which begins on page 593. Both the fixed and the movable dates in the Christian church year may be located through the index.

Gregorian Calendar Months	*Movable Days of the Christian Church Year*
November–December	Advent Sunday, marks the beginning of the Christian church year, on the Sunday of or nearest to Saint Andrew's Day, November 30; the Advent season is a period of preparation for Christmas and includes four Sundays; varies in length from twenty-two to twenty-eight days.
January	The Feast of the Holy Family, observed by the Roman Catholic church on the Sunday after Epiphany to honor Jesus, Mary, and Joseph.
February–March	Ash Wednesday, the first day of Lent, the period of Christian penance in preparation for Easter; derives its name from the use of ashes in marking the sign of the cross on the forehead of the worshipper; observed forty-six days before Easter.
March–April	Palm Sunday, the Sunday before Easter, the beginning of Holy Week; the memorial of Christ's entrance into Jerusalem; named for the palms that were placed in his path by the multitude and for the palms that are distributed at the Palm Sunday services of many denominations.
March–April	Maundy Thursday, or Holy Thursday, observed during Holy Week in commemoration of the day of the Last Supper.
March–April	Good Friday, the Friday before Easter; the commemoration of the Passion and death by crucifixion of Jesus Christ; a day of fasting, abstinence, and penitence, which is a public holiday in sixteen states of the United States and in sixty-four nations of the world.
March–April	Easter Day; the Sunday of the Resurrection of Jesus Christ; the greatest day in the Christian calendar; Easter Monday, the day following Easter, is a holiday in sixty-four nations of the world. 423–38.
April–June	Ascension Day; the commemoration of the ascension of the Lord into heaven; a holy day of obligation observed forty days after Easter; a holiday in forty-two nations in the world.
May–June	Pentecost, or Whitsunday, the birthday of the Church commemorating the coming of the Holy Spirit and the gift of faith to the apostles and disciples; observed on Sunday fifty days after Easter; Whitmundy, the Monday following Pentecost, is observed as a holiday in many European countries.
May–June	Trinity Sunday, the first Sunday after Pentecost; a special commemoration in the name of the Father, Son, and Holy Spirit.

May–June   Corpus Christi, the popular name for the Feast of the Most Holy Body
            of Christ; a festival in honor of the Holy Eucharist; celebrated the
            Thursday after Trinity Sunday; also called "Day of Wreaths" in central
            Europe and France, in recognition of the wreaths that are carried in
            procession; a holiday in twenty-two nations.

October   Feast of Christ the King, observed in the Roman Catholic church on
            the last Sunday in October, and by Protestant churches on the last
            Sunday in August, to honor Christ as the ruler of all nations.

The Islamic Calendar

The Islamic, or Mohammedan, calendar is based on the moon's course, without regard to seasons. There are twelve lunar months totaling 354 or 355 days. Time is figured on a basis of cycles thirty years long. During each cycle, nineteen years have 354 days, and an extra day is added to each of the other eleven years.

Since the months and the seasons do not correspond in the Islamic calendar, the Moslem New Year and its related religious festivals occur in all seasons in the course of the overall time cycle. An unusual characteristic of the Islamic calendar is that these festivals move backward. The United Nations calendars, for example, show that the first month in the Islam year, Muharram, began on January 25 in the Gregorian year 1974, and on January 14 in 1975. The backward movement of the festivals will continue until the thirty-year cycle is complete.

The Islamic calendar dates from the emigration, or hijrah, of the Prophet Mohammed from Mecca to Medina in A.D. 622. The weekly day of rest is Friday, Yawm al-Jum'ah. It is observed by all of the faithful of Islam who believe that Adam was born on Friday, and taken into paradise on Friday.

Some Islamic nations have adopted fixed dates for the commemoration of contemporary civil or national events. It is reported, however, that the orthodox recognize only the following festivals. No attempt has been made to indicate the Gregorian time equivalent, because of the continuing movement of the five important religious periods in the lunar Islamic calendar.

Movable Islamic Festivals

Variable Seasons   Muharram, the first month of the Islamic calendar year; the first ten
                    days celebrate the beginning of the Moslem New Year, and are dedi-
                    cated to the martyrdom of Hezret Iman Husain.

                    Ashura, the Mohammedan commemoration of Noah's completion of the
                    ark on Mount Aarat; celebrated about the tenth day of the first moon
                    month, Muharram.

                    Ramadan, the ninth month of the Mohammedan calendar, commem-
                    orates the period during which Mohammed received divine revelations;
                    special observance of this month is one of the five great tenets of Islam
                    and is marked by a strict fast from sunrise to sundown.

                    'Id al-Fitr, a three-day celebration marking the end of the observance of
                    the fast of Ramadan; begins on the first day of Shawwai, the tenth lunar
                    month of the Moslem calendar; known as "the Breaking of the Fast."

                    'Id al-Adha, a three-day festival of sacrifice celebrated on the twelfth
                    day of Zu'lhijjah, the twelfth Moslem month, in tribute to Abraham's
                    obedience to God in sending his son Ishmael into the desert. Ishmael is
                    considered to be the forefather of the Arabs.

149

The Jewish Calendar

The Jewish calendar is lunisolar. It is regulated by the positions of both the moon and the sun. Thus the day upon which an annual festival falls varies from year to year, even though that day may be fixed in the history of the Jews.

The Jewish calendar consists of twelve alternating months of twenty-nine and thirty days each. Adjustments are made in the calendar when necessary to reconcile the average lunar year of 355 days to the solar year of 365¼ days in order to assure that the major festivals fall into their proper season.

The great Jewish holy days are the heritage of all Jewish people. Reform, Orthodox, and Conservative congregations, however, may vary in the length of the observances and in the prescribed form of observance.

Gregorian Calendar Months	*The Jewish Holy Days and Holidays*
September–October	Rosh Hashanah, the New Year of the Jewish people, which "ushers in the Days of Judgment for all mankind"; observed as the first day of the interlunar month of Tishri. 693–96.
September–October	Yom Kippur, or Day of Atonement, the holiest day of the Jewish year, and the most solemn of the Jewish holy days; a day of fasting, penitence, and prayer observed on the tenth day of the month of Tishri. 875, 876.
September–October	Sukkot, the Jewish Feast of the Tabernacles; originally a seasonal celebration of the ingathering of summer crops, it has a historical relationship to the Flight from Captivity, when the Israelites lived in sukkots, or booths; a joyous festival celebrated for seven days in the middle of the month of Tishri.
September–October	Shemini Atzeret, the eighth day of the Festival of Sukkot; observed on the twenty-second day of Tishri.
September–October	Simhat Torah, a day of "Rejoicing in the Law" and completion of the Torah reading cycle; observed on the twenty-third day of Tishri.
November–December	Chanukah, or Hanukkah, the Jewish Feast of Lights, also called the "Feast of Dedication"; commemorates the Maccabean victories but focuses on the relighting of the Temple Eternal Light; observed for eight days beginning with the twenty-fifth day of the month of Kislev. 505–13.
January–February	B'Shevat, the New Year of Trees, observed on the fifteenth of Shevat, is the Arbor Day of the Jewish people.
February–March	Ta'anit Esther, the Fast of Esther, commemorates the memory of Queen Esther and the fast she proclaimed following the demands of Ahasuerus for the annihilation of her people; observed on the thirteenth of Adar.
February–March	Purim, or the Feast of Lots, celebrates the deliverance of the Jews in Persia from the machinations of Haman; observed on the fourteenth day of Adar. 685–88.
March–April	Passover, or Pesah, the Jewish Feast of Unleavened Bread, instituted in commemoration of the deliverance of the Jews from Egypt; observed for eight days beginning with the fifteenth day of the month of Nisan. 638–45.
March–April	Yom Hashoa, or Holocaust Day, commemorates the suffering and systematic destruction of European Jewry between 1933 and 1945; occurs on the seventh day of Nisan.

April–May   Lag b'Omer, the thirty-third day of the forty-nine days between Pass-over and Shavuot; its origin is attributed to the cessation of a plague that was decimating the student body of Akiba, a rabbinic sage in the second century; a semiholiday celebrated in Israel with bonfires and dancing; Jewish communities in other nations plan programs for Lag B'Omer to express love of the Holy Land; observed on the eighteenth day of Iyar.

May–June   Shavuot, or Feast of Weeks, marking the completion of seven weeks from the second day of Passover; celebrates the presentation of the Ten Commandments to Israel at Mount Sinai and the offering of the first fruits of the harvest at the Temple in Jerusalem; observed on the sixth and seventh days of the month of Sivan.

The Festival Calendar in the Eastern World

The lunar calendar, the varying monastic years of Buddhism, Jainism, and other religious faiths, and the weather are factors that determine the time patterns for the holidays and festivals on the Asian continent and the islands of the Pacific.

Many local and religious variations of the lunar calendar prevail in Asia. It has been reported that there were more than thirty lunar calendars in use in India in the 1950s. In Bali, in the 1970s, there are two New Years. One is set by the Wauku calendar, which represents a year totaling 210 days. The other is determined by the Sakata calendar, composed of 420 days.

Many variations of the same kind of holiday or festival are to be found in the Far East, molded by differing religious concepts or folk customs. Buddhism, for example, originated as a monastic order. Its festivals center around the monastic year and on commemorations of the events in the life of Buddha. However, there is no single Buddhist calendar. There are many Buddhist sects; consequently, the Buddhist tradition in one area is not necessarily the same as in another. Mahayana Buddhism recognizes several mythological Buddhas and some sectarian founders. The Theravada Buddhists worship the historical Buddha. The Japanese recognize both, and it is said that the Japanese observances honoring a favorite Buddha are frequently more elaborate than the ceremonies for the historical Buddha.

The movable festivals of India are derived from the sectarian Hinduism of the period after the writing of the Puranas. Ancient India celebrated festivals at the end of winter, the beginning of the rainy season, and in the autumn. These seasonal customs had an influence on the timing of the twentieth-century seasonal holidays. The contemporary religious festivals are associated with the great gods, Shiva, Vishnu, and Shakti.

For the Westerner, the most familiar festivals of the Far East are the Chinese festivals. The Chinese influence is also to be seen in many of the festivals of other Asian nations. The observance of the traditional festival on mainland China has diminished with the rise of a new national spirit in the People's Republic of China. The old festivals, however, are kept alive by Taiwan and the Chinese communities around the world.

There are hundreds of festivals in the Near and the Far East. The following calendar of movable festivals of the Eastern world is selective. It includes samples of the historic and the popular and gives some indication of the variety of festivals enjoyed by the people in the Eastern hemisphere.

Gregorian Calendar Months	*Movable Festivals in the Eastern World*
January	Ume Matsuri, or Apricot Festival, observed in many places in Japan with ceremonials related to the ume, or apricot blossom, the Japanese symbol of strength and nobility; ume-viewing events are occasions of quiet dignity.
January	Black Nazarene Fiesta, observed in Manila, Philippine Islands, for eight days, honoring the patron saint of the Quiapo district of Manila.
January	Magh Mela Fair, an annual purification pilgrimage to Allahabad, where devout Hindus bathe in the River Ganges; Allahabad is also the site for the Kumbh Mela Festival, which occurs every twelfth year.
January	Ta-Uchi, the Rice-Field Work Festival, observed in rural Japan with rites and customs in petition for a good rice harvest.
January–February	Chinese New Year, Hs'in Nien, begins with the first new moon after the sun enters Aquarius; occurs between January 21 and February 19; observed in many parts of the Near and Far East; called the "Narcissus Festival" in some areas, since the narcissus symbolizes good fortune.
January–February	Shivaratra, a Hindu day of fasting in honor of the Lord Shiva.
January–February	Tet Nguyenden, commonly known as "Tet," the New Year festival of Vietnam; celebrated during the first seven days of the first month of the lunar calendar.
February	Baika-sai, the Plum Blossom Festival, observed in Japan; commemorating Sugawara Michizane, the ninth-century patron saint of literature and school examinations.
February	Li Chum, a traditional Chinese seasonal observance celebrating the coming of spring. Li Chum means "Spring is here."
February	Thaipusam, an annual Hindu religious festival observed in Malaysia, commemorating the birthday of Lord Subramian; a period of penitence.
February	Tibetan New Year, a three-day holiday celebrated by visiting, feasting, and the relaxation of monastic discipline. It is followed by sMon-lan, a major religious festival of supplication.
February–March	Hari Raya Haji, a Malay festival honoring the Mohammedan pilgrims who return from Mecca.
February–March	Holi, or Hola, a Hindu springtime festival commemorating the burning of Holika, a witch that once tormented all of India; also observed by the Sikhs to honor Krishna; a special time of omens, auguries, and divination in India.
February–March	The Lantern Festival, originally marking the end of the Chinese New Year's season; observed on the fifteenth day of the first moon with lantern rituals and customs; observed in Hong Kong and other parts of Asia.
March	Day of the Moon, the end of the lunar New Year season; observed in Korea with games, feasting, and moon-watching.
March	Kannon Festival, a two-day event observed in mid-March, at the Asakusa Kannon Temple in Japan; a festival of Chigo, or celestial children, honoring the better-behaved children of the parish.
March	Omizutori, a two-week ascetic training ritual combining elements of the Shinto and Buddhist traditions; observed in Japan.

March	O-Mizutori Matsuri, or Water-drawing Ceremony, a fifteen-day festival at Nara in Japan; observed for twelve centuries in commemoration of ancient rites in which holy water is drawn from the Wakasa Well near the temple.
March–April	Birthday of the Goddess of Mercy; observed in Malaysia by the Malayan Chinese, and in Singapore.
March–April	Trut, or New Year; a three-day holiday in Thailand with mixed observances: oblations are made to various gods of Hindu origin; the Buddhist monks exorcise ghosts from the community; and gambling is permitted.
April	Anjin Matsuri, observed in Yokosuka, Japan, as a memorial to William Adams, an Englishman who taught Western navigation, mathematics, and other technical subjects to the Japanese during the time of Shogun Tokugawa Ieyasu.
April	Feast of A-Ma, observed in Macau, an overseas province of Portugal off the China coast, honoring A-Ma, patroness of fishermen and seamen, with rituals in a six-hundred-year-old temple.
April	Maha Thingan Festival, the three-day New Year festival in Burma; observed with periods of prayer and fasting, combined with fun and amusement.
April	Nagasaki Takoage, or Kite-flying Contest; features competing teams of costumed men and gaily decorated kites; observed in late April at Nagasaki, Japan; comparable events are held on varying dates in other parts of Japan and in other nations of the Eastern world.
April	Tsurugaoka Hachiman Spring Festival, a week-long event at Kamakura in Japan; honors the city as the first seat of government seven centuries ago and pays tribute to the cherry blossoms as a symbol of gallant knighthood.
April	Yasukini Matsuri, observed in Tokyo at the Yasakuni Shrine for four days to honor the deified spirits of the Japanese soldiers who died for their country in wars at home or abroad.
April	Zojoji Matsuri, observed in Tokyo, Japan, by the Jodo sect of Buddhism; commemorates the anniversary of the death of Saint Honen, the founder of the Jodo sect; the greatest event in the Jodo calendar.
April–May	Buart Nark, the Buddhist ordination day, usually observed in the spring when young men of Thailand are taken into the priesthood for varying periods of service.
April–May	Buddha Vaisakha Purnima, the celebration of the birthday of Lord Buddha in India; the most outstanding celebration is reported to be at Buddha-Gaya in the province of Hihar, where Buddha received enlightenment.
April–May	Cherry Blossom Festival, observed throughout Japan for about two weeks to celebrate the spring season and the cherry blossoms.
April–May	Toshogu Shrine Grand Festival, observed for two days in Japan in commemoration of the death of Tokugawa Ieyasu in 1616, a Buddhist ceremony re-creating the customs, dress, and dances of the Tokugawa period.
April–May	Wesak, Pali Vishakha-puja, a three-day, or more, holiday celebrated in all of the countries of the Near and Far East during the full month of Vishakha; commemorates the birthday, enlightenment, and death of Buddha; called the "Full Moon of Waso" in Burma.

May	Santa Cruz de Mayo, a month-long Philippine festival; celebrated with processions of costumed Filipinos, parades, and gifts for children.
May–June	Birthday of the Prophet Mohammed, observed in Muslim communities in the Far East with processions or Koran reading, competitions, and other events.
May–June	Guru Arjun's Martyrdom Day, a commemorative holiday of the Sikhs.
June	The Dragon Boat Festival, an old Chinese festival observed on the fifth day of the fifth moon to honor a Chinese poet and statesman; celebrated in many Asian nations.
June	Tano Festival, one of Korea's major holidays, celebrating the end of the spring planting.
July	Tenjin Matsuri, a shrine festival observed in Japan, featuring a river parade of decorated boats carrying the shrine palanquins.
July–August	Bon Festival, or Feast of the Dead, a Buddhist ceremonial of lighting lanterns for deceased ancestors, observed in mid-July in metropolitan areas and mid-August after the harvest in rural regions; a traditional festival in many parts of Asia.
July–August	Lantern-floating Festival, observed in rural Japan after the harvest with the floating of paper lanterns on the waters.
July–August	Narali Purnima, the Hindu holiday of the full moon of Sravan, sometimes called "Coconut Full-Moon day."
August	Awa Odori, the Fools' Dance, a Japanese event of dancing in the street all night.
August	Ch'usok, a day of honor to the dead, observed by the Koreans on a day determined by the lunar calendar, usually in August at the end of the harvest period.
August	Esala Perahera, a festival held in the lunar month of Esala in Ceylon; originally celebrated in tribute to Hindu gods, it is now a colorful festival in honor of a tooth of Buddha preserved in the temple at Kandy.
August	Krishna's Birthday, commemorated in India in honor of the Baby Krishna, with ceremonials of prayer and anointment of an image of the infant God and recountings of his life.
August	Pajjusana, an eight-day period of penance observed by the followers of Jainism; commemorating the birth of Mahavira, founder of the Jain order, and honoring Kalpa Sutra, the sacred scripture.
August	Raksha Bandhan Day, observed in India during the first part of August; sometimes called "Sisters' Day," since it is the day when a sister ties a rakhi, or treasured scarf, to her brother's wrist to protect him.
August	Rokusai Nembutsu and O-Bon, observed in Japan with danced prayer and folk-dance events combined with O-Bon, the Buddhist festival for the souls of the dead.
August–September	Feast of the Hungry Ghosts, or All Soul's Day, a day of honoring the spirits of ancestors; observed in Malaysia and Singapore.
September	Choosuk, or Moon Festival, observed in Korea as Thanksgiving Day, a time to tend the graves of ancestors, hold hunting contests, and enjoy the year's biggest feast.
September	Confucian Festival, a Korean day honoring Confucius; another is held in the spring.

September–October	Quarrel Festival at Matsubara Shrine in Japan, re-creating the clash between bearers of portable shrines.
October	Durga Puja, the festival of the Divine Mother, a ten-day holiday in India celebrating the creative force of the universe and honoring the ten-armed Durga, wife of Shiva; the day is also known as "the Festival of Victory," to commemorate the victory of the goddess Durga over the demon Mashishasura.
October	Festival of the Emperor Gods, celebrated in Penang, Malaysia, to commemorate the return of nine celestial kings to heaven.
October	Full Moon of Thadingyut, the end of Buddhist Lent, observed in Burma and other Buddhist countries; a tradition time for engagements and weddings.
October	Paung-daw-U Festival, observed in Yawnghe in the Shan states of Burma; a Buddhist festival featuring a water procession honoring three Buddha images.
October	Tod Kathin and Procession of Golden Barges of the King; a Thailand observance commemorating the king's annual presentation of new yellow robes to the monks.
October–November	Deepavali, or Festival of Lights, an annual celebration in Malaysia and in Singapore, commemorating the slaying of a mythological king by Lord Krishna.
October–November	Diwali, or Festival of Lights, a holiday commemorating one of the four New Year's days celebrated in India; Diwali is a five-day celebration observing in succession Dhana Trayodashi, the New Year of business; the triumph of the god Vishnu over Narakasura; the virtues of Lakshmi, Vishnu's wife; Bali worship day; and Yamma, a day devoted to brothers and sisters.
October–November	Mooncake Festival, celebrated in Singapore, commemorating the overthrow of the Mongol overlords in ancient China.
December	Guru Tegh Bahadur's Martyrdom Day, a commemorative day of the Sikhs.
December–January	Anniversary of the birth of Guru Govind Singh, a commemorative holiday observed by the Sikhs.

The Festival Calendar in the Western World

The Gregorian calendar, the church calendar, the seasons, and local customs regulate the movable festivals of the Western world. Many are associated with fixed days but are movable in the extension of the festival period before or after a traditional date. The following selected festivals are representative of the countless movable festivals that are a part of the heritage of the Western world. The festivals are arranged alphabetically within the corresponding time frame of the Gregorian calendar. The location of a specific festival may be determined through the index.

Gregorian Calendar Months	Movable Festivals in the Western World
January	Chalma pilgrimage; observed at Chalma, Mexico, during the first week of January in veneration of the Chalma image of Christ; the last mile of the pilgrimage must be on foot or horseback.
January	Tsao Chun, Festival of the Kitchen God, observed by Chinese-American communities in preparation for the Chinese New Year. The custom is based on a traditional farewell ceremony for T'sao Wang, Prince of the Oven, or Kitchen God, before he leaves on an annual trip to heaven to report on the family's behavior during the year.
January–February	Carnival Days, observed in all Roman Catholic countries on varying days between Epiphany and Ash Wednesday; a public holiday period in at least ten nations; a time of revelry and feasting.
January–February	American-Chinese New Year, determined by the Chinese lunar calendar; observed in San Francisco and by Chinese-American communities throughout the United States, featuring cavorting dragons, silken lions, and ancient customs of Old China.
February	Charro Days, a four-day festival celebrated at Brownsville, Texas, featuring the traditions and customs of a two-nation border city.
February	Festival du Voyageur, celebrated at Saint Boniface, Manitoba, for five days in late February to honor the early *coureur-de-bois* and the founding of the French-speaking community in Manitoba.
February–March	Bun Day, a children's festival of Iceland, held on the Monday before Shrove Tuesday, a traditional day for sharing whipped-cream buns with children.
February–March	Carnaval-Souvenir de Chicoutimi, celebrated in Chicoutimi, Quebec, from late February into early March to honor the history and the folkways of the region.
February–March	Collop Monday, the Monday before Shrove Tuesday; the traditional day for the faithful to stop eating meat; the day was once known as "Poets' Monday" because of the many poems that were written about this penitential day in England and Europe.
February–March	Fasching, a Shrovetide festival observed in Austria and Germany on Rose Monday and Shrove Tuesday, between Fasching Sunday and Ash Wednesday; also called "Fasnacht," "Fasnet," or "Feast of Fools"; features processions of masked figures and generations of old customs.
February–March	Mardi Gras, the best-known Lenten carnival in the United States; celebrated in New Orleans, Louisiana, since 1830 during the week before Lent, with a king and a queen, parades, masqued balls, music, and gay pageantry.
February–March	Marfeh, meat-fare and cheese-fare days, observed in the Orthodox Catholic communities of Syria and Lebanon preceding the Lenten fast; carries out old customs such as eating a boiled egg last at meals.
February–March	Pancake Day, always observed on Shrove Tuesday; a day for eating pancakes; a special event is the International Pancake Race between the housewives of Liberal, Kansas, and Olney, England, in which they run a quarter mile while tossing pancakes in a skillet.
February–March	Rosemontag, or Rose Monday; the Monday before Lent, celebrated in Germany with processions, mummery, and masquerades.

March	Fallas de San José, the Bonfires of Saint Joseph, a week-long festival in Valencia, Spain; originated in medieval times when the carpenter's guild burned the annual accumulation of shop chips; a spectacular competition of ingenious bonfires and other events; honors Saint Joseph, father of Jesus and patron of carpenters.
March–April	The Cherry Blossom Festival in Washington, D.C., is held when the cherry trees bloom that were presented by Japan and planted around the Potomac River Tidal Basin; the season varies from approximately March 20 to April 15.
March–April	Emaischen Day, a traditional festival of old customs celebrated in Luxembourg on Easter Monday.
March–April	Festival of States, a spring festival held in Saint Petersburg, Florida, in late March and early April to welcome spring; a special feature is the band competition, with representatives from the various states vying for the Governor's Cup.
March–April	Saint Lazarus Day, an ancient Slav holiday observed in Bulgaria on the Saturday preceding Easter, a special day for young girls.
March–April	White House Easter Egg Roll, a traditional event held annually on Easter Monday on the south lawn of the White House in Washington, D.C.
April	Daffodil Festival, the first Puyallup Valley Daffodil Festival was held on April 6, 1926, near Sumner, Washington; now observed in Tacoma, Sumner, and Puyallup in April, with floral parades and picturesque coronation ceremonies for the daffodil queen.
April	Jaudes Days, a two-day festival observed in Vianden, Luxembourg, in early April; a youth festival with traditions dating from the pre-Christian era.
April	Sechseläuten, Six Ringing Festival, observed in Zurich, Switzerland, on a Sunday and Monday early in April; originally a medieval guild holiday commemorating the ringing of the cathedral bells at six instead of seven o'clock for the end of the working day; a public holiday with events symbolizing the driving out of Böög, a huge snowman, the traditional embodiment of Old Man Winter.
April–May	Alp Aufzug, Procession to the Alps, observed in the valley villages of Switzerland on varying days in April and May, to honor the herdsmen and the flower-decked cattle on their slow march to the mountaintop pastures.
May	Cartagena de Indias Festival, an annual event in the fortress city of Cartagena, Colombia, celebrated in late May; a distinguished celebration of the arts with concerts, recitals, dance presentations, and lectures.
May	Holland Tulip Time Festival, observed in mid-May in Holland, Michigan, to display the tulip gardens and to share the Dutch cultural heritage of the area.
May	Our Lady of Fátima pilgrimages to Fátima, Portugal, to commemorate the appearance of the Virgin to three children tending their sheep in 1917; Fátima pilgrimages are also held in other months.
May	Saint Isidro Labrador's festival, a time of general fiesta merriment and feasting in Madrid to honor San Isidro, patron of Madrid and of farmers; an eight-day event in mid-May of colorful parades, street dancing, and bullfights.

May	Midnight Sun Days, observed at North Cape, Norway, beginning in mid-May and lasting two months; a series of festivals in honor of the round-the-clock sunshine.
May–June	Ecaussines, Belgium, matrimonial party, given on Whitmonday by neighborhood girls for the bachelors of the community.
June	Sitges Carnation Show, takes place in early June in Sitges, Spain, where carnations grow like weeds. The carnations are gathered by the community and woven into a decorated carpet a quarter of a mile long. At the close of the show, the local Catalan dance crushes the carpet into perfume. The Fiesta of Corpus Christi is celebrated with this event.
June	Xiquets de Valls, a part of the celebration of the Feast of Saint John at Valls in Spain, which goes back to 1633; observed in June as a gymnastic specialty that forms human towers with musical accompaniment from a clarinet and a drum.
June–July	Common Ridings Day, observed in June and July in the towns and villages of Scotland, commemorates "the riding of the borders of the town common" to retain royal charters; repeats ceremonies that were established four or five centuries ago.
June–August	The Pilgrimage to Lough Derg, the greatest of the popular pilgrimages of Ireland, takes place between June 1 and August 15; during this season, only the pilgrims may visit the island, and they must take only one meal a day, drink "pilgrim's wine," and go barefoot; also called the Pilgrimage of Saint Patrick's Purgatory.
June	Festival of Good Neighbours; observed at Dumfries, Scotland, in late June; commemorating an age-old custom of resolving complaints between neighbors; a week of festivities, including the Riding of the Marches.
July	Battle of Flowers; celebrated on the Island of Jersey, usually in the fourth week of July; a spectacular floral carnival that began in 1902 as a part of the celebration honoring the coronation of Edward VII.
July	The Days of Ezra Meeker, presented at the end of July in Puyallup, Washington, to re-create the life of the pioneer who is credited with the marking of the Oregon Trail and whose work led to the establishment of the Oregon Trail Association and the American Trails Association.
July	Festa do Colete Encarnado, the Red Waistcoat Festival, celebrated in July at Vila Franca de Xira in Portugal; a festival honoring the bull herders in their red waistcoats and the chase of the black bulls down the streets.
July	Festa dos Tabuleiros, Festival of the Tabuleiros, observed in Tomar, in the province of Ribatejo, Portugal, for four days in mid-July every third year in odd years; a six-hundred-year event celebrating a thanksgiving for the harvest and expressing Tomar's charity for the poor and the afflicted.
July	Festival of the Holy Queen Isabel, observed in Coimbra, Portugal, during the first fortnight in July in even years; commemorates the memory of Queen Isabel, who saved Portugal's first capital from calamity and was canonized in 1625.

July	The Festival of the Magdalene, La Fête de la Madeleine, observed in Sainte Baume, a region of Provence, by pilgrimages to the Holy Cave where the Magdalene reputedly lived in repentance of her sins. The shrine is visited at all times of the year, but July 22 is the day when many young girls visit the grotto to seek the help of Magdalene in finding husbands.
July	Jasper Outdoor Spectacle, held annually in mid-July since 1955, with pageants showing the growth of the Canadian West from the time of the voyageurs.
July	Kutztown Fair, a Pennsylvania Dutch festival, Kutztown, Pennsylvania, always held around the July 4 weekend, presenting authentic re-creations of early Pennsylvania Dutch life, art, and handicrafts.
July	Les Trois Glorieuses, a French celebration commemorating the three Glorious Days, July 27, 28, and 29, 1830, when a popular uprising in France replaced one king with another; special honors are given to Burgundy wine; the same fete is celebrated in the fall to mark the end of the grape harvest.
July	The National Cherry Festival; held annually at Traverse City, Michigan, since 1928 in mid- or late July, with programs, festivities, and ceremonies attending the departure of the first loads to market.
July	The Royal Tournament, an annual event in London providing a showcase for the British armed services, with mock battles, gymnastics, and precision marching.
July	Sunflower Festival, celebrated by the Mennonites, descendants of the nineteenth-century settlers of Manitoba; the festival honors more than a century of accomplishments, including the success of extracting oil from sunflower plants.
July	Wild Pony Round-up on Virginia's Chincoteague Island, held in July; also called "Pony-penning Day." The wild ponies of the island are supposedly descendants of Arabian horses left by the pirates or early colonists.
July–August	The Fiesta of Santiago, observed at Loiza Aldea in Puerto Rico for ten days beginning in late July; combines a religious festival with a masquerade carnival in which citizens dress as Christian Spaniards or infidel Moors.
July–August	Salzburg Festival, a musical event of international fame scheduled annually in July and August.
July–August	Schutzenfeste, a marksmen's festival that originated in Biberach, Germany; a traditional folk festival with marksmen's societies as the principal participants; a popular event in other regions in Germany as well, observed on varying days in July or August.
August	American Indian Exposition, held annually in August at Anadarko, Oklahoma, the site of Indian City, U.S.A., where authentic reproductions of several Indian villages and murals by Kiowa artists in the intertribal Indian agency may be found.
August	David and Goliath Day, a re-creation of the biblical story, part of a centuries-old fall festival at Ath, Belgium; Goliath is vanquished but has the last line "I'm not dead yet."

August	Doggett's Coat and Badge Race up the Thames River, an English event scheduled around August 1; originated as a tribute to the company of Watermen of the River Thames; reported to be the world's oldest annually staged sporting event and the longest rowing race; now kept up under the supervision of the Fishmongers' Company.
August	Hobo Days; a gathering of people with wanderlust; observed in late August in Britt, Iowa, with celebrations in the carnival manner and with the crowning of a king of the hoboes.
August	Pilgrims' Progress, observed on five separate days in August and on November 2 in Plymouth, Massachusetts; an observance re-creating the Sabbath procession of the Pilgrims to church services.
August	The Royal National Eisteddfod of Wales; held annually in August in North and South Wales alternately, to encourage Welsh literature and music. Other Eisteddfodau are held in separate Welsh communities from May until early November for the preservation of the Welsh language and national customs.
August– September	The Highland Games of Scotland, begin around the first of August and continue at varying dates and places into September; the most important features are competitions in bagpipe music, Highland dancing, and the tossing of the caber, a fir-tree competition that displays coordination.
September	Almabtrieb, a gala festival day in the German Alps celebrating the return to winter shelter of the herdgirls and flower-decked cattle from summer pasture in the mountains.
September	Braemar Gathering, an annual event in the village of Braemar in Scotland; a festive occasion with Highland dancing, games, and athletic competitions demanding skill and prowess.
September	Fiesta de la Vendimia, or Vintage Feast, celebrated in mid-September in Jerez de la Frontera, Spain; an annual thanksgiving for the grape harvest, honoring Saint Gines de la Jara, patron of vineyards; celebrated with religious services, cavalcades of Andalusian-bred horses, bullfights, and feasting.
September	The Pendleton Round-up, celebrated at Pendleton, Oregon, since pioneer days, and regularly since 1910, during the last four days of the second or third week in September. Its purpose is to recall and honor pioneer life.
September– October	National Gaelic Mod, observed in Scotland during the first two weeks in October, or occasionally beginning in the last week of September; a major cultural event since 1892, organized to promote the Gaelic language and the history and arts of the Highlands and the islands of Scotland.
September– October	Oktoberfest, one of Germany's most famous festivals, began on October 17, 1810, the wedding day of King Ludwig I; now held from mid-September into October to celebrate with the best beers, foods, and entertainment of the season.
October	Mop Fairs at Stratford-on-Avon in England; originally a harvest festival when the farmers picked their hired help for the next year; now a two-part carnival, including a time-honored ox-roasting ceremony during the first fair, and a traditional Runaway Mop Fair a few days later to recall early employment practices.

October– November	Aloha Festival, the largest of all Hawaiian festivals, is celebrated in Hawaii from mid-October through mid-November; known as the "Mardi Gras of the Pacific," it is observed with pageantry, street dancing, hula festivals, luaus, parades, and balls.
October	Virgen del Pilar, Virgin of the Pillar, celebrated with a ten-day festival in Saragossa, Spain; honoring the legend that the Virgin revealed herself from a pillar to Saint James the Apostle when he was evangelizing Spain; the secular events include the famous parade of giants and dwarfs.
November	State Opening of Parliament, a colorful British ritual dating back to Plantagenet times; observed in London after a general election and preceding the beginning of each parliamentary session; involves the queen in traditional royal ceremonies.
December	Kriss Kringle's Fair; presented in Nuremberg, Germany, from early December until Christmas; reportedly began in the Middle Ages to display the arts of the Nuremberg craftsmen and specialty cooks.
December	The annual Christmas Novena, the nine-day ritual preceding the celebration of Christ's birth, begins on December 16 in Popayan, Colombia, and officially opens the Christmas season. The observance is a combination of religious fervor and fiesta and evening devotions, opening with the singing of traditional Christmas carols, prayers at the *pesebre*, and special prayers for the novena, followed by fireworks, dancing, and small parties during the nine days.
December	Caribbean Christmas Festival, begins on December 23 in Christiansted in Saint Croix and lasts for two weeks, with wandering guitarists singing to the Christ child. A unique feature of this festival is the jig-dance carried on since Elizabethan days, with the recitation of old poems and stories, such as *Saint George and the Dragon*.
December	Philippine Christmas, held in the Philippine Islands from December 16 to January 6, with the observance of traditions and special Christmastime events; reported to be one of the longest and gayest Christmas festivals in the world.

PART

Books Related to Anniversaries and Holidays

Source Books and Background Readings

Almanacs and Dictionaries of Days

1. The black almanac. Rev. and enl. by Alton Hornsby, Jr. Woodbury, N.Y.: Barron's Educational Series, 1973.
Brief commentaries on the facts and events in Afro-American history from 1619 to 1972 that are subject to commemoration or recognition; arranged chronologically; indexed.

2. Bowker annual of library and booktrade information. Sponsored by the Council of National Library Associations. New York: Bowker, annual.
An annual handbook of book-trade and library statistics and surveys; includes calendars of meetings and promotional events, information on library prizes and awards, best sellers, and notable books.

3. Canadian almanac and directory for the year. Toronto: Copp Clark, annual.
Source for current Canadian statistics; data on holidays includes listing of public statutory holidays for the Dominion of Canada, major provincial holidays, and a summary list of special days.

4. Carruth, Gorton, ed. The encyclopedia of American facts and dates. 5th ed. New York: Crowell, 1971.
A compilation of dates, facts, and developments in many fields in American life; arranged chronologically in parallel columns for comparative reference; indexed.

5. Catholic almanac. Ed. by Felician A. Foy. Huntington, Ind.: Our Sunday Visitor, annual.
A handbook of current information on the Roman Catholic church; includes the liturgical calendar, background dates in the United States Catholic chronology, a list of saints, and a description of awards and honors.

6. Chase, William D. Chase's calendar of annual events. Flint, Mich.: Apple Tree Press, annual.
A handy publication listing the events of each day of the month, special weeks, and month-long observances; particularly useful for ascertaining specific dates for movable events in a one-year period; arranged chronologically; indexed.

7. Cullen, Marion Elizabeth. Memorable days in music. Metuchen, N.J.: Scarecrow, 1970.
A chronological compilation of important events in classical music: dates of important musicians, opera premieres, and famous performances.

8. Douglas, George William. The American book of days: a compendium of information about holidays, festivals, notable anniversaries and Christian and Jewish holy days with notes on other American anniversaries worthy of remembrance. Rev. by Helen Douglas Compton. New York: Wilson, 1948.
Descriptive articles on the origin and observance of holidays and special days in the United States; arranged by the calendar year; indexed.

9. The Ebony handbook, by the editors of Ebony. Chicago: Johnson Pub., 1974.
A handbook of information about black Americans, including a chronology of contemporary events, 1954–73; a military chronology, 1969–73; lists of winners of the Congressional Medal of Honor and winners of the Spingarn Medal.

10. Eggenberger, David. A dictionary of battles. New York: Crowell, 1967.
Dates and data on famous military engagements, from the first Battle of Megiddo in 1479 B.C. to the Arab-Israeli War, June 1967.

11. Emrich, Duncan, comp. The hodge-podge book: an almanac of American folklore. New York: Four Winds Press, 1972.
An almanac of curious fancies and information, drawn from American folklore, about seasons, months, and special days.

12. Europa year book. 2 vols. London: Europa Pub., annual.
An international statistical survey; vol. 1 covers the United Nations and Europe; vol. 2 includes the nations in Africa, the Americas, Asia, and Australia; the survey of each nation includes a simple listing of public holidays observed during the last half of one year and the first half of the following year; useful for determining specific dates of movable feasts; volumes arranged alphabetically by country.

13. Everyman's dictionary of dates. 6th ed. Rev. by Audrey Butler. New York: Dutton, 1971.
A frequently revised handbook, beginning with a section on the Gregorian, Jewish, Roman, and Orthodox calendars; the main entries provide dates for all periods in history; alphabetically arranged by dictionary topic.

14. Harbottle, Thomas. Dictionary of battles. Rev. and updated by George Bruce. New York: Stein & Day, 1971.
A dictionary of battles from ancient times through the Vietnam War; arranged alphabetically.

15. Harper encyclopedia of the modern world: a concise reference history from 1760 to the present. Ed. by Richard B. Morris and Graham W. Irwin. New York: Harper, 1970.
A chronology providing dates for political, military, and diplomatic events, followed by topical studies of world developments; indexed.

16. Information please almanac, atlas, and yearbook. New York: Simon & Schuster, annual.
An annual review of the year on topics of current interest; identifies major religious and secular holidays; lists the legal holidays of the fifty states, the District of Columbia, and Puerto Rico; projects Gregorian calendar dates for movable Christian, secular, and Jewish holidays, a decade in advance of the current year.

17. Jahn, Raymond. Concise dictionary of holidays. New York: Philosophical Lib., 1958.
A dictionary with brief entries defining terms or names associated with holidays and other days of observance; arranged alphabetically by principal word.

18. Langer, William Leonard. An encyclopedia of world history: ancient, medieval, and modern. 5th ed. Boston: Houghton, 1972.
Outlines of events in world history from the prehistoric period into the twentieth century; arranged chronologically; appendix includes dates for world rulers and the year in which universities and colleges in the New World were founded, prior to 1900.

19. Lipkind, William. Days to remember: an almanac. New York: Obolensky, 1961.
An almanac of traditional holidays, special days, and birthdays, identified with drawings and very simple descriptions or quotations; arranged by the calendar year.

20. Mirkin, Stanford M. What happened when. Rev. ed. New York: Washburn, 1966.
A compilation of dates of notable events, primarily of the nineteenth and twentieth centuries through 1965; arranged chronologically by year; indexed.

21. Official Associated Press almanac. Maplewood, N.J.: Hammond, annual.
Information on holidays; lists dates for foreign national holidays, and includes a check-off chart of American public holidays indicating observance practices in each of the states in the United States; holiday facts may be located through the index.

22. Spinrad, Leonard, and Spinrad, Thelma. Instant almanac of events, anniversaries, observances, and birthdays for every day of the year. West Nyack, N.Y.: Parker Pub., 1972.
A month-by-month, day-by-day listing of holidays, events, birthdays, and special weeks, with brief identification; includes quotations, notations on birthstones, and the signs of the zodiac.

23. Steinberg, Sigfrid H. Historical tables. 8th ed. London: Macmillan, 1966.
A tabular chronology of world history, arranged by period in parallel columns; includes dates for political, constitutional, and economic history, and natural-science and cultural developments.

24. Whitaker, Joseph. An almanack. London: Clowes, annual.
A British compilation of current information, including the annual dates for bank holidays in England, Wales, Northern Ireland, Scotland, and the Channel Islands; a table of Easter days and Sunday letters from 1500 to 2000; a table of movable religious feasts; and other quick-reference calendar tables.

25. World almanac and book of facts. New York: New York Newspaper Enterprise Assn., annual.

A comprehensive American almanac of miscellaneous information; the section on holidays includes an up-to-date listing of American and Canadian holidays, data on the Jewish holidays, the Greek Orthodox calendar, the Islamic calendar, the lunar calendar for the Chinese New Year and the Vietnamese Tet, Old English holidays, and an annual calendar of events.

Calendars and the Measurement of Time

26. Adler, Irving. Time in your life. Rev. ed. New York: Day, 1969.

An examination of time in relation to the planets, the calendar, clocks and watches, and time zones.

27. Asimov, Isaac. The clock we live on. Rev. ed. New York: Abelard-Schuman, 1965.

A study of the complexities of measuring time, the numbering of years and naming of days, and the problems of calendar reform.

28. Bell, Thelma Harrington, and Bell, Corydon. The riddle of time. New York: Viking, 1963.

A review of the philosophical concepts of time, the use of the calendar, and the standardization of public time.

29. Buxton, David Roden. The Abyssinians. New York: Praeger, 1970.

Appendix B of this introduction to the life and culture of the Abyssinian people provides an explanation of the Coptic/Ethiopian calendar, an ancient time-instrument that survives nowhere else in the world.

30. "Calendar," Encyclopaedia Judaica 5:43–54. Jerusalem: Keter, 1971.

A concise explanation of the Jewish calendar, the fixing of New Year's Day, the character of the year, and the present order of intercalation; followed by short articles on sectarian calendars and on calendar reform.

31. Coleman, Lesley. A book of time. New York: Nelson, 1971.

An account of calendars, sundials, sandglasses, clocks, clockmakers, time zones, and international date lines from the era of the Sumerian priests to the atomic clocks at Greenwich.

32. Cousins, Frank W. Sundials: the art and science of gnomonics. New York: Pica Press, 1970.

Descriptions and illustrations of various types of the sundial, mankind's oldest astronomical instrument, with technical information on astronomy, geometry, and other factors involved in their development.

33. Couzens, Reginald C. The stories of the months and days. London: Blackie, 1922; Detroit: Gale Research, 1970.

A reprint of a book on the history, myths, and legends of the names of the days of the week and the months.

34. Duran, Fray Diego. Book of the gods and rites and the ancient calendar. Norman: Univ. of Oklahoma Press, 1971.

A translation of the work of a sixteenth-century Dominican friar, which includes an explanation of the Aztec system of measuring time.

35. Fredregill, Ernest J. One thousand years. New York: Exposition Press, 1970.

"A Julian-Gregorian perpetual calendar, 1100 A.D. to 2099 A.D."—subtitle.

36. Freeman-Grenville, Greville S. Muslim and Christian calendars. New York: Oxford, 1963.

"Tables for the conversion of Muslim and Christian days from the Hijra to the year A.D. 2000."—subtitle.

37. Guye, Samuel, and Michel, Henri. Time and space: measuring instruments from the 15th to the 19th century. New York: Praeger, 1971.

A history of the development of clocks and such measuring instruments as terrestrial and celestial globes, sundials, and hourglasses.

38. Irwin, Keith Gordon. The 365 days. New York: Crowell, 1963.

An account of the evolution of the calendar from the Egyptian calendar based on the flooding cycles of the Nile River to the Gregorian calendar; explains variable months and the progression of dates for the days of the week, tree-ring records, temperature studies, and radiocarbon dating.

39. Krythe, Maymie Richardson. All about the months. New York: Harper, 1966.

Information on the months of the Gregorian calendar, including birthstones, flowers, important birthdays, holidays, and happenings.

40. León Portilla, Miguel. Time and reality in the thought of the Maya. Boston: Beacon Press, 1973.

A scholarly interpretation of the time-space concepts of the ancient Mayans, beginning with a description of the Mayan calendar system.

Commemorative Events and Collections

41. Bloomgarten, Henry S. American history through commemorative stamps. New York: Arco, 1969.
A depiction of notable events and memorable people in the history of the United States as honored through commemorative stamps; illustrated with black-and-white enlargements of individual stamps; not indexed.

42. Davis, Norman M. The complete book of United States coin collecting. New York: Macmillan, 1971.
Information on major mintages, changing designs, and coin lore from the colonial period to the present, with charts of commemorative coins.

43. Fales, Martha Gandy. Early American silver. Rev. and enl. ed. New York: Dutton, 1973.
An overview of the regional characteristics, design sources, and forms of American silver from the seventeenth to the early nineteenth century; background material for commemorative exhibits.

44. Hartje, Robert G. Bicentennial U.S.A.: pathways to celebration. Nashville, Tenn.: American Assn. for State and Local History, 1973.
An examination of centennials of the Civil War, the Canadian Confederation, and several American states, with guidelines for planning by organizations on the local, state, and national levels.

45. Klamkin, Marian. American patriotic and political china. New York: Scribner, 1973.
Highlights in the history and production of commemorative china honoring the presidents of the United States, the Apollo flights, and centennials.

46. Maass, John. The glorious enterprise: the Centennial Exhibition of 1876 and H. J. Schwarzmann, architect-in-chief. Watkins Glen, N.Y.: American Life Foundation, 1973.
A study of the Philadelphia Centennial Exhibition of 1876, its chief designer, and its place among nineteenth-century world's fairs.

47. Michael, George. George Michael's treasury of Federal antiques. New York: Hawthorn Books, 1972.
A study of American craftsmanship in the years between 1770 and 1830, the last era of hand creativity and manufacture in the United States; useful background material for commemorative programs.

48. Nathan, Adele. How to plan and conduct a bicentennial celebration. Harrisburg, Pa.: Stackpole, 1971.
A handbook on the organization and management of community bicentennials and other anniversary events, from the production of pageants, parades, and dedications to restorations and vignettes.

49. Preserving a heritage: final report to the president and congress of the National Parks Centennial Commission. Washington, D.C.: The Commission, 1973.
An official report covering nationwide centennials honoring the establishment of Yellowstone; also lists commemorative stamps and gives recommendations from world conferences.

Historic Fetes and Public Entertainment

50. Barber, Richard. The knight and chivalry. New York: Scribner, 1970.
Background reading on the interrelationship of chivalry and ancient tournaments, epics, and military orders; based on the literature and history of the Middle Ages.

51. Beijer, Agne. Court theatres of Drottningholm and Gripsholm. New York: Benjamin Blom, 1972.
A description of the eighteenth-century Swedish court theaters at Gripsholm Castle and Drottningholm Palace, the sites of contemporary theatrical revivals.

52. Brody, Alan. The English mummers and their plays: traces of ancient mystery. Philadelphia: Univ. of Pennsylvania Press, 1970.
An examination of three types of mummers' plays: the hero-combat, the sword play, and the wooing ceremony; indexed.

53. Calder, Alexander. Calder's circus. Ed. by Jean Lipman. New York: Dutton, 1972.
A description of the traveling miniature circus of the early twentieth century designed and produced by Alexander Calder, creator of the mobile and the stabile.

54. Fried, Frederick. Artists in wood: American carvers of cigar-store Indians, show figures, and circus wagons. New York: Potter, 1970.
A biography of thirty-seven wood carvers of the United States and Canada who contributed to the popular visual arts and to the entertainment devices of the nineteenth century.

55. **Greene, Theodore P.** America's heroes. New York: Oxford, 1970.
A study of the American hero as reflected in periodical literature in four major historical periods, from 1787 to 1918; provides insight into the public interest in days of recognition for popular heroes.

56. **Jones, William.** Crowns and coronations: a history of regalia. London: Chatto & Windus, 1902; Detroit: Singing Tree Press, 1968.
A history of royal coronation days, regalia, rituals, and pageantry in various ages and countries, primarily British.

57. **Lewis, Philip C.** Trouping: how the show came to town. New York: Harper, 1973.
A popular history of the road show era, showing the interaction between the traveling theater and the American public from 1850 to 1905; recalls the legendary careers of playwrights, minstrels, actors, and actresses on the road.

58. **McKennon, Joe.** A pictorial history of the American carnival. Sarasota, Fla.: Carnival Pub., 1972.
A trouper's recall of carnivals in the United States, types of performances, performers, and companies; includes a glossary of carnival terms and many illustrations.

59. **Morley, Henry.** Memoirs of Bartholomew Fair. London: Chatto & Windus, 1880; Detroit: Singing Tree Press, 1968.
A detailed account of Saint Bartholomew's Fair, once the greatest of English festivals.

60. **Morrison, Theodore.** Chautauqua: a center for education, religion, and the arts in America. Chicago: Univ. of Chicago Press, 1974.
A history of the seasonal offerings and experimental programs of Chautauqua, the most popular out-of-school educational movement of the nineteenth century in the United States.

61. **Strong, Roy.** Splendour at court: Renaissance spectacle and the theater of power. Boston: Houghton, 1973.
A history of Renaissance court fetes, the impact of celebrations in sixteenth- and seventeenth-century society, and their influence on later creative forms.

62. **Thiselton-Dyer, Thomas Firminger.** British popular customs, present and past: illustrating the social and domestic manners of the people. London: Bell, 1876; Detroit: Singing Tree Press, 1968.
A book of days recording Old English customs and commemorations; indispensable for history of obsolete days.

63. **Toll, Robert C.** Blacking up: the minstrel show in nineteenth-century America. New York: Oxford, 1974.
A study of the minstrel show and its influence on public opinion and popular culture for fifty years in the nineteenth century.

64. **Weatherwax, Paul.** "Corn and the culture of Old America." In his Indian corn in Old America, pp. 208–38. New York: Macmillan, 1954.
A chapter on the stories of the origin of corn, its symbolism in ceremonies of birth, its use in the fetes for the maize deities, and early harvest festivals.

Religious Days: Background Readings

The Christian Year

65. **Chambers, Robert.** Book of days. 2 vols. Philadelphia: Lippincott, 1899; Detroit: Gale Research, 1967.
A miscellany of information on days related to the church calendar, with descriptions of festivals and customs; arranged chronologically by days; indexed.

66. **Child, Heather, and Colles, Dorothy.** Christian symbols, ancient and modern. New York: Scribner, 1973.
A description of Christian symbols, correlating the evolution of symbolism with developments in theology; well illustrated with black-and-white plates and line drawings.

67. Cowie, L. W., and Gummer, John S. The Christian calendar: a complete guide to the seasons of the Christian year. Springfield, Mass.: Merriam-Webster, 1974.
A two-part interpretation of the Christian calendar; Part 1 is focused on the feasts and festivals associated with the life of Christ; Part 2 lists the saints for each day of the year and events in the life of the Virgin.

68. Deems, Edward Mark. Holy-days and holidays. New York: Funk & Wagnalls, 1902; Detroit: Gale Research, 1968.
Source material on the origin of church festivals and national holidays; excerpts from the work of nineteenth-century writers on the meaning of holy days and holidays.

69. Epton, Nina Consuelo. Spanish fiestas, including romerias, excluding bull-fights. New York: Barnes & Noble, 1969.
Outstanding Spanish religious fiestas, from the Easter cycle to the pre-Lenten carnival season; dates are given for the fixed observances.

70. Forsyth, Ilene H. The throne of wisdom: wood sculptures of the Madonna in Romanesque France. Princeton, N.J.: Princeton Univ. Press, 1972.
A study of the origin, function, and character of the carvings of the enthroned Virgin and child in Western Europe up to the end of the twelfth century.

71. Gardner, Helen, ed. A book of religious verse. New York: Oxford, 1972.
An anthology of religious verse from the seventh to the twentieth century; the majority are Christian poems.

72. Gerhard, H. P. The world of icons. New York: Harper, 1972.
An introduction to the creation and use of icons as religious symbols and art forms from the time of Justinian to the seventeenth century.

73. Horn, Edward T., III. The Christian year. Philadelphia: Muhlenberg Press, 1957.
An analysis of the evolution of the church calendar, focusing on the ways in which the Lutheran, Anglican, and Roman churches carry out liturgical traditions.

74. Laliberte, Norman, and West, Edward V. The history of the cross. New York: Macmillan, 1960.
An illustrated history of the cross as a Christian symbol and an important element in ecclesiastical observances, with identification of individual crosses of all periods of history; illustrated with line drawings.

75. Long, Kenneth R. The music of the English Church. New York: St. Martins, 1972.
A history of Anglican liturgical music, projected against the religious, cultural, social, and political backgrounds, and musical trends of four hundred years.

76. MacKay, Ruth. They sang a new song: stories of great hymns. Nashville, Tenn.: Abingdon, 1959.
A narrative history of the circumstances that inspired the writing of twenty hymns used for Christmas, Thanksgiving, and other religious services.

77. Maus, Cynthia Pearl, comp. Christ and the fine arts. Rev. ed. New York: Harper, 1959.
A classic anthology of pictures, poetry, stories, and music related to the life of Christ.

78. Miller, Madeleine S. A treasury of the cross. New York: Harper, 1956.
A comprehensive study of the background, symbolism, and designs of crosses used in the Christian church; includes a section on hymns, poems, and sayings about the cross.

79. Spicer, Dorothy Gladys. Festivals of Western Europe. New York: Wilson, 1958.
Descriptions of local customs in feasts and festivals of Western Europe related to the church year; arranged alphabetically by country, chronologically within the country; indexed.

80. Weiser, Francis Xavier. Handbook of Christian feasts and customs: the year of the Lord in liturgy and folklore. New York: Harcourt, 1958.
An explanation of the origin and development of Christian feasts, symbols, customs, traditions, and liturgy.

See also Christmas; Easter; and the section on Planning and Preparing for Anniversaries and Holidays

The Islamic Year

81. Farid al-Din 'Attar. Muslim saints and mystics. Chicago: Univ. of Chicago Press, 1966.
A translation of a major thirteenth-century study of the saints and mystics of Islam, their times, and their deeds.

82. Fitch, Florence Mary. Allah, the god of Islam: Moslem life and worship. New York: Lothrop, 1950.
An interpretation of the life of Mohammed, the Koran, the five pillars of the faith, pilgrimages, holy days and festivals, and the place of the Islamic faith in the culture of many nations.

83. Glubb, Sir John Bagot. The life and times of Muhammad. New York: Stein & Day, 1970.
A biography of Mohammed, the founder of Islam, emphasizing the impact of his teaching on the Arabs; includes lists of notable dates.

84. Kamal, Ahmad. The sacred journey, being a pilgrimage to Makkah. New York: Duell, 1961.
A description of Makkah, the holiest of Islamic cities, with an explanation of the significance of the prescribed traditions in the great pilgrimage to Mecca.

85. The message of the Qur'an, presented in perspective by Hashim Amir-Ali. Rutland, Vt.: Tuttle, 1974.
A translation into English of the Koran, the holy book of Islam, with explanatory prefaces and appendixes.

86. Pike, E. Royston. Mohammed: prophet of the religion of Islam. New York: Praeger, 1969.
An introduction to the life of Mohammed, the teachings of the Koran, and the faith and religious traditions of Islam.

87. Stewart, Desmond. Early Islam. New York: Time, 1967.
Illustrated essays on Islam as the religion revealed to Mohammed, enshrined in the Koran, and reflected in the way of life of the Islamic state and culture.

88. Suskind, Richard. The sword of the prophet: the story of the Moslem empire. New York: Grosset, 1971.
An introduction to Islam, beginning with the revelations of Mohammed in A.D. 610.

89. Williams, John Alden, ed. Islam. New York: Braziller, 1962.
A collection of major writings on the messages of Mohammed and the law of Islam, with selections from the work of theologians, traditionalists, and dissidents.

The Jewish Year

90. Baron, Joseph L., ed. A treasury of Jewish quotations. New rev. ed. New York: Yoseloff, 1965.
A collection of quotations, including proverbs, maxims, and comments on themes from both the Jewish secular and religious world.

91. Charry, Elias, and Segal, Abraham. The eternal people. New York: United Synagogue, 1967.
A study of Judaism and Jewish thought through the ages.

92. Cone, Molly. The Jewish Sabbath. New York: Crowell, 1966.
An introduction to the significance of the Sabbath for the Jewish people.

93. Donin, Hayim H. To be a Jew: a guide to Jewish observance in contemporary life. New York: Basic Books, 1972.
An introduction to the laws and observances for all aspects of Jewish life, including special occasions of the year; summaries of customs and ceremonies are accompanied by biblical quotations.

94. Eisenberg, Azriel. The story of the Jewish calendar. New York: Abelard-Schuman, 1958.
An explanation of the Jewish calendar, the names of the months, and differences in observances of holy days and festivals.

95. ———. The synagogue through the ages. New York: Bloch, 1974.
An introduction to the history of the synagogue and its influence on society in China, North Africa, Europe, and the United States.

96. Eisenberg, Hattie. Bar Mitzvah with ease. New York: Doubleday, 1966.
A look at the Bar Mitzvah as an important religious ceremony, with suggestions and a timetable for celebrations appropriate to the significance of the occasion.

97. Eisenstein, Judith Kaplan. Heritage of music: the music of the Jewish people. New York: Union of American Hebrew Congregations, 1972.
A survey of Jewish music through the ages; with varied examples of chants and folk tunes; examples are arranged topically and suggestions are made for their use.

98. Gaster, Theodor Herzl. Festivals of the Jewish year: a modern interpretation and guide. New York: Sloane, 1953.
History and description of the observances of the great Jewish festivals, with comparisons to observances of other faiths.

99. Gilbert, Arthur, and Tarcov, Oscar. Your neighbor celebrates. New York: Friendly House Pub., 1957.
Designed for interfaith and intergroup use, this book interprets the ways in which American Jews celebrate their holy days and festivals; includes a glossary of Hebrew words.

100. Gittelsohn, Roland Bertram. The meaning of Judaism. New York: World Pub., 1970.
An interpretation of the fundamentals of Judaism, including an examination of the origins and the traditions behind the observances of holy days.

101. Glazer, Nathan. American Judaism. 2d ed. Chicago: Univ. of Chicago Press, 1973.
A new edition of a near-classic study of the Jews and the Jewish faith in the United States.

102. Goldin, Hyman E. A treasury of Jewish holidays: history, legends, traditions. New York: Twayne, 1952.
A history of Jewish holidays, with an explanation of the ways they are celebrated.

103. Kanof, Abram. Jewish ceremonial art and religious observance. New York: Abrams, 1970.
A contribution to the understanding of the history and role of ceremonial art in the Jewish home and synagogue and its associations with such holy days as the Sabbath, Passover, Hanukkah, and Purim.

104. Kitov, Eliyahu. The book of our heritage: the Jewish year and its days of significance. 3 vols. New York: Feldheim, 1970.
A comprehensive study of the Jewish year, with interpretations of the celebratory cycle and descriptions of the rituals.

105. Lamm, Maurice. The Jewish way in death and mourning. New York: Jonathan David, 1969.
An interpretation of Jewish teaching, customs, and practices of mourning.

106. Levin, Marlin. Balm in Gilead: the story of Hadassah. New York: Schocken, 1973.
The story of Hadassah in Israel, with accounts of Henrietta Szold and other leaders and their contributions to Jewish life.

107. Millgram, Abraham E. Sabbath: the day of delight. Philadelphia: Jewish Pub. Soc., 1944.
A standard interpretation of the Sabbath as "the cornerstone of Judaism" and a guide to observances in the home and the synagogue; includes a music supplement for Sabbath services.

108. Morrow, Betty, and Hartman, Louis. Jewish holidays. Champaign, Ill.: Garrard, 1967.
An examination of the traditions and meaning of the major Jewish holidays, comparing the spirit of freedom in Jewish and American traditions.

109. Purdy, Susan Gold. Jewish holidays, facts, activities, and crafts. Philadelphia: Lippincott, 1969.
A history of Jewish holidays, their origins, and traditional ways of celebration; each holiday is followed by suggestions for craft projects, such as greeting cards, decorations, and preparing programs and food.

110. Rubin, Ruth, ed. Jewish folk songs in Yiddish and English. New York: Oak Pub., 1965.
A collection of Yiddish wedding songs, ballads, love songs, lullabies, children's songs, work songs, and military songs, with English translations.

111. Siegel, Richard, Strassfeld, Michael, and Strassfeld, Sharon, comps. and eds. The Jewish catalog. Philadelphia: Jewish Pub. Soc., 1973.
A comprehensive compendium of tools and resources "for use in Jewish education and Jewish living," covering every aspect of Jewish life from understanding and observing the Jewish holidays to building a personal library on the Jewish way of life.

112. Silver, Daniel Jeremy, and Martin, Bernard. A history of Judaism. 2 vols. New York: Basic Books, 1974.
A comprehensive study of the history, faith-culture, literature, values, world outlook, and customs of the Jewish people.

113. Sindrey, Alfred. Music in the social and religious life of antiquity. Cranbury, N.J.: Fairleigh Dickinson Univ. Press, 1974.
A survey of ancient music from the Sumerians to the Greeks and Romans, with a major emphasis on Jewish music.

114. Suhl, Yuri. An album of the Jews in America. New York: Watts, 1972.
An illustrated history of Jewish immigrants and their contributions to the United States.

115. Zeligs, Dorothy F. The story of Jewish holidays and customs for young people. New York: Bloch, 1942.
An account of the Jewish holy days and festivals, beginning with the calendar as it affects the Jewish year and concluding with special blessings in Hebrew and English.

See also Hanukkah; Passover; Purim; Rosh Hashanah; and the section on Holiday Costumes and Crafts.

Religious Beliefs and Customs around the World

116. Ahern, Emily M. The cult of the dead in a Chinese village. Stanford, Calif.: Stanford Univ. Press, 1973.
An ethnographic study of the relationships between social organization and the beliefs and behavior related to the cult of the dead; background material on the festivals of the dead.

117. Bahá'i holy places at the world centre. Haifa: Bahá'i World Centre, 1968.
A description of the communities, gardens, and shrines associated with Bahá'u'lláh, the important sites of the Baha'i faith.

118. Bahá'i world faith. 2d ed. Wilmette, Ill.: Bahá'i Pub. Trust, 1956.
A compilation of the sacred writings of the Baha'i faith, including selected writings of Bahá'u'lláh and Abdu'l-Bahá.

119. Black, Algernon David. Without burnt offerings: ceremonies of humanism. New York: Viking, 1974.
A presentation of ceremonies of naming, marriage, memorials, and invocations, each prefaced with a short commentary underscoring the philosophy of the Ethical Culture movement.

120. Buxton, David. "The Abyssinians: their religion and their way of life." In his The Abyssinians, pp. 57–85. New York: Praeger, 1970.
A short contribution to an understanding of the Abyssinian culture, including an explanation of the cycle of the Abyssinian year, with the feasts and fasts ordained by the church and the cycle of life, including baptism, marriage, and mourning.

121. Cunnington, Phillis, and Lucas, Catherine. Costume for births, marriages and deaths. New York: Barnes & Noble, 1972.
An illustrated history of English dress associated with the symbolism and ceremonies related to birth, marriage, and death from medieval times to 1900.

122. Encyclopaedia of religion and ethics. Ed. by James Hastings, with the assistance of John A. Selbie and other scholars. 13 vols. New York: Scribner, 1908–27.
A basic encyclopedia on world religions, ethical systems, and movements; a major source for ascertaining historic distinctions among various Oriental sects, and for interpretation of founding beliefs, philosophical ideas, ceremonials, rites, and customs of major and lesser-known faiths.

123. Frazer, Sir James George. The golden bough: a study in magic and religion. Abridged ed. New York: Macmillan, 1960.
An abridgement of a classic study of primitive religion and ancient deities, with background information on such customs as prevail in the midsummer, midwinter, and Lenten festivals of Europe.

124. Gaer, Joseph. Holidays around the world. Boston: Little, 1953.
An interpretation and comparison of the holy days and festivals of Buddhism, Judaism, Hinduism, Christianity, and the Islamic faith.

125. Harper, Howard V. Days and customs of all faiths. New York: Fleet Press, 1957.
A collection of essays, with facts and legends about holy days, special days, folk beliefs, traditions, customs, and people of many faiths and denominations; includes some secular days with religious associations; arranged by the calendar year; indexed.

126. Haskins, James. Religions. Philadelphia: Lippincott, 1973.
A survey of Buddhism, Christianity, Hinduism, Islam, and Judaism, which includes major holy days and ritual practices and an analysis of attitudes toward ethical behavior and mores.

127. Helfman, Elizabeth S. Celebrating nature: rites and ceremonies around the world. New York: Seabury, 1969.
A study of the rites performed in honor of Mother Earth in Africa, the East Indies, China, and Japan, and among the Hindus, Moslems, and some North American Indian tribes.

128. Hume, Robert E. The world's living religions, with special reference to their sacred scriptures and in comparison with Christianity: an historical sketch. Completely rev. New York: Scribner, 1959.
"A concise survey of the origin, the sacred scriptures, the historical career, and the chief values of the organized religions of culture which have lived for more than a century."—preface.

129. Hunter, Louise H. Buddhism in Hawaii: its impact on a Yankee community. Honolulu: Univ. Press of Hawaii, 1971.
A study of the relationship of the Japanese-Buddhist and the American-Christian communities from 1868 through World War II, with evidence of the contributions of the Buddhist community to Hawaiian society.

130. Ickis, Marguerite. The book of festival holidays. New York: Dodd, 1964.
A history of the origins and customs of the major Christian and Jewish holidays; includes suggestions on holiday crafts, musical games, and dances.

131. ——. The book of festivals and holidays the world over. New York: Dodd, 1970.
A description of international customs in observance of New Year's Day, Epiphany, Lent, Holy Week, Easter, the seasonal festivals, Advent, and Christmas.

132. ——. The book of religious holidays and celebrations. New York: Dodd, 1967.
Background material on Christmas, Easter, Pentecost, Holy Trinity, the major Jewish holidays, and several Oriental festivals; includes suggestions on programming.

133. Kettelkamp, Larry. Religions, East and West. New York: Morrow, 1972.
A study of the history and beliefs of Hinduism, Buddhism, Taoism, Confucianism, Zoroastrianism, Judaism, Christianity, and Islam, surveying their similarities and differences.

134. King, Noel Q. Religions of Africa: a pilgrimage into traditional religions. New York: Harper, 1970.
An interpretation of the religious life of tribal groups in equatorial and tropical Africa, with an examination of the roles of leaders and sacred persons.

135. Koller, John M. Oriental philosophies. New York: Scribner, 1970.
An introduction to the dominant characteristics and philosophies of Hinduism, Buddhism, Confucianism, Taoism, and Neo-Confucianism.

136. Mulholland, John F. Hawaii's religions. Rutland, Vt.: Tuttle, 1970.
An overview of the world's religions as represented in Hawaii; background material for Hawaii's religious festivals.

137. National Geographic Society. Great religions of the world. Washington, D.C.: The Society, 1971.
A survey of the basic beliefs of Hinduism, Buddhism, Judaism, Islam, and Christianity, with brief commentaries on the customs of each faith.

138. Negev, Avraham, ed. Archaeological encyclopedia of the Holy Land. New York: Putnam, 1972.
A commentary on the Bible, combined with a survey of archaeological discoveries in the Holy Land and an identification of the sites of biblical events associated with religious observances and studies.

139. Pike, Royston. Round the year with the world's religions. New York: Schuman, 1950.
A book of historic customs associated with religious observances around the world; arranged by months; indexed.

140. Rice, Edward E. The Ganges, a personal encounter. New York: Four Winds Press, 1974.
A tour to the Ganges, the sacred river that has 108 names which form a prayer, with an interpretation of its religious significance, the rites that are performed along its banks, its geology, and its history.

141. Saddhatissa, H. The Buddha's way. New York: Braziller, 1971.
An introduction to Buddha's teachings; the appendixes include listings of Buddhist countries, shrines, historical events, and festivals.

142. Seeger, Elizabeth. Eastern religions. New York: Crowell, 1973.
An explanation of Buddhism, Confucianism, Hinduism, Shinto, and Taoism, which interprets the rituals, holidays, and legends and discusses the concepts, founders, and subsequent development of each faith.

143. Trigg, Elwood B. Gypsy demons and divinities: the magic and religion of the Gypsies. Secaucus, N.J.: Citadel, 1973.
A study of Gypsy magico-religious beliefs, practices, and folklore.

144. Wray, Elizabeth, and others. Ten lives of the Buddha: Siamese temple paintings and Jataka tales. New York: Weatherhill, 1972.
An account of Buddhism, including birth stories of the Buddha demonstrating the ten virtues; illustrated with fine reproductions.

Celebrations, Ceremonials, and Festivals: International

145. Basche, James. "Phuket." In his Thailand: land of the free, pp. 236–45. New York: Taplinger, 1971.
Firsthand impressions of the Thai New Year's festival, the First Plowing ceremony, Buddhist celebrations, loy krathong and other religious days, and civic holidays.

146. Bauer, Helen, and Carlquist, Sherwin. Japanese festivals. New York: Doubleday, 1965.
An interpretation of Japanese national, community, religious, and seasonal festivals, with a comprehensive calendar of Japan's festival year; indexed.

147. Belting, Natalia. Winter's eve. New York: Holt, 1969.
A poetic calendar of traditional English festivities from Winter's Eve to Halloween, which provides understanding of the people who believed in the legends associated with folk practices.

148. Buell, Hal. Festivals of Japan. New York: Dodd, 1965.
Descriptive sketches of religious and historical celebrations, athletic events, holidays for children, and other matsuri, or festivals, of Japan; illustrated with photographs.

149. Casal, U. A. The five sacred festivals of ancient Japan. Rutland, Vt.: Tuttle, 1967.
An account of the symbolism and historical development of five major festivals of Japan: the New Year festival, the girls' festival, the boys' festival, the star festival, and the chrysanthemum festival.

150. Dobler, Lavinia G. Customs and holidays around the world. New York: Harper, 1963.
A history of the significance and customs of holidays around the world; arranged according to the calendar, beginning with spring.

151. Eberhard, Wolfgram. Chinese festivals. New York: Schuman, 1952.
Descriptions of the Chinese New Year, dragonboat and seasonal festivals, the feast of souls, and festivals of the dead.

152. Fox, Lilla M. Costumes and customs of the British Isles. Boston: Plays, 1974.
A description of contemporary occupational dress and ceremonial costumes worn in England, Scotland, Ireland, and Wales for traditional rituals and special events.

153. Fujioka, Ryoichi, and others. Tea ceremony utensils. New York: Weatherhill, 1973.
A brief explanation of the Japanese tea ceremony, with a major focus on each category of utensil used in the ceremonial; beautifully illustrated.

154. Hill, Errol. The Trinidad carnival. Austin: Univ. of Texas Press, 1972.
History of the great folk festival of Trinidad and Tobago, introducing the calypso, rituals, dramas, and masquerades that catch the spirit of the carnival and hopes for a national theater.

155. Hogg, Garry. Customs and traditions of England. New York: Arco, 1971.
Brief descriptions of festivals, fairs, religious services, dances, sports, and military events observed in England; arranged alphabetically by county.

156. Krythe, Maymie Richardson.. All about American holidays. New York: Harper, 1962.
A history and description of observances for religious, patriotic, and ethnic holidays in the United States; arranged chronologically from New Year's Day to Christmas.

157. Lu, Yu. The classic of tea. Trans. and introd. by Frances Ross Carpenter. Boston: Little, 1974.
The first Western-language version of a one-thousand-year-old interpretation of the ritual of tea drinking and its significance as a celebration of life.

158. McSpadden, J. Walker. The book of holidays. New York: Crowell, 1958.
Background material on American holidays and days of observance, with brief chapters on those of other countries; includes a list of United States holidays.

159. Marcus, Rebecca B. Fiesta time in Mexico. Champaign, Ill.: Garrard, 1974.
An explanation of Mexican national and religious holidays, beginning with November's Day of the Dead; discusses the significance of each festive occasion and describes ways of celebrating it.

160. Meyer, Robert, Jr. Festivals U.S.A. and Canada. Rev. ed. New York: Washburn, 1970.
A guide to annual events celebrated in the United States and Canada; organized by type of observance.

161. Milne, Jean. Fiesta time in Latin America. Los Angeles: Ward Ritchie Press, 1965.
A month-by-month review of the new and old religious, civic, and tribal fiestas or fetes celebrated regularly or irregularly in the cities and interior of the Latin American countries.

162. Morton, William Scott. "Festivals." In his The Japanese: how they live and work, pp. 65–67. New York: Praeger, 1973.
A brief description of the major festivals celebrated throughout all of modern Japan; the book concludes with hints for visitors, listing several festivals by region and time schedules.

163. Myers, Robert J., and others. Celebrations: the complete book of American holidays. Garden City, N.Y.: Doubleday, 1972.
The history, symbols, and special features of forty-two holidays observed in the United States; includes a listing of selected state holidays, with commentary on the origin of the holidays and past and present observances, information on holy days of major American faiths, federal legal holidays, and ethnic and local or regional events; indexed.

164. Palmer, Geoffrey, and Lloyd, Noel. A year of festivals: a guide to British calendar customs. London: Warne, 1972.
An interpretation of the origins of customs and rites carried on in the modern-day British Isles; begins with the month of May and follows through the calendar year; special sections describe London customs and fairs; concludes with a calendar of events by counties.

165. Price, Christine. Talking drums of Africa. New York: Scribner, 1973.
An explanation of how various drums are made and played in the countries of West Africa; includes poems from Nigeria and Ghana that illustrate the use of the drum in festivals and ceremonials.

166. Seaburg, Carl. Great occasions: readings for the celebration of birth, coming-of-age, marriage, and death. Boston: Beacon Press, 1968.
An anthology of readings on four major life-events—birth, adulthood, marriage, and death—collected for use in group or public observances; the appendix includes a ceremony for adoption, a rite for divorce, and a memorial service; indexed by author, first lines, and subjects.

167. Spicer, Dorothy Gladys. Yearbook of English festivals. New York: Wilson, 1954.
A calendar outline to British folk festivals; indexed by customs and regions.

168. Stein, R. A. "Festivals of the year." In his Tibetan civilization, pp. 212–21. Stanford, Calif.: Stanford Univ. Press, 1972.
A brief description of Tibetan festivals, with a major focus on the rites and customs of the movable New Year celebrations in twentieth-century Tibet.

169. Steiner, Stan. "The African masks." In his The islands: the worlds of the Puerto Ricans, pp. 63–66. New York: Harper, 1974.
A short commentary on the use of masks in the pageantry of the annual Fiesta de Santiago.

Anniversaries, Holidays, and Special-Events Days

American Indian Days

170. Belting, Natalia. Our fathers had powerful songs. New York: Dutton, 1974.
An anthology of free-verse poems expressing the beliefs of several western and southwestern tribes of the United States; the poems are related to ceremonials of mourning and healing, and to communal activities.

171. Bierhorst, John, ed. In the trail of the wind: American Indian poems and ritual orations. New York: Farrar, 1971.
A collection of the prayers, incantations, song texts, myths, and legends reflecting the tribal beliefs of American Indians; arranged by theme.

172. ——, comp. Songs of the Chippewa. Adapted from the collections of Frances Densmore and Henry Rowe Schoolcraft. New York: Farrar, 1974.
A collection of the ritual chants, dream songs, medicine charms, and lullabies of the Chippewa Indians; translated for solo or group singing with piano and guitar arrangements.

173. Clark, Ann Nolan. Circle of seasons. New York: Farrar, 1970.
A description of Pueblo Indian ceremonial customs related to the seasons and such special occasions as the Day of the Dead.

174. Culin, Robert Stewart. Games of the North American Indians. New York: AMS, 1973.
Information on Indian games of chance and dexterity, minor amusements, and competitions; indicates where appropriate the relationship between games and religious ceremonies; originally published in 1907 as the 24th Annual Report of the United States Bureau of Ethnology; indexed.

175. Erdoes, Richard. The sun dance people. New York: Knopf, 1972.
A history of the Plains Indians and other tribes, interpreting their cultures and the relationship of the Indian and the white man; arranged topically; indexed.

176. Jorgensen, Joseph G. The sun dance religion: power for the powerless. Chicago: Univ. of Chicago Press, 1972.
A scholarly treatise on the structure, role, and variations of the sun dance of the Utes and Shoshones of Utah, Colorado, Wyoming, and Idaho, with documentation on the political and spiritual significance of the dance for the contemporary Indian.

177. Kubiak, William J. Great Lakes Indians. Grand Rapids, Mich.: Baker Book House, 1970.
An illustrated study of the Indian tribes of the Great Lakes area of the United States; text and drawings illustrate their physical characteristics, weapons, tools, ceremonial dress; includes lists of synonymous names.

178. Lavine, Sigmund A. The games the Indians played. New York: Dodd, 1974.
An introduction to the ceremonial origins of the games of the Eskimos and Indians of North America, with chapters on types of games and tribal variations in play.

179. Niethammer, Carolyn. American Indian food and lore. New York: Macmillan, 1974.
A book of traditional Indian recipes, with ethnic information on plant identification, tribal love, and festival dishes.

180. Oswalt, Wendell H. This land was theirs: a study of the North American Indian. 2d ed. New York: Wiley, 1973.
A look at twelve native American Indian groups in the United States and Canada, which examines the question of who is an Indian, digs into history, and analyzes the mid-twentieth-century status and circumstances of each tribe.

181. Sanders, Thomas E., and Peek, Walter W. Literature of the American Indian. New York: Glencoe Press, 1973.
An anthology of myths, poems, oratory, laws, rituals, and memoirs of American Indian tribes, Mexican and South American aborigines, and Eskimos; arranged chronologically, and by literary form.

182. Taxay, Don. Money of the American Indians and other primitive currencies of the Americas. Flushing, N.Y.: Nummus Press, 1970.
A history of the currency of the American Indians in pre-Columbian and early colonial America; organized geographically; indexed.

183. Turner, Frederick W., III, ed. The portable North American Indian reader. New York: Viking, 1974.
An anthology of literature by and about the American Indian; divided into sections on "Myths and Tales," "Poetry and Oratory," "Culture Contact," and "Image and Anti-Image."

Arbor Day

184. Banker, Harry J. "Arbor day: the first hundred years." American Forests 78, no. 4: 8–10 (April 1972.)
A brief review of the one-hundred years of activity behind Arbor Day, beginning with J. Sterling Morton's resolution of April 10, 1872, sparking the establishment of Arbor Day in the state of Nebraska and concluding with the presidential proclamation of April 24, 1970, establishing the last Friday in April as National Arbor Day.

185. Barney, Daniel Rhodes. The last stand: Ralph Nader's study group report on the national forests. New York: Grossman, 1974.
A study of the management of the national forests in the United States, with recommendations on policies and practices to enhance the quality of natural-resource preservation and American life.

186. Clepper, Henry. Professional forestry in the United States. Baltimore: Johns Hopkins Univ. Press, 1971.
Data on American forest use from the earliest records to the 1970s; includes information on professional education, legal and legislative issues, and viewpoints on ecological problems.

187. Earle, Olive L. State trees. Rev. ed. New York: Morrow, 1973.
An account and a description of the official trees designated by individual states of the United States.

188. Frome, Michael. The forest service. New York: Praeger, 1971.
A survey of the United States Forest Service from its beginnings in the late nineteenth century, through the Pinchot era, to the application of the multiple use-sustained yield act.

189. Johnson, Hugh. The international book of trees: a guide to the trees of our forests and gardens. New York: Simon & Schuster, 1973.
An introduction to tree species in the temperate regions of the world; words and pictures distinguish among great groups of trees; the text covers reproduction, cultivation, use, and survival factors.

190. Menninger, Karl. "Trees are forever—we hope." The Morton Arboretum Quarterly 9, no. 1: 7–9 (Spring 1973).
A statement by a well-known psychiatrist and author on the meaning of Arbor Day and its significance for all mankind.

191. Randall, Janet. To save a tree: the story of the coast redwoods. New York: McKay, 1971.
A description of the California redwoods from prehistoric times to the passage of the act creating the Redwood National Park in 1968 and subsequent efforts to preserve additional redwood acreage.

192. Roberts, Martha McMillan. Public gardens and arboretums of the United States. New York: Holt, 1962.
An illustrated introduction to the gardens and arboretums of the United States, including the Morton Arboretum at Lisle, Illinois, established by J. Sterling Morton, originator of Arbor Day.

193. Stone, Christopher D. Should trees have standing? Toward legal rights for natural objects. Los Altos, Calif.: William Kaufmann, 1974.
The development of a concept that trees and natural resources might be legally represented in court by organizations or groups; based on a California court case involving the Sierra Club.

Armed Forces Day

194. Berg, Fred Anderson. Encyclopedia of Continental army units—battalions, regiments, and independent corps. Harrisburg, Pa.: Stackpole, 1972.
A concise history of each unit serving in the Continental army, the militia, and the state troops.

195. Borklund, C. W. The Department of Defense. New York: Praeger, 1968.
A report on the organization, growth, and change in the United States Department of Defense, including significant actions, interrelationships with other agencies, and problem issues.

196. Carrison, Daniel J. The United States Navy. New York: Praeger, 1968.
An account of the traditions, organizations, and missions of the United States Navy, including its role in the space program; the appendixes include a list of navy career opportunities.

197. De Chant, John A. The modern United States Marine Corps. New York: Van Nostrand, 1966.
A history of the Marine Corps, reporting its role in war and peace.

198. Dupuy, R. Ernest. The compact history of the United States Army. 2d ed. rev. New York: Hawthorn Books, 1973.
A review of the history, organization, administration, and development of the United States Army, with short accounts of important battles.

199. Glines, Carroll W., and Walker, G. I. The compact history of the United States Air Force. New York: Hawthorn Books, 1973.
A history of American military aeronautics from the first successful ascension of a balloon in 1783 to the experimental aircraft of the contemporary air force.

200. Greene, Robert Ewell. Black defenders of America, 1775–1973. Chicago: Johnson Pub., 1974.
A pictorial history documenting the service records of Negro men and women in the armed forces in ten wars from the American Revolution to the Vietnam conflict; the appendix includes the contributions that are recognized as milestones in black military history.

201. Gurney, Gene. The United States Coast Guard. New York: Crown, 1973.
An illustrated history of the United States Coast Guard from its beginning in 1790 as a revenue fleet to its current global responsibilities as the guardian of maritime safety, ocean stations, and pollution control; includes reproductions of insignia and cap devices.

202. Heinl, Robert Debs, Jr. Dictionary of military and naval quotations. Annapolis, Md.: U.S. Naval Institute, 1966.
A compilation of quotations on the traditions, personalities, and participants in the military services, and on modes of war on land and sea and in the air; arranged alphabetically by topic.

203. Miller, Nathan. Sea of glory: the Continental navy fights for independence. New York: McKay, 1974.
A study of the American Continental navy, covering all aspects of the naval war, correlated with a narrative on eighteenth-century shipbuilding, privateering, the life of seamen, and the role of John Paul Jones, John Barry, and other naval patriots.

204. North, Rene. Military uniforms, 1686–1918. New York: Grosset, 1970.
An illustrated guide to the campaign and dress uniforms of American and European soldiers from the late seventeenth century through World War I.

205. Reynolds, Clark G. The fast carriers: the forging of an air navy. New York: McGraw, 1968.
An account of the events that led to establishment of the fleet of aircraft carriers in the United States Navy, with documentation on the record of the carriers in World War II; the appendixes include dates of commissioning.

Author's Day

206. Anderson, Margaret J. The Christian writer's handbook. New York: Harper, 1974.
A standard handbook for the beginner in the field of church-related publications; suggestions for articles, examples, and practical advice.

207. "Author's day, national." The world book encyclopedia 1:913. Chicago: Field Enterprises Education Corp., 1973.
A paragraph explaining the origin of Author's Day in the United States.

208. Barzun, Jacques. On writing, editing, and publishing: essays explicative and hortatory. Chicago: Univ. of Chicago Press, 1971.
A collection of essays interpreting good writing and how it is achieved, with reflections on the problems of editing and publishing.

209. Bowen, Catherine Drinker. Biography: the craft and the calling. Boston: Little, 1969.
Musings and observations on the art of the biographer: the problems of interpreting original source material, the importance of form, and personal experiences in research and writing.

210. Burack, A. S., ed. The writer's handbook. Rev. ed. Boston: Writer, 1972.
A frequently updated handbook on all phases of authorship, from developing an idea to consulting lists of markets; includes illustrative pieces by contemporary authors.

211. Hersey, John, ed. The writer's craft. New York: Knopf, 1974.
An anthology of commentary about the art of writing, representing the viewpoints of thirty-two authors, including James, Tolstoy, Coleridge, Faulkner, Mailer, and others.

212. Wyndham, Lee. Writing for children and teen-agers. Rev. ed. Cincinnati: Writers Digest, 1972.
A manual for the beginning writer on work habits, planning a book, handling characterization, plots, and dialogues, and preparing and marketing the manuscript.

Aviation Day

213. Angelucci, Enzo. Airplanes: from the dawn of flight to the present date. New York: McGraw, 1973.
A well-illustrated survey of historic and contemporary aircraft, with information on important dates and designers and data on size, characteristics, and performance.

214. Freudenthal, Elsbeth Estelle. Flight into history: the Wright brothers and the air age. Norman: Univ. of Oklahoma Press, 1949.
A study of Orville and Wilbur Wright that evaluates their major contribution to aviation history and acknowledges their debt to Chanute.

215. Green, William. The warplanes of the Third Reich. New York: Doubleday, 1970.
A definitive contribution to aircraft history which appraises each type of warplane developed in Germany between 1933 and 1945 and relates it to the rise and fall of the Luftwaffe.

216. Harris, Sherwood. The first to fly: aviation's pioneer days. New York: Simon & Schuster, 1970.
A review of the experiences of pioneer pilots, beginning with the ordeal of Dr. Samuel Langley in 1900 and concluding with the death of Lincoln Beachey in 1915.

217. Hart, Clive. The dream of flight: aeronautics from classical times to the Renaissance. New York: Winchester Press, 1973.
The story of man's initial concepts of flight and early experiments with kites, windmills, rockets, ornithopters, and other devices; covers the period from 400 B.C. to A.D. 1600.

218. Holliday, Joe. Mosquito! The wooden wonder aircraft of World War II. New York: Doubleday, 1970.
A history of the *Mosquito,* called "the most versatile aircraft of World War II," including its achievements as well as anecdotes and biographies of pilots and technicians.

219. King, Horace Frederick. Milestones of the air. New York: McGraw, 1969.
Descriptions of one-hundred significant aircraft representing important steps in aviation since the Wright flyer went into the air on December 17, 1903; selections were made to honor the diamond jubilee of Jane's *All the World's Aircraft.*

220. Lindbergh, Charles A. The Spirit of St. Louis. New York: Scribner, 1953.
Lindbergh's personal story of the first solo transatlantic flight from New York to Paris; the appendix includes the log of the flight and reproductions of headlines from the world press.

221. Smith, Richard K. First across! The U.S. Navy's transatlantic flight of 1919. Annapolis, Md.: Naval Institute Press, 1973.
The record of the history-making 1919 flight of the United States Navy's NC-4 flying boat, the first aircraft to carry men over the Atlantic.

222. Wright, Wilbur, and Wright, Orville. Miracle at Kitty Hawk. Ed. by Fred C. Kelly. New York: Farrar, 1951.
Selections from the letters of the Wright brothers from 1881 to 1946, which reveal their personalities and tell of their experiments with aeronautical problems, their achievements, litigations, and commercial negotiations; arranged chronologically.

Awards and Honors Days

223. Abbott, P. E. British gallantry awards. New York: Doubleday, 1972.
A history of British awards for gallantry, with information on origin and development, verification, and number awarded.

224. Bonin, Jane F. Prize-winning American drama: a bibliographical and descriptive guide. Metuchen, N.J.: Scarecrow, 1973.
A compilation of data on prizewinning American drama from 1917 through 1970–71; chronologically arranged; indexed.

225. Farber, Eduard. Nobel Prize winners in chemistry, 1901–1961. Rev. ed. New York: Abelard-Schuman, 1953.
Brief biographical sketches revealing some of the human factors in the lives of the Nobel laureates in chemistry up to 1961, combined with statements on the importance of each individual's prizewinning work.

226. **French, Warren G.** American winners of the Nobel literary prize. Norman: Univ. of Oklahoma Press, 1968.
Essays on seven American authors awarded the Nobel Prize in literature up to 1962: Sinclair Lewis, Eugene O'Neill, Pearl Buck, T. S. Eliot, William Faulkner, Ernest Hemingway, and John Steinbeck.

227. **Frenz, Horst.** Literature, 1901–1967. Amsterdam: Elsevier Pub., 1969.
Nobel lectures, including presentation speeches and laureates' biographies.

228. **Hieronymussen, Paul.** Orders and decorations of Europe in color. New York: Macmillan, 1967.
A guide to the official national and international decorations of all European countries; their purpose, the privileges and obligations of those honored, and other information, such as the international ranking system; illustrations of the international orders are in full color.

229. **Hohenberg, John, ed.** The Pulitzer Prizes. Rev. ed. New York: Columbia Univ. Press, 1974.
An account of the Pulitzer Prizes, with essays on the significance of the prizes in American history from 1917 to 1973.

230. **Kerrigan, Evans E.** American war medals and decorations. New York: Viking, 1971.
Descriptions of military award insignia from the Revolution to the Vietnam War; also includes the National Aeronautics and Space Administration awards.

231. **Kidd, Walter E.** British winners of the Nobel literary prize. Norman: Univ. of Oklahoma Press, 1973.
Essays on the Nobel Prize winners: Kipling, Yeats, Shaw, Galsworthy, Russell, Churchill, and Beckett, with biographical notes and identification of the unique qualities of each author.

232. **Kingman, Lee, ed.** Newbery and Caldecott Medal books: 1956–1965. Boston: Horn Book, 1965.
Acceptance papers, biographical notes, and lists of runners-up.

233. **Lee, Irvin H.** Negro Medal of Honor men. 3d ed. New York: Dodd, 1969.
The record of heroic actions of Negro Medal of Honor winners in American wars.

234. **Literary and library prizes.** 8th ed. Rev. and enl. New York: Bowker, 1973.
A frequently revised reference source on literary and library awards: American, British, Canadian, and international.

235. **Miller, Bertha Mahony, ed.** Caldecott Medal books: 1938–1957. Boston: Horn Book, 1957.
A collection of winners' acceptance papers, with biographical notes on the artists and descriptive notes on the books.

236. ———. Newbery Medal books: 1922–1955. Boston: Horn Book, 1955.
Brief history of Newbery awards, commentaries on winning books, notes on the authors, and acceptance papers.

237. **Morello, Theodore, ed.** The Hall of Fame for Great Americans. New York: New York Univ. Press, 1962.
Official handbook to the Hall of Fame; rules of election; biographical sketches of honored individuals up to 1960.

238. **Riedman, Sarah R., and Gustafson, Elton T.** Portraits of Nobel laureates in medicine and physiology. New York: Abelard-Schuman, 1963.
An account of the Nobel Prize winners in medicine and physiology from 1901 through 1963, based on scientific reports, biographical sketches, institutional records, and memories of associates; concludes with a chronological table of award winners.

239. **Robles, Philip K.** United States military medals and ribbons. Rutland, Vt.: Tuttle, 1971.
A history and description of the military medals of the United States; includes data on origin, purpose, and rank in relation to other medals.

240. **Roland, Albert.** Profiles from the new Asia. New York: Macmillan, 1970.
A review of the accomplishments of eleven men and women of Asian countries who have received the Magsaysay Awards–Asian counterparts of the Nobel Prizes.

241. **Schuck, H.** The man and his prizes. Amsterdam: Elsevier Pub., 1962.
Background material on Alfred Nobel, the Nobel Foundation, and the prizes and prizewinners.

242. **United States Architect of the Capitol.** Compilation of works of art and other objects in the United States Capitol. Washington, D.C.: U.S. Govt. Printing Office, 1965.
A review of the art forms in the Capitol, including sketches of famous Americans represented in Statuary Hall.

243. Wasserman, Paul, ed. Awards, honors, and prizes: a source book and directory. 2d ed. Detroit: Gale Research, 1973.
A major source of information on contemporary honors for notable achievements in all fields; arranged alphabetically by sponsors; indexed.

Battle of New Orleans Day

244. Carter, Samuel, III. Blaze of glory: the fight for New Orleans, 1814–1815. New York: St. Martins, 1971.
A popular history of the issues, strategies, and personalities involved in the Battle of New Orleans, which ended on January 8, 1815.

245. Falkner, Leonard. "Like a sea of blood." In his For Jefferson and liberty: the United States in war and peace, 1800–1815; pp. 207–55. New York: Knopf, 1972.
A brief review of the Battle of New Orleans and the tactics of General Andrew Jackson; includes a ballad called *The Hunters of Kentucky,* which recreates the spirit of Jackson's militia in facing the enemy.

246. Lawson, Don. The War of 1812: America's second war for independence. New York: Abelard-Schuman, 1966.
The concluding chapter of this account of the War of 1812 deals with the Battle of New Orleans as one of the remarkable conflicts in military history.

247. Mason, F. Van Wyck. The battles for New Orleans. Boston: Houghton, 1962.
The history of four battles for the city of New Orleans during the War of 1812, indicating the military strategy utilized by both the Americans and the British.

248. Reilly, Robin. The British at the gates: the New Orleans campaign in the War of 1812. New York: Putnam, 1974.
A British view of the New Orleans campaign and the generalship of Andrew Jackson.

Bill of Rights Day

249. Brownlie, Ian, ed. Basic documents on human rights. New York: Oxford, 1971.
Source material on human rights; includes the bills of rights and constitutions of twelve countries and documents of the United Nations and other international organizations.

250. Dorsen, Norman, ed. The rights of Americans: what they are—what they should be. New York: Pantheon Books, 1971.
A compilation of articles on the rights of American citizens, published in honor of the fiftieth anniversary of the American Civil Liberties Union; includes, in addition to the basic rights, those of separate groups, such as women, teachers, and students.

251. Downs, Robert B., ed. First freedom: liberty and justice in the world of books and reading. Chicago: ALA, 1960.
A basic collection of material on freedom of speech and of the press, which examines the issues related to restraints on reading, community pressures, censorship, and court decisions, with positive affirmations of the essentiality of intellectual freedom in a democracy.

252. Ernst, Morris L. The first freedom. New York: Plunum, 1971.
A reprint of a 1946 classic on the erosion of freedom in the press, movies, and radio, with specific pointers on techniques for the protection of media freedom.

253. Hand, Learned. The bill of rights. Cambridge, Mass.: Harvard Univ. Press, 1958.
A classic volume; includes three lectures on the responsibility of the American Supreme Court in the interpretation of the Bill of Rights.

254. Hole, Clarke, ed. Magna Carta and the idea of liberty. New York: Wiley, 1972.
Selections dealing with the formation of the Magna Carta, studies of its long-lasting impact; includes a section on comparable medieval charters.

255. Konvitz, Milton Ridvas, ed. Bill of Rights reader: leading constitutional cases. 5th ed. rev. Ithaca, N.Y.: Cornell Univ. Press, 1973.
A compilation of Supreme Court opinions on major cases dealing with the Bill of Rights; the appendix reprints the Universal Declaration of Human Rights adopted by the United Nations on December 10, 1948.

256. Pallister, Anne. Magna Carta: the heritage of liberty. New York: Oxford, 1971.
A study of interpretations of the Magna Carta from the seventeenth century to the present, with documentation on change through the centuries.

Bird Day

257. Anderson, John M. The changing world of birds. New York: Holt, 1973.
An environmental approach to ornithology; covers the adaptability of birds, their life cycles, and mortality rates.

258. Berger, Andrew. Hawaiian birdlife. Honolulu: Univ. Press of Hawaii, 1972.
A survey of the birds of the Hawaiian Islands, including the Leeward Islands, written from a historical standpoint and with an emphasis on contemporary conservation.

259. Choate, Ernest A. A dictionary of American bird names. Boston: Gambit, 1973.
A dictionary of common and scientific names for birds, with essays on the origin and meaning; the appendix includes information on European and American namers of birds.

260. Gruson, Edward S. Words for birds: a lexicon of North American birds with biographical notes. Chicago: Quadrangle Books, 1972.
A scholarly study designed to provide etymologies of the common names of birds in North America, to translate scientific names, and to tell of the people for whom birds are named.

261. Hartshorne, Charles. Born to sing: an interpretation and world survey of bird song. Bloomington: Indiana Univ. Press, 1973.
A comprehensive study of the function and significance of bird songs of species from all over the world; indexed.

262. McElroy, Thomas P. The habitat guide to birding. New York: Knopf, 1974.
A bird-watcher's guide to species of birds, field techniques, and nature lore, which relates birds to their environments.

263. Murton, R. K. Man and birds. New York: Taplinger, 1971.
A study of the interrelationships between humans and birds in a technological society; concludes with an analysis of wildlife management practices related to bird problems.

264. Peterson, Roger Tory. The birds. New York: Time, 1967.
An overview of bird life: migration; conservation; habits and protective devices; the language of birds; oddities; and adaptations.

265. Schutz, Walter E. How to attract, house, and feed birds. Rev. ed. Milwaukee: Bruce Pub., 1970.
Bird watching as a hobby, with supplementary information on suitable feeds, nesting accommodations, water supplies, and shelters.

Birthdays

266. Brewton, Sara, and Brewton, John E., comps. Birthday candles burning bright: a treasury of poetry. New York: Macmillan, 1960.
An anthology of British and American poems about christenings, the birthdays of individuals, twins, youth, and birthday parties.

267. Commins, Dorothy Berliner. Lullabies of the world. New York: Random House, 1967.
Over one-hundred lullabies expressing the cultures of the world, in original languages with English translations, explanatory notes, and piano settings.

268. Johnson, Lois S. Happy birthdays round the world. Chicago: Rand McNally, 1963.
An account of birthday customs and traditions, with translations of the typical birthday songs or saints' songs of twenty-four nations of the world, from Belgium to Venezuela.

269. Poston, Elizabeth. The baby's song book. New York: Crowell, 1972.
A collection of traditional English-language nursery songs, with basic piano accompaniment; also includes songs in French, German, Italian, and Spanish, with English translations.

270. Price, Christine. Happy days: a UNICEF book of birthdays, name days, and growing days. New York: U.S. Committee for UNICEF, 1969.
Descriptions of landmark days for children throughout the world: the day when a baby is named; the birthday anniversary; and the day of initiation into adulthood. The appendix includes the music and words, with English translations, of birthday songs from Egypt, Holland, Japan, Mexico, and Venezuela.

271. Rinkoff, Barbara. Birthday parties around the world. New York: Morrow, 1967.
Descriptions of the ways in which birthday parties are celebrated in lands around the world.

272. Smith, Elsdon C. Naming your baby: rules to follow when you name your baby. 2d ed. Radnor, Pa.: Chilton, 1970.
A list of over 2,500 first names with their meanings and suggestions on appropriate choice of names.

See also sections on Holiday Poetry, Songs, and Observance Ideas

Children's Day

273. De Mause, Lloyd, ed. The history of childhood. New York: Psychohistory Press, 1974.
A collection of essays on child rearing from early times to the nineteenth century appraising the rationale for child-care practices in Western Europe and the United States.

274. De Vries, Leonard. Little wide-awake. Cleveland: World Pub., 1967.
"An anthology from Victorian children's books and periodicals in the collection of Anne and Fernand G. Renier."—subtitle.

275. Egoff, Sheila. The republic of childhood: a critical guide to Canadian children's literature in English. Toronto: Oxford, 1967.
Essays and annotated bibliographies on books for children written primarily by Canadians or by writers long resident in Canada; a contribution to the literature and to Canada's centennial year.

276. ———, Stubbs, G. T., and Ashley, L. F., comps. Only connect: readings on children's literature. Toronto: Oxford, 1969.
A collection of essays representing the reflections and judgments of North American and British writers who consider children's books an important part of human expression and literary creativity.

277. First graces. Illus. by Tasha Tudor. New York: Walck, 1955.
A little book of table graces with a special grace for the Fourth of July, United Nations Day, Thanksgiving, and Christmas.

278. Foley, Dan. Toys through the ages. Philadelphia: Chilton, 1962.
"Dan Foley's story of playthings filled with history, folklore, romance, and nostalgia: a book for all ages."—subtitle.

279. Frye, Burton C., comp. A St. Nicholas anthology: the early years. New York: Meredith, 1969.
A nostalgic selection of stories, poems, and articles from the world's most famous children's magazine; arranged by seasons; the contributors range from Kipling to a very young Edna St. Vincent Millay.

280. Haviland, Virginia, and Coughlan, Margaret N., comps. Children's literature: a guide to reference sources, first supplement. Washington, D.C.: Library of Congress, 1972.
An annotated supplement to an outstanding bibliography of children's literature published in 1966 under the same title; a source of information on evaluation, particularly for international publications in the field of children's literature.

281. ———. Yankee Doodle's literary sampler of prose, poetry and pictures. New York: Crowell, 1974.
An anthology of children's literature and art from colonial times to 1900; selected from the rare-book collection at the Library of Congress.

282. Hein, Lucille E. Entertaining your child. New York: Harper, 1971.
An idea book for parents, teachers, and volunteers in services to children; focused on activities for both the independent child and children who need direction.

283. Hurlimann, Bettina. Picture-book world. Trans. and ed. by Brian W. Alderson. Cleveland: World Pub., 1969.
A survey of artistically satisfying picture books for children created in German-speaking countries, America, Scandinavia, the Netherlands, England, France, Eastern Europe, the Mediterranean area, and Asia.

284. McCaslin, Nellie. Theatre for children in the United States. Norman: Univ. of Oklahoma Press, 1971.
A history of the theater for children in the United States, from the settlement-house productions for immigrant children of the early twentieth century to the professional theater of 1960–70.

285. Miller, Carl S., ed. Sing, children, sing: songs, dances, and singing games of many lands and peoples. New York: Chappell, 1972.
Words and scores for songs and singing games from Brazil to Yugoslavia; a collection arranged with the assistance of the United States Committee for UNICEF through its Information Center on Children's Cultures.

286. Morton, Miriam, ed. A harvest of Russian children's literature. Berkeley: Univ. of California Press, 1967.
A substantial sampling of Russian verses, folktales, short stories, and selections from novels organized by age-group interests; authors include Turgenev, Tolstoi, Chekhov, and Gorky, as well as contemporary authors.

287. Mulac, Margaret E. Educational games for fun. New York: Harper, 1971.
Thinking games and team games for classroom or group use, as distinguished from party games; graded with suggestions on variations for simplification or increased sophistication.

288. Nickerson, Betty. Celebrate the sun: a heritage of festivals interpreted through the art of children from many lands. Philadelphia: Lippincott, 1969.
A collection of children's paintings of seasonal celebrations from thirty-two nations, with text describing the origin and the nature of each occasion.

289. Opie, Iona, and Opie, Peter. Children's games in street and playground: chasing, catching, seeking, hunting, racing, duelling, exerting, daring, guessing, acting, pretending. New York: Oxford, 1969.
A survey of the "games that children, aged about 6–12, play on their own accord when out-of-doors, and usually out of sight."

290. Pellowski, Anne, comp. Have you seen a comet? Children's art and writing from around the world. New York: Day, 1971.
Examples of children's and young people's art and writing from seventy-five countries; the writing is in the original language with English translations.

291. Phelps, William Lyon, sel. The children's anthology. Garden City, N.Y.: Doubleday, 1941.
A source for the old, the sentimental, and the traditional poems about children, from Eugene Field to William Wordsworth.

292. Sawyer, Ruth. The way of a storyteller. New York: Viking, 1962.
A classic volume on storytelling as a creative folk art for modern times; includes personal experiences in story collecting, presents lists of favorite stories, and gives suggestions on techniques.

293. Staudacher, Rosemarian V. Children welcome: villages for boys and girls. New York: Farrar, 1963.
A report on the care of the homeless children of the world from Japan to Canada and the United States.

294. Sutherland, Zena, ed. The best in children's books: the University of Chicago guide to children's literature, 1966–1972. Chicago: Univ. of Chicago Press, 1973.
Annotated reviews of children's books published from 1966–72; indexed by title, developmental values, curricular use, reading level, subjects, and types of literature.

295. Vinton, Iris. The folkways omnibus of children's games. Harrisburg, Pa.: Stackpole, 1970.
An international approach to playing games shared by all nations or molded by traditions, cultures, and geography; also includes games for special days, street games, and games for travelers; indexed.

See also section on Planning and Preparing for Anniversaries and Holidays.

Christmas

296. Abisch, Roz. 'Twas in the moon of wintertime: the first American Christmas carol. Englewood Cliffs, N.J.: Prentice-Hall, 1969.
An adaptation of a carol written for the Huron Indians by Father Jean de Brebeuf in the 1840s; musical accompaniment and words in both English and Huron.

297. Anderson, Raymond, and Anderson, Georgene. The Jesse tree: stories and symbols of Advent. Philadelphia: Fortress Press, 1966.
A guide to readings and prayers to be correlated with the symbolism of the Jesse tree during the Advent season and in preparation for Christmas.

298. Auld, William Muir. Christmas traditions. New York: Macmillan, 1931; Detroit: Gale Research, 1968.
A standard history of the religious and secular aspects of Christmas traditions, origins, antecedents, and customs, with excerpts from literary and historical records.

299. Barth, Edna. Holly, reindeer and colored lights: the story of Christmas symbols. New York: Seabury, 1971.
An explanation of the origins and meaning of such Christmas symbols as the tree, Yule logs, bells, ornaments, Santa Claus and his ancestors, cards and greetings, shepherds, angels, colors, and candles; indexed.

300. Belting, Natalia. Christmas folk. New York: Holt, 1969.
A description in free verse of the celebration of the "hallow days of Yule" in Elizabethan England, with the mummers starting the revelries on Saint Andrews Day on November 30 and closing them on Twelfth Night, January 5.

301. Bishop, Claire Huchet, ed. Happy Christmas! Tales for boys and girls. New York: Daye, 1956.
An anthology of tales about the first Christmas, Saint Nicholas and Santa Claus, Christmas Day, and Twelfth Night.

302. Bjorn, Thyra. Once upon a Christmas time. New York: Holt, 1964.
Reminiscence of the Christmas season in the Swedish Lapland in the early twentieth century; customs extending from the Festival of Lights to Epiphany.

303. Boni, Margaret Bradford, ed. Favorite Christmas carols. New York: Simon & Schuster, 1957.
Fifty-nine Yuletide songs with piano arrangements; brief introductions on the origin of the carols; indexed.

304. The book of Christmas. Pleasantville, N.Y.: Reader's Digest Assn., 1973.
A Christmas book containing the stories of the Nativity, a history of Christmas by Rummer Godden, selections from traditional and modern literature, and color photographs of Christmas in Germany, Italy, Spain, Mexico, and other parts of the world.

305. Braybrooke, Neville, comp. A partridge in a pear tree: a celebration for Christmas. Westminster, Md.: Newman Press, 1960.
An anthology of Christmas poems, stories, dramas, and devotional literature, ranging from the works of Virgil to W. H. Auden.

306. Brewton, Sara, and Brewton, John E. Christmas bells are ringing. New York: Macmillan, 1951.
An anthology of both gay and reverent poems for the Christmas season; indexed by author, title, and first lines.

307. Buday, George. The history of the Christmas card. London: Rockliff, 1954.
A history of the Christmas card: its forerunners, the influence of the valentine on Christmas cards, the creators and card makers, with a commentary on sentiments expressed in verses and types of cards.

308. Carroll, Gladys Hasty. Christmas through the years. Boston: Little, 1968.
A collection of reminiscences of Christmas, reflecting the moods and customs of fifteen periods from 1898 to 1968.

309. Chrisman, Irma. Christmas trees, decorations and ornaments. New York: Hearthside Press, 1956.
A handbook on the selection of trees, the making of artificial trees, ornaments, and decorations.

310. Christmas: an American annual of Christmas literature and art. Ed. by Randolph E. Haugan. Minneapolis: Augsburg, annual.
A yearly compilation of articles, stories, and pictures of the religious and secular observance of Christmas.

311. Coffin, Tristram Potter. The book of Christmas lore. New York: Continuum-Seabury, 1973.
A scholarly study of the development of Christmas lore and traditions in relation to older mythologies; topics include superstitions, mumming and folk drama, the symbolism of food, drink, Christmas trees, and cards, the transformation of Saint Nicholas into Santa Claus, and Christmas literature.

312. Cooney, Barbara. The little juggler. New York: Hastings House, 1961.
An adaptation of the old French legend of the little street juggler of Notre Dame, who had no gift for the Virgin Mary; the illustrations are French sites where the little juggler might have wandered.

313. Dalphin, Marcia. Light the candles: a list for Christmas reading. Rev. by Anne Thaxter Eaton. Boston: Horn Book, 1960.
An annotated list of stories, poems, legends, carols, and books about Christmas enjoyed by American families and families around the world, as reviewed in the *Horn Book* up to 1960; updated for 1960–72 by Sidney Long in *And All the Dark Make Bright like Day*. See *also* no. 340.

314. Dawson, William Francis. Christmas: its origin and associations, together with historical events and festive celebrations during nineteen centuries. London: Stock, 1902; Detroit: Gale Research, 1968.
An account of Christmas origins, rituals, historical events, and celebrations from the first to the nineteenth centuries.

315. Dickens, Charles. A Christmas carol. Philadelphia: Lippincott, 1915.
An edition of the most famous of all Christmas stories; illustrated by Arthur Rackham.

316. Duncan, Edmonstoune. The story of the carol. New York: Scribner, 1911; Detroit: Singing Tree Press, 1968.
A standard history of carols, their antecedents and forms, related to ecclesiastical days and seasonal celebrations.

317. Eaton, Anne Thaxter, comp. The animals' Christmas: poems, carols, and stories. New York: Viking, 1944.
Christmas legends and poems in which animals have the important roles.

318. Ehret, Walter. The international book of Christmas carols. Englewood Cliffs, N.J.: Prentice-Hall, 1963.
Carols in their original language, with translations and scores, from England, France, Germany, Scandinavia, the Slavic countries, Italy, Spain, and the United States; arranged by nationality; indexed by title and first lines.

319. Engle, Paul. An old fashioned Christmas. New York: Dial Press, 1964.
Verses and sketches describing a typical midwestern Christmas in the United States of the early twentieth century.

320. Fields, Nora. New ideas for Christmas decorations. New York: Hearthside Press, 1967.
Ideas and instructions for making wreaths, swags, mobiles, hanging ornaments, and corsages out of greens, pods, cones, and scrap; includes a section on Christmas for the birds, with suggestions for pine-cone cookies and feeders.

321. Foley, Daniel J. Christmas the world over: how the season of joy and good will is observed and enjoyed by peoples here and everywhere. Philadelphia: Chilton, 1963.
An account of Christmas celebrations in Bethlehem, Australia, China, Japan, the United States, and parts of Europe and Latin America.

322. Gardner, Horace J. Let's celebrate Christmas. New York: Ronald, 1950.
An idea book on Christmas celebrations, including parties suitable for specific age groups, with icebreakers and games, plays, poetry, quizzes, and stories.

323. Gibson, George M. The story of the Christian year. Nashville, Tenn.: Abingdon, 1945.
An account of the evolution of Christian festivals from the time of the primitive church to the modern era.

324. The glory and pageantry of Christmas, by the editors of Time-Life books. Maplewood, N.J.: Hammond, 1974.
A Christmas anthology centered on the significance of Christmas; Part I deals with the biblical story from Isaiah's prophecy to the holy birth and the life of Christ; the second section covers 2,000 years of observance from ancient times to the modern word; full-color reproductions of art and photographs.

325. Hadfield, Miles, and Hadfield, John. The twelve days of Christmas. Boston: Little, 1961.
A historical survey of the customs and traditions of the period from Christmas Eve to Epiphany.

326. Harper, Wilhelmina, comp. Merry Christmas to you. Rev. ed. New York: Dutton, 1965.
A collection of Christmas stories from Poland, Australia, Denmark, Sweden, Germany, France, Bulgaria, and England.

327. Henderson, Yorke, and others. Parents' magazine's Christmas holiday book. Bergenfield, N.Y.: Parents' Magazine Press, 1972.
A book of time-tested ingredients for a reverent Christmas involving the entire family; includes seasonal lore, customs, selections for reading, recipes, and the all-time favorite Christmas carols, with music; indexed.

328. Horder, Mervyn. On Christmas day: first carols to play and sing. New York: Macmillan, 1969.
Welsh, French, and Old English carols are among the thirteen Christmas songs presented in this volume for unison singing; simple piano arrangements.

329. Hottes, Alfred Carl. 1001 Christmas facts and fancies. 2d ed. New York: Dodd, 1944.
A collection of Christmas legends, stories, carols, toasts, superstitions, omens, and customs around the world, with ideas for making Christmas cards, decorating, and cooking.

330. Ickis, Marguerite. The book of Christmas. New York: Dodd, 1960.
A description of Christmas traditions in the United States, England, and Europe, with ideas for activities.

331. Johnson, Lois S., ed. Christmas stories around the world. Chicago: Rand McNally, 1970.
A collection of Christmas stories from many nations, including one from Colonial America; each story is prefaced by a brief note on the Christmas customs of the country of origin.

332. Kainen, Ruth Cole. America's Christmas heritage. New York: Funk & Wagnalls, 1969.
A compilation of observances and recipes brought to the United States by the English, Dutch, Germans, Mexicans, Greeks, Orientals, and others; arranged by geographical regions and national groups; indexed.

333. Kamerman, Sylvia E., ed. A treasury of Christmas plays: royalty-free stage and radio dramas for young players. Boston: Plays, 1972.
A collection of traditional and modern one-act plays on the theme of the real meaning of Christmas.

334. Kane, Harnett T. The southern Christmas book: the full story from earliest times to present: people, customs, conviviality, carols, cooking. New York: McKay, 1958.
A book of Christmas customs in the American South from the first genial season in Virginia through the years to the Confederate Christmas and a cowboy's Christmas ball and other festivities in the "many Souths"; concludes with recipes, such as Martha Washington's "Great Cake."

335. Langstaff, John, comp. American Christmas songs and carols. New York: Doubleday, 1974.
A collection of American Christmas carols with piano and guitar arrangements; grouped by such sections as folk, Shaker, Moravian, Indian, black traditions, spirituals, shape-note hymns, and part songs.

336. ———, comp. On Christmas day in the morning. New York: Harcourt, 1959.
A collection of carol verses from different places in the world to supplement the familiar verses of four traditional carols, such as *On Chris-i-mas day in the morning*.

337. ———, adapter. Saint George and the dragon. New York: Atheneum, 1973.
A version of the Saint George folk play performed at Christmastime in English communities by local actors and mummers; includes music, costume suggestions, and directions for a sword dance.

338. Lewis, Taylor. Christmas in New England. New York: Holt, 1972.
Full-color photographs and descriptive text on the Christmas season throughout New England.

339. Lohan, Robert, ed. Christmas tales for reading aloud. Enl. ed. New York: Daye, 1966.
A collection of legends and humorous, adventurous, and sentimental stories suitable for reading aloud in the home, classroom, or club meeting; opens with the Nativity story and concludes with twelve great poems.

340. Long, Sidney. And all the dark make bright like day: Christmas books, 1960–1972. Boston: Horn Book, 1972.
An annotated list of books on Christmas reviewed in the *Horn Book* from 1960–72; includes titles on the Nativity, miracles and legends, Christmas in America, and Christmas make-believe; a companion list to Dalphin's *Light the Candles. See also* no. 313.

341. Luckhardt, Mildred C. Christmas comes once more. Nashville, Tenn.: Abingdon, 1962.
A collection of poems and stories to be used with the lighting of each candle on the Advent wreath in preparation for Christmas.

342. McGinley, Phyllis. A wreath of Christmas legends. New York: Macmillan, 1967.
The retelling in verse of fifteen medieval legends of the first Christmas, such as *The Ballad of the Red Breast of the Robin* and *The Canticle of the Bees*.

343. The Metropolitan Museum of Art. The Nativity: the Christmas crèche at the Metropolitan Museum of Art. New York: Doubleday, 1969.
Superb photographs of figures from an eighteenth-century Neapolitan crèche recounting the Christmas story, with explanatory text.

344. Meyer, Carolyn. Christmas crafts: things to make the 24 days before Christmas. New York: Harper, 1974.
A guide to Advent crafts, with unique projects for each day beginning December 1, correlated with customs; illustrated with project drawings and sketches.

345. Miles, Clement A. Christmas in ritual and tradition, Christian and pagan. London: T. F. Unwin, 1912; Detroit: Gale Research, 1968.
A study of the intermingling of customs of Christmas and pagan festivals; cross-referenced index.

346. Moore, Clement Clarke. A visit from St. Nicholas: a facsimile of the 1848 edition. New York: Simon & Schuster, 1971.
A small volume with the old-fashioned engravings and text of the 1848 edition of the all-time favorite among Christmas poems.

347. The Oxford book of carols. New York: Oxford, 1964.
First published in 1928; a collection of traditional and twentieth-century carols; well indexed.

348. Patterson, Lillie. Christmas in Britain and Scandinavia. Champaign, Ill.: Garrard, 1970.
A description of Christmas observances in Norway, Denmark, Sweden, Finland, England, Scotland, Wales, and Ireland; illustrated with photographs.

349. Payne, Alma Smith. Jingle bells and pastry shells: holiday baking favorites for all year round. Cleveland: World Pub., 1968.
A cookbook with an international flavor, linking recipes for holiday breads, cakes, and cookies with customs in different lands; describes Early American Christmas customs and traditional Christmas menus from Greece to the West Indies, and includes some adaptations of these recipes for the dieter.

350. Perry, Margaret. Christmas card magic: the art of making decorations and ornaments with Christmas cards. Garden City, N.Y.: Doubleday, 1970.
Suggestions for keeping Christmas cards out of the wastepaper basket: ideas and decorations for transforming used cards into card trees, centerpieces, crèches, mobiles, mats, candle ruffs, and even next summer's birthday party.

351. Petersham, Maud, and Petersham, Miska. The Christ Child as told by Matthew and Luke. Garden City, N.Y.: Doubleday, 1931.
The classic among picture books re-creating the biblical record of the Nativity.

352. Politi, Leo. The poinsettia. Palm Desert, Calif.: Best-West Pub., 1967.
A picture book blending the legend of the moment the poinsettia became the Christmas flower with recollections of the mood of Christmas in Los Angeles: on Olvera Street, in representative churches, and in Watts.

353. Preston, Carol. A trilogy of Christmas plays for children. New York: Harcourt, 1967.
Three Christmas plays for school or club use; concludes with a suggested list of appropriate music and its use for each play.

354. Rand, Christopher. Christmas in Bethlehem; and Holy Week at Mount Athos. New York: Oxford, 1963.
A report on the Latin, Greek, and Armenian Christmas services at Bethlehem, combined with a description of Holy Week on Mount Athos peninsula.

355. Reed, Will, comp. The second treasury of Christmas music. New York: Emerson, 1968.
A collection of traditional carols and spirituals of international origin, with modern compositions from Asia, Africa, Latin America, and Oceania.

356. ———. The treasury of Christmas music. New York: Emerson, 1961.
Words and music for traditional and modern Christmas carols and hymns; includes some seasonal instrumental music.

357. Reeves, James, comp. The Christmas book. New York: Dutton, 1968.
A selection of modern and traditional carols, stories, poems, legends, and verse, representing a wide variety of authors from Dickens to Dylan Thomas.

358. Rockwell, Anne. El Toro Pinto and other songs in Spanish. New York: Macmillan, 1971.
Christmas carols, folk songs, lullabies, and comic songs from Spain, Latin America, and southwestern United States, with translations.

359. Rollins, Charlemae, comp. Christmas gif'. Chicago: Follett, 1963.
An anthology of Christmas poems, stories, and songs written by and about Negroes; includes some unique holiday recipes.

360. Sansom, William. A book of Christmas. New York: McGraw, 1968.
Informative essays on Christmas customs, literature, food, gifts, and special performances, such as Christmas pantomimes and galanty shows.

361. Sawyer, Ruth. Joy to the world: Christmas legends. Boston: Little, 1966.
Christmas legends and tales from ancient Arabia, Ireland, old and modern Spain; each is preceded by a Christmas carol.

362. Sayre, Eleanor, ed. A Christmas book: fifty carols and poems from the 14th to the 17th centuries. New York: Potter, 1966.
A multilingual collection of Christmas carols and poems with English translations; notes on history and source.

363. Scovel, Myra. The gift of Christmas. New York: Harper, 1972.
A memoir of "Christmases Past" spent in China, Thailand, India, and the United States; instructions for making a partridge-berry wreath and other decorations are interspersed with poems and recollections.

364. Sechrist, Elizabeth Hough, ed. Christmas everywhere: a book of Christmas customs of many lands. Rev. ed. Philadelphia: Macrae Smith, 1962.
Christmas customs as celebrated in many nations, and by national and communal groups.

365. Seeger, Ruth Crawford, comp. American folk songs for Christmas. Garden City, N.Y.: Doubleday, 1953.
A collection of carols and folk songs arranged to tell the Christmas story from song to song; simple accompaniments.

366. Seibel, Kathryn Holley. The joyful Christmas craft book. New York: Van Nostrand, 1963.
A guidebook to the personal pleasures of making Christmas decorations with paper, foodstuffs, wood, baskets, straw, sea shells, cones, nuts, greens, clay, glass, plastics, sheet metal, and copper screen.

367. Seymour, William Kean, and Smith, John, comps. Happy Christmas. Philadelphia: Westminster, 1968.
An anthology for the Christmas season, with selections from English and American novels, autobiographies, and poetry; includes some carols with musical scores.

368. Shekerjian, Haig, and Shekerjian, Regina. A book of Christmas carols. New York: Harper, 1963.
A collection, with interpretative essays, of shepherd, dance, lullaby, magi, nativity, and legendary carols, carols of custom, and miscellaneous carols.

369. Simon, Henry W., ed. A treasury of Christmas songs and carols. Boston: Houghton, 1955.
A collection of Christmas carols, hymns, chorales, solo songs, rounds, and canons from Britain, the United States, and other parts of the world; indexed by titles, first lines, and musical and literary sources.

370. Spicer, Dorothy Gladys. 46 days of Christmas: a cycle of Old World songs, legends, and customs. New York: Coward-McCann, 1960.
An interpretation of the celebration of Christmas in eighteen European and Asiatic countries; arranged in chronological order from Saint Barbara's day to Old Twelfth Night; indexed by countries.

371. Thompson, Jean McKee, sel. Our own Christmas: an anthology. Boston: Beacon Press, 1967.
A collection of prose and poetry expressing the meaning of Christmas as light, love, and everlasting life; the authors range from John Donne to Dick Gregory.

372. Thurman, Howard. The mood of Christmas. New York: Harper, 1973.
A book of Christmas meditations exploring the quality and the spiritual symbolism of the season.

373. Tudor, Tasha, ed. Take joy! Cleveland: World Pub., 1966.
An anthology of Christmas thoughts, stories, poems, carols, lore, and legends, which concludes with the traditions of Advent calendars and wreaths, the filling of cornucopias, the animal Christmas, the marionette show, and other activities observed by the Tudor family in New England.

374. Walsh, William Shepard. The story of Santa Klaus, told for children of all ages from six to sixty, and illustrated by artists of all ages from Fra Angelico to Henry Hutt. Detroit: Gale Research, 1970.
Reprint of the 1909 edition of the history of the Santa Claus legend and its relationship to Saint Nicholas, with an account of the Santa Claus traditions.

375. Wasner, Franz, ed. The Trapp family book of Christmas songs. New York: Pantheon Books, 1950.
Christmas songs from many lands and many periods of Christian history, with English translations of foreign songs.

376. Watts, Franklin, ed. The complete Christmas book. Rev. ed. New York: Watts, 1961.
A manual of suggestions on celebrating Christmas, from homemade cards to recipes.

377. Weiser, Francis X. The Christmas book. New York: Harcourt, 1952.
An interpretation of the origin and meaning of the customs, ceremonies, and legends of Christmas.

378. Wernecke, Herbert H., ed. Celebrating Christmas around the world. Philadelphia: Westminster, 1962.
A collection of material on Christmas customs arranged alphabetically by continent and country.

379. ———. Christmas customs around the world. Philadelphia: Westminster, 1959.
A record of Christmas customs focused on geographical and cultural influences; arranged by continent and by country.

380. ———, ed. Christmas stories from many lands. Philadelphia: Westminster, 1961.
A collection of stories reflecting the universal spirit of the Christmas season.

381. Wheeler, Opal. Sing for Christmas: a round of Christmas carols and stories of the carols. New York: Dutton, 1943.

A collection of twenty-four Christmas carols with music and accounts of how most of them came to be written.

See also section on Planning and Preparing for Anniversaries and Holidays

Citizenship Day

382. Angle, Paul. By these words: great documents of American liberty, selected and placed in their contemporary settings. Chicago: Rand McNally, 1966.

A selection, with explanatory introductions, of charters, compacts, proclamations, and addresses of significance in American history; the documents range from the Mayflower Compact of November 11, 1620, to Lyndon Johnson's March 15, 1965, address to Congress on the civil rights bill.

383. Blevins, Leon W. The young voter's manual. Totowa, N.J.: Littlefield, 1973.

A topical dictionary dealing with the basic functions of American government; includes the Constitution through the twenty-sixth amendment; indexed.

384. Brewton, Sara Westbrook, and Brewton, John Edmund, comps. America forever new. New York: Crowell, 1968.

A collection of poems with patriotic themes directed to the United States of America; indexed by author, title, and first lines.

385. Cavanah, Frances, and Crandall, Elizabeth L. Freedom encyclopedia: American liberties in the making. Chicago: Rand McNally, 1968.

A book about the fundamental rights of citizens, the responsibilities of freedom, the heritage of liberty from the Old World, basic American documents, and leaders of liberty; organized as an encyclopedia with entries in alphabetic order; indexed.

386. Emerson, Ralph Waldo. The sound of trumpets. New York: Viking, 1971.

Selections from the work of Emerson, illustrated by James Daugherty, expressing a personal faith in the goodness of life and in America as the country of the future.

387. Hine, Al. This land is mine: an anthology of American verse. Philadelphia: Lippincott, 1965.

A collection of poetry for patriotic occasions, reflecting the history of the United States beginning with Philip Frenau's *The Indian Burying Ground* and concluding with Phyllis McGinley's *Star-Spangled Ode*; indexed by author and first line.

388. Hoke, Helen, sel. Patriotism, patriotism, patriotism. New York: Watts, 1963.

An anthology of prose and poetry on the themes of freedom, equality, justice, brotherhood, and love of country.

389. Jessup, Libby F. How to become a citizen of the United States. 4th ed. rev. Dobbs Ferry, N.Y.: Oceana, 1972.

A guidebook for prospective citizens on the requirements of the naturalization process, eligibility, facts about the government, and the Constitution.

390. Moffett, Toby. Nobody's business: the political intruder's guide to everyone's state legislature. Riverside, Conn.: Chatham Press, 1973.

Guidelines for citizens' groups based on the Connecticut Citizen Action Group's experience in studying the records of candidates standing for reelection.

391. Niebuhr, Reinhold, and Sigmund, Paul E. The democratic experience: past and prospects. New York: Praeger, 1969.

Essays on the origin, growth, and development of Western democracy as compared with European experiences; followed by assessments of the situation relative to democracy in Africa, the Middle East, Asia, and Latin America.

392. Wood, Dorothy Carrico. This nation: the spirit of America in songs, speeches, poems, and documents. Cleveland: World Pub., 1967.

A collection of poems and prose excerpts on the promise of America, the Declaration of Independence, the idealism and heroism of its founders, and the meaning of its flag.

Columbus Day

393. Bradford, Ernie Dusgate Selby. Christopher Columbus. New York: Studio-Viking, 1973.

A re-creation of the life of Columbus: his personality, efforts to obtain funds, voyages of discovery, colonial administration, and eventual downfall.

394. Divine, David. The opening of the world: the great age of maritime exploration. New York: Putnam, 1973.
A survey of maritime explorations and discoveries from ancient times to the sixteenth century, focusing on Prince Henry the Navigator and chronicles on Diaz, da Gama, Magellan, and Columbus.

395. Foster, Genevieve. The world of Columbus and sons. New York: Scribner, 1965.
An account of the world of Christopher Columbus and his sons Ferdinand and Diego; a chronicle of the time of Isabella, Gutenberg, Luther, Mohammed II, and other greats of history.

396. Frye, John. The search for the Santa Maria. New York: Dodd, 1973.
An account of the underwater search off Cape Haitien for the *Santa Maria,* the vessel used by Columbus in his voyage to the New World.

397. Horizon magazine. Ferdinand and Isabella, by the editors of Horizon magazine. New York: American Heritage, 1965.
A history of Spain in 1492, in the reign of Ferdinand and Isabella, with background material on the queen and her support of the ventures of Christopher Columbus.

398. Meredith, Robert, and Smith, E. Brooks, eds. The quest of Columbus. Boston: Little, 1966.
An account of the discovery of America, based on the writings of Ferdinand, the son of Columbus.

399. Morison, Samuel Eliot. Christopher Columbus, mariner. Boston: Little, 1955.
A rewritten version of *Admiral of the Ocean Sea,* a study of Columbus as a seaman and navigator.

400. Sanderlin, George. Across the ocean sea: a journal of Columbus's voyage. New York: Harper, 1966.
A look at the theories of early explorers about unknown worlds, combined with a description of the voyages of Columbus and other mariners; based primarily on the journals of Columbus and his son Ferdinand.

D Day

401. Eisenhower Foundation. D-day: the Normandy invasion in retrospect. Lawrence: Univ. Press of Kansas, 1971.
A collection of retrospective articles on the planning for D-Day on June 6, 1944, and its aftermath; prepared in commemoration of the day's twenty-fifth anniversary.

402. Howarth, David. D day, the sixth of June 1944. New York: McGraw, 1959.
A chronicle of the planning, the strategy, and the military movements in the invasion of Normandy on June 6, 1944, called "the greatest day of World War II."

403. Tute, Warren, and others. D-day. New York: Macmillan, 1974.
A British view of the planning, organization, and execution of the 1944 Normandy invasion, based on eyewitness reports; illustrated with photographs, maps, and diagrams.

Jefferson Davis' Birthday

404. Catton, William, and Catton, Bruce. Two roads to Sumter. New York: McGraw, 1963.
A contribution to the history of pre-Civil War conflict comparing the backgrounds, personalities, ideals, and principles of Jefferson Davis and Abraham Lincoln.

405. Green, Margaret. President of the Confederacy: Jefferson Davis. New York: Messner, 1963.
A biography of Jefferson Davis as soldier, congressman, secretary of war, senator, and president of the Confederacy.

406. Randall, Ruth Painter. I, Varina. Boston: Little, 1962.
A biography of Varina Davis, wife of Jefferson Davis and first lady of the South; based on family letters and the Jefferson Hayes-Davis collection.

407. Smith, Whitney. "Confederate States of America." In his The flag book of the United States, pp. 263–73. New York: Morrow, 1970.
A history of the Confederate flags as symbols of regional unity and as battle flags, with a brief account of the selection of the design of the official national flag.

408. Strode, Hudson. Jefferson Davis. 3 vols. New York: Harcourt, 1955–1964.
A three-volume study of Jefferson Davis as an American patriot, the president of the Confederacy, and a tragic hero.

409. ———, ed. Jefferson Davis: private letters, 1823–1889. New York: Harcourt, 1966.
A collection of the personal letters of Jefferson Davis, with commentaries by the editor explaining the circumstances of the communications between Jefferson Davis, his father, wife, children, friends, and associates.

Defenders' Day

410. Key, Francis Scott. The star-spangled banner. Garden City, N.Y.: Doubleday, 1973.
A pictorial interpretation of the national anthem of the United States, illustrated by Peter Spier, including a historical note on the event that inspired its writing, and a reproduction of Francis Scott Key's original manuscript.

411. Krythe, Maymie R. "The star-spangled banner." In her Sampler of American songs, pp.15–39. New York: Harper, 1969.
A chapter on the national anthem and Francis Scott Key, with human-interest stories about American attitudes on the anthem's singability and references to Fort McHenry as a national shrine; the book also includes background material on other songs sung on patriotic occasions and three Christmas songs.

412. Lyons, John Henry. Stories of our American patriotic songs. New York: Vanguard, 1942.
An introduction to the history of the patriotic songs of the United States, beginning with an account of Francis Scott Key and the writing of *The Star Spangled Banner.*

413. Woods, Ralph L. "The star-spangled banner." In his Famous poems and the little known stories behind them, pp. 309–11. New York: Hawthorn Books, 1961.
A brief account of Francis Scott Key and the writing of *The Star-Spangled Banner* on September 14, 1814, and its adoption as the national anthem 117 years later.

Earth Day

414. Ault, Phil. These are the Great Lakes. New York: Dodd, 1972.
A report on the Great Lakes, beginning with the glacial period, moving into the times of Indians, explorers, and settlers, and concluding with the age of ecological problems; suggests solutions; indexed.

415. Brooks, Paul. The house of life: Rachel Carson at work. Boston: Houghton, 1972.
An account of the work of Rachel Carson as a biologist and author whose books inspired conservation-minded Americans and laid the foundation for the ecological movement.

416. Clement, Roland C. Hammond nature atlas of America. Maplewood, N.J.: Hammond, 1973.
A handsome survey of the natural resources of the United States, designed to provide information on man-nature relationships and to underscore citizen responsibility for conservation.

417. Passmore, John. Man's responsibility for nature: ecological problems and Western traditions. New York: Scribner, 1974.
An examination of problems of pollution, conservation, preservation, and population control from the viewpoint of society's obligation to transform the world into a civilized state.

418. The Rand McNally atlas of world wildlife. Foreword by Sir Julian Huxley. New York: Rand McNally, 1973.
A comprehensive atlas on the diversity of the world's wildlife resources, underscoring the essentiality of conservation in the interrelations of organisms and their environments.

419. Udall, Stewart L. America's natural treasures: national native monuments and seashores. Waukesha, Wis.: Country Beautiful Corp., 1971.
A handsome introduction to the heritage provided by nature for the American people; includes national nature monuments from stone arches to white sands, wildlife refuges, seashores, and wild and scenic rivers.

420. Ward, Barbara. Who speaks for earth? Seven citizens of the world on major issues of the global environment. New York: Norton, 1973.
An anthology of papers prepared for the 1972 United Nations Conference on International Environmental Issues; includes material on pollution, environmental management, human settlement, social and biological problems.

421. The wild places: a photographic celebration of unspoiled America. Text by Ann and Myron Sutton. New York: Harper, 1973.
A photographic record, with a supplementary text by a geologist-botanist team, on the untouched natural resources of America.

422. Wilderness, U.S.A. Washington, D.C.: National Geographic Soc., 1973.
Illustrated essays on the heritage of the wilderness of the Far West, the Southwest, the Great Divide, the Midlands, the East, and Alaska, underscoring the importance of conservation.

Easter

423. Adams, Charlotte. Easter idea book. New York: Barrows, 1954.
Suggestions for celebrating Easter, from luncheon centerpieces and favors to gifts to make for children and grown-ups.

424. Barth, Edna. Lilies, rabbits, and painted eggs: the story of the Easter symbols. New York: Seabury, 1970.
An explanation of the meaning of the Easter symbols: the sunrise, flowers, fire and fireworks, hot cross buns, eggs, lambs, rabbits, colors, bells, chants, and rituals.

425. Benoit, Pierre, Leube, Konrad, and Hagolani, Elhanan, eds. Easter: a pictorial pilgrimage. Nashville, Tenn.: Abingdon, 1970.
A photographic record of the holy places associated with Easter, with accompanying text and reproductions of religious art.

426. Coskey, Evelyn. Easter eggs for everyone. Nashville, Tenn.: Abingdon, 1973.
The comprehensive book on the Easter egg: lore, legend, customs, descriptions of dyed eggs, batik-process and collage eggs, novelties; concludes with Easter entertainments and egg games; indexed.

427. Fisher, Aileen. Easter. New York: Crowell, 1968.
A simple retelling of the life of Christ, prefaced by a short introduction on Easter customs in different sections of the world.

428. Harper, Wilhelmina, comp. Easter chimes: stories for Easter and the spring season. Rev. ed. New York: Dutton, 1965.
An anthology of legends, poems, and stories of Easter and springtime, including such authors as Padraic Colum, Marchette Chute, and Hans Christian Andersen.

429. Hartman, Rachel. The joys of Easter. New York: Meredith, 1967.
Essays on the significance of the customs of the Easter season, concluding with a commentary on spiritual values in typical celebrations and in communication through art, spirituals, and hymns; indexed.

430. Hazeltine, Alice Isabel, and Smith, Elva Sophronia. The Easter book of legends and stories. New York: Lothrop, 1947.
An anthology of stories, poems, and plays on the first Easter, the waking year, and the spirit of faith and worship; indexed by author and title.

431. Hole, Christina. Easter and its customs. New York: Barrows, 1961.
A review of customs associated with Eastertide, Shrovetide, Mothering Sunday, Good Friday, Easter, Easter Monday, and Hocktide; indexed.

432. Lord, Priscilla Sawyer, and Foley, Daniel J. Easter garland. Philadelphia: Chilton, 1963.
A collection of material on Easter, ranging from the biblical story and the lore of Easter plants to the winter demons and Mardi Gras.

433. ———. Easter the world over. Philadelphia: Chilton, 1971.
A comprehensive survey of Easter as it is celebrated in European countries from Austria to Wales, in Bermuda, the islands of the Caribbean, Latin America, the United States, and the Orient; includes sections on Easter music and Easter and the fine arts; indexed.

434. Maier, Paul L. First Easter: the true and unfamiliar story in words and pictures. New York: Harper, 1973.
The scriptural events of Holy Week examined in the light of recent archaeological and historical research on the religious, social, and political situations prevailing during the "week that changed the world."

435. Newall, Venetia. An egg at Easter: a folklore study. Bloomington: Indiana Univ. Press, 1971.
A study of the folklore and symbolism of decorated eggs and the varying concepts of their use.

436. Newsome, Arden J. Egg craft. New York: Lothrop, 1973.
A guide to becoming an egger, with detailed advice on materials and tools, special instructions and diagrams for unique decorations, and a list of sources of supply; indexed.

437. Patterson, Lillie. Easter. Champaign, Ill.: Garrard, 1966.
A simply written account of the Sunday of joy and the traditions of eggs, rabbits, gifts, and greetings that are a part of the Easter season; the last chapter briefly covers Easter in legend, poetry, and song.

438. Sechrist, Elizabeth Hough, and Woolsey, Janette. It's time for Easter. Philadelphia. Macrae Smith, 1961.
A collection including the Gospel story of Easter and sections on Easter customs around the world, legends, music, and poetry; indexed.

See also section on Planning and Preparing for Anniversaries and Holidays

Leif Ericson Day

439. Enterline, James Robert. Viking America: the Norse crossings and their legacy. Garden City, N.Y.: Doubleday, 1972.
An examination of the evidence for Norse explorations, the saga of Leif Ericson, the Columbus controversy, and other segments of the question of who first discovered America.

440. Golding, Morton J. The mystery of the Vikings in America. Philadelphia: Lippincott, 1973.
An account of the explorations of the Vikings, with scattered commentaries on Leif Ericson; indexed.

441. Klindt-Jensen, Ole. The world of the Vikings. Washington, D.C.: Luce, 1970.
A handsome volume on the Viking period and the world known by Leif Ericson.

442. Pohl, Frederick J. The Viking settlements of North America. New York: Potter, 1972.
A contribution to research on the Viking settlements, with descriptions of Leif Ericson's three landings and his voyage home from Vinland; indexed.

443. Ray, Frederic, comp. "Landing of Leif Ericson in the New World in 1001." In his O! say can you see: the story of America through great paintings, pp. 21–23. Harrisburg, Pa.: Stackpole, 1970.
A reproduction of Edward Moran's painting of Leif Ericson's arrival on the coast of Newfoundland in 1001, with a brief historic note; one of the fifty-four full-color reproductions of paintings on subjects of historic significance in the history of the American continent.

Father's Day

444. Brussell, Eugene E. Dictionary of quotable definitions. Englewood Cliffs, N.J.: Prentice-Hall, 1970.
A collection of aphorisms and metaphors for speakers and writers; includes a baker's dozen of definitions of a father; arranged alphabetically by topic.

445. Doud, Margery, and Parsley, Cleo M. Father: an anthology of verse. New York: Dutton, 1931.
An old but still useful collection of poems in tribute to fathers; the brief introduction includes the 1910 petition to the Spokane Ministerial Association asking support for the setting aside of the third Sunday in June as a tribute to fathers.

446. Prescott, Orville, ed. A father reads to his children. New York: Dutton, 1965.
An anthology of poems, fairy tales, ancient myths, stories about knights and heroes, the Old West, animals, and adventures collected to bring pleasure to fathers reading to their children.

447. Schwartz, Alvin. To be a father: stories, letters, essays, poems, comments, and proverbs on the delights and despairs of fatherhood. New York: Crown, 1967.
An anthology of writings about fathers as proud parents, friends, protectors, teachers, disciplinarians, including an address given by Adlai E. Stevenson before the National Father's Day Committee on May 25, 1961.

448. Swinnerton, Frank Arthur. A galaxy of fathers. Garden City, N.Y.: Doubleday, 1966.
Literary essays on the father-daughter relationship in eighteenth-century England, with special attention to the fathers of four prominent women authors.

Fire Prevention Day

449. Andrews, Ralph W. Historic fires of the West. Seattle: Superior Pub., 1966.
A pictorial history of volunteer firemen, bucket brigades, early pumping stations, and the historic fires of early days in the western American states, Alaska, and British Columbia.

450. Ditzel, Paul C. Firefighting: a new look in the old firehouse. New York: Van Nostrand, 1969.
A history of the development of fire-fighting techniques and fire prevention.

451. Kogan, Herman, and Cromie, Robert. The great fire: Chicago, 1871. New York: Putnam, 1971.
A pictorial history of Chicago's great fire of October 8–10, 1871, which is commemorated annually by fire-prevention days and weeks.

452. Naden, Corinne, J. The Chicago Fire —1871: the blaze that nearly destroyed a city. New York: Watts, 1969.
A detailed account of the Chicago Fire, with maps of sections of the city to assist the reader in following the spread of one of the nation's most dramatic fires.

Flag Days and Patriotic Holidays

453. Barraclough, E. M. C. Flags of the world. Rev. ed. London: Warne, 1965.
A history of flags in Great Britain, the British Commonwealth of Nations, the United States, Latin America, Africa, the Middle East, and Europe, including the new nations established by the early 1960s.

454. Dobler, Lavinia. National holidays around the world. New York: Fleet Press, 1968.
A brief description of the patriotic holidays of 134 countries of the world, their flags, anthems, and manner of celebrating; arranged by date of holiday; indexed by country.

455. Elting, Mary, and Folsom, Franklin. Flags of all nations and the people who live under them. New York: Grosset, 1969.
A history of flags, beginning with the ancient Egyptians; the descriptions of modern flags are correlated with capsule histories of individual nations and their people.

456. Evans, I. O. Flags of the world. New York: Grosset, 1970.
Brief descriptions of the flags of all nations, states, provinces, and possessions.

457. Ickis, Marguerite. The book of patriotic holidays. New York: Dodd, 1962.
Ideas for patriotic holiday programs from making a patriotic mural to displaying patriotic collections; includes material for specific patriotic holidays, such as Flag Day, the Fourth of July, and other patriotic days of the United States, patriotic games and songs, patriotic symbols, and facts about the fifty American states.

458. Krythe, Maymie R. What so proudly we hail: all about our American flag, monuments, and symbols. New York: Harper, 1968.
A background study of such American symbols as the flag, the presidential seal, the great seal, the American eagle, the national motto, the Liberty Bell, and Independence Hall.

459. Mastai, Boleslaw, and Mastai, Marie-Louise D'Otrange. The Stars and Stripes: the American flag as art and history from the birth of the republic to the present. New York: Knopf, 1973.
A comprehensive illustrated history of the flag of the United States, its use on land, sea, and on the moon; includes descriptions of flag souvenirs, commemorative flags, decorative, political, and patriotic flag functions, and other historic data; concludes with a list of official American flags and their stars.

460. Nettl, Paul. National anthems. 2d enl. ed. New York: Ungar, 1967.
Source material on national anthems, with texts in the original language and in English; indexed by first lines.

461. Parrish, Thomas. The American flag. New York: Simon & Schuster, 1973.
A history of the flag of the United States; takes a look at the banners that have flown over American soil and discusses the events and legends associated with the flag and its changes.

462. Pedersen, Christian Fogd. The international flag book in color. New York: Morrow, 1971.
An illustrated review of national, state, naval, mercantile, and other official flags of the world.

463. Smith, Whitney. The flag book of the United States. New York: Morrow, 1970.
A history of the flag of the United States, the flags of the fifty states and territories, official governmental units, and the armed forces; includes flag etiquette.

See also Fourth of July; section on Planning and Preparing for Anniversaries and Holidays

Forefather's Day

464. Caffrey, Kate. The Mayflower. New York: Stein & Day, 1974.
A chronicle of the Pilgrims in America: their doctrines, leaders, and settlement decisions; the appendix includes passenger lists, the Mayflower Compact, representative Pilgrim letters, and other historic materials.

465. Fleming, Thomas J. One small candle: the Pilgrim's first year in America. New York: Norton, 1964.
A narrative history of the Pilgrim's first year at Plymouth, beginning with the negotiations for passage and concluding with the arrival of new recruits from England after the first Thanksgiving Day.

466. Hall-Quest, Olga W. How the Pilgrims came to Plymouth. New York: Dutton, 1946.
An account of the Pilgrims' flight to Holland, voyage to the New World, and settlement at Plymouth; includes an introductory note on the first use of the term *Pilgrims* in a celebration of Forefather's Day in 1798.

467. Hays, Wilma Pitchford. Christmas on the Mayflower. New York: Coward-McCann, 1956.
A story, based on historical records, of the Pilgrims' Christmas in the company of the rebellious sailors on the *Mayflower* in 1620.

468. McGovern, Ann. . . . if you sailed on the Mayflower. New York: Four Winds Press, 1969.
A report on the daily life of the Pilgrims, presented through questions and answers; concludes with the first Thanksgiving.

469. Morison, Samuel Eliot. The story of the "Old Colony" of New Plymouth, 1620–1692. New York: Knopf, 1956.
A chronological record of the Plymouth Colony from its beginnings as an offshoot of the Separatist movement in England to its annexation by the Massachusetts Bay Colony in 1692; includes details on laws and government, manners and customs, homes and clothing, and the Pilgrims' first Thanksgiving.

470. Myers, Robert J. "Forefathers' Day." In his Celebrations: the complete book of American holidays, pp. 295–301. Garden City, N.Y.: Doubleday, 1972.
A history of Forefathers' Day from its first observance on December 22, 1796, at Plymouth, Massachusetts.

471. Speare, Elizabeth George. "New England neighbors." In her Life in colonial America, pp. 24–51. New York: Random House, 1963.
A contribution to the history of the first colonists in New England, their homes, their Sabbath, town meetings, beliefs, and conduct.

472. Stearns, Monroe. "Poor little Plymouth." In his The story of New England, pp. 13–32. New York: Random House, 1967.
An account of the arrival of the *Mayflower* and its passengers: the "Saints" or "Separatists" and the nonsaints, known as "Strangers," who accompanied them; discusses their choice of Plymouth for the first settlement, and gives a quick overview of their problems up to the dissolution of the colony in 1692.

473. Walsh, John E. The Mayflower Compact, November 11, 1620: the first democratic document in America. New York: Watts, 1971.
An identification of the Pilgrims as a distinctive group, with an interpretation of the events and problems that led to the creation of the covenant known as "the Mayflower Compact"; includes a commentary on the lives of the signers and on the significance of the document.

474. Willison, George F. The Pilgrim reader: the story of the Pilgrims as told by themselves and their contemporaries, friendly and unfriendly. Garden City, N.Y.: Doubleday, 1953.
The firsthand record of the settlers of the Plymouth Colony; based on their own letters, journals, and documents; arranged chronologically with connecting commentaries.

475. Wright, Louis B. Everyday life in colonial America. New York: Putnam, 1965.
An insight into the lives of the individuals and families of the first colonists in the United States; scattered references to the first Thanksgiving at Plymouth, to a few other activities of the Pilgrims, and to the holidays of all the early colonies; indexed.

Fourth of July

476. Booth, Sally Smith. The women of '76. New York: Hastings House, 1974.
An account of the courage, ingenuity, and contributions of women participants in the American Revolution.

477. Brand, Oscar. Songs of '76: a folksinger's history of the Revolution. New York: Evans, 1973.
Words and music to Tory and Rebel songs of the American Revolution, with commentary on the historical and social background of each song.

478. Cooke, Donald Ewin. Fathers of America's freedom: the story of the signers of the Declaration of Independence. Maplewood, N.J.: Hammond, 1969.
An insight into the personal convictions and circumstances of the fifty-six men who signed the Declaration of Independence, with a follow-up on the course of their later lives.

479. Ferris, Robert G. Signers of the Declaration. Washington, D.C.: U.S. Dept. of the Interior, Natl. Park Service, 1973.
The history of the Declaration of Independence, with biographical sketches of the signers, a listing of historic sites and homes associated with the signers, and the text of the declaration.

480. Furneaux, Rupert. The pictorial history of the American Revolution as told by eyewitnesses and participants. Chicago: Ferguson Pub., 1973.
A re-creation of the events, the locations, and the experiences of soldiers and citizens, from the Boston Tea Party of December 16, 1773, to Washington's Farewell Address to his troops at Fraunces Tavern on December 4, 1783.

481. Handlin, Oscar. Statue of Liberty. New York: Newsweek Book Div., 1971.
An illustrated history of Auguste Bartholdi's Statue of Liberty, conceived as a monument to Franco-American friendship and dedicated in New York harbor on July 4, 1886; concludes with a chronology of immigration and a brief description of colossal statues through the ages.

482. Hatch, Eric. The little book of bells. New York: Duell, 1964.
A brief history of bells, inspired by a broadcast of bells ringing across the United States in honor of July 4; concludes with a chapter on the Liberty Bell.

483. Kavenagh, W. Keith, ed. Foundations of colonial America: a documentary history. 3 vols. New York: Chelsea House, 1973.
Over one thousand documents of American colonial history of the seventeenth and eighteenth centuries.

484. Murfin, James V. National Park Service guide to the historic places of the American Revolution. Washington, D.C.: U.S. Dept. of the Interior, 1974.
An illustrated guide to the national, state, and local historic sites associated with the American Revolution, with a chronology of political and military events of the period.

485. Rabson, Carolyn. Songbook of the American Revolution. Peaks Island, Maine: NEO Press, 1974.
A collection of ballads, national songs, and hymns of both the Rebels and the Loyalists of early America; useful for patriotic programming.

486. Randel, William Pierce. The American Revolution: mirror of a people. Maplewood, N.J.: Hammond, 1973.
An illustrated description of the way of life in American cities and on the farms in the era that produced the Declaration of Independence, combined with a history of events that sparked the fuse for independence.

487. Ross, George E. Know your Declaration of Independence and the 56 signers. Chicago: Rand McNally, 1963.
A summary of the events leading up to the signing of the Declaration of Independence, with concise biographies of the signers.

488. Silber, Irwin, ed. Songs of independence. Harrisburg, Pa.: Stackpole, 1973.
A study of the earliest patriotic music in the United States; includes ninety-seven songs reflecting the revolutionary spirit as seen in the words and tunes of colonial times.

489. Wright, Esmond. A time for courage: the story of the Declaration of Independence. New York: Putnam, 1971.
An examination of the American Revolution from the standpoint of the positions on independence taken by Jefferson, Patrick Henry, George Washington, Sam and John Adams, John Hancock, and others.

See also section on Planning and Preparing for Anniversaries and Holidays

Halloween/Houdini Day

490. Anderson, Jean. The haunting of America: ghost stories from our past. Boston: Houghton, 1973.
Accounts of ghosts and supernatural beings of American folklore from the ghost ship of the Great Lakes to the ghost of Abraham Lincoln.

491. Barth, Edna. Witches, pumpkins, and grinning ghosts: the story of the Halloween symbols. New York: Seabury, 1972.
An account of the symbols of Halloween, from ancient Britain to modern times; for young readers.

492. Christian, Roy. Ghosts and legends. North Pomfret, Vt.: David & Charles, 1973.
A look at the British historical legends and ghostly tales connected with places such as Glastonbury and people like Ann Boleyn.

493. Christopher, Milbourne. Houdini: the untold story. New York: Crowell, 1969.
A study of the character, personality, and career of the celebrated magician whose birthday is observed on Halloween.

494. ———. The illustrated history of magic. New York: Crowell, 1973.
A survey of magic from the time of the Egyptian sorcerer-priests to the age of Houdini, Blackstone, and Dunninger; includes a chapter on American Indian magic.

495. Coxe, Antony H. Haunted Britain: a guide to supernatural sites frequented by ghosts, witches, poltergeists, and other mysterious beings. New York: McGraw, 1973.
A guide to places in England, Scotland, Wales, and the Isle of Man where ghostly and other supernatural manifestations occur.

496. Green, Roger Lancelyn, ed. A cavalcade of magicians. New York: Walck, 1973.
An anthology of traditional and modern tales about magicians gathered from scattered sources.

497. Gresham, William Lindsay. Houdini, the man who walked through the walls. New York: Holt, 1959.
An account of Houdini's career as a magician and a crusader against fakery, and an explanation of some of his magic.

498. Harper, Wilhelmina, comp. Ghosts and goblins: stories for Halloween. Rev. ed. New York: Dutton, 1965.
An anthology of folktales of Halloween from several different countries.

499. Hopkins, Lee Bennett, comp. Hey-how for Halloween! Poems. New York: Harcourt, 1974.
A collection of poems with Halloween themes for personal reading, storytelling hours, and reading-aloud sessions.

500. Kaye, Marvin. The Stein and Day handbook of magic. New York: Stein & Day, 1973.
A book for the beginning magic entertainer, with descriptions and instructions for over eighty tricks; includes a section on entertaining children, the hospitalized, and others.

501. Leach, Maria. Whistle in the graveyard: folktales to chill your bones. New York: Viking, 1974.
Tales for Halloween; includes White House ghosts, Anne Boleyn, treasure ghosts, bogeys and bugaboos, ghostly things, witch lore, and fakes.

502. Linton, Ralph, and Linton, Adelin. Halloween through twenty centuries. New York: Schuman, 1950.
An account of Halloween in relation to All Hallows' Day and All Souls' Day, folk beliefs, witchcraft in Europe and New England, and the custom of trick-or-treat.

503. Ross, Laura. "Halloween." In her Holiday puppets, pp. 159–80. New York: Lothrop, 1974.
A puppeteer's suggestions for making a scarecrow puppet, a pumpkin puppet, and a witch puppet for Halloween.

504. Sechrist, Elizabeth Hough, ed. Heigh-ho for Halloween! Philadelphia: Macrae Smith, 1948.
Halloween material, including its origins, poems, stories, costumes, and entertainment.

See also section on Planning and Preparing for Anniversaries and Holidays

Hanukkah

505. Chiel, Kinneret. The complete book of Hanukkah. New York: Friendly House Pub., 1959.
A Hanukkah anthology, including history, traditions, legends, stories, songs, prayers, and typical recipes.

506. Cohen, Lenore. Came liberty beyond our hope: a story of Hanukkah. Los Angeles: Ward Ritchie Press, 1963.
An interpretation of the historic facts behind the commemoration of Hanukkah.

507. Epstein, Morris. "Hanukkah." In his A pictorial treasury of Jewish holidays and customs, pp. 49–61. New York: Ktav Pub., 1959.
Background reading on Hanukkah as a historic saga of courage and fortitude, with an explanation of Hanukkah lights, menorahs, dreidels, and Hanukkah customs.

508. Morrow, Betty. A great miracle: the story of Hanukkah. New York: Harvey House, 1968.
A narrative account of the overthrow of the Syrians by the Jewish people of two thousand years ago as background for the modern observance of Hanukkah.

509. Pearlman, Moshe. The Maccabees. New York: Macmillan, 1973.
An illustrated history of the Maccabees and their role in firmly establishing the identity of the Jewish people; a retelling of the Hanukkah epic.

510. Rosenblum, William F., and Rosenblum, Robert J. The story of Chanukah. Garden City, N.Y.: Doubleday, 1967.
Insight into the lessons to be learned by all men in the eight-day observance of the Jewish Festival of Lights.

511. Scharfstein, Edythe, and Scharfstein, Sol. The book of Chanukah. 2d ed. New York: Ktav Pub., 1959.
A short introduction to Hanukkah with "poems, riddles, stories, songs, and things to do."

512. Simon, Norma. Hanukkah. New York: Crowell, 1966.
A simple explanation of the history, customs, and significance of Hanukkah as the Festival of Lights, a symbol of religious freedom.

513. Solis-Cohen, Emily, Jr., comp. Hanukkah: the feast of lights. Philadelphia: Jewish Pub. Soc., 1937.
A collection of articles on the significance of Hanukkah, with a section on its commemoration from religious services to a candle drill and a Hanukkah party.

Humane Day

514. Alexander, Lloyd. Fifty years in the doghouse. New York: Putnam, 1964.
The adventures of William Michael Ryan, special agent for the American Society for the Prevention of Cruelty to Animals, the oldest humane society in the Western hemisphere.

515. Carson, Gerald. Men, beasts, and gods: a history of cruelty and kindness to animals. New York: Scribner, 1972.
A survey of animal treatment in Europe from the Stone Age to Victorian England, followed by an examination of practices in the United States from the colonial period to the present; concludes with a plea for animal rights.

516. Chrystie, Francis N. Pets: a complete handbook on the care, understanding, and appreciation of all kinds of animal pets. Boston: Little, 1974.
A third edition of a classic book on the intelligent care of pets.

517. Curry-Lindahl, Kai. Let them live: a worldwide survey of animals threatened with extinction. New York: Morrow, 1972.
Facts about 982 mammals, birds, reptiles, amphibians, and fishes endangered by extinction on the land masses and waters of the world; indexed.

518. Harlow, Alvin F. Henry Bergh: founder of the A.S.P.C.A. New York: Messner, 1957.
The life of Henry Bergh and his twenty-two years of leadership in the American Society for the Prevention of Cruelty to Animals and in the organization of the Society for the Prevention of Cruelty to Children.

Independence Days around the World

519. Archer, Jules. African firebrand: Kenyatta of Kenya. New York: Messner, 1969.
An account of Kenya's freedom from British dominion, coupled with a biography of Kenyatta, the hero of the independence movement.

520. ———. Congo: the birth of a new nation. New York: Messner, 1970.
A historical account of the problems of Congolese independence.

521. ———. The Philippines' fight for freedom. New York: Crowell, 1970.
A review of the struggle of the Filipinos to throw off successively Spanish, American, and Japanese rule and establish an independent nation.

522. Bebler, Anton, ed. Military rule in Africa: Dahomey, Ghana, Sierra Leone, and Mali. New York: Praeger, 1973.
A study of coups d'etat in four West African states and the effect of military intervention in the life and freedom in each nation.

523. Cornwall, Barbara. The bush rebels: a personal account of black revolt in Africa. New York: Holt, 1972.
A journalist's report on the struggle for independence in Mozambique and Portuguese Guinea.

524. Dakin, Douglas. The Greek struggle for independence, 1821–1833. Berkeley: Univ. of California Press, 1973.
A short history of the Greek independence movement and the events leading to the establishment of the modern Greek state.

525. Eyck, Frank, comp. The revolutions of 1848–49. New York: Harper, 1972.
A collection of documents on the relationships of the European revolutions of 1848–49 to events in France, Germany, Austria, and Italy.

526. Franke, Wolfgang. A century of Chinese revolution. Columbia: Univ. of South Carolina Press, 1970.
A description of the Taiping Rebellion, the reform movement, the Boxer uprising, the republican revolution of 1911, the May 4 movement of 1919, the victory and ultimate collapse of the Kuomintang, and the victory of the Chinese Communists.

527. Godechot, Jacques. The taking of the Bastille, July 14th, 1789. New York: Scribner, 1970.
An interpretation of the significance of the revolutionary movement that resulted in the fall of the Bastille on July 14, 1789, honored each year by French citizens.

528. Goldston, Robert. The Cuban revolution. Indianapolis: Bobbs, 1970.
A chronological history of Cuba focused on the Twenty-Sixth of July movement.

529. ———. The Vietnamese revolution. Indianapolis: Bobbs, 1972.
An analysis of Vietnamese independence, the conflict between the Vietnamese people, and the involvement of United States forces.

530. Lomask, Milton. The first American revolution. New York: Farrar, 1974.
A history of the American Revolution that challenges some legends and records the contributions of the blacks.

531. Mitchell, Broadus. The price of independence: a realistic view of the American Revolution. New York: Oxford, 1974.
Insights into the civic and governmental community problems, and the alterations in the social fabric, that resulted from the Revolution.

532. Niemeyer, E. V., Jr. Revolution at Queretaro: the Mexican Constitutional Convention of 1916–1917. Austin: Univ. of Texas Press, 1974.
A study of the personalities, issues, and developments of the convention that gave Mexico its present constitution.

533. Ott, Thomas O. The Haitian revolution, 1789–1804. Knoxville: Univ. of Tennessee Press, 1973.
A concise history of the Haitian revolution that continued from 1804 and its consequences for the independent nation.

534. Postal, Bernard, and Levy, Henry. And the hills shouted for joy: the day Israel was born. New York: McKay, 1973.
A history of the events leading to the creation of the state of Israel; the appendix includes biographical sketches of the signers of Israel's declaration of independence.

535. Prago, Albert. The revolutions in Spanish America: the independence movements of 1808–1825. New York: Macmillan, 1970.
A history of the independence movement of the early 1800s in Latin America.

536. Sterne, Emma Gelders. Benito Juárez: builder of a nation. New York: Knopf, 1967.
A history of the Mexican struggle for independence, combined with the life story of Benito Juárez, the leader of the common man.

537. Stewart, Rhea Tulley. Fire in Afghanistan, 1914–1929: faith, hope, and the British Empire. New York: Doubleday, 1973.
An analysis of Britain's relations with Afghanistan, centered on the rise and fall of the Afghan ruler Amanullah and the country's emergence as an independent nation.

See also Fourth of July.

Jefferson's Birthday

538. Brodie, Fawn McKay. Thomas Jefferson: an intimate history. New York: Norton, 1974.
A biography of Jefferson focused on the philosophy, experiences, and personality traits that molded his career; the appendix includes reminiscences written by his sons.

539. Guinness, Desmond, and Sadler, Julius T. Mr. Jefferson, architect. New York: Studio-Viking, 1973.
A review of Jefferson's interests and talents as an architect, from the first plans for Monticello to the design of the University of Virginia, combined with a record of his influence on the architecture of colonial America.

540. Jefferson, Thomas. Thomas Jefferson: a biography in his own words. By the eds. of Newsweek Books. New York: Newsweek Book Div., 1974.
Excerpts from *The Papers of Thomas Jefferson,* volumes 1–19, illuminating Jefferson as a statesman, humanist, and draftsman of the Declaration of Independence.

541. Krythe, Maymie. "The Jefferson Memorial." In her What so proudly we hail, pp. 236–47. New York: Harper, 1968.
A brief history and description of the Jefferson Memorial in Washington, D.C.

542. Malone, Dumas. Jefferson and his time. Vol. 5. Jefferson the president: second term, 1805–1809. Boston: Little, 1974.
The fifth volume of a monumental study of Jefferson; an appraisal of Jefferson's last years of public service.

543. Peterson, Merrill D. Thomas Jefferson and the new nation. New York: Oxford, 1970.
A study of the strengths and weaknesses of Thomas Jefferson: his philosophy, concepts of individual freedom, views on education, and leadership skills as governor of Virginia and minister to France.

544. Weymouth, Lally, comp. Thomas Jefferson: the man, his world, his influence. New York: Putnam, 1974.
A scholarly collection of studies dealing with Jefferson's relationship to the Enlightenment and the Renaissance, his interpretation of the political scene, and his contributions to architecture and to libertarian thought.

545. Wibberley, Leonard P. O. Man of liberty: a life of Thomas Jefferson. New York: Farrar, 1968.
A one-volume edition of a four-volume study of Thomas Jefferson as father, farmer, and president of the United States.

Martin Luther King's Birthday/Human Relations Day

546. Bennett, Lerone. What manner of man. 3d rev. ed. Chicago: Johnson Pub., 1968.
A biography of Martin Luther King, Jr., which points to the factors that influenced his development as a leader in the civil-rights movement and the nation.

547. Brooks, Thomas R. Walls come tumbling down: a history of the civil rights movement—1940–1970. Englewood Cliffs, N.J.: Prentice-Hall, 1974.
An account of thirty years of the civil-rights movement in the United States, including studies of A. Philip Randolph, Martin Luther King, Jr., and other outstanding leaders.

548. Clayton, Ed. Martin Luther King: the peaceful warrior. 3d ed. Englewood Cliffs, N.J.: Prentice-Hall, 1968.
A short biography focused on the efforts of Martin Luther King, Jr., to achieve equality through nonviolent methods.

549. Fager, Charles. Selma 1965: the town where the South was changed. New York: Scribner, 1974.
A report on the civil-rights confrontations in Selma in 1965 and the leadership of Martin Luther King, Jr.

550. Friedman, Leon, ed. The civil rights reader: basic documents of the civil rights movement. New York: Walker, 1967.
A collection of major civil-rights documents up to the middle of the 1960s.

551. Harris, Middleton. The black book. New York: Random House, 1974.
A visual record of three hundred years of American black history, made up of photos, newspaper articles, posters, and songs demonstrating the Negro's contribution to American society.

552. Hirsch, S. Carl. The riddle of racism. New York: Viking, 1972.
A social history of racism in the United States from the 1880s to the 1970s; participants in the account range from Jefferson to Martin Luther King, Jr., and other contemporaries.

553. King, Coretta Scott. My life with Martin Luther King, Jr. New York: Holt, 1969.
The autobiography of Martin Luther King's widow, with reminiscences and reflections on her marriage to the great black leader.

554. King, Martin Luther, Jr. Strength to love. New York: Harper, 1963.
A collection of King's sermons, concluding with a statement of his personal credo explaining his understanding of the Christian faith and way of life.

555. Lincoln, C. Eric, ed. Martin Luther King, Jr.: a profile. New York: Hill & Wang, 1970.
Selections and essays assessing King's philosophy on nonviolence, his response to social problems, and his leadership role.

556. Smith, Kenneth L., and Zepp, Ira G., Jr. Search for the beloved community: the thinking of Martin Luther King, Jr. Valley Forge, Pa.: Judson Press, 1974.
An examination of King's intellectual concepts of social justice and nonviolence as they stemmed from the theology and ethics of his Christian faith.

Kosciuszko Day

557. Abodaher, David J. Warrior on two continents. New York: Messner, 1968.
A fictionalized account of Thaddeus Kosciuszko, Polish hero and American revolutionary officer, with major credit for his contributions to the American cause.

558. Pilarski, Laura. "Thaddeus Kosciuszko." In her They came from Poland: the stories of famous Polish-Americans, pp. 37–51. New York: Dodd, 1969.
A biographical sketch of General Kosciuszko, the Polish hero, fortifications engineer, and military strategist who served seven years with the American revolutionary troops.

559. Reeder, Red. Bold leaders in the American Revolution. Boston: Little, 1973.
Biographical sketches of twelve men and women involved in the American Revolution, including Thaddeus Kosciuszko, Polish patriot-soldier, whose major life concern was freedom for all mankind.

Labor Day

560. Coffin, Tristram Potter, and Cohen, Hennig, eds. Folklore from the working folk of America. New York: Doubleday, 1973.
An anthology of folklore articles selected from archives and journals and including tales, proverbs, songs, riddles, and verse of diverse occupational groups.

561. Davis, Daniel S. Mr. Black Labor: the story of A. Philip Randolph, father of the civil rights movement. New York: Dutton, 1972.

A biography of A. Philip Randolph focused on his lifelong campaign to bring black workers into American trade unions and his strategy for civil-rights action.

562. Grossman, Jonathan Philip. The Department of Labor. New York: Praeger, 1973.

A history of the Department of Labor, established in 1913, and an examination of its organization, function, projects, and role as a mediator.

563. Labor on the march: the story of America's unions. By the editors of American Heritage magazine; narrated by Joseph L. Gardner. New York: American Heritage, 1969.

An illustrated history of American labor, beginning with the Homestead strike of 1842, describing earlier and later struggles for fair working conditions, and telling of such leaders as Debs, Gompers, and Lewis.

564. Lens, Sidney. The labor wars: from the Molly Maguires to the sitdowns. Garden City, N.Y.: Doubleday, 1973.

An account of the battles, the issues, and the leaders in the first three generations of the labor movement in the United States.

565. Lingenfelter, Richard E. The hardrock miners: a history of the mining labor movement in the American West, 1863–1893. Berkeley: Univ. of California Press, 1974.

A contribution to the history of the labor movement, centered on the lives, aspirations, and problems of the hard-rock miners of the American West, from the establishment of the first union in 1863 to the federation of hardrock unions in 1893.

566. Lomax, Alan, comp. Hard-hitting songs for hard-hit people: notes on the songs by Woody Guthrie. New York: Oak Pub., 1967.

A collection of ballads and folk songs of longshoremen, miners, farmers, and other groups of American laborers.

567. Meltzer, Milton. Bread—and roses: the struggle of American labor, 1865–1915. New York: Knopf, 1967.

An illustrated history of the era of child labor, sweatshops, and company towns, which led to strikes, strikebreakers, and the eventual establishment of a successful labor movement.

568. Myers, Robert J. "Labor day." In his Celebrations: the complete book of American holidays, pp. 209–12. Garden City, N.Y.: Doubleday, 1972.

A brief history of Labor Day in the United States and Peter J. McGuire, its founder, with short paragraphs contrasting the first Labor Days with modern-day observances.

569. Pflug, Warner. The U.A.W. in pictures. Detroit: Wayne State Univ. Press, 1971.

A pictorial history of the growth and development of the union of automobile workers and its leaders.

570. Schnapper, M. B. American labor: a pictorial social history. Washington, D.C.: Public Affairs Press, 1972.

An illustrated history of American labor, beginning with a typical indenture contract of 1726, following through the years to the 1972 election; indexed.

571. Taft, Philip. Defending freedom: American labor and foreign affairs. Los Angeles: Nash, 1974.

An examination of the influence of American labor on foreign affairs from World War II to 1971, with a focus on labor's opposition to totalitarianism.

Law Day

572. Barth, Alan. Prophets with honor: great dissents and great dissenters in the Supreme Court. New York: Knopf, 1974.

An account of the circumstances, philosophy, and issues behind six historic dissents in the United States Supreme Court involving individual rights and liberties; the dissenters are Harlan, Brandeis, Black, Stone, and Douglas.

573. Friedman, Lawrence M. A history of American law. New York: Simon & Schuster, 1973.

An examination of United States law from colonial times to 1900, showing the effect of American traditions, milestone cases, and great legal minds on the evolution of legal concepts and the administration of the law.

574. Guice, John D. W. The Rocky Mountain bench: the territorial supreme courts of Colorado, Montana, and Wyoming, 1861–1890. New Haven, Conn.: Yale Univ. Press, 1972.

A contribution to American legal history that examines the courts and the law in the territorial West of the nineteenth century.

575. Ireland, Robert M. The county courts in antebellum Kentucky. Lexington: Univ. Press of Kentucky, 1972.
A monograph on the county courts of Kentucky, relating the courts to the politics, economy, and government of the state.

576. Norwick, Kenneth P., ed. Your legal rights: making the law work for you. New York: Day, 1972.
A collection of articles on special fields of the law, such as consumer rights and student rights.

577. Schwartz, Bernard. The life of the law: American legal history, 1776–1973. New York: Dial Press, 1973.
American legal history which examines the evolution of the law and its relation to the achievement of national stability.

578. Swiger, Elinor Porter. The law and you. Indianapolis: Bobbs, 1973.
A study of the principles of the law as they relate to the rights, responsibilities, and questions of young adults.

579. Switzer, Ellen. There ought to be a law! How laws are made and work. New York: Atheneum, 1972.
An explanation of local, state, and federal legislation, the responsibilities of lawyers, judges, and prosecutors, and the function of the Supreme Court.

Robert E. Lee Day

580. Catton, Bruce. Gettysburg: the final fury. Garden City, N.Y.: Doubleday, 1974.
A contribution to Civil War history that interprets Lee's strategy at the Battle of Gettysburg and throws light on his futile fight against a man who did not wear a uniform, Abraham Lincoln.

581. Commager, Henry Steele. America's Robert E. Lee. Boston: Houghton, 1951.
An account of Robert E. Lee's military training and career, the quality of his leadership of the Confederate forces, and his farewell to the Army of Northern Virginia.

582. Dowdey, Clifford. Lee. Boston: Little, 1965.
An interpretation of the personal relationships and the events that shaped the character of Robert E. Lee and established his "timeless view of timeless values."

583. Earle, Peter. Robert E. Lee. New York: Saturday Review Press, 1974.
A biography of Lee, focused on his role in the Civil War and on his image as an unusually fine leader and person.

584. Freeman, Douglas Southall. R. E. Lee: a biography. 4 vols. New York: Scribner, 1934–35.
A definitive four-volume study of the character, talents, and times of the great Confederate general, Robert E. Lee.

Lincoln's Birthday

585. Bullard, Frederic L. Lincoln in marble and bronze. New Brunswick, N.J.: Rutgers Univ. Press, 1952.
A publication of the Abraham Lincoln Association, describing sixty-seven Lincoln statues and their sites, with details on sponsorship, dedication services, sculptors, and locations of replicas.

586. Davis, Michael. The image of Lincoln in the South. Knoxville: Univ. of Tennessee Press, 1971.
A study of the changes in attitudes toward Lincoln from the period preceding the Civil War into the early twentieth century.

587. Hamilton, Charles, and Ostendorf, Lloyd. Lincoln in photographs: an album of every known pose. Norman: Univ. of Oklahoma Press, 1963.
One of the most comprehensive compilations of photographs of Lincoln, with informative captions and documentation.

588. Horgan, Paul. Citizen of New Salem. New York: Farrar, 1961.
A biographical essay on Lincoln's young manhood; a retelling of the familiar stories of the example of Mentor Graham, the reading of books, and life in New Salem.

589. Johnson, James Weldon, and Johnson, J. Rosamond. Lift every voice and sing. New York: Hawthorn Books, 1970.
Words and music for a song written in 1900 to celebrate Lincoln's Birthday; considered to be the black national anthem.

590. Kerner, Fred, comp. A treasury of Lincoln quotations. Garden City, N.Y.: Doubleday, 1965.
A collection of authenticated quotations from Lincoln's own writings or self-edited speeches; arranged alphabetically by topics, from abolition to youth; indexed.

591. Mearns, David Chambers. Largely Lincoln. New York: St. Martins, 1961.
A collection of essays, of which nine deal with Lincolniana and include such topics as Lincoln as an inexhaustible story, Lincoln and the image of America, and the great day in "Ottaway" when Douglas and Lincoln met fact to face.

592. Miller, Edward, and Mueller, Betty Jean. The halls of Lincoln's greatness. New York: Meredith, 1968.
Photographs, with brief essays, introducing the residences, places, and memorials associated with Abraham Lincoln, from Hodgenville, Kentucky, to New Salem and Springfield, Illinois, and on to Ford's Theater and the Lincoln Memorial in Washington, D.C.

593. Mitgang, Herbert. The fiery trial: a life of Lincoln. New York: Viking, 1974.
A study of Lincoln as a president who found in the Constitution his solutions to the problems of states' rights and other issues; the text is preceded by a Lincoln chronology and concludes with an analysis of Lincoln's image in the world.

594. Nevins, Allan, ed. Lincoln and the Gettysburg Address; commemorative papers. Urbana: Univ. of Illinois Press, 1964.
A collection of addresses by specialists on such subjects as Lincoln's religion, Lincoln and the law, and the significance of the Gettysburg Address; the authors include Allan Nevins, John Dos Passos, Arthur Goodhart, Reinhold Niebuhr, Robert Lowell, Paul H. Douglas, and David C. Mearns.

595. Sandburg, Carl. Lincoln: the prairie years and the war years. New York: Harcourt, 1970.
A condensation of the two volumes of *The Prairie Years* and the six volumes of *The War Years,* biographical studies of Lincoln that achieved great popular acclaim.

596. Sigelschiffer, Saul. The American conscience: the drama of the Lincoln-Douglas debates. New York: Horizon Press, 1973.
A study of the Lincoln-Douglas debates of 1858.

597. Van Doren, Mark. Last days of Lincoln. New York: Hill & Wang, 1959.
A verse play, in six scenes, covering the last few weeks of Lincoln's life and centering on the Civil War president's thinking about such issues as the surrender terms for a defeated South.

Memorial Day

598. Garnett, Emmeline. A cycle of verse. New York: Farrar, 1965.
Poems on the seasons, with a section called "And the city was pure gold," a group of poems useful for Memorial Day programs.

599. Goudge, Elizabeth, ed. A book of comfort: an anthology. New York: Coward-McCann, 1964.
A treasury of British and American poetry and prose selected as sources of inspiration and consolation; includes sections on the comfort of faith and comfort in tribulation.

600. Greenberg, Sidney, ed. A treasury of comfort. New York: Crown, 1954.
Prose and poetry reflecting the heritage of Jewish thought and wisdom on such themes as time as the healer, memory as life's afterglow, and faith as the strength for the living.

601. Mary Immaculate, Sister, ed. The cry of Rachel: an anthology of elegies on children. New York: Random House, 1966.
Poems mourning and memorializing children from the sixth century B.C. to the 1960s; the poets represent six countries and twenty-six nations.

602. Morrison, James Dalton, ed. "Memorial day." In his Masterpieces of religious verse, pp. 524–40. New York: Harper, 1948.
Selections of poems honoring men fallen in battle; the poets range from Joyce Kilmer and John McCrae to Edna Jaques and Jessie Rittenhouse.

Moon Day

603. Alter, Dinsmore. Pictorial guide to the moon. Rev. by Joseph H. Jackson, 3d rev. ed. New York: Crowell, 1973.
An illustrated guide to the topography of the moon, based on manned and unmanned surface explorations and moon probings, and presenting revised scientific opinions.

604. Bodechtel, Johann, and Gierloff-Enden, Hans-Gunter. The earth from space. New York: Arco, 1974.
Maps and photographs from the Gemini and Apollo flights and lunar and meteorological satellites, with narrative texts; shows earth-crust movements, landscapes, and the earth's environment in relation to surroundings and the moon.

605. Davies, Merton. The view from space. New York: Columbia Univ. Press, 1971.
A report on photographic exploration of the moon and the planets, with an introduction on the significance of space photography and an appendix on space-camera design.

606. First on the moon: a voyage with Neil Armstrong, Michael Collins, and Edwin Aldrin, Jr. Boston: Little, 1970.
A journalistic, authorized report of the flight of *Apollo II*, the astronauts, and their families; concludes with a rationale for the space program by Arthur Clarke.

607. Kopal, Zdenek. A new photographic atlas of the moon. New York: Taplinger, 1971.
A description of the moon based on terrestrial and space photographs; includes a chronology of moon studies; space photographs taken during the United States Ranger, Surveyor, Orbiter, and Apollo projects.

608. Lewis, Richard S. The voyages of Apollo. New York: Quadrangle Books/New York Times, 1974.
A summary of the results of the American exploration of the moon, indicating the extent of scientific knowledge accumulated by each of the Apollo series.

609. Slote, Alfred. The moon in fact and fancy. Rev. ed. Cleveland: World Pub., 1971.
A look at the moon by both storytellers and scientists; the legends are from Africa, Burma, the Philippines, South America, Scandinavia, and the South Pacific.

610. Thomas, Davis, ed. Moon: man's greatest adventure. New York: Abrams, 1971.
A beautifully illustrated study of lunar lore, exploration, and the findings of the Apollo missions.

Mother's Day

611. Applegarth, Margaret T. "Women." In her Heirlooms, pp. 291–99. New York: Harper, 1967.
A collection of proverbs, epitaphs, quotations about women in general and Mary Slessor, "Everybody's Mother," and Jane Addams in particular; useful material for adaptation to Mother's Day programs.

612. Faber, Doris. The mothers of American presidents. New York: New American Library, 1968.
A study of the backgrounds, personal characteristics, and attitudes of the mothers of twelve American presidents, with brief sketches of twenty-three others.

613. Felleman, Hazel, ed. "Home and mother." In her Best loved poems of the American people, pp. 369–81. Garden City, N.Y.: Doubleday, 1936.
A section including traditional and familiar poems associated with mothers.

614. Fremantle, Anne, ed. Mothers: a Catholic treasury of great stories. New York: Daye, 1951.
An anthology of prose, with some poems, in tribute to mothers; authors are representative of various nations and range in time from Saint Augustine to W. H. Auden and Charles Péguy.

615. Phelan, Mary Kay. Mother's Day. New York: Crowell, 1965.
A simply written, short introduction to the history of Mother's Day, from the myths and festivities of the ancient world to the spread of the Mother's Day idea from the United States to other parts of the world.

616. Phelps, William Lyon. The mother's anthology. Garden City, N.Y.: Doubleday, 1940.
A collection of prose and poetry expressing sentiments for and memories of mothers; the authors range through generations from William Blake to Pearl Buck.

617. Spellman, John W., ed. "Mother's day." In his The beautiful blue jay and other tales of India, pp. 26–27. Boston: Little, 1967.
A short legend from India that explains the fast observed by many mothers in Maharashtra on the last day of the month of Shravana.

New Year's Day

618. Clark, Thomas Curtis, and Clark, Robert Earle. "New Year's day." In their Poems for the great days, pp. 11–21. Nashville, Tenn.: Abingdon, 1948.
Traditional poems on bells and resolutions for the New Year; authors range from Alfred Tennyson to Theodore Parker.

619. Hadfield, Miles, and Hadfield, John. "New Year's day." In their The twelve days of Christmas, pp. 146–52. Boston: Little, 1961.
An account of a few customs associated with New Year's Day: gift-giving on the European continent; firstfooting in Scotland; eating roast beef in England; and a remembrance of a one-time custom of writing odes to the New Year.

620. Johnson, Lois S. Happy new year round the world. Chicago: Rand McNally, 1966.
The customs and traditions of New Year celebrations from twenty-five nations in Africa, Asia, Europe, the Far and Middle East, and North and South America.

621. Krythe, Maymie R. "New Year's Day." In her All about American holidays, pp. 1–20. New York: Harper, 1962.
A discussion of the symbolic importance of New Year's Day, its history, including early celebrations, omens and portents, foods, gifts, and New Year's in the United States.

622. Spicer, Dorothy Gladys. "New Year's Eve in the Netherlands" and "New Year's Eve in Bulgaria." In her 46 days of Christmas: a cycle of Old World songs, legends, and customs, pp. 77–81. New York: Coward-Mc-Cann, 1960.
A description of New Year's Eve services and family parties in Holland and an account of the tradition of the "switch in," which accompanies good wishes for the new year in the Bulgarian tradition.

623. Thurman, Howard. "The end of the year." In his The mood of Christmas, pp. 121–27. New York: Harper, 1973.
A brief meditation on the blessings at the year's end and the meaning and promise of a new year.

Pan-American Day

624. Augelli, John P. American neighbors. Grand Rapids, Mich.: Fideler, 1973.
An introduction to the ways of life, resources, and culture of Canada, Mexico, the Caribbean lands, and South America; includes representative fiestas and festivals for the lands south of the border.

625. Benson, Elizabeth P. The Mochica: a culture of Peru. New York: Praeger, 1972.
A study of the pre-Columbian civilization of the Mochica Indians of Peru, as seen in particular in ceramics as a cultural and ceremonial expression.

626. Castedo, Leopoldo. A history of Latin American art and architecture: from pre-Columbian times to the present. New York: Praeger, 1969.
A history of the fusion of Indian, European, and African elements in Latin American art and architecture.

627. Engber, Marjorie, comp. Caribbean fiction and poetry. New York: Center for Inter-American Relations, 1970.
A bibliography of Caribbean fiction and poetry published from 1900 through September 1970; brief annotations or listings of writers for anthologies; indexed by authors, titles, and countries.

628. Geyer, Georgie Anne. The new Latins: fateful change in South and Central America. Garden City, N.Y.: Doubleday, 1970.
A journalist's view of the new directions in leadership and attitudes, relationships with the United States, and the world scene.

629. Hardoy, Jorge Enrique. Pre-Columbian cities. New York: Walker, 1973.
A study of the ancient cities of Latin America, the life of their inhabitants, and the temples, palaces, and markets that formed the origins of American civilization.

630. Harvey, Marian. Crafts of Mexico. New York: Macmillan, 1973.
An introduction to the indigenous culture of Mexico found in the work of craftsmen who create from reeds, metals, paper, clay, and wood; includes details of processes, suggestions on materials, and how-to-do-it illustrations.

631. Hemming, John. The conquest of the Incas. New York: Harcourt, 1970.
A history of Pizarro's conquest of the Incas, with a description of the fragment of the Inca empire that survived in the jungle.

632. Ickis, Marguerite. "Pan American Day." In her The book of patriotic holidays, pp. 43–58. New York: Dodd, 1962.
A chapter devoted to Pan American Day, with program ideas and suggestions on appropriate dances, games, and musical instruments representative of South America.

633. Nolen, Barbara, ed. Mexico is people: land of three cultures. New York: Scribner, 1973.
A study of the Indian, Spanish, and mestizo heritage in contemporary Mexico; a chapter on festivals interprets the art of the fiesta and describes the fiesta of the flyers, the blessing of the animals, the Day of the Dead, and the bullfight.

634. Paulmier, Hilah, and Schauffler, Robert Haven. Pan-American Day. New York: Dodd, 1943.
A partially dated anthology of prose and verse on Pan-Americanism and the good-neighbor policy; includes a useful section on the origin of Pan American Day and the ideals of the Pan American Union.

635. Rothchild, John, ed. Latin America yesterday and today. New York: Praeger, 1973.
A collection of essays, primarily by Latin American writers, on the Latin American myths of geography, the historical and cultural influences, current social conditions, and relationships with the United States.

636. Schmitt, Karl Michael. Mexico and the United States, 1821–1973: conflict and coexistence. New York: Wiley, 1974.
An examination of the issues and policies in United States-Mexican relations from 1822 to 1973 which reflect Anglo-Spanish differences in religion, tradition, culture, and historical development.

637. Worcester, Donald E. Brazil: from colony to world power. New York: Scribner, 1973.
A political history of Brazil, with good summaries of social, economic, intellectual, and artistic developments.

See also section on Planning and Preparing for Anniversaries and Holidays

Passover

638. Bial, Morrison David. The Passover story. New York: Behrman House, 1952.
A brief narrative on the history of Passover, with a description of the Pesah holiday and its customs.

639. Gaster, Theodor Herzl. Passover: its history and traditions. New York: Schuman, 1949.
A study of the history, ceremonials, and significance of Passover in terms of tradition and twentieth-century research; includes seder and Passover songs.

640. Goldin, Hyman E. "Passover." In his A treasury of Jewish holidays, pp. 128–88. New York: Twayne, 1952.
An explanation of Passover as a festival of freedom, with descriptions of the seder and the customs of Pesah; includes a retelling of the biblical account of the Egyptian bondage.

641. Goodman, Philip. Passover anthology. Philadelphia: Jewish Pub. Soc., 1961.
A Passover anthology, including accounts of its origin and the history of observance in many lands, with chapters on the Passover in literature, art, and music, ideas for programs and projects, and a section on the ceremonies of observance.

642. Raphael, Chaim. A feast of history: Passover through the ages as a key to Jewish experience. New York: Simon & Schuster, 1972.
A history of Passover; its rituals, prayers, and songs, with a contemporary translation of the Haggadah read at the seder in commemoration of the exodus from Egypt; includes a section on the preparations for the seder; illustrated in color.

643. Segal, J. B. The Hebrew Passover, from the earliest times to A.D. 70. London: Oxford, 1963.
A full-scale examination of Passover up to the destruction of the Temple in A.D. 70, developed from the viewpoint of twentieth-century religious research into historical documents and theories.

644. Silverman, Morris, comp. Passover Haggadah. Hartford, Conn.: Prayer Book Press, 1959.
An edition of the Haggadah designed for adult study groups, Passover institutes, and home use; explanations and comments interpolated in the text.

645. Simon, Norma. Passover. New York: Crowell, 1955.
A simple explanation of the events behind the first Passover and of the traditions of commemoration that have passed down from generation to generation.

Patriots' Day

646. Beach, Stewart. Lexington and Concord in color. New York: Hastings House, 1974.
A description of the sites of the beginning of the American Revolution, with full-color photographs by Samuel Chamberlain.

647. Colby, Jean Poindexter. Lexington and Concord, 1775: what really happened. New York: Hastings House, 1974.
A history of the first battles of the American Revolution, combined with a tour of the sites of major events; based on diaries, letters, and eyewitness accounts.

648. Fisher, Leonard Everett. Two if by sea. New York: Random House, 1970.
An account of the historic events during the evening of April 18, 1775, and the actions of the patriots Joseph Warren, Paul Revere, and Robert Newman, and the British general Thomas Gage.

649. Forbes, Esther. America's Paul Revere. Boston: Houghton, 1946.
An account of Paul Revere, artisan and patriot; the events that led up to his famous ride and to the Revolution, combined with an appreciation of his skill as a silversmith.

650. Revere, Paul. Paul Revere's three accounts of his famous ride. 2d ed. Boston: Massachusetts Historical Soc., 1968.
Facsimiles of Paul Revere's personal accounts of the events of April 18, 1775.

651. Russell, Francis. Lexington, Concord, and Bunker Hill. New York: American Heritage, 1963.
A history of the last days of British rule in colonial America, beginning with Paul Revere's report of the night of April 18, 1775, and interpreting the first events of the Revolution.

652. Schackburg, Richard. Yankee Doodle. Englewood Cliffs, N.J.: Prentice-Hall, 1965.
An illustrated account of the song *Yankee Doodle,* written by a British surgeon, sung by the British as they marched to Lexington, and taken over by the Americans as they drove the British to Boston.

653. Stubenrauch, Bob. Where freedom grew. New York: Dodd, 1970.
Photographs and word sketches of buildings and sites associated with the Revolutionary War, including Paul Revere House and Old North Church in Boston, the Hancock-Clarke house and the Battle Green in Lexington, and the *Minute Man* and Old North Bridge at Concord.

Pearl Harbor Day

654. Farago, Ladislas. The broken seal: the story of "Operation Magic" and the Pearl Harbor disaster. New York: Random House, 1967.
A record of Japanese and American code-breaking operations between 1921 and 1941 in relation to the attack on Pearl Harbor.

655. Feis, Herbert. The road to Pearl Harbor: the coming of the war between the United States and Japan. Princeton, N.J.: Princeton Univ. Press, 1950.
A well-balanced account of the negotiations and diplomatic maneuvering that resulted in the attack on Pearl Harbor.

656. Goldston, Robert. Pearl Harbor! December 7, 1941: the road to Japanese aggression in the Pacific. New York: Watts, 1972.
A concise review of the militarism in Japanese history that culminated in the attack on Pearl Harbor in 1941.

657. Lord, Walter. Day of infamy. New York: Holt, 1957.
A detailed account of the action and the human drama in the attack on Pearl Harbor on Sunday, December 7, 1941.

658. Taylor, Theodore. Air raid—Pearl Harbor! The story of December 7, 1941. New York: Crowell, 1971.
A history of the events that culminated with the attack on Pearl Harbor; written from both the American and Japanese points of view.

Pioneer Days

659. Felton, Harold W. Cowboy jamboree: western songs and lore. New York: Knopf, 1951.
A collection of cowboy songs that tell the "most about the cowboy and at the same time make the best singing."—foreword.

660. Frazer, Robert W. Forts of the West: military forts and presidios, and posts commonly called forts, west of the Mississippi River to 1898. Norman: Univ. of Oklahoma Press, 1972.
Information on the military posts in the western United States in the expansion era; arranged alphabetically within the boundaries of modern-day states; the appendix lists Civil War forts of both the Union and the Confederacy.

661. Haines, Francis. Horses in America. New York: Crowell, 1971.
A popularly written account of the inter-relationship of the horse and the progress of the nation; explains the uses of horses in the early days of the East and the frontier days of the West, along with tales of the skills and feats of the horsemen.

662. Katz, William Loren. The black West. Garden City, N.Y.: Doubleday, 1971.
A history of black frontiersmen, cowboys, and homesteaders, and their contributions to America's westward movement.

663. McCracken, Harold. The American cowboy. Garden City, N.Y.: Doubleday, 1973.
A history of the cowboy and the American West, beginning with the Spanish conquistadors and ending with the range wars of the 1890s; includes graphic descriptions of the cattle drives, cattle rustling, vigilante committees, cowboy-homesteader conflicts, and tall tales.

664. Pettengill, Samuel B. The Yankee pioneers: a saga of courage. Rutland, Vt.: Tuttle, 1971.
Information on the daily life of the first generation to live in Vermont and New Hampshire.

665. Rathjen, Frederick W. The Texas panhandle frontier. Austin: Univ. of Texas Press, 1974.
A regional history of the Texas panhandle, dealing with geography, Spanish exploration, buffalo hunters, Indian wars, settlements, and the coming of the railroads.

666. Utley, Robert M. Frontier regulars: the United States Army. New York: Macmillan, 1974.
A contribution to the history of national expansion in the United States, centered on the life of the frontier soldier, military leadership, and Indian problems in the post-Civil War period.

Presidents' Days

667. American Heritage. The American Heritage pictorial history of the presidents of the United States. 2 vols. New York: American Heritage, 1968.
A picture portfolio, with narrative essays, on the presidents from Washington through Johnson, with brief biographical sketches of their associates; indexed.

668. Armbruster, Maxim Ethan. The presidents of the United States, and their administrations from Washington to Nixon. 5th ed. New York: Horizon Press, 1973.
A study of the American presidents as individuals and leaders.

669. Bonnell, John Sutherland. Presidential profiles: religion in the life of American presidents. Philadelphia: Westminster, 1971.
Brief background information on the place of religion in the lives and careers of American presidents.

670. Collins, Herbert Ridgeway. Presidents on wheels. Washington, D.C.: Acropolis, 1971.
An illustrated history of the vehicles used by American presidents, from Washington's neat, plain horse-drawn coach to the armored cars of contemporary times.

671. Cunliffe, Marcus. American presidents and the presidency. New York: American Heritage, 1972.
A study of the presidency of the United States from the time of Washington, showing how politics, events, and the social fabric affected the conduct of the office.

672. Freidel, Frank. Our country's presidents. 4th ed. Washington, D.C.: National Geographic Soc., 1972.
Biographical sketches of the presidents, their contributions, leadership style, and families.

673. Johnson, Richard T. Managing the White House: an intimate study of six presidents. New York: Harper, 1974.
A study of the managerial styles of Presidents Roosevelt, Truman, Eisenhower, Kennedy, Johnson, and Nixon.

674. Jones, Olga. Churches of the presidents in Washington. New York: Exposition, 1961.
A look at sixteen churches in the nation's capital in which the presidents have worshipped, from the Friends' Meeting House to the Washington Cathedral.

675. Kane, Joseph Nathan. Facts about the presidents: a compilation of biographical and historical data. 3d ed. New York: Wilson, 1974.
A souce book of election data and information about the presidents of the United States, their lives and families, and the major events of their terms of office, with comparative statistics, lists, and tables.

676. Leish, Kenneth W. The White House. New York: Newsweek Book Div., 1972.
A history of the White House as a symbol of the presidency and the home of America's chief executive, with special chapters on selected periods, such as the Lincoln years and the Teddy Roosevelt era.

677. Sinkler, George. The racial attitudes of American presidents, from Abraham Lincoln to Theodore Roosevelt. New York: Doubleday, 1971.
An examination of the writings of ten American presidents who served between 1860 and 1908, designed to determine their attitudes toward the Southern blacks and other minority groups.

678. Taylor, John M. From the White House inkwell. Rutland, Vt.: Tuttle, 1968.
An account of presidential autographs, with black-and-white reproductions of letters and documents signed by the presidents, from Washington through Johnson.

679. Taylor, Tim. The book of presidents. New York: Arno Press, 1972.
Facts about the presidents of the United States, from Washington through Nixon, listing significant events and decisions associated with each man; data on his vice-president, cabinet, Supreme Court, governmental agencies, and family; arranged chronologically.

680. Youngblood, Rufus W. 20 years in the secret service: my life with five presidents. New York: Simon & Schuster, 1973.
Behind-the-scenes memoirs of a secret-service agent assigned to guard the American presidents, from Truman to Nixon.

Pulaski Day

681. Abodaher, David J. Freedom fighter: Casimir Pulaski. New York: Messner, 1969.
A biography of Casimir Pulaski, leader of the Pulaski Legion in the American Revolutionary War, who is honored annually by Polish Americans.

682. Army times, Washington, D.C. "The revolution on horseback." In its Great American cavalrymen, pp. 13–30. New York: Dodd, 1964.
An account of Pulaski: the "great grand-daddy of the United States cavalry," and his role in organizing the scattered cavalry units of Washington's army.

683. Douglas, George William. "Pulaski Day." In his The American book of days, pp. 525–27. New York: Wilson, 1948.
A brief statement of the origin of Pulaski Day, the founding of the Military Order of Pulaski, and a summary of General Pulaski's career.

684. Sobol, Donald J. Lock, stock and barrel. Philadelphia: Westminster, 1965.
Sketches of forty participants in the American Revolution, including Casimir Pulaski, patriot from Poland.

Purim

685. Epstein, Morris. "Purim." In his A pictorial treasury of Jewish holidays and customs, pp. 71–83. New York: Ktav Pub., 1959.
An explanation of the history of Purim and the special vocabulary of the holiday.

686. Gaster, Theodor Herzl. Purim and Hanukkah in custom and tradition. New York: Schuman, 1950.
A sketch of the history, development, and observance of Purim and Hanukkah, with samples of Purim plays and mummeries.

687. Goldberg, David. "Purim—the Feast of Lots." In his Holidays for American Judaism," pp. 158–66. New York: Bookman Associates, 1954.
An explanation of the history and significance of Purim, or the Feast of Lots, with explanatory notes, including a reproduction of the prayer entitled "Purim, the feast of mirth."

688. Goodman, Philip. Purim anthology. Philadelphia: Jewish Pub. Soc., 1949.
A Purim anthology that tells of the origin of the holiday, identifies special Purims and observances by nations, considers Purim in literature, art, music, and Jewish law, and describes customs of commemoration; includes a supplement of appropriate music.

Will Rogers Day

689. Croy, Homer. Our Will Rogers. Boston: Little, 1953.
A biography of Will Rogers, based on personal friendship, interviews with his cowboy friends and neighbors, and an examination of scrapbooks and documents at the Will Rogers Memorial at Claremore, Oklahoma.

690. Day, Donald. Will Rogers: a biography. New York: McKay, 1962.
A review of the life of Will Rogers and an appraisal of his role as America's commonsense philosopher.

691. Ketchum, Richard M. Will Rogers: his life and times. New York: American Heritage, 1973.
An illustrated biography of the quotable and unforgettable commentator on the American scene of the 1920s and 1930s; the book was developed in cooperation with the Will Rogers Memorial at Claremore, Oklahoma.

692. Love, Paula McSpadden, comp. The Will Rogers book. Indianapolis: Bobbs, 1961.
A compilation of the quotable observations of Will Rogers on such subjects as the presidents of the United States and various aspects of life in "America, U.S.A."

Rosh Hashanah

693. Barish, Louis. High holiday liturgy. New York: Jonathan David, 1959.
An interpretation of the theology, history, and artistry of the Machzor, the prayer book of Rosh Hashanah and Yom Kippur.

694. Cone, Molly. The Jewish New Year. New York: Crowell, 1966.
An explanation of the origin and meaning of the Jewish New Year, with a description of a traditional observance.

695. Goodman, Philip, comp. The Rosh Hashanah anthology. Philadelphia: Jewish Pub. Soc., 1970.
A collection of material on the solemn Jewish New Year, selected from biblical and post-biblical writings, medieval literature, and modern periods; covers law, music, the culinary arts, and special programming for the cycle known as "the Days of Awe."

696. Snaith, Norman H. The Jewish New Year festival. London: Soc. for Promoting Christian Knowledge, 1947.
A history that includes the pre-exilic New Year feast, a study of the exile and the change of calendar, and Tishri as the day of memorial; also gives an interpretation of the benedictions of Rosh Hashanah and a description of selected New Year festivals in Mesopotamia and Syria.

Saint Patrick's Day

697. Cantwell, Mary. St. Patrick's Day. New York: Crowell, 1967.
A simple introduction to Saint Patrick and the ways in which his day has been celebrated by different countries.

698. Farjeon, Eleanor. Ten saints. New York: Oxford, 1936.
A book about ten saints, which includes a story about Saint Patrick and *A Rhyme for Patrick,* in honor of March 17.

699. Gallico, Paul. The steadfast man: a biography of St. Patrick. Garden City, N.Y.: Doubleday, 1958.
A study of Patrick, Ireland's patron saint, beginning with a brief reference to Saint Patrick's Day and the wearing of the green, then proceeding to tell of Patrick's life and work; the appendix includes translations of the *Confession* of Saint Patrick and of his letter to the soldiers of Coroticus.

700. Gogarty, Oliver St. John. I follow Saint Patrick. New York: Reynal & Hitchcock, 1938.
A pilgrimage taken in the 1930s to the places in Wales and Ireland that legend or history has associated with Saint Patrick.

701. Irvine, John. A treasury of Irish saints: a book of poems. New York: Walck, 1964.
A little book of poems about Saint Patrick and other Irish saints; concludes with brief explanatory and biographical notes.

702. Reynolds, Quentin. The life of Saint Patrick. New York: Random House, 1955.
A narrative blending facts, folk beliefs, and legends as a reconstruction of the life and adventures of Saint Patrick.

703. Ward, Maisie. Saints who made history: the first five centuries. New York: Sheed, 1959.
A review of the contributions of the saints of the early centuries of the Christian church, which includes a chapter on Saint Patrick, his boyhood, his preparation for the apostolate, and his tenure as bishop of Ireland.

Saints' Days

704. Ancelet-Hustache, Jeanne. Saint Nicholas. New York: Macmillan, 1962.
A biography of Nicholas of Myra, patron saint and friend of children; traces his activities in Lycia, Lorraine, and the West.

705. Butler, Alban. Lives of the saints. Complete ed., rev., and supplemented by Herbert Thurston and Donald Attwater. 4 vols. New York: Kenedy, 1956.
Sketches of the lives of the principal saints and beati venerated liturgically by the Roman Catholic church; arranged by the calendar year; indexed.

706. Cluny, Roland. Holiness in action. New York: Hawthorn Books, 1963.
A volume in the Twentieth Century Encyclopedia of Catholicism series; an examination of Christian holiness in the lives of Paul of Tarsus, Augustine, Bernard of Clairvaux, Francis, and Loyola.

707. Haughton, Rosemary. Six saints for parents. New York: Sheed, 1962.
Essays on the lives of Joseph, Louise de Marillac, Augustine, Rose of Lima, Thomas Aquinas, and Marie-Thérèse de Soubiran, written from the point of view of a mother concerned with standards of conduct and moral training in the home.

708. McGinley, Phyllis. Saint-watching. New York: Viking, 1969.
A look at a selected group of saints and human beings, dissenters and leaders, dreamers, friends of animals, and molders of history; concludes with a list of saints, their dates, and feast days.

Senior Citizens Day

709. Cooley, Leland Frederick, and Cooley, Lee Morrison. How to avoid the retirement trap. Los Angeles: Nash, 1972.
An identification of the socioeconomic problems faced by older citizens, coupled with advice for planning.

710. Fish, Harriet U. Activities program for senior citizens. West Nyack, N.Y.: Parker Pub., 1971.
Guidelines for planning holiday celebrations and other activities and events by and for senior citizens.

711. Hepner, Harry W. Retirement: a time to live anew. New York: McGraw, 1969.
A practical guide for the recent or prospective retiree; includes projects, retirement activities, and the development of a mature philosophy.

712. Jonas, Doris, and Jonas, David. Young till we die. New York: Coward, McCann, 1973.
An examination of a program to make positive use of the expertise and wisdom of the older generations in a youth-oriented society.

713. Moses, Anna Mary Robertson. Grandma Moses: my life's history. Ed. by Otto Kaller. New York: Harper, 1952.
The personal story of Grandma Moses, who turned from "fancy work" to oil painting at the age of eighty.

714. Percy, Charles H. Growing old in the country of the young. New York: McGraw, 1974.
A look at the problems of adequacy in income, food, health care, and housing for older citizens of the United States, with suggested solutions for handling critical concerns, including loneliness; includes an "Action Resource Guide," with information on agencies that provide assistance.

Shakespeare's Birthday

715. Campbell, Oscar James, ed. The reader's encyclopedia of Shakespeare. New York: Crowell, 1966.
A compilation of facts and information about all facets of Shakespeare's life and work, his associates, celebrated Shakespearian actors, critics, and scholars.

716. Charney, Maurice. How to read Shakespeare. New York: McGraw, 1971.
An invitation to rediscover the multiplicity of interests and delights in Shakespeare's plays by replacing "Shakespearizing" with a personalized approach to reading and to theatrical productions.

717. Deelman, Christian. The great Shakespeare jubilee. New York: Viking, 1964.
A unique account of the pageantry, the follies, and the values of the first jubilee organized by David Garrick in the fall of 1769; based on original letters, diaries, and other documents.

718. Frye, Roland Mushat. Shakespeare's life and times: a pictorial record. Princeton, N.J.: Princeton Univ. Press, 1967.
A pictorial history showing the environment and the life-styles of Shakespeare and his contemporaries through reproductions of Elizabethan illustrations.

719. Horizon magazine. Shakespeare's England, by the editors of Horizon magazine in consultation with Louis B. Wright. New York: American Heritage, 1964.
An illustrated picture of Shakespeare, the touring companies, and life in England under Elizabeth I and James I.

720. Lamb, Charles, and Lamb, Mary. Ten tales from Shakespeare. New York: Watts, 1969.
A classic retelling of the stories from ten of Shakespeare's plays; includes the original preface to the 1807 edition.

721. Martin, Michael Rheta, and Harrier, Richard C. The concise encyclopedia guide to Shakespeare. New York: Horizon Press, 1971.
A guide to Shakespeare's plays and characters, with synopses of plays, explanation of words and phrases from the plays, charts of historical characters, biographical sketches of actors, critics, and others.

722. Milward, Peter. Shakespeare's religious background. Bloomington: Indiana Univ. Press, 1973.
An examination of the religious climate and controversies of the Elizabethan age in relationship to the work of Shakespeare and his ethical and religious viewpoints.

723. Phillips, O. Hood. Shakespeare and the lawyers. New York: Harper, 1972.
An examination of Shakespeare's continuing and lively interest in the law as reflected in his connections with the Inns of Court, his use of legal terms, and the trial scenes in his plays.

724. Shakespeare, William. Seeds of time. Comp. by Bernice Grohskopf. New York: Atheneum, 1963.
A selection of lyric poetry from the plays of Shakespeare.

725. Swinden, Patrick. An introduction to Shakespeare's comedies. New York: Barnes & Noble, 1973.
An introduction to Shakespeare's comedies, the comic theme, and the Elizabethan audience, actors, and stage.

726. Webb, Nancy, and Webb, Jean Francis. Will Shakespeare and his America. New York: Viking, 1964.
A history of Shakespearean productions in America and presentations by European theatrical troupes from colonial days to the twentieth century.

Sports Anniversary Days

727. Bochroch, Albert R. American automobile racing: an illustrated history. New York: Studio-Viking, 1974.
A history of automobile racing in the United States, with an appendix listing race winners from 1895 to 1972.

728. Chew, Peter. The Kentucky Derby: the first 100 years. Boston: Houghton, 1974.
A historical tribute commemorating the one-hundredth anniversary of the Kentucky Derby, with facts about horses, tracks, and jockeys.

729. Devaney, John. The World Series: a complete pictorial history. Chicago: Rand McNally, 1972.
A pictorial history of the World Series, with descriptions of series highlights, players, and scores from 1903 through 1972.

730. Durso, Joseph. Yankee Stadium: fifty years of drama. Boston: Houghton, 1972.
The history of baseball's most renowned arena, its players, the great games, and the nonsporting spectaculars.

731. Fetros, John G. This day in sports: a diary of major sports events. Novato, Calif.: Gregg, 1974.
A day-by-day record of happenings in the world of sports; arranged by date of occurrence, subarranged by year.

732. Fleming, Alice, comp. Hosannah the home run! Poems about sports. Boston: Little, 1972.
A collection of poems about baseball, fishing, tennis, and other sports; authors range from Izaak Walton to Carl Sandburg.

733. Harris, H. A. Sport in Greece and Rome. Ithaca, N.Y.: Cornell Univ. Press, 1972.
A history of Greek and Roman sporting activity, from the first Olympic games in 776 B.C. to chariot racing in the Byzantine era.

734. Lewis, Guy, and Redmond, Gerald. Sporting heritage: a guide to halls of fame, special collections, and museums in the United States and Canada. New York: Barnes, 1974.
Information on sport museums and sport collections in the United States and Canada, ranging from the Baseball Hall of Fame to a cricket library; arranged by regions in the United States and provinces in Canada.

735. Lipscomb, F. W. A hundred years of the America's Cup. New York: New York Graphic, 1972.
An informal history of the first hundred years of yachting's most elite event, the America's Cup races.

736. Longrigg, Roger. The history of horse racing. New York: Stein & Day, 1972.
An illustrated history of horse racing from ancient times into the twentieth century.

737. Morrison, Lillian, comp. Sprints and distances: sports in poetry and the poetry in sport. New York: Crowell, 1965.
An anthology of poems about sports, arranged by topics, such as "Races and Contests"; indexed by first line, title, and sport.

738. Setright, L. J. K. The grand prix, 1906 to 1972. New York: Norton, 1973.
An illustrated history of international motor racing, centered around the technical development of racing from 1906 to 1972.

States' Days

739. Boatner, Mark Mayo, III. Landmarks of the American Revolution: a guide to knowing what happened at the sites of independence. Harrisburg, Pa.: Stackpole, 1973.
A descriptive guide to Revolutionary War sites, state by state and in Canada; locations plotted on contemporary maps.

740. Boland, Charles Michael. Ring in the jubilee: the epic of America's Liberty Bell. Riverside, Conn.: Chatham Press, 1973.
An account of the Pennsylvania statehouse bell, a symbol of liberty in the United States, from its first casting to its final tolling at the death of John Marshall.

741. The book of the states. Lexington, Ky.: The Council of State Governments, biennial.
An authoritative source of information on the governments of the individual states of the United States, including historical data on each state, such as source of state lands, date admitted to the Union, and chronological order of admission.

742. Drotning, Phillip T. An American traveler's guide to black history. Garden City, N.Y.: Doubleday, 1968.
Data on the history made by black men and women in specific places in the United States and the District of Columbia; organized alphabetically by states and by sites within each state.

743. Folsom, Franklin. America's ancient treasures: guide to archeological sites and museums. Chicago: Rand McNally, 1971.
An illustrated guide to archaeological sites and museums, featuring prehistoric Indian life; arranged by geographical regions, with specific sites and museums organized by states.

744. Gebhart, John Robert. Your state flag. Philadelphia: Franklin Pub., 1973.
Descriptions of each of the flags of the fifty states, with interpretations of their symbolism; full-color illustrations; the appendix includes names of designers of twenty-eight state flags.

745. Goetz, Delia. State capital cities. New York: Morrow, 1971.
An introduction to the capitals of the fifty states, with brief history and commentary on the community and cultural events; arranged alphabetically by states.

746. Great historic places, by the editors of American Heritage. New York: American Heritage, 1973.
A state-by-state guide to a thousand historic sites in the United States; landmarks associated with the American Revolution are identified with a Liberty Bell symbol; arranged alphabetically by state and by town.

747. Jordan, E. L. Pictorial travel atlas of scenic America. Bicentennial ed. Maplewood, N.J.: Hammond, 1973.
A travel atlas focusing on the scenic areas, high points of interest, and regional foods of six areas of the United States, Puerto Rico, and Hawaii; the last section is called "1776 Revisited—See and Relive the American Revolution."

748. Kane, Joseph Nathan. The American counties: origin of names, dates of creation and organization, area, population, historical data, and published sources. 3d ed. Metuchen, N.J.: Scarecrow, 1972.
A source book of data on over 3,000 counties in the United States, with dates of formation, nicknames, and other historic and current facts.

749. Kane, Joseph Nathan, and Alexander, Gerald L. Nicknames and sobriquets of U.S. cities and states. 2d ed. Metuchen, N.J.: Scarecrow, 1970.
An index to the well-known and little-known nicknames of states, cities, and towns of the United States; separate indexes for cities and states arranged according to geography and nicknames.

750. Kelley, Joseph J. Life and times in colonial Philadelphia. Harrisburg, Pa.: Stackpole, 1973.
A social history of late seventeenth- and eighteenth-century Philadelphia, with accounts of such leading citizens as William Penn, Ben Franklin, Benjamin West, and Dr. Benjamin Rush.

751. Konikow, Robert B. Discover historic America. Chicago: Rand McNally, 1973.
A descriptive listing of battlefields, shrines, monuments, homes, cemeteries, and other sites that are visual representations of historic America; includes the fifty states and the District of Columbia.

752. Landmarks of liberty. Maplewood, N.J.: Hammond, 1970.
Brief descriptions of twenty-two historic landmarks located in various states of the United States, beginning with Abraham Lincoln's birthplace in Hodgenville, Kentucky, and concluding with the memorial to the Wright brothers at Kitty Hawk, North Carolina.

753. Lefler, Hugh T., and Powell, William S. Colonial North Carolina: a history. New York: Scribner, 1973.
A history of the influences that shaped North Carolina, from the first exploration to the Mecklenburg declaration and the ultimate affiliation with the Union.

754. Main, Jackson Turner. The sovereign states, 1775–1783. New York: New Viewpoints, 1973.
A survey of the thirteen distinct political units that comprised the American states during the Revolutionary War.

755. Naske, Claus. An interpretative history of Alaskan statehood. Anchorage: Alaska Northwest Pub., 1973.
A detailed examination of the events and the national climate under which Alaska achieved statehood.

756. Peirce, Neal R. The deep South states of America: people, politics, and power in the seven deep South states. New York: Norton, 1974.
A survey of twenty years of change in political and economic conditions and life-styles in Alabama, Arkansas, Florida, Georgia, Louisiana, Mississippi, and South Carolina.

757. Sechrist, Elizabeth Hough, comp. "State's day." In her Poems for red letter days, pp. 246–94. Philadelphia: Macrae Smith, 1951.
Poems honoring each of forty-three states in the United States; the section is introduced with Walt Whitman's *A Song for the States.*

758. Sprague, Marshall. So vast, so beautiful a land: Louisiana and the purchase. Boston: Little, 1974.
A history of Louisiana, ranging from the psychology of the explorers to the diplomatic and cartographic problems of the acquisition of the territory by the United States.

759. Stember, Sol. The bicentennial guide to the American Revolution. 3 vols. New York: Saturday Review Press, 1974.
A guide to the sites of the American Revolution in the various states and Canada, with suggested routes and commentaries on the significance of forts, battlefields, and other locations of historic interest.

760. U.S. National Park Service. Explorers and settlers: historic places commemorating the early exploration and settlement of the United States. Washington, D.C.: U.S. Dept. of the Interior, 1968.
A history of explorers on the North American continent, with a survey of historic sites and buildings in the national park system and historic districts eligible for registry as national landmarks in the states of the United States.

761. Trienens, Roger J. Pioneer imprints from fifty states. Washington, D.C.: Library of Congress, 1973.
A description of early examples of broadsides, pamphlets, books, and newspapers published within the present boundaries of each state in the United States, with brief notes on the establishment of printing in each state; based on the Library of Congress holdings.

762. Wood, Frances, and Wood, Dorothy. America: land of wonders. New York: Dodd, 1973.
A description of the natural wonders of the American continent, such as waterways, deserts, mountains, rivers, national parks, and monuments; includes notes on the history, ecological facts, and problems of each region; indexed.

763. Zook, Nicholas. Museum villages, U.S.A. Barre, Mass.: Barre, 1970.
A guide to 120 restored villages and residences located in various states of the United States.

Steuben Day

764. Davis, Burke. "Friedrich von Steuben: the drillmaster." In his Heroes of the American Revolution, pp. 78–88. New York: Random House, 1971.
A chapter on von Steuben, the German teacher of the art of war, and an account of his efforts to transform Washington's ragged army into a knowledgeable military force.

765. Douglas, George William. "Birthday of Baron von Steuben." In his The American book of days, pp. 486–89. New York: Wilson, 1948.
A brief review of the military career of Baron von Steuben, his contributions to the Revolutionary army, the establishment of the Steuben society, and notes on Steuben anniversaries.

766. Hayman, LeRoy. "1778—". . . an old blanket or woolen bedcovers . . ." In his Leaders of the American Revolution, pp. 141–47. New York: Four Winds Press, 1970.
A short description of the skill of Baron von Steuben as drillmaster at Valley Forge in 1778, a specialty that brought him the appointment as inspector general of Washington's armies.

767. O'Connor, Richard. The German-Americans. Boston: Little, 1968.
A report on the contributions of German-Americans, including short descriptions of the arrival of Baron von Steuben, Washington's drillmaster, his plan for Revolutionary vengeance on Benedict Arnold, and his role in the siege at Yorktown; indexed.

768. Ray, Frederic, comp. "Von Steuben at Valley Forge." In his O! say can you see: the story of America through great paintings, pp. 53–55. Harrisburg, Pa.: Stackpole, 1970.
A reproduction of Edwin Abbey's painting of von Steuben at Valley Forge, with brief notes; one of fifty-four full-color reproductions of paintings on subjects of historic significance in the history of the American continent.

769. Wheeler, Richard, comp. Voices of 1776. New York: Crowell, 1972.
A re-creation of the observations and opinions of the men of the American Revolution, from diaries, reports, and letters; includes a short firsthand appreciation of the qualifications of Baron von Steuben as a teacher of military tactics; indexed.

Thanksgiving Day

770. Bartlett, Robert Merrill. Thanksgiving Day. New York: Crowell, 1965.
A simple explanation of the custom of giving thanks at harvest time, with special attention to the Pilgrims and their Thanksgiving celebrations of 1621 and 1623.

771. Colby, Jean Poindexter. Plimouth Plantation, then and now. New York: Hastings House, 1970.
Background material on the Pilgrims, correlated with information on Plymouth Plantation, a re-creation of the original Pilgrim settlement; brief statement on the first Thanksgiving; indexed.

772. Cowie, Leonard W. The Pilgrim fathers. New York: Putnam, 1972.
Brief notes on the first harvest and thanksgiving in a history of the Pilgrims in England, Holland, and the Plymouth colony.

773. Dalgliesh, Alice. The Thanksgiving story. New York: Scribner, 1954.
A classic interpretation of the meaning of Thanksgiving, expressed through a story of the first Thanksgiving in America; illustrated in autumn colors.

774. Earle, Alice Morse. Home and child life in colonial days. Ed. by Shirley Glubok. New York: Macmillan, 1969.
A combined abridgement of Alice Earle's *Home Life in Colonial Days* and *Child Life in Colonial Days,* constituting a standard social history of the colonists, their way of life, customs, and observances.

775. Hanson, Gertrude, comp. This is America. Minneapolis: National Thanksgiving Assoc., 1950.
A collection of Thanksgiving poems submitted in contests sponsored by the National Thanksgiving Association.

776. Harper, Wilhelmina, comp. The Harvest feast: stories of Thanksgiving, yesterday and today. Rev. ed. New York: Dutton, 1965.
Stories of the first Thanksgiving and of Thanksgivings of the twentieth century, from books by Dorothy Canfield Fisher, Carl Sandburg, Elizabeth Coatsworth, and others.

777. Luckhardt, Mildred C., comp. Thanksgiving: feast and festival. Nashville, Tenn.: Abingdon, 1966.
An anthology of poetry and prose about Thanksgiving and harvest-festival observances, with some information on customs.

778. Sechrist, Elizabeth H., ed. It's time for Thanksgiving. Philadelphia: Macrae Smith, 1957.
A collection of stories, poems, plays, recipes, and games for the Thanksgiving season.

779. Untermeyer, Louis, ed. Songs of joy from the book of Psalms. New York: World Pub., 1967.
A selection of passages from the Psalms, chosen as expressions of praise and thanksgiving.

780. Weisgard, Leonard. The first Thanksgiving. Garden City, N.Y.: Doubleday, 1967.
An attractively illustrated interpretation of the Pilgrims and the events leading up to the first Thanksgiving; based on the old-style calendar dates and William Bradford's diary.

781. Wirt, Sherwood Eliot, comp. "Thankfulness" and "Thanksgiving." In his Living quotations for Christians. pp. 238–40. New York: Harper, 1974.
The quotations on Thanksgiving include excerpts from the Thanksgiving proclamations of George Washington in 1789, Abraham Lincoln in 1863, Dwight Eisenhower in 1956, John Kennedy in 1961, and Lyndon Johnson in 1964.

See also Forefather's Day; section on Planning and Preparing for Anniversaries and Holidays

United Nations Day

782. Barros, James, ed. The United Nations: past, present, and future. New York: Free Press, 1972.
Essays on the organization of the United Nations which assess the effectiveness of the world organization in resolving conflicts and furthering cooperation.

783. Epstein, Edna. United Nations. Rev. ed. New York: Watts, 1973.
A concise, simply written explanation of the United Nations, its organization, membership, specialized agencies, problems, and achievements; lists the member nations as of 1972.

784. Everyman's United Nations: a complete handbook of the activities and evolution of the United Nations during its first twenty years, 1945–1965. 8th ed. New York: United Nations, 1968.
A history of the growth of the United Nations in all major fields of activity from 1945 to 1965; a supplement continues the record through 1970.

785. Fehrenbach, T. R. The United Nations in war and peace. New York: Random House, 1968.
An examination of the role of the United Nations in maintaining world peace since 1945, with consideration of organizational and financial limitations and conflicting national interests.

786. Kelen, Emery. Stamps tell the story of the United Nations. Des Moines: Meredith, 1968.
An introduction to the design, the designers, and the symbolism of the stamps issued by the United Nations.

787. Robertson, A. H. Human rights in the world. New York: Humanities Press, 1972.
". . . being an account of the United Nations covenants on human rights, the European convention, the American convention, the Permanent Arab commission, the proposed African commission, and recent developments affecting humanitarian law."—subtitle.

788. Savage, Katharine. The story of the United Nations. Rev. and enl. ed. New York: Walck, 1970.
A survey of the United Nations from its establishment through the 1960s; includes a review of major issues and problems.

789. Scott, George. The rise and fall of the League of Nations. New York: Macmillan, 1974.
A journalist's report on the hopeful beginnings and sad decline of the League of Nations, predecessor of the United Nations, with an analysis of the styles of Wilson, Briand, Lloyd-George, and other statemen working for peace in their time.

Valentine's Day

790. Barth, Edna. Hearts, cupids, and red roses: the story of the Valentine symbols. New York: Seabury, 1974.
The origin, development, symbols, and customs of the world's most sentimental holiday, named for the third-century Saint Valentine but going back to the Roman festival of Lupercalia.

791. Guilfoile, Elizabeth. Valentine's Day. Champaign, Ill.: Garrard, 1965.
A simply written account of the origins of Saint Valentine's Day, old customs, symbols, the first paper valentines, and a brief history of valentines in America.

792. Lee, Ruth Webb. A history of valentines. Wellesley Hills, Mass.: Lee Pub., 1952.
A history of the valentine from Roman times, with illustrations of collector's items and commentaries on their artists and publishers.

793. Manley, Seon, and Lewis, Gogo. A treasury of great romantic literature. Philadelphia: Macrae Smith, 1969.
A collection of romantic stories, poems, and love letters useful for Valentine's Day.

794. Staff, Frank. The valentine and its origin. New York: Praeger, 1969.
A review of the history and customs of the exchange of valentines from the time of Chaucer to the mid-twentieth century; appendixes include notes on the legend, love tokens, and information for collectors.

795. Untermeyer, Louis, ed. Men and women: the poetry of love. New York: American Heritage, 1970.
An anthology of romantic poetry, from the *Song of Songs* to the work of Judith Viorst; indexed.

Veterans' Day

796. Essame, H. The battle for Europe, 1918. New York: Scribner, 1972.
A British view of the last year of World War I, crediting the Allied victory to the courage and spirit of the ordinary soldier who is honored on Veterans' Day.

797. Greene, Robert E. Black defenders of America, 1775–1973: a reference and pictorial history. Chicago: Johnson Pub., 1974.
Biographical sketches of blacks who fought in wars from the Revolution to Vietnam; arranged by war; indexed.

798. Huston, James A. Out of the blue: U.S. Army airborne operations in World War II. Lafayette, Ind.: Purdue Univ. Studies, 1972.
A comprehensive study of American army parachute and glider experience from the late 1930s to 1945 and a review of the specific contributions of airborne operations to Allied victory.

799. Jones, Barbara. Popular arts of the first World War. New York: McGraw, 1972.
A well-illustrated study of the popular arts that appealed to ordinary people in all of the nations involved in World War I, with a major emphasis on the morale-boosting popular art forms of Britain and France.

800. MacCloskey, Monro. Hallowed ground: our national cemeteries. New York: Richards Rosen Press, 1968.
A history of the development of the national cemetery system from 1862 to date; includes national and overseas cemeteries and memorials, with separate chapters on Arlington and the Tomb of the Unknowns.

801. Meyer, Frank S., ed. Breathes there the man: heroic ballads of the English-speaking peoples. La Salle, Ill.: Open Court, 1973.
Patriotic ballads and lyrics chosen from four centuries of English verse; the section on American poetry includes McCrae's *In Flanders Fields* and other poems appropriate for Veterans' Day.

802. Middlebrook, Martin. The first day on the Somme, 1 July 1916. New York: Norton, 1972.
A history of the tragic Battle of the Somme which evokes the courage of the ordinary soldier in World War I.

803. Sulzberger, C. L. World War II. New York: American Heritage, 1970.
An abridged version of the *American Heritage Picture History of World War II,* providing an overview of World War II from the Hitler era to the Japanese surrender in 1945.

804. Toland, John. Battle: the story of the Bulge. New York: Random House, 1959.
A historical narrative of the Battle of the Ardennes, known as "the Battle of the Bulge," which began on December 15, 1944.

805. ———. The last 100 days. New York: Random House, 1966.
A survey of the military and diplomatic strategy, the governmental and military leaders, the successes and failures of the period between January 27 and May 8, 1945, the last days of World War II in Europe.

Washington's Birthday

806. Billias, George A. George Washington's generals. New York: Morrow, 1964.
Essays examining the careers of the most important Continental Army commanders, including Lafayette, who were associated with Washington in major capacities or campaigns.

807. Busch, Noel P. Winter quarters: Washington and the Continental Army at Valley Forge. New York: Liveright, 1974.
An account of the bleak winter of 1777–78 at Washington's winter quarters at Valley Forge.

808. Callahan, North. George Washington: soldier and man. New York: Morrow, 1972.
A concise biography of Washington, with a major focus on his years as commander-in-chief of the Revolutionary forces.

809. Fleming, Thomas J. First in their hearts: a biography of George Washington. New York: Norton, 1968.
A biography of Washington as a young man, surveyor, soldier, husband, businessman, and president.

810. Flexner, James Thomas. George Washington: anguish and farewell. Boston: Little, 1972.
The last in a four-volume biography that examines Washington's second term in office and his retirement; a definitive personal biography of America's first president.

811. Freidel, Frank, and Aikman, Lonnelle. G. Washington: man and monument. Washington, D.C.: Washington National Monument Assn., 1965.
A brief review of the life of George Washington and a history of the Washington Monument, and some of the events associated with it, since the laying of the cornerstone on July 4, 1848.

812. Heusser, Albert H. George Washington's map maker. New Brunswick, N.J.: Rutgers Univ. Press, 1966.
A study of Robert Erskine, the surveyor-general of the Continental army whose knowledge and maps helped Washington outmaneuver the British.

813. Ketchum, Richard M. The winter soldiers. Garden City, N.Y.: Doubleday, 1973.
A view of Washington's army from the autumn of 1776 to the spring of 1777, with brief accounts of his generals, their shortcomings, and talents.

814. Krythe, Maymie. "The Washington Monument." In her What so proudly we hail, pp. 186–214. New York: Harper, 1968.
A history of the monument to the first president of the United States in the nation's capital; site of major patriotic and ceremonial events of national significance.

815. McDonald, Forrest. The presidency of George Washington. Lawrence: Univ. Press of Kansas, 1974.
A study of the first president of the United States, his influence on the symbolic qualities of the office, and the achievements of his administration.

816. Wright, Esmond. Washington: the man and the myth. Edinburgh: Oliver & Boyd, 1967.
A British view of Washington as a leader of men and an assessment of the legends that surround him.

Wedding Days

817. Arisian, Khoren. The new wedding: creating your own marriage ceremony. New York: Knopf, 1973.
Observations on contemporary nontraditional marriage ceremonies, with suggestions on the choice of music and poetry or prose readings.

818. **Carter, Charles Frederick.** The wedding day in literature and art: a collection of the best descriptions of weddings, from the works of the world's leading novelists and poets. New York: Dodd, 1900; Detroit: Singing Tree Press, 1969.
Excerpts from the era of Elizabeth Browning, Longfellow, and Dickens, describing the festivities of the wedding day.

819. **Kirschenbaum, Howard, and Stensrud, Rockwell.** The wedding book: alternative ways to celebrate marriage. New York: Seabury, 1974.
A practical guide to planning a nontraditional wedding, with sample texts of personally planned ceremonies, readings and prayers, checklists for budgeting and planning; includes a brief history of the traditions of wedding ceremonies.

820. **Routtenberg, Lilly S.** The Jewish wedding book: a practical guide to the traditions and social customs of the Jewish wedding. New York: Schocken, 1967.
A guide to the ceremonial variations among the three divisions of American Jewry, with advice on rituals, customs, and planning procedures.

821. **Seligson, Marcia.** The eternal bliss machine: America's way of weddings. New York: Morrow, 1973.
A journalist's report on the traditions and values revealed in the pageantry and theater of weddings in the United States.

Woman's Equality Day

822. **Chamberlin, Hope.** A minority of members: women in the U. S. Congress. New York: Praeger, 1973.
A collective biography examining the lives and careers of eighty-five women who have been elected to the United States Congress; the emphasis is on political careers; chronologically arranged.

823. **Clarke, Elizabeth.** Bloomers and ballots: Elizabeth Cady Stanton and women's rights. New York: Viking, 1972.
A portrayal of Elizabeth Cady Stanton as a seeker for her own individuality and a leader in the nineteenth-century suffragette movement.

824. **Cleverdon, Catherine L.** The woman suffrage movement in Canada. Toronto: Univ. of Toronto Press, 1974.
A history of the woman's-suffrage movement in Canada from about 1870 to the 1940s; originally published in 1950; organized by regions.

825. **Douglas, Emily Taft.** Remember the ladies: the story of great women who helped shape America. New York: Putnam, 1966.
A narrative history of the leaders in the advancement of the social, economic, and intellectual life of women in the United States; includes Anne Hutchinson, Abigail Adams, Anne Royal, Margaret Fuller, Dorothy Dix, the civil-rights and suffrage crusaders, Jane Addams, and Eleanor Roosevelt.

826. **Faber, Doris.** Petticoat politics: how American women won the right to vote. New York: Lothrop, 1967.
An introduction to the woman's-suffrage movement, with a strong interest in the qualities that marked the leaders of the movement.

827. **Flexner, Eleanor.** Century of struggle: the woman's rights movement in the United States. Cambridge, Mass.: Harvard Univ. Press, 1959.
A history of woman's-rights movements in the United States from the 1820s to the adoption of the woman's-suffrage amendment.

828. **Hahn, Emily.** Once upon a pedestal: an informal history of women's lib. New York: Crowell, 1974.
A popular account of women in America, from the arrival of Anne Forrest at Jamestown in 1607 to the present; includes commentaries on authors who wrote about women, books that women read, and the varying movements that influenced women.

829. **Huber, Joan, ed.** Changing women in a changing society. Chicago: Univ. of Chicago Press, 1973.
Essays on the changing status of women and the woman's movement—past, present, and future.

830. **Ireland, Norma Olin.** Index to women of the world, from ancient to modern times. Westwood, Mass.: Faxon, 1970.
A source book for the identification of 13,000 women, with data on dates, nationality, vocations, and sources for further information; the introduction deals with the contributions of women through the ages.

831. **Janeway, Elizabeth.** Between myth and morning: women awakening. New York: Morrow, 1974.
An examination of the need for women to disengage themselves from the myths about women and an analysis of the woman's movement in the context of general social change in society.

832. ———. Man's world, woman's place: a study in social mythology. New York: Morrow, 1971.
A study of the social and psychological situations behind the contemporary woman's-rights movement.

833. **Krichmar, Albert.** The women's rights movement in the United States, 1848–1970. Metuchen, N.J.: Scarecrow, 1972.
A bibliography and source book providing essential information on books, articles, manuscript collections, and serials dealing with the woman's-rights movement.

834. **Lerner Gerda, ed.** Black women in white America: a documentary history. New York: Pantheon Books, 1972.
A collection of documents, letters, articles, excerpts from books, and other material on major issues written by American women from the 1830s up to 1970.

835. **Maimon, Ada.** Women build a land. New York: Herzl, 1962.
A history of the working-woman's movement in early twentieth-century Israel, before statehood.

836. **Noble, Iris.** Emmeline and her daughters: the Parkhurst suffragettes. New York: Messner, 1971.
A study of Emmeline Parkhurst and her three daughters, who spent thirty years in a struggle for equality for women.

837. **Stoddard, Hope.** Famous American women. New York: Crowell, 1970.
A collective biography of such distinguished American women as Jane Addams and Harriet Tubman, who made contributions to American life in the nineteenth and twentieth centuries.

838. **Tremain, Rose.** The fight for freedom for women. New York: Random House, 1973.
A comparison of the woman's-suffrage movements in Britain and the United States, with consideration of the lessons learned by American leaders from British suffragettes.

World Health Day

839. **Anderson, Odin W.** Health care: can there be equity? New York: Wiley, 1972.
A comparative study of the development of health care in England, Sweden, and the United States.

840. **Bickel, Lennard.** Facing starvation: Norman Borlaug and the fight against hunger. New York: Reader's Digest Press, 1974.
A study of Norman Borlaug, Nobel prize-winning agronomist, and his worldwide effort to increase the world's food supply to alleviate the threats of starvation.

841. **Cahill, Kevin M., ed.** The untapped resource. Maryknoll, N.Y.: Orbis Books, 1971.
A collection of essays by specialists in medicine, economics, and international relations on the importance of sharing American medical knowledge and techniques with less technologically advanced societies.

842. **Camp, John.** Magic, myth and medicine. New York: Taplinger, 1974.
A study of medicinal folklore through the ages, ranging from purification rituals to patent medicines.

843. **Marks, Geoffrey, and Beatty, William K.** Women in white. New York: Scribner, 1972.
A study of the role of women in the healing arts from the Stone and Bronze Ages to the 1970s; recalls the years of struggle for women's rights in medicine and reviews the achievements of Elizabeth Blackwell, Florence Nightingale, Dorothea Lynde Dix, Marie Curie, and others in medicine, nursing, and research; indexed.

844. **Simon, Paul, and Simon, Arthur.** The politics of world hunger, grass roots, politics, and world poverty. New York: Harper's Magazine Press, 1973.
Information and documentation on the problems of hunger, malnutrition, and underdevelopment in the world as related to the participation of the United States in world development.

World Literacy Day

845. **La Pray, Margaret.** Teaching children to become independent readers. New York: Center for Applied Research in Education, 1972.
A useful text on individualizing reading programs, with suggestions for informal diagnostic testing, techniques, games, motivational devices, and activities for teaching reading skills.

846. **Laubach, Frank C.** Thirty years with the silent billion. Westwood, N.J.: Revell, 1960.
An account of the period from 1929 to 1957 in the worldwide career of Frank Laubach, literacy crusader, who coined the phrase "Each one teach one."

847. Lyman, Helen Huguenor. Library materials in service to the adult new reader. Chicago: ALA, 1973.
Important research data on the reading of the adult new literate in the United States, with an analysis of criteria for the evaluation of needed materials.

848. Palmer, Julia Reed. Read for your life: two successful efforts to help people read and an annotated list of the books that made them want to. Metuchen, N.J.: Scarecrow, 1974.
A contribution to the literature on illiteracy, with descriptions of literacy programs, practical advice, and an annotated bibliography of materials that appeal to different ages and interests.

849. Smith, Carl B., and Fay, Leo C. Getting people to read. New York: Delacorte, 1973.
A report, sponsored by the National Book Committee, on volunteer programs and techniques designed to alleviate the illiteracy problem in the United States.

World Poetry Day

850. Abdul, Raoul. The magic of black poetry. New York: Dodd, 1972.
A collection of poems by black people of the world on fourteen subjects, such as the seasons, Christmas, and heroes; concludes with brief notes on the poets.

851. Allen, Terry, ed. The whispering wind. New York: Doubleday, 1972.
A collection of poems by young American Indians, students at the Institute of American Indian Arts in Santa Fe, New Mexico.

852. Cole, William, sel. The sea, ships, and sailors: poems, songs, and shanties. New York: Viking, 1967.
A collection of poems representing all of the moods of the sea and buccaneers, sailors, and adventurers who sailed the waters of the world.

853. Downie, Mary Alice, and Robertson, Barbara, comps. The wind has wings: poems from Canada. New York: Walck, 1968.
A collection of the work of Canadian poets, including translations from the Eskimo, French, and Yiddish.

854. Emrich, David, ed. American folk poetry: an anthology. Boston: Little, 1974.
A collection of songs, poems, and ballads arranged by subjects: children's ballads, hymns, songs of occupations, of cowboys, Mormons, and outlaws.

855. Figueroa, John, sel. Caribbean voices. New York: Luce, 1973.
The work of leading poets of the West Indies.

856. Flores, Angel, ed. An anthology of French poetry from Nerval to Valéry in English translation. New York: Doubleday, 1962.
A collection of the work of nine major French poets of the nineteenth and early twentieth centuries.

857. Gill, John, ed. New American and Canadian poetry. Boston: Beacon Press, 1971.
A collection of contemporary American and Canadian poetry, with biographical notes.

858. Granger's index to poetry. Ed. by William James Smith. 6th ed. New York: Columbia Univ. Press, 1973.
An index to anthologies of poetry published through December 31, 1970; a source book for locating poems for traditional holidays and such special days as Arbor Day or Commencement Day.

859. Howe, Irving, ed. A treasury of Yiddish poetry. New York: Holt, 1969.
Translations of Yiddish poems from the earliest period to modern times, chosen for variety of theme and style.

860. Hughes, Langston, and Bontemps, Arna, eds. The poetry of the Negro, 1746–1970: an anthology. Rev. ed. Garden City, N.Y.: Doubleday, 1970.
An anthology of the work of Negro poets of the United States; includes a section on work by non-Negroes, and a selection of poems by black poets of the Caribbean; indexed.

861. Hughes, Ted. Poetry is. Garden City, N.Y.: Doubleday, 1970.
A discussion of poetry, based on a BBC series, with advice for beginning poets and interesting examples for poetry readers.

862. Lewis, Richard, ed. I breathe a new song. New York: Simon & Schuster, 1971.
Examples of Eskimo poetry and sacred and secular songs selected from journals of Arctic expeditions and other sources.

863. ———, comp. Miracles: poems by children of the English-speaking world. New York: Simon & Schuster, 1966.
A collection of poems written by children in eighteen countries where English is the native tongue or an important second language.

864. McDowell, Robert E., and Lavitt, Edward, eds. Third world voices for children. New York: Third Press, 1971.
An anthology of folklore, prose, poetry, and song selections from Africa, the West Indies, and Papua New Guinea.

865. Malkoff, Karl. Crowell's handbook of contemporary poetry. New York: Crowell, 1973.
Essays on the development of philosophies and themes associated with major movements in American poetry published since 1940.

866. Morton, Miriam, ed. The moon is like a silver sickle: a celebration of poetry by Russian children. New York: Simon & Schuster, 1972.
A translation of ninety-two poems written by young Russians, interpreting their lives and sentiments.

867. Parker, Elinor Minor, comp. Four seasons five senses. New York: Scribner, 1974.
An anthology of seasonal poems by Shakespeare, Longfellow, Frost, and other traditional poets, along with a few modern poets; arranged by seasons.

868. Peck, Richard E., ed. Sounds and silences. New York: Delacorte, 1970.
A collection of poems on life as reality; arranged in categories, such as the family, identity, communication, illusion, dissent, love, war, and pain; indexed.

869. Rasmussen, Knud. Eskimo poems from Canada and Greenland. Trans. by Tom Lowenstein. Pittsburgh: Univ. of Pittsburgh Press, 1974.
A collection of Eskimo songs and poems reflecting the Eskimo culture and way of life.

870. Rexroth, Kenneth, ed. Love and the turning year: one hundred more poems from the Chinese. New York: New Directions, 1970.
A collection of Chinese verse on reverie, love, and meditation from the third to the twentieth centuries.

World Red Cross Day

871. Epstein, Beryl, and Epstein, Sam. The story of the International Red Cross. New York: Nelson, 1963.
A report on the organization, development, and contributions of the International Red Cross from its inception through three world wars and into the middle of the twentieth century.

872. Nolan, Jeannette Covert. The story of Clara Barton of the Red Cross. New York: Messner, 1941.
A biography of Clara Barton, founder of the American Red Cross; the major time focus in this biography is the Civil War period.

873. Ross, Ishbel. Angel of the battlefield. New York: Harper, 1956.
The story of the dedicated career of Clara Barton on the battlefields of the Civil War as an inspiration for the establishment of the American Red Cross.

874. Rothkopf, Carol Z. The Red Cross. New York: Watts, 1971.
An introduction to the history, ideals, and work of the Red Cross, which includes information on the International Committee of the Red Cross, national societies, Red Cross youth, and a brief chapter on Clara Barton.

Yom Kippur

875. Goodman, Philip. Yom Kippur anthology. Philadelphia: Jewish Pub. Soc., 1971.
An anthology designed to demonstrate the meaning of Yom Kippur through the interpretations of biblical, talmudical, and midrashic selections, inspirational essays, prayers, modern literature, art, and music.

876. Schauss, Hayyim. "Yom Kippur—in olden days" and "Yom Kippur—in Temple days." In his The Jewish festivals, pp. 119–42. New York: Union of American Hebrew Congregations, 1938.
An account of the observance of Yom Kippur in early periods of Jewish history, with a brief description of rituals and ceremonies.

Planning and Preparing
for Anniversaries and Holidays

Holiday and Festival Foods:
International

877. Aaberg, Jean, and Bolduc, Judith H.
Classics in the kitchen: an edible anthology for the literary gourmet. Los Angeles: Ward Ritchie Press, 1969.
A menu for each month of the year, correlated with a quotation from a famous author.

878. Born, Wina. Famous dishes of the world. New York: Macmillan, 1973.
An introduction to the world of international cooking; recipes are correlated with brief information on the history of the dish.

879. Brown, Helen. Holiday cook book. Boston: Little, 1952.
Ideas and recipes for thirty-one secular and religious holidays and such special days as Chinese New Year and Bastille Day.

880. Corey, Helen. The art of Syrian cookery: a culinary trip to the land of Bible history—Syria and Lebanon. Garden City, N.Y.: Doubleday, 1962.
A compilation of recipes, introduced with a description of Middle Eastern customs and holidays; includes Arabic menus, a section on Lenten foods, and an interpretation of the significance of foods planned for the twelve great feasts of the Orthodox Catholic church; indexed.

881. Ellison, Virginia H. The Pooh cook book: inspired by *Winnie-the-Pooh* and *The House at Pooh Corner*. New York: Dutton, 1969.
A cookbook for all ages and many occasions, with a section on Christmas specialties; each recipe is accompanied by a quotation from A. A. Milne.

882. Fitzgibbon, Theodora. A taste of Ireland: Irish traditional food. Boston: Houghton, 1969.
A collection of recipes from rural and urban Ireland, including colcannon, traditionally eaten at Halloween, spiced beef for Christmas, dulse, sloke, and willicks for Easter Monday, and goose for Michaelmas Day.

883. Frucht, Phyllis, ed. The best of Jewish cooking. Ed. by Phyllis Frucht, Joy Rothschild, and Gertrude Katz, with the Ladies Auxiliary of Temple Beth Israel. New York: Dial Press, 1974.
A cookbook beginning with a section of recipes for Jewish holidays: the Sabbath, Rosh Hashanah and Yom Kippur, Sukkot, Hannukah, Purim, Passover, Shavuot, and Thanksgiving, and concluding with foreign foods enjoyed by Jewish families around the world.

884. Goodman, Hanna. Jewish cooking around the world. Philadelphia: Jewish Pub. Soc., 1974.
International variations of Jewish food from China, Europe, North Africa, and the Middle East; includes special menus for the Sabbath, Passover, and other religious days, correlated with Jewish traditions, dietary laws, and customs.

885. Gupta, Pranati Sen. The art of Indian cuisine: everyday menus, feasts, and holiday banquets. New York: Hawthorn Books, 1974.
A book of Indian recipes adapted for American use; a brief introduction correlates food with special events: the wedding feast and the holy festival of Durga puja, and others.

886. Herman, Judith, ed. The cornucopia. New York: Harper, 1973.
". . . being a kitchen entertainment and cookbook; containing good reading and good cookery from more than 500 years of recipes, food lore, etc., as conceived and expounded by the great chefs & gourmets of the Old and New Worlds between the years of 1390 and 1899"—subtitle.

887. Jervey, Phyllis. A world of parties: the busy gourmet's guide to exciting entertaining. Rutland, Vt.: Tuttle, 1964.
Round-the-world dishes representing many nations, from a Spanish Gypsy outing and a North African banquet to an American Thanksgiving and a New Year's Eve in Germany.

888. Kaufman, William I. The Catholic cookbook. New York: Citadel, 1965.
Foods for Catholic feast days, holidays, and days of fast and abstinence; indexed by category and country of origin.

889. Krieg, Saul. What's cooking in Portugal. New York: Macmillan, 1974.
The traditional dishes of Portugal and regional specialities of the Portuguese provinces; indexed.

890. Langseth-Christensen, Lillian. The holiday cook. New York: Lion Press, 1969.
A cookbook for young people and their parents, with recipes for holidays from Happy New Year beans to plum pudding for Christmas; arranged by the calendar year.

891. Lesberg, Sandy. At the table of Israel: a unique collection of three hundred traditional and modern Israeli recipes. Indianapolis: Bobbs, 1973.
A cookbook reflecting the diversity of Israeli food culture; arranged by types of dishes; includes a section of colored photographs of people at festival occasions.

892. Mazda, Maideh. In a Persian kitchen: favorite recipes from the Near East. Rutland, Vt.: Tuttle, 1960.
An introduction to Persian culinary arts and hospitality, with commentaries on special foods and recipes and a sample menu for New Year's dinner and seasonal lunches or dinners; indexed.

893. Meyer, Carolyn. The bread book: all about bread and how to make it. New York: Harcourt, 1971.
A history of bread and instructions for making it, with references to holy-day and holiday use by various faiths and to the once-a-year traditions, such as barmbrack for the Irish Halloween.

894. Moore, Eva. The cookie book. New York: Seabury, 1973.
A collection of cookie recipes for celebrating one special day of each month, such as coconut drops for Valentine's Day and molasses cookies for April Fool's Day.

895. Nightingale, Marie. Out of old Nova Scotia kitchens: a collection of traditional recipes of Nova Scotia and stories of people who cooked them. New York: Scribner, 1971.
A history of the table traditions of the Micmac Indians, the French, English, Scots, Irish, and Negroes of Nova Scotia; their food beliefs, traditional festivals, pie socials, and other events.

896. Norman, Barbara. Tales of the table: a history of Western cuisine. Englewood Cliffs, N.J.: Prentice-Hall, 1972.
An account of Western cooking linked to the history of civilization; concludes with menus from every era from the time of the ancient Greeks, through the Dark and Middle ages and the age of the Revolution, to the nineteenth century.

897. Perl, Lila. Foods and festivals of the Danube lands. Cleveland: World, 1969.
An overview of traditional menus and food customs associated with German and Austrian festivals, the celebrations of the Hungarian Gypsies, Yugoslav saints' days, and the major festivities of Bulgaria, Romania, and Russia.

898. ———. Red flannel hash and shoo-fly pie. Cleveland: World, 1965.
An account of good eating for four-hundred years in all parts of the United States: the food of the Indians, Pilgrims, pioneers, Cornish, and other national groups; includes recipes; arranged by regions of the mainland, Alaska, and Hawaii.

899. ———. Rice, spice and bitter oranges: Mediterranean foods and festivals. Cleveland: World, 1967.
A history of the cuisines and dining customs of Portugal, Spain, Syria, Lebanon, Israel, and North Africa, correlated with feast days, festivals, weddings, and funerals.

900. Roden, Claudia. A book of Middle Eastern food. New York: Knopf, 1972.
Culinary traditions and recipes from Syria, Lebanon, Egypt, Iran, Turkey, Greece, Iraq, Saudi Arabia, Yemen, Sudan, Algeria, Tunisia, Morocco, and Israel; includes interpretations of origins of foods, the rules for being a host or a guest, superstitions, and dietary laws.

901. Root, Waverly Lewis. The food of Italy. New York: Atheneum, 1971.
A gastronomical tour of Italy, with narrative descriptions of regional specialties and foods for Christmas, Easter, and other holidays; indexed.

902. Shapiro, Rebecca. A whole world of cooking. Boston: Little, 1972.
Recipes from around the world, beginning with Canadian fish cakes; table of contents arranged alphabetically by country; indexed by type of dish.

903. Turgeon, Charlotte Snyder. Cooking for many on holidays and other festive occasions. New York: Crown, 1962.
Holiday recipes and menus for club, church, and home functions; includes Christian and Jewish holidays.

904. Wilson, Ellen Gibson. A West African cookbook. New York: Evans, 1971.
Recipes from Ghana, Liberia, Sierra Leone, and Nigeria, with a brief chapter on *awoojah,* a feast of Thanksgiving, and the customs involving foods at funerals, weddings, baptisms, and harvest festivals.

905. Wolfert, Paula. Couscous and other good food from Morocco. New York: Harper, 1973.
A combination of culinary experiences with Moroccan cooking styles and Moroccan recipes for all occasions, including the lamb-eating holy period of Aid-el-Kebit, the festival of the Sacrifice of the Lamb.

Holiday Costumes and Crafts

906. Airey, Graham, and others. New ideas in card and paper crafts. New York: Van Nostrand, 1973.
Ideas and instructions for making objects from cards and paper that are adaptable for such holiday needs as the Three Kings for Epiphany or an owl for Halloween.

907. Bachmann, Manfred, and Hansmann, Claus. Dolls the world over. New York: Crown, 1973.
A study of the doll from its primitive use as a religious object to its role as a toy; various categories are depicted that suggest the use of dolls to illustrate national costumes or folk art.

908. Creekmore, Betsey B. Traditional American crafts. New York: Hearthside Press, 1968.
A study of Early American decorations and crafts, including a section on Christmas specialities and customs of the seventeenth, eighteenth, and nineteenth centuries.

909. Cummings, Richard. 101 costumes for all ages, all occasions. New York: McKay, 1970.
Suggestions for making historical, ethnic, and unusual costumes, for impromptu or special occasions.

910. Cutler, Katherine N., and Bogle, Kate Cutler. Crafts for Christmas. West Caldwell, N.J.: Lothrop, 1974.
Instructions for Christmas projects, including gifts and decorations to be made from commonly available materials.

911. D'Amato, Alex, and D'Amato, Janet. African crafts for you to make. New York: Messner, 1969.
A guide to African craftwork, with an explanation of the use of symbols and the function of the craft item; includes directions and illustrations.

912. Drehman, Vera L. Holiday ornaments from paper scraps. New York: Hearthside Press, 1970.
Patterns and directions for paper-scrap ornaments for Christmas, New Year's, Valentine's Day, Mother's Day, Father's Day, Halloween, Thanksgiving, and birthdays, with suggestions for wrapping presents; indexed.

913. Elicker, Virginia Wilk. Biblical costumes for church and school. New York: Ronald, 1953.
Ideas, principles, and directions for costuming biblical plays, particularly for the eras of Abraham, Joseph, David, Esther, the Nativity, and Jesus in his ministry.

914. Freehof, Lillian S., and King, Bucky. Embroideries and fabrics for synagogue and home. New York: Hearthside Press, 1966.
A manual on handworked Jewish ceremonial art for the synagogue and the home, with ideas, designs, and instructions.

915. Gilbreath, Alice. Making costumes for parties, plays, and holidays. New York: Morrow, 1974.
Instructions for making ghost, valentine, firecracker, and other kinds of costumes for special days; arranged in order of difficulty.

916. Greenhowe, Jean. Making costume dolls. New York: Watson-Guptill, 1973.
Instructions for making dolls for dioramas and displays; includes ideas for representing historical periods, fairy-tale characters, and imaginative scenes.

917. In praise of hands: contemporary crafts of the world, published in association with the World Crafts Council. New York: New York Graphic, 1974.
An illustrated study of the primitive, traditional, and innovative crafts of fifty-four nations of the world; based on the first World's Crafts Exhibition held in Toronto in the summer of 1974.

918. Ives, Suzy. Creating children's costumes in paper and card. New York: Taplinger, 1973.
A British costume manual on making children's costumes from inexpensive materials; instructions for creating masks, disguises, Halloween guises, theatrical costumes, and fun extravaganzas.

919. Joseph, Joan. Folk toys around the world and how to make them. New York: Parents' Magazine Press, 1972.
A guidebook, published in cooperation with UNICEF, on making toys of various nations; provides geographical and historical information as well as directions for making twenty-three toys, from a Russian bear to a cymbal-clacking Egyptian clown.

920. Leeming, Joseph. Holiday craft and fun. Philadelphia: Lippincott, 1950.
A craft book with directions for making decorations, novelties, and gadgets for Christmas, New Year's Day, Lincoln's Birthday, Valentine's Day, Washington's Birthday, Saint Patrick's Day, Easter, April Fools' Day, Arbor Day, May Day, Flag Day, Mother's Day, Father's Day, the Fourth of July, Columbus Day, Halloween, and Thanksgiving Day.

921. Listaite, Sister M. Gratia, and Hildebrand, Norbert A. A new look at Christmas decorations. Milwaukee: Bruce Pub., 1957.
Directions for creating Christmas bells, wreaths, and other decorations that incorporate the art forms and customs of many lands; illustrated with color photographs of Christmas trees featuring the decorative specialties of nations on the European, Asiatic, and North and South American continents.

922. Newman, Lee Scott, and Newman, Jay Hartley. Kite craft: the history and processes of kitemaking throughout the world. New York: Crown, 1974.
A history of kites, with special chapters on Oriental kites and their symbolism and on the kites of the last thirty years; includes basic construction techniques and decorating ideas; useful for seasonal observances and kite competitions; indexed.

923. Parish, Peggy. Costumes to make. New York: Macmillan, 1970.
Simple directions for making costumes for Valentine's Day, Halloween, and Christmas, as well as for special-events days, utilizing storybook or animal characters, or historical or national costumes.

924. Pettit, Florence H. How to make whirligigs and whimmy diddles and other American folkcraft objects. New York: Crowell, 1972.
Instructions for making replicas of objects used by Indians, Eskimos, and pioneer settlers of America, from candles to Eskimo masks and Kachina dolls.

925. Pflug, Betsy. You can. New York: Van Nostrand, 1969.
Ideas and directions for making Christmas ornaments, lanterns, candleholders, and other objects from tin or aluminum cans; for adept youngsters and group leaders.

926. Purdy, Susan. Costumes for you to make. Philadelphia: Lippincott, 1971.
Ideas and instructions for designing and making costumes, hats, masks, disguises, suits of armor, and animals for theatrical productions or parties.

927. ———. Festivals for you to celebrate. Philadelphia: Lippincott, 1969.
An activity-craft book providing background information on American nonpatriotic holidays and festivals, with directions for projects; arranged by seasons; entries in the subject index key such activities as the making of costumes or puppets to the level of difficulty.

928. ———. Holiday cards for you to make. Philadelphia: Lippincott, 1967.
Suggestions and directions for creating handmade marbleized, collage, pressed-flower, cut-out, and boxed cards, with ideas on the use of old greeting cards.

929. Rockland, Mae Shafter. The work of our hands: Jewish needlecraft for today. New York: Schocken, 1973.
Ideas and instructions on the arts of Jewish needlecraft.

930. Ross, Laura. Holiday puppets. New York: Lothrop, 1974.
Suggestions for puppet shows for Lincoln's Birthday, Valentine's Day, Washington's Birthday, Saint Patrick's Day, Purim, Easter, Columbus Day, Halloween, Thanksgiving Day, and Christmas.

931. Sargent, Lucy. Tincraft for Christmas. New York: Morrow, 1969.
A manual on tools, materials, and techniques for using tin for Christmas gifts and decorations: stars, wreaths, wind chimes, and trinkets.

932. Sattler, Helen Roney. Holiday gifts, favors, and decorations. New York: Lothrop, 1971.
An idea and instruction book for making table decorations, party favors, and gifts for major holidays, mother-daughter or father-son banquets for club, school, or home festivities; arranged by the four seasons of the year.

933. Shannon, Alice, and Shirrod, Barbara. Decorative treasures from papier-mâché. Great Neck, N.Y.: Hearthside Press, 1970.
Suggestions and instructions for making Christmas ornaments and objects for other purposes from papier-mâché.

934. Slivka, Rose, ed. The crafts of the modern world. New York: Horizon Press, 1968.
A pictorial compendium of over four-hundred objects of contemporary craft from over seventy countries; useful as an idea book for the holiday crafts.

935. Van Zandt, Eleanor. Crafts for fun and profit. Garden City, N.Y.: Doubleday, 1974.
A manual on craft projects ranging from candlemaking to polished stones; includes a special section on Christmas ideas.

936. Waltner, Willard, and Waltner, Elma. Holiday hobbycraft. New York: Lantern Press, 1964.
A craft book with directions for making favors, gifts, and decorations for thirty special-events days, ranging from suggestions for the traditional holidays to ideas for April Fools' Day and a witch's den for Halloween.

937. Wendorff, Ruth. How to make cornhusk dolls. New York: Arco, 1973.
Basic instructions for making cornhusk dolls for Thanksgiving decorations, Nativity scenes, decorations, and holiday souvenirs.

938. Wilcox, R. Turner. Folk and festival costume of the world. New York: Scribner, 1965.
A description of folk costumes around the world, from Afghanistan to Yugoslavia, including selected American states such as Alaska and Wisconsin; illustrations are black-and-white line drawings.

Holiday Poetry, Songs, and Observance Ideas

939. Bennett, Rowena. Creative plays and programs for holidays. Boston: Plays, 1966.
Plays, group and choral readings, and poems for the traditional holidays, the seasons, special days such as Mother's Day, and Book Week.

940. Bormann, Ernest G., and Bormann, Nancy C. Effective committees and groups in the church. Minneapolis: Augsburg, 1973.
An approach to group functioning through objectives, definitions, and practical procedures; organized by sections on group dynamics, leadership, and small-group communication; adaptable for organizational needs for planning large-scale observances.

941. Britton, Dorothea S. The complete book of bazaars. New York: Coward, McCann, 1973.
A guide to the planning and promotion of bazaars, with advice on enlisting local talent and suggestions for bookkeeping and handling financial problems that are applicable to similar community activities as well.

942. Brussell, Eugene F. Dictionary of quotable definitions. Englewood Cliffs, N.J.: Prentice-Hall, 1970.
A collection of quotations useful for talks on democracy, Lincoln's Birthday, Washington's Birthday, and other special days; arranged alphabetically by topic.

943. Cavanah, Frances, and Pannell, Lucile, comps. Holiday roundup. Rev. ed. Philadelphia: Macrae Smith, 1968.
A collection of stories to tell on Christian and Jewish holy days, American holidays, and such special days as Arbor Day, Patriots' Day, Mother's Day, and Father's Day.

944. Christian, Roy. "May day customs." In his Old English customs, pp. 34–45. London: Country Life Ltd., 1966.
A description of English May Day traditions of the past and May Day dances and revelries of modern England; background material for May Day revival observances.

945. Cole, William, ed. Poems for seasons and celebrations. Cleveland: World Pub., 1961.
An anthology of poems related to the four seasons and to twenty-two holidays and observances, including Book Week; indexed by author and title.

946. Copland, Margaret L. Fun and festival from the rim of East Asia. New York: Friendship Press, 1962.
A booklet on festival folklore, games, songs, and food from Korea, Okinawa, Taiwan, and Hongkong.

947. Duran, Dorothy, and Duran, Clement A. The new encyclopedia of successful program ideas. New York: Association Press, 1967.
A manual of basic steps in program planning; includes a chapter on holidays as program possibilities and lists sponsors of special day and week observances; holidays and events listed chronologically.

948. Ellison, Virginia. The Pooh party book. New York: Dutton, 1971.
A party book inspired by the works of A. A. Milne; includes options for five parties, such as a spring party correlated with Easter or May Day; a sequel to *The Pooh Cook Book.*

949. Ford, James Lauren. Every day in the year: a poetical epitome of the world's history. New York: Dodd, 1902; Detroit: Gale Research, 1969.
A collection of poetry on memorable events and people, from the assassination of Julius Caesar to the sinking of the *Maine*; arranged in order of the days in the calendar.

950. Gunn, Mary Kemper. A guide to academic protocol. New York: Columbia Univ. Press, 1969.
Advice for preparing for commencement days, receptions, and other college and university affairs.

951. Hallock, Constance M. Fun and festival from Southeast Asia. Rev. ed. New York: Friendship Press, 1968.
Suggestions for learning the customs of Burma, the Philippines, Thailand, Vietnam, and Southeast Asia through the games and songs of each country.

952. Harrington, Mildred P., and Thomas, Josephine H. Our holidays in poetry. New York: Wilson, 1929.
A standard collection of useful poetry for Lincoln's Birthday, Washington's Birthday, Easter, Arbor Day, Mother's Day, Memorial Day, Thanksgiving, and Christmas.

953. Hazeltine, Alice I., and Smith, Elva S., eds. The year around: poems for children. Nashville, Tenn.: Abingdon, 1956.
Poems for the seasons, the traditional American holidays, such special days as Arbor Day and Columbus Day, and Book Week.

954. Hoffmann, Detlef. The playing card: an illustrated history. New York: New York Graphic, 1974.
A history of playing cards in Europe and the Orient; includes a section on playing cards used in education, propaganda, and fortune-telling.

955. Humphrey, Marylou, and Humphrey, Ron. Cheerleading and song leading. Rutland, Vt.: Tuttle, 1970.
A manual on tryouts, techniques for effective leadership, and ideas on rousing maximum group participation in cheers and songs.

956. Ikerman, Ruth C. Women's programs for special occasions. Nashville, Tenn.: Abingdon, 1966.
Program ideas and devotional exercises for group or organizational use.

957. Katz, William Loren. Teachers' guide to American Negro history. Rev. ed. Chicago: Quadrangle Books, 1971.
Major units of study begin with "dates to remember," expressed in years without specific days; includes annotated lists of printed and audiovisual materials to aid studies in Negro history.

958. Keppel, Ella Huff. Fun and festival from Latin America. New York: Friendship Press, 1961.
A booklet on games, poems, stories, and recipes of Latin America; suggests program outlines for a fun festival, a staged festival, and a banquet festival.

959. Kipnis, Claude. The mime book. Ed. by Neil Kleinman. New York: Harper, 1974.
An interpretation, through text and photographs, of the mime as an art of movement; includes directives from basic exercise to full pantomimes; indexed.

960. Lane-Palagyi, Addyse. Successful school assembly programs. West Nyack, N.Y.: Parker Pub., 1971.
Guidelines for planning, organizing, and producing assembly programs for elementary and secondary schools; includes sample tested program ideas, such as colonial Thanksgiving tableaus and Labor Day dramatizations.

961. Larrick, Nancy, sel. Poetry for holidays. Champaign, Ill.: Garrard, 1966.
Little poems for little people for Halloween, Thanksgiving, Christmas, New Year's Day, Valentine's Day, Saint Patrick's Day, Easter, May Day, the Fourth of July, and their own birthdays.

962. Leisy, James. The good times song-book: 160 songs for informal singing, with resources for song leaders, accompanists, and singers. Nashville, Tenn.: Abingdon, 1974.
A collection of folk, camp, and cumulative songs, ballads, hymns, and carols, with notes on their origins or idioms; includes suggestions on performance techniques; useful for observance of patriotic days, Christmas, and Thanksgiving, and for ideas on opening and closing songs for all kinds of observances; indexed by song categories.

963. Manning-Saunders, Ruth, comp. Festivals. New York: Dutton, 1973.
An anthology of poems, stories, and songs for major and minor festivals; international in scope, with brief introductions for selected days; arranged by the calendar year.

964. Naylor, Penelope. Black images: the art of West Africa. New York: Doubleday, 1973.
An explanation of the use of masks, carvings, and bronzes in the religious customs of West African societies.

965. Newland, Mary Reed. The year and our children: planning the family activities for Christian feasts and seasons. New York: Kenedy, 1956.
A Christian approach to family participation in activities for Christmas and other important days in the church calendar; ranges from the Advent wreath and the Jesse tree to preparing for the feast of Thanksgiving; concludes with a list of liturgical symbols.

966. Sechrist, Elizabeth Hough, comp. Poems for red letter days. Philadelphia: Macrae Smith, 1951.
A traditional collection of poems for patriotic and religious days and such special days as commencements and birthdays; indexed.

967. Seranne, Ann, and Gaden, Eileen. The church and club woman's companion. Garden City, N.Y.: Doubleday, 1964.
A practical guide to the management of club and church functions; includes recipes, ideas for fund-raising events, group festivities for the Christmas season and other special occasions.

968. The speaker's special occasion book. Ed. by the staff of Quote magazine. Anderson, S.C.: Droke House, 1965.
A collection of quotations suitable for speeches at holiday observances; arranged by calendar year and chronologically within each month; not indexed.

969. Stoudt, John Joseph. Sunbonnets and shoofly pies: a Pennsylvania Dutch colonial history. Cranbury, N.J.: Barnes, 1973.
A pictorial history of the cultural celebrations and folk arts of the Pennsylvania Dutch, including useful children's lore, proverbs, superstitions, and recipes.

970. Wade, Carlson. Shower parties for all occasions. Cranbury, N.J.: Barnes, 1973.
Ideas for traditional showers, plus brief suggestions for "special holiday" showers on New Year's Day, Saint Patrick's Day, Halloween, and other days of observance.

971. Warren, Lee. The dance of Africa. Englewood Cliffs, N.J.: Prentice-Hall, 1972.
A description of the traditional ritual dance in the African tribal culture in a changing society; includes instructions for a singing-game dance and a modern dance.

972. Wasserman, Paul, and Herman, Esther, eds. Museum media: a biennial directory and index of publications and audiovisuals available from United States and Canadian institutions. Detroit: Gale Research, 1973.
Data on books, pamphlets, catalogs, films, and other media available from large national and local museums, galleries, and state agencies; a source book of value to planners of observances and special events.

973. Wells, Irene. Fun and festival from India, Pakistan, Ceylon, and Nepal. Rev. ed. New York: Friendship Press, 1963.
Background information on the festivals, music, games, and food of India, Pakistan, Ceylon, and Nepal, with concise directions for learning the songs and games of each country.

974. Whitman, Wanda Wilson, ed. Songs that changed the world. New York: Crown, 1969.
Music and words and a brief commentary on songs from all over the world dealing with revolution, hard times, patriotism, religion, and folk interests.

975. Wright, Rose H. Fun and festival from Africa. Rev. ed. New York: Friendship Press, 1959.
A booklet on the music, games, stories, and feasting of Africa, with suggestions for adaptation and use.

Books about Persons Related to the Calendar

976. Archer, Jules. Famous young rebels. New York: Messner, 1973.
Short biographical sketches of the early lives of famous people considered as radicals in their day: Jawaharal Nehru, Elizabeth Gurley Flynn, Marcus Garvey, Robert La Follette, Margaret Sanger, Léon Blum, Lázaro Cárdenas, Sam Gompers, Mussolini, Elizabeth Cody Stanton, and Sam Adams.

977. Asimov, Isaac. Asimov's biographical encyclopedia of science and technology. Rev. ed. Garden City, N.Y.: Doubleday, 1972.
"The lives and achievements of 1,195 great scientists from ancient times to the present, chronologically arranged"—subtitle; indexed.

978. Ayre, Leslie. The Gilbert and Sullivan companion. New York: Dodd, 1972.
An encyclopedic study of the partnership between W. S. Gilbert and Arthur Sullivan, including plot summaries of their operettas, the major artists, and the texts of their songs; arranged alphabetically.

979. Brooks, H. Allen. The prairie school: Frank Lloyd Wright and his Midwest contemporaries. Toronto: Univ. of Toronto Press, 1972.
A history of the careers and achievements of over two-dozen American architects in the nineteenth and early twentieth centuries who were influenced by Frank Lloyd Wright and Louis Sullivan.

980. Chicorel, Marietta, ed. Chicorel index to biographies. 2 vols. New York: Chicorel, 1974.
A bibliography of book-length biographies of individuals; arranged by name, period, vocation, and nationality.

981. Clark, Kenneth. The romantic rebellion: romantic versus classic art. New York: Harper, 1973.
A study of the conflict between romanticism and classicism in art, featuring thirteen famous artists, including Blake, Constable, Degas, Millet, Rodin, and others.

982. Cook, Fred J. The muckrakers: crusading journalists who changed America. Garden City, N.Y.: Doubleday, 1972.
An account of the influence of crusading journalists, such as Lincoln Steffens and Ida Tarbell, who stimulated reform through the pages of newspapers in the late 1800s and early 1900s.

983. Ewen, David. Great men of American popular song. Englewood Cliffs, N.J.: Prentice-Hall, 1970.
A review of changing song styles from the Revolutionary period to modern times, as seen in the works of Stephen Foster, the Gershwins, and others.

984. Haber, Louis. Black pioneers of science and invention. New York: Harcourt, 1970.
A collective biography focusing on the professional contributions of Benjamin Benneker, George Washington Carver, and twelve other outstanding black scientists and inventors.

985. Kinton, Jack F. American ethnic groups. Mount Pleasant, Iowa: Social Science and Sociological Resources, 1973.
A guide to material on ethnic groups in the United States, with citations from American history, anthropology, sociology, and other fields related to minorities.

986. Kronenberger, Louis. Atlantic brief lives: a biographical companion to the arts. Boston: Little, 1971.
Brief essays on over a thousand men and women associated with literature, art, and music of the Western world; includes vital statistics and dates of major works; arranged alphabetically.

987. ———. The last word: portraits of fourteen master aphorists. New York: Macmillan, 1972.
An introduction to the careers and talents of fourteen aphorists, including Shaw, Chesterton, Butler, Johnson, Goethe, Emerson, and others.

988. McCarthy, Harold T. The expatriate perspective: American novelists and the idea of America. Cranbury, N.J.: Fairleigh Dickinson Univ. Press, 1974.
Essays on ten Americans—Cooper, Hawthorne, Melville, James, Twain, Cummings, Hemingway, Miller, Wright, and Baldwin, examining the use of expatriate experiences to assess American values; indexed.

989. Matlaw, Myron. Modern world drama. New York: Dutton, 1972.
An encyclopedic review of major playwrights, notable plays, and theatrical productions of the nineteenth and twentieth centuries; arranged alphabetically, with general and character indexes.

990. Merriam, Eve. Independent voices. New York: Atheneum, 1968.
Portraits in verse of Benjamin Franklin, Elizabeth Blackwell, Frederick Douglass, Henry Thoreau, Lucretia Mott, Ida Tarbell, and Fiorello La Guardia.

991. Morris, Richard B. Seven who shaped our destiny: the founding fathers as revolutionaries. New York: Harper, 1973.
Interpretations of Franklin, Jay, Washington, Jefferson, John Adams, Madison, and Hamilton, with insight into their positions on independence from England and their individual contributions to the unique character of the American Revolution.

992. Nicholsen, Margaret E. People in books: a selective guide to biographical literature arranged by vocations and other fields of reader interest. New York: Wilson, 1969.
"The purpose of this reference tool is to identify by vocation or field of activity, by country, and by century the subjects of biographies and other biographical writings which are recommended for libraries serving children, young adults, and adults."—preface.

993. Peters, Margaret. The Ebony book of black achievement. Chicago: Johnson Pub., 1970.
Sketches of black contributors to the progress of nations and mankind from the fourteenth to the twentieth centuries, as represented by Jean Baptiste Pointe du Sable, Frederick Douglass, Mary McLeod Bethune, and W. E. B. Du Bois.

994. Silverman, Judith. An index to young readers' collective biographies: elementary and junior high school level. New York: Bowker, 1970.
A source book on biographical material about 4,600 individuals representing specific vocations or contributions to society; arranged by both alphabetical and subject listings, supplemented with an index of subject headings and indexed books by title.

995. Story, Norah. The Oxford companion to Canadian history and literature. Toronto: Oxford, 1967.
An encyclopedia on Canadian explorers, public figures, authors, important places, and events in Canadian history; arranged alphabetically; indexed.

996. Sulzberger, C. L. The last of the giants. New York: Macmillan, 1970.
A reporter's view of De Gaulle, Churchill, Eisenhower, Adenauer, and Kennedy.

997. Tregaskis, Richard William. The warrior king: Hawaii's Kamehameha the Great. New York: Macmillan, 1973.
The life and achievements of the Polynesian warrior who unified the islands in 1810 and reigned until his death in 1819.

998. Tunney, Christopher. Biographical dictionary of World War II. New York: St. Martin's, 1972.
A compilation of brief biographies of soldiers, sailors, airmen, secret agents, politicians, propagandists, entertainers, journalists, and poets who were engaged in activities related to World War II; arranged alphabetically.

999. Wagenknecht, Edward. Ambassadors for Christ: seven American preachers. New York: Oxford, 1972.
Biographical sketches of seven influential preachers of the nineteenth century, such as Phillips Brooks, D. L. Moody, and Henry Ward Beecher, with commentaries on the interest of each in literature and the arts, science and nature, the social-economic climate, and religion.

1000. Wagner, Jean. Black poets of the United States from Paul Laurence Dunbar to Langston Hughes. Urbana: Univ. of Illinois Press, 1973.
A survey of the lives and works of major black poets in the United States from the days of slavery to Langston Hughes; discusses the social conditions revealed by both major and minor poets; bibliography.

1001. White, Hilda. Truth is my country: portraits of eight New England authors. Garden City, N.Y.: Doubleday, 1971.
Emerson, Dickinson, Frost, Hawthorne, Millay, Robinson, Stowe, and Thoreau are presented in the light of the times that affected their work.

1002. Wilder, Alec. American popular song: the great innovators, 1900–1950. New York: Oxford, 1972.
A history of distinctive contributions to the popular song in the United States; separate chapters deal with the work of Kern, Berlin, Gershwin, Rodgers, and Arlen.

Index

231